D1263429

BERLITZ BASIC SPANISH DICTIONARY

Berlitz BASIC SPANISH Dictionary

BY THE EDITORIAL STAFF OF
BERLITZ PUBLICATIONS, INC.

PUBLISHERS Grosset & Dunlap NEW YORK

ISBN: 0-448-01434-3

1971 PRINTING

PRINTED IN THE UNITED STATES OF AMERICA

HOW THIS DICTIONARY CAN HELP YOU SPEAK SPANISH

AS FAR BACK as the end of the first World War at the inception of the League of Nations, the Berlitz Schools (then already nearly half a century old) were requested to prepare a list of the 800 most important words in any language. It was found that a mastery of this list would enable a person to deal adequately with most conversational situations.

This new dictionary, the first ever to be offered by the Berlitz Schools, is the result of constant research based on this original list, but now expanded to more than 4000 words to cover reading and writing as well as conversation. Although this list represents but a small portion of the rich Spanish vocabulary, the student who wishes to express himself easily and fluently in Spanish will find it a compact and ready word collection that he will use regularly. Such a selection is infinitely more valuable than a long unwieldy word list which tends to swamp the student who needs a quick and ready grasp of Spanish. In fact, a native Spaniard rarely uses more than a few thousand words in everyday speech. Therefore, when these words are pre-selected for the student, he automatically has a considerable start in his study of Spanish. This is precisely what the Berlitz Schools have accomplished in this dictionary.

In the English-to-Spanish section the exact equivalent of an English word or expression is given, thereby eliminating for the student a difficult choice from among as many as ten possibilities.

Although most dictionaries are designed for those who already have a considerable command of the language, this dictionary can be used with advantage by people who do not as yet speak any Spanish at all. Numerous notes and hints throughout the dictionary itself indicate how complete sentences may be formed. Key expressions such as "give me," "tell me," "come in," etc., are offered along with the infinitive of the verb; for in actual usage an expression such as "How much does it cost?" is certainly as useful and more common than the infinitive form "to cost," just as "go away!" may prove more helpful than "to go."

When there has been a choice of Spanish equivalent for an English word, the one of highest conversational frequency has been indicated.

Pronunciation of the Spanish words and expressions is indicated in the simplified Berlitz phonetic system, so that an English speaking person can easily approximate the correct sound without having to learn an additional system of complicated symbols. However, no phonetic system is more than an approximation and, while we consider ours as close to the original as practicable, we urge our readers to observe and then practice the sound of these words as spoken by a native of a Spanish-speaking country.

The second part, the Spanish-to-English section, is not an exact equivalent of the first part, the English-to-Spanish. This is because the words you will see and hear most frequently in any Spanish speaking country do not correspond to those that have top frequency in English. Moreover, certain complete expressions are often pronounced almost as one word by Spanish speaking people and have therefore been included under the letter with which the phrase begins. The most important public signs and notices you may see in Spanish speaking countries have also been included. Your understanding of them may be more than useful; it may keep you out of trouble!

The basic words and expressions in Spanish and English respectively have been marked with a star. These are the three or four hundred indispensable words. You should leaf through the dictionary and test yourself on these whenever you have time. Get them down pat and you will have at your command the backbone of the language.

How to use this dictionary

As this dictionary is designed to enable you to use Spanish in conversation the Berlitz phonetic system has been employed so that you may pronounce each Spanish word and expression. To get the approximate pronunciation of any word, see the phonetic rendition in italics. For example, the word for "hat," *sombrero,* should be pronounced som-BREH-roh. Say it aloud and place the emphasis on the syllable in capital letters. The word pronounces itself! By paying close attention to the phonetics, you will gradually develop a sense of the values of Spanish sounds.

Here are the Spanish names of the letters of the alphabet in terms of our phonetic rendition:

A [*ah*] B [*beh*] C [*theh* or *seh*] CH [*tcheh*] D [*deh*]
E [*eh*] F [EH-*feh*] G [*heh*] H [AH-*cheh*] I [*ee*]
J [HOH-*tah*] K [*kah*] L [EH-*leh*] LL [EH-*l'yeh*]
M [EH-*meh*] N [EH-*neh*] Ñ [EH-*n'yeh*] O [*oh*] P [*peh*]
Q [*koo*] R [EH-*reh*] RR [EH-*rreh*] S [EH-*seh*] T [*teh*]
U [*oo*] V [*veh*] W [DOH-*bleh veh* or DOH-*bleh oo*]
X [EH-*keess*] Y [*yeh*] Z [THEH-*tah* or SEH-*tah*]

Certain letters have quite a different pronunciation from English and you will do well to remember them from the very beginning. They are:

j, which is always pronounced like the English "h";
h, which is never pronounced;
ll, which is pronounced like the combination "l'y";
ñ, which is pronounced like the combination "n'y";
z, which never has a "z" sound but is generally pronounced like "th" in Spain and like "ss" in Latin America.

The principal use of the written accent, as in the words está ("is"), aquí ("here"), árbol ("tree"), and María, is to indicate that the vowel carrying the accent is to be stressed.

In using this dictionary to form original sentences, certain essential differences between Spanish and English should be noted.

1. Spanish nouns are classified as either masculine or feminine. *El* (meaning "the") is used for the masculine, while *la* (also meaning "the") is used for the feminine gender. *Los* for the masculine and *las* for the feminine are the plural words for "the." The gender of all nouns given is indicated by (m) or (f).

The plural of all nouns and adjectives ends in *s*.

2. Spanish adjectives always agree with the noun they modify in gender and number and usually come after the noun. In this dictionary the feminine form of the adjective is given following the masculine. Also remember that Spanish adjectives can be used as nouns when so desired.

3. The different forms of subject, object and possessive pronouns are given in their alphabetical sequence; simply turn to the word you want to translate and you will find its equivalent. Remember that even object and indirect object pronouns precede the verb, except when the verb is an affirmative command or an infinitive.

4. Spanish verbs have six forms for every tense; these are given in a condensed verb table at the end of the dictionary which shows in detail the different Spanish tenses and their English equivalents. Some of the forms most frequent in conversation are given in phrases under the infinitive form entered in the body of the dictionary.

You will find short notes inserted after some of the entries. Read these carefully, as they will bring out the principal differences between the two languages and will aid you to construct your own sentences. Most of them are pointed up by the little professor.

With a minimum of effort in the use of this dictionary you will be able to get off to a good start in basic Spanish conversation. Remember to practice your pronunciation on any Spanish-speaking person you meet. For that matter, drop in at any Berlitz School in the world to have your accent checked. You will be most welcome, or as we say in Spanish: *¡Ud. será muy bienvenido!*

A

★ **a,** un (m) una (f) [*oon, oo-nah*]
able, capaz [*kah*-PAHTH]
Are you able to do it? ¿Puede hacerlo? [*p'*WEH-*deh ah*-THEHR-*loh*]
to be able, poder [*poh*-DEHR] (followed by infinitive of other verb)
aboard, a bordo [*ah* BOHR-*doh*]
★ **about** (adv), casi [KAH-*see*]
about (prep), sobre [SOH-*breh*]
to be about to, estar a punto de [*ehs*-TAHR *ah* POON-*toh deh*]
above, encima de [*ehn*-THEE-*mah deh*]
abroad, en el extranjero [*ehn ehl ehks-trahn*-HEH-*roh*]
absent, ausente [*ah-oo*-SEHN-*teh*]
absent-minded, distraído, -a [*dees-trah*-EE-*doh, -dah*]
absolutely, absolutamente [*ahb-soh-loo-tah*-MEHN-*teh*]
(to) **absorb,** absorber [*ahb-sohr*-BEHR]
abundant, abundante [*ah-boon*-DAHN-*teh*]
(to) **abuse,** abusar [*ah-boo*-SAHR]
academy, academia [*ah-kah*-DEH-*m'yah*]
accelerator, acelerador [*ah-theh-leh-rah*-DOHR]
accent, acento [*ah*-THEHN-*toh*]
(to) **accept,** aceptar [*ah-thep*-TAHR]
accident, accidente (m) [*ahk-thee*-DEHN-*teh*]
(to) **accompany,** acompañar [*ah-kohm-pah-n'*YAHR]
accordion, acordeón (m) [*ah-kohr-deh*-OHN]
according to, según [*seh*-GOON]

account, cuenta [KWEHN-*tah*]
  bank account, cuenta de banco [KWEHN-*tah de* BAHN-*koh*]
  on account of, a causa de [*ah* KOW-*sah deh*]
  to pay the account, pagar la cuenta [*pah*-GAHR *lah* KWEHN-*tah*]
  to settle an account, arreglar una cuenta [*ah-rreh*-GLAHR OO-*nah* KWEHN-*tah*]
accountant, contador [*kohn-tah*-DOHR]
accurate, exacto, -a [*ehk*-SAHK-*toh, -tah*]
(to) **accuse,** acusar [*ah-koo*-SAHR]
(to be) **accustomed to,** estar acostumbrado a [*ehs*-TAHR *ah-kohs-toom*-BRAH-*doh ah*]
ace, as (m) [*ahs*]
ache, dolor (m) [*doh*-LOHR]
(to) **ache,** doler [*doh*-LEHR]
  My head aches, Tengo dolor de cabeza [TEHN-*goh doh*-LOHR *deh kah*-BEH-*thah*]
(to) **achieve,** lograr [*loh*-GRAHR]
acid (n, adj), ácido [AH-*thee-doh*]
(to) **acknowledge,** reconocer [*reh-koh-noh*-THEHR]
  to acknowledge receipt of a letter, acusar recibo de una carta [*ah-koo*-SAHR *reh*-THEE-*boh deh* OO-*nah* KAHR-*tah*]
acquaintance, conocido, -a [*koh-noh*-THEE-*doh, -dah*]
(to) **acquire,** adquirir [*ahd-kee*-REER]
across, a través de [*ah trah*-VEHS *deh*]
  across the street, al otro lado de la calle [*ahl* OH-*troh* LAH-*doh deh lah* KAH-*l'yeh*]
act, acto [AHK-*toh*]
(to) **act,** actuar [*ahk-too*-AHR]
action, acción (f) [*ahk-th'*YOHN]
active, activo, -a [*ahk*-TEE-*voh, -vah*]
actor, actress, actor, actriz [*ahk*-TOHR, *ahk*-TREETH]
actual, verdadero, -a [*vehr-dah*-DEH-*roh, -rah*]
actually, verdaderamente [*vehr-dah-deh-rah*-MEHN-*teh*]
acute, agudo, -a [*ah*-GOO-*doh, -dah*]
(to) **add,** añadir [*ah-n'yah*-DEER]
(to) **add** (in arithmetic), sumar [*soo*-MAHR]

address, dirección (f) [*dee-rehk-th'*YOHN]
address (speech), discurso [*dees-*KOOR-*soh*]
(to) **address** (a person or group), dirigir la palabra a [*dee-ree-*HEER *lah pah-*LAH-*brah ah*]
(to) **address** (a letter), dirigir una carta [*dee-ree-*HEER OO-*nah* KAHR-*tah*]
addressee, destinatario, -a [*dehs-tee-nah-*TAH-*r'yoh, -r'yah*]
adequate, adecuado, -a [*ah-deh-*KWAH-*doh, -dah*]
adhesive tape, esparadrapo [*ehs-pah-rah-*DRAH-*poh*]
adjective, adjetivo [*ahd-heh-*TEE-*voh*]
(to) **adjust,** ajustar [*ah-hoos-*TAHR]
administration, administración (f) [*ahd-mee-nees-trah-th'*YOHN]
admiral, almirante [*ahl-mee-*RAHN-*teh*]
admiration, admiración [*ahd-mee-rah-th'*YOHN]
(to) **admire,** admirar [*ahd-mee-*RAHR]
admission, admisión, entrada (f) [*ahd-mee-s'*YOHN, *ehn-*TRAH-*dah*]
How much is the admission? ¿Cuánto cuesta la entrada? [KWAHN-*toh* KWEHS-*tah lah ehn-*TRAH-*dah*]
(to) **admit,** admitir [*ahd-mee-*TEER]
admittance, entrada [*ehn-*TRAH-*dah*]
No admittance! ¡Se prohibe entrar! [*seh proh-*EE-*beh ehn-*TRAHR]
(to) **adopt,** adoptar [*ah-dohp-*TAHR]
adorned, adornado, -a [*ah-dohr-*NAH-*doh, -dah*]
adult, adulto, -a [*ah-*DOOL-*toh, -tah*]
(to) **advance,** avanzar [*ah-vahn-*THAHR]
in advance, de antemano [*deh ahn-teh-*MAH-*noh*]
advantage, ventaja [*vehn-*TAH-*hah*]
adventure, aventura [*ah-vehn-*TOO-*rah*]
adventurer, aventurero, -a [*ah-vehn-too-*REH-*roh, -rah*]
adverb, adverbio [*ahd-*VEHR-*b'yoh*]
advertisement, anuncio [*ah-*NOON-*th'yoh*]
advice, consejo [*kohn-*SEH-*hoh*]
(to) **advise,** aconsejar [*ah-kohn-seh-*HAHR]
affair, asunto [*ah-*SOON-*toh*]
(to) **affect,** afectar [*ah-fehk-*TAHR]
affection, afecto, cariño [*ah-*FEHK-*toh, kah-*REE-*n'yoh*]

affectionate, afectuoso, -a, cariñoso, -a [*ah-fehk-too-*OH*-soh, -sah, kah-ree-n'*YOH*-soh, -sah*]

(to) **afford,**

NOTE: No exact equivalent in Spanish. The closest way of saying "I cannot afford ..." is: *No puedo pagar ...* (lit. "I cannot pay ...")

afraid, miedoso, -a [*m'yeh-*DOH*-soh, -sah*]
  to be afraid, tener miedo [*teh-*NEHR *m'*YEH*-doh*]
Africa, Africa [AH*-free-kah*]
African, africano, -a [*ah-free-*KAH*-noh, -nah*]
★ **after,** después [*dehs-*PWEHS]
  after all, después de todo [*dehs-*PWEHS *deh* TOH*-doh*]
★ **afternoon,** tarde (f) [TAHR*-deh*]
  in the afternoon, por la tarde [*pohr lah* TAHR*-deh*]
afterwards, más tarde, después [*mahs* TAHR*-deh, dehs-*PWEHS]
★ **again,** otra vez [OH*-trah vehth*]
  once again, una vez más [OO*-nah vehth mahs*]
  never again, nunca más [NOON*-kah mahs*]
★ **against,** contra [KOHN*-trah*]
age, edad (f) [*eh-*DAHD]
  to be of age, ser de edad [*sehr deh eh-*DAHD]
  to be under age, ser menor de edad [*sehr meh-*NOHR *deh eh-*DAHD]
agency, agencia [*ah-*HEHN*-th'yah*]
  travel agency, agencia de viajes [*ah-*HEHN*-th'yah deh v'*YAH*-hehs*]
agent, agente [*ah-*HEHN*-teh*]
(to) **aggravate,** agravar [*ah-grah-*VAHR]
ago, hace [AH*-theh*]
  long ago, hace mucho tiempo [AH*-theh* MOO*-choh t'*YEHM*-poh*]
  how long ago? ¿cuánto tiempo hace? [KWAHN*-toh t'*YEHM*-poh* AH*-theh*]
  two days ago, hace dos días [AH*-theh dohs* DEE*-ahs*]

(to) **agree,** estar de acuerdo [*ehs*-TAHR *deh ah*-KWEHR-*doh*]

agreeable, agradable [*ah-grah*-DAH-*bleh*]

agreed, convenido [*kohn-veh*-NEE-*doh*]

agreement, acuerdo [*ah*-KWEHR-*doh*]

ahead (in front), por delante [*pohr deh*-LAHN-*teh*]

Go ahead!, ¡adelante! [*ah-deh*-LAHN-*teh*]

aid, ayuda [*ah*-YOO-*dah*]

first aid, primeros auxilios [*pree*-MEH-*rohs ow*-KSEE-*l'yohs*]

First Aid Station, Casa de Socorro [KAH-*sah deh soh*-KOH-*rroh*]

(to) **aim,** apuntar [*ah-poon*-TAHR]

air, aire (m) [EYE-*reh*]

airline, línea aérea [LEE-*neh-ah ah*-EH-*reh-ah*]

airplane, avión (m) [*ah-v'*YOHN]

airport, aeropuerto [*ah-eh-roh*-PWEHR-*toh*]

by air mail, por avión [*pohr ah-v'*YOHN]

alarm, alarma [*ah*-LAHR-*mah*]

alarm-clock, despertador [*dehs-pehr-tah*-DOHR]

alcohol, alcohol (m) [*ahl-koh*-OHL]

alike, igual [*ee*-GWAHL]

alive, vivo, -a [VEE-*voh, -vah*]

★ **all,** todo, -a, todos, -as [TOH-*doh, -dah,* TOH-*dohs, -dahs*]

★ **all right!** ¡está bien! [*ehs*-TAH *b'yehn*]

not at all, de ningún modo [*deh neen*-GOON *moh-doh*]

that's all! eso es todo [EH-*soh ehs* TOH-*doh*]

allied, aliado [*ah-l'*YAH-*doh*]

(to) **allow,** permitir [*pehr-mee*-TEER]

Allow me! ¡Permítame! [*pehr*-MEE-*tah-meh*]

almond, almendra [*ahl*-MEHN-*drah*]

★ **almost,** casi [KAH-*see*]

★ **alone,** solo, -a [SOH-*loh, -ah*]

Leave me alone! ¡Déjeme tranquilo! [DEH-*heh-meh trahn*-KEE-*loh*]

along, a lo largo de [*ah loh* LAHR-*goh deh*]

alongside of, al lado de [*ahl* LAH-*doh deh*]

Come along with me! ¡Venga usted conmigo! [VEHN-*gah oos*-TEHD *kohn*-MEE-*goh*]

aloud, en voz alta [*ehn voth* AHL-*tah*]

★ **also,** también [*tahm-b'*YEHN]
altar, altar (m) [*ahl-*TAHR]
although, aunque [AH-*oon-keh*]
altogether, enteramente [*ehn-teh-rah-*MEHN-*teh*]
★ **always,** siempre [*s'*YEM-*preh*]
★ (I) **am** (for general use), (yo) soy [*soy*]
★ (I) **am** (indicating location), (yo) estoy [*ehs-*TOY]
ambassador, -dress, embajador, -a [*ehm-bah-hah-*DOHR, -DOH-*rah*]
ambitious, ambicioso, -a [*ahm-bee-th'*YOH-*soh, -sah*]
ambulance, ambulancia [*ahm-boo-*LAHN-*th'yah*]
America, América [*ah-*MEH-*ree-kah*]
North America, América del Norte [*dehl* NOHR-*teh*]
South America, América del Sur [*dehl* SOOR]
Central America, América Central [*thehn-*TRAHL]
American, americano, -a [*ah-meh-ree-*KAH-*noh, -nah*]

NOTE: We suggest the alternate use of *norteamericano,* as Latin Americans prefer this term for U.S. citizens. They consider themselves Americans too.

among, entre [EHN-*treh*]
amount, cantidad [*kahn-tee-*DAHD]
(to) **amuse,** divertir [*dee-vehr-*TEER]
amusement, diversión (f) [*dee-vehr-s'*YOHN]
amusing, divertido, -a [*dee-vehr-*TEE-*doh, -dah*]
ancestor, antepasado [*ahn-teh-pah-*SAH-*doh*]
anchor, ancla [AHN-*klah*]
anchovy, anchoa [*ahn-*CHOH-*ah*]
ancient, antiguo, -a [*ahn-*TEE-*gwoh, -ah*]
★ **and,** y, e [*ee, eh*]
NOTE: ***e*** is only used when the following word begins with an ***i***.
angel, ángel (m) [AHN-*hehl*]
anger, enojo [*eh-*NOH-*hoh*]

angle, ángulo [AHN-*goo-loh*]
angry, enojado, -a [*eh-noh*-HAH-*doh, -dah*]
animal, animal [*ah-nee*-MAHL]
ankle, tobillo [*toh*-BEE-*l'yoh*]
anniversary, aniversario [*ah-nee-vehr*-SAH-*r'yoh*]
(to) **announce,** anunciar [*ah-noon-th'*YAHR]
announcement, aviso, anuncio [*ah*-VEE-*soh, ah*-NOON-*th'yoh*]
(to) **annoy,** molestar [*moh-lehs*-TAHR]
annoying, molestoso, -a [*moh-lehs*-TOH-*soh, -sah*]
another, otro, -a [OH-*troh, -trah*]
answer, contestación [*kohn-tehs-tah-th'*YOHN]
★ (to) **answer,** contestar [*kohn-tehs*-TAHR]
ant, hormiga [*ohr*-MEE-*gah*]
anxious, ansioso, -a [*ahn-s'*YOH-*soh, -sah*]
★ **any,** cualquier, -a, algún, alguno, -a [*kwahl-k'*YEHR, *-k* YEH-*rah, ahl*-GOON, *ahl*-GOO-*noh, -nah*]
NOTE: "Any" used for quantity is usually not translated. Have you any money? *¿Tiene dinero?* No I haven't any. *No, no tengo.*
★ **anybody** (anyone), alguien, alguno, cualquiera [*ahl-g'*YEHN, ahl-GOO-*noh, kwahl-k'*YEH-*rah*]
★ **anyhow** (anyway), de cualquier modo [*deh kwahl-k'*YEHR MOH-*doh*]
★ **anything,** cualquier cosa [*kwahl-k'*YEHR KOH-*sah*]
★ **anywhere,** dondequiera [DOHN-*deh-k'*YEH-*rah*]
apartment, apartamiento [*ah-pahr-tah-m'*YEHN-*toh*]
apartment house, casa de apartamientos [KAH-*sah deh ah pahr-tah-m'*YEHN-*tohs*]
(to) **apologize,** excusar(se) [*ehks-koo*-SAHR-*seh*]
(to) **appear,** aparecer(se), parecer [*ah-pah-reh*-THEHR-*seh, pah-reh*-THEHR]
appearance, apariencia, aspecto [*ah-pah-r'*YEHN-*th'yah, ahs*-PEHK-*toh*]
appendicitis, apendicitis [*ah-pehn-dee*-THEE-*tees*]
appetite, apetito [*ah-peh*-TEE-*toh*]
(to) **applaud,** aplaudir [*ah-plow*-DEER]

apple, manzana [*mahn*-THAH-*nah*]
  apple pie, pastel de manzanas [*pahs*-TEHL *deh mahn*-THAH-*nahs*]
(to) **apply,** aplicar [*ah-plee*-KAHR]
(to) **apply for,** solicitar [*soh-lee-thee*-TAHR]
appointment, compromiso [*kohm-proh*-MEE-*soh*]
(to) **appreciate,** apreciar [*ah-preh-th'*YAHR]
(to) **approach,** acercar(se) [*ah-thehr*-KAHR-*seh*]
appropriate, apropiado, -a [*ah-proh-p'*YAH-*doh, -dah*]
(to) **approve,** aprobar, sancionar [*ah-proh*-BAHR, *sahn-th'yoh*-NAHR]
April, abril [*ah*-BREEL]
apron, delantal (m) [*deh-lahn*-TAHL]
Arab, árabe [AH-*rah-beh*]
Arabia, Arabia [*ah*-RAH-*b'yah*]
architect, arquitecto [*ahr-kee*-TEHK-*toh*]
architecture, arquitectura [*ahr-kee-tehk*-TOO-*rah*]
★ **are,**

NOTE: for general use:
(we) **are,** somos [SOH-*mohs*]
(you *or* they) **are,** son [*sohn*]
  to indicate location:
(we) **are,** estamos [*ehs*-TAH-*mohs*]
(you *or* they) **are,** están [*ehs*-TAHN]

area, superficie, área [*soo-pehr*-FEE-*th'yeh,* AH-*reh-ah*]
Argentina, Argentina [*ahr-hehn*-TEE-*nah*]
Argentine, argentino, -a [*ahr-hehn*-TEE-*noh, -nah*]
argument, disputa [*dees*-POO-*tah*]
arithmetic, aritmética [*ah-reet*-MEH-*tee-kah*]
arm (part of body), brazo [BRAH-*thoh*]
arm (weapon), arma [AHR-*mah*]
armchair, butaca [*boo*-TAH-*kah*]
army, ejército [*eh*-HEHR-*thee-toh*]
around, alrededor [*ahl-reh-deh*-DOHR]
  around 6 o'clock, alrededor de las seis [*ahl-reh-deh*-DOHR *deh lahs* SEH-*ees*]

(to) **arrange,** arreglar [*ah-rreh-*GLAHR]
arrangement, arreglo [*ah-*RREH-*gloh*]
(to) **arrest,** detener [*deh-teh-*NEHR]
arrival, llegada [*l'yeh-*GAH-*dah*]
(to) **arrive,** llegar, arribar [*l'yeh-*GAHR, *ah-rree-*BAHR]
art, arte (m) [AHR-*teh*]
article, artículo [*ahr-*TEE-*koo-loh*]
artificial, artificial [*ahr-tee-fee-th'*YAHL]
artillery, artillería [*ahr-tee-l'yeh-*REE-*ah*]
artist, artista (m & f) [*ahr-*TEES-*tah*]
★ **as,** como [KOH-*moh*]
  as . . . as, tan . . . como [*tahn* . . . KOH-*moh*]
  as big as, tan grande como [*tahn* GRAHN-*deh* KOH-*moh*]
  as much as, tanto como [TAHN-*toh* KOH-*moh*]
ash, ceniza [*theh-*NEE-*thah*]
ash-tray, cenicero [*theh-nee-*THEH-*roh*]
ashamed, avergonzado, -a [*ah-vehr-gohn-*THAH-*doh, -dah*]
Asia, Asia [AH-*s'yah*]
asiatic, asiático, -a [*ah-s'*YAH-*tee-koh, -kah*]
aside, aparte [*ah-*PAHR-*teh*]
★ (to) **ask** (a question), preguntar [*preh-goon-*TAHR]
★ (to) **ask** (for something), pedir [*peh-*DEER]
asleep, dormido, -a [*dohr-*MEE-*doh, -dah*]
  (to) **fall asleep,** dormirse [*dohr-*MEER-*seh*]
asparagus, espárragos [*ehs-*PAH-*rrah-gohs*]
aspirin, aspirina [*ahs-pee-*REE-*nah*]
(to) **assemble** (people or things), reunir [*reh-oo-*NEER]
(to) **assemble** (a machine), montar [*mohn-*TAHR]
(to) **assist,** ayudar [*ah-yoo-*DAHR]
assistant, ayudante [*ah-yoo-*DAHN-*teh*]
associate (also) **associated,** asociado [*ah-soh-th'*YAH-*doh*]
(to) **assure,** asegurar [*ah-seh-goo-*RAHR]
(to) **astonish,** asombrar [*ah-sohm-*BRAHR]
  How astonishing! ¡Qué asombroso! [*keh ah-sohm-*BROH-*soh*]
asylum, asilo [*ah-*SEE-*loh*]

★ **at,** a, en [*ah, ehn*]
at first, al principio [*ahl preen*-THEE-*p'yoh*]
at last, al fin [*ahl feen*]
at once, en seguida [*ehn seh*-GHEE-*dah*]
at the same time, al mismo tiempo [*ahl* MEES-*moh t'*YEHM-*poh*]
at eight o'clock, a las ocho [*ah lahs* OH-*choh*]
athletics, deportes [*deh*-POHR-*tehs*]
Atlantic, Atlántico [*aht*-LAHN-*tee-koh*]
atmosphere (air), atmósfera [*aht*-MOHS-*feh-rah*]
atomic, atómico, -a [*ah*-TOH-*mee-koh, -kah*]
atom bomb, bomba atómica [BOHM-*bah ah*-TOH-*mee-kah*]
(to) **attach,** fijar [*fee*-HAHR]
(to) **attack,** atacar [*ah-tah*-KAHR]
(to) **attempt to,** probar [*proh*-BAHR]
(to) **attend,** asistir a [*ah-sees*-TEER *ah*]
(to) **attend to,** atender a [*ah-tehn*-DEHR *ah*]
attendant, encargado [*ehn-kahr*-GAH-*doh*]
attention, atención (f) [*ah-tehn-th'*YOHN]
attentive, atento, -a [*ah*-TEHN-*toh, -tah*]
attic, desván (m) [*dehs*-VAHN]
attitude, actitud (f) [*ahk-tee*-TUHD]
attorney, abogado [*ah-boh*-GAH-*doh*]
(to) **attract,** atraer [*ah-trah*-EHR]
attractive, atractivo, -a [*ah-trahk*-TEE-*voh, -vah*]
audience, auditorio [*ow-dee*-TOH-*r'yoh*)
August, agosto [*ah*-GOHS-*toh*]
aunt, tía [TEE-*ah*]
Australia, Australia [*ows*-TRAH-*l'yah*]
Australian, australiano, -a [*ows-trah-l'*YAH-*noh, -nah*]
Austria, Austria [ows-*tree-yah*]
Austrian, austriaco, -a [*ows-tree*-AH-*koh, -kah*]
author, autor, -a [*ow*-TOHR, *-rah*]
authority, autoridad (f) [*ow-toh-ree*-DAHD]
automobile, automóvil [*ow-toh*-MOH-*veel*]
autumn, otoño [*oh*-TOH-*n'yoh*]

available, disponible [*dees-poh*-NEE-*bleh*]
avenue, avenida [*ah-veh*-NEE-*dah*]
average, promedio [*proh*-MEH-*d'yoh*]
  on the average, por termino medio [*pohr* TEHR-*mee-noh* MEH-*d'yoh*]
(to) **avoid,** evitar [*eh-vee*-TAHR]
(to) **awake,** despertar(se) [*dehs-pehr*-TAHR-*seh*]
awake (adj), despierto, -a [*dehs-p'*YEHR-*toh, -tah*]
aware, enterado, -a [*ehn-teh*-RAH-*doh, -dah*]
away (for a person), ausente [*ow*-SEHN-*teh*]
away (for a place), lejos [LEH-*hohs*]
  far away, muy lejos [*mwee* LEH-*hohs*]
  (to) **go away,** irse [EER-*seh*]
awe, pavor, terror [*pah*-VOHR, *teh*-RROHR]
awful, terrible [*teh*-RREE-*bleh*]
ax, hacha [AH-*chah*]
  NOTE: *hacha* is a feminine word but nevertheless uses the article *el* in the singular.
axle, eje [EH-*heh*]

B

baby, bebé, nene [*beh*-BEH, NEH-*neh*]
bachelor, soltero, -a [*sohl*-TEH-*roh, -rah*]
back (n), espalda [*ehs*-PAHL-*dah*]
back (adv), atrás [*ah*-TRAHS]
  When will you (he, she) be back? ¿Cuándo estará de vuelta? [KWAHN-*doh ehs-tah*-RAH *deh v'*WEHL-*tah*]
backward (adj), atrasado, -a [*ah-trah*-SAH-*doh, -dah*]
(to) **go backward,** retroceder [*reh-troh-theh*-DEHR]
bacon, tocino [*toh*-THEE-*noh*]
★ **bad,** malo, -a [MAH-*loh, -lah*]
  That's too bad! ¡Qué lástima! [*keh* LAHS-*tee-mah*]
badly, mal [*mahl*]
bag, saco, bolsa [SAH-*koh,* BOHL-*sah*]
baggage, equipaje (m) [*eh-kee*-PAH-*heh*]

bakery, panadería [*pah-nah-deh-*REE-*ah*]
bald, calvo [KAHL-*voh*]
ball (for playing), pelota [*peh-*LOH-*tah*]
balloon, globo [GLOH-*boh*]
banana, plátano [PLAH-*tah-noh*]
band (music), banda [BAHN-*dah*]
bandage, vendaje [*vehn-*DAH-*heh*]
bandit, bandido [BAHN-*dee-doh*]
bank, banco [BAHN-*koh*]
  bank note, billete de banco [*bee-l'*YEH-*teh deh* BAHN-*koh*]
bankruptcy, quiebra [*k'*YEH-*brah*]
banquet, banquete (m) [*bahn-*KEH-*teh*]
baptism, bautizo [*bow-*TEE-*thoh*]
bar (metal), barra [BAH-*rrah*]
barber, barbero [*bahr-*BEH-*roh*]
bare, desnudo, -a [*dehs-*NOO-*doh, -dah*]
bargain (merchandise) ganga [GAHN-*gah*]
(to) **bargain,** regatear [*reh-gah-teh-*AHR]
bark (of tree), corteza [*kohr-*TEH-*thah*]
bark (of dog), ladrido [*lah-*DREE-*doh*]
barracks, cuartel [*kwahr-*TEHL]
barrel, barril [*bah-*RREEL]
base, base [BAH-*seh*]
basement, sótano [SOH-*tah-noh*]
basic, básico, -a [BAH-*see-koh, -kah*]
basket, canasta [*kah-*NAHS-*tah*]
bath, baño [BAH-*n'yoh*]
  to take a bath, tomar un baño [*toh-*MAHR *oon* BAH-*n'yoh*]
bathing-suit, traje de baño [TRAH-*heh deh* BAH-*n'yoh*]
★ **bathroom,** cuarto de baño [KWAHR-*toh deh* BAH-*n'yoh*]
bathtub, bañera [*bah-n'*YEH-*rah*]
battalion, batallón (m) [*bah-tahl-l'*YOHN]
battery, batería [*bah-teh-*REE-*ah*]
battle, batalla [*bah-*TAH-*l'yah*]
battleship, acorazado [*ah-koh-rah-*THAH-*doh*]
bay, bahía [*bah-*EE-*ah*]

(to) **be,** ser, estar [*sehr, eh-*STAHR]

NOTE: There are two words for "to be": *estar* is used for location and position; *ser* covers most other uses.
Attention: Many important idioms used in English with "to be" are expressed by *tener* as follows:

to be afraid, tener miedo [*teh-*NEHR *m'*YEH-*doh*]
to be ashamed, tener verguenza [*teh-*NEHR *vehr-*GWEHN-*thah*]
to be cold, tener frío [*teh-*NEHR FREE-*oh*]
to be warm, tener calor [*teh-*NEHR *kah-*LOHR]
to be sleepy, tener sueño [*teh-*NEHR *s'*WEH-*n'yoh*]
to be right, tener razón [*teh-*NEHR *rah-*THOHN]
to be wrong, estar equivocado [*ehs-*TAHR *eh-kee-voh-*KAH-*doh*]
to be sorry, sentir [*sehn-*TEER]
to be hungry, tener hambre [*teh-*NEHR AHM-*breh*]
to be thirsty, tener sed [*teh-*NEHR *sehd*]

beach, playa [PLAH-*yah*]
bean, habichuela, frijol, judía, haba [*ah-bee-ch'*WEH-*lah, free-*HOHL, *hoo-*DEE-*ah,* AH-*bah*]
NOTE: The translation of "bean" as well as several other vegetables and fruits, varies from place to place.
bear, oso [OH-*soh*]
(to) **bear** (endure), aguantar [*ah-gwahn-*TAHR]
(to) **bear** (children), dar a luz [*dahr ah looth*]
(to) **bear** (animals), parir [*pah-*REER]
(to) **bear** (fruit), producir [*proh-doo-*THEER]
beard, barba [BAHR-*bah*]
beast, bestia [BEHS-*t'yah*]
(to) **beat** (defeat), derrotar [*deh-rroh-*TAHR]
beautiful, hermoso, -a, bello, -a [*ehr-*MOH-*soh, -sah,* BEH-*l'yoh, -l'yah*]
beauty, belleza [*beh-l'*YEH-*thah*]

beauty parlor, salón de belleza (m) [*sah*-LOHN *deh beh-l'*YEH-*thah*]
because, porque [*pohr*-KEH]
because of you, por causa de Ud. [*pohr* KOW-*sah deh oos*-TEHD]
(to) **become,** llegar a ser [*l'yeh*-GAHR *ah sehr*]
bed, cama [KAH-*mah*]
bedroom, dormitorio [*dohr-mee*-TOH-*r'yoh*]
bee, abeja [*ah*-BEH-*hah*]
beef, carne (f) de res [KAHR-*neh deh rehs*]
beer, cerveza [*thehr*-VEH-*thah*]
beet, remolacha [*reh-moh*-LAH-*chah*]
★ **before** (conj), antes [AHN-*tehs*]
★ (prep), delante de [*deh*-LAHN-*teh deh*]
before he comes, antes que venga [AHN-*tehs keh* VEHN-*gah*]
beforehand, de antemano [*deh ahn-teh*-MAH-*noh*]
★ (to) **begin,** empezar [*ehm-peh*-THAHR]
beginning, principio [*preen*-THEE-*p'yoh*]
(to) **behave,** conducir(se) [*kohn-doo*-THEER-*seh*]
Behave yourself! ¡Pórtese bien! [POHR-*teh-seh b'yehn*]
behavior, comportamiento [*kohm-pohr-tah-m'*YEHN-*toh*]
★ **behind,** detrás de, atrás [*deh*-TRAHS *deh, ah*-TRAHS]
belief, creencia [*kreh*-EHN-*th'yah*]
★ (to) **believe,** creer [*kreh*-EHR]
Belgian, belga (m and f) [BEHL-*gah*]
Belgium, Bélgica [BEHL-*hee-kah*]
bell, campana [*kahm*-PAH-*nah*]
bellboy, botones [*boh*-TOH-*nehs*]
belong (to), pertenecer [*pehr-teh-neh*-THEHR]
It belongs to me, Me pertenece. [*meh pehr-teh*-NEH-*theh*]
below, abajo, debajo de [*ah*-BAH-*hoh, deh*-BAH-*hoh deh*]
belt, cinturón [*theen-too*-ROHN]
bench, banco [BAHN-*koh*]
(to) **bend,** doblar [*doh*-BLAHR]
benefit, beneficio [*beh-neh*-FEE-*th'yoh*]
beside, al lado de [*ahl* LAH-*doh deh*]
besides, además [*ah-deh*-MAHS]

★ (the) **best,** (el or la) mejor [*meh*-HOHR]
bet, apuesta [*ah*-PWEHS-*tah*]
(to) **bet,** apostar [*ah-pohs*-TAHR]
(to) **betray,** traicionar, vender [*try-th'yoh*-NAHR, *vehn*-DEHR]
better, mejor [*meh*-HOHR]
★ **between,** entre [EHN-*treh*]
Beware! ¡cuidado! [*kwee*-DAH-*doh*]
Beware of the dog, Cuidado con el perro. [*kwee*-DAH-*doh kohn ehl* PEH-*rroh*]
beyond, más allá [*mahs ah-l'*YAH]
bible, biblia [BEE-*bl'yah*]
bicycle, bicicleta [*bee-thee*-KLEH-*tah*]
★ **big,** grande [GRAHN-*deh*]
bill, cuenta [KWEHN-*tah*]
bill of fare, lista de platos [LEES-*tah deh* PLAH-*tohs*]
Send me the bill, Mándeme la cuenta [MAHN-*deh-meh lah* KWEHN-*tah*]
billion, mil millones [*meel mee-l'*YOH-*nehs*]
(to) **bind,** atar [*ah*-TAHR]
★ **bird,** pájaro [PAH-*hah-roh*]
birth, nacimiento [*nah-thee-m'*YEHN-*toh*]
birthday, cumpleaños [*koom-pleh*-AH-*n'yohs*]
Happy Birthday! ¡Feliz cumpleaños! [*feh*-LEETH *koom-pleh*-AH-*n'yohs*]
biscuit, bizcocho [*beeth*-KOH-*choh*]
bishop, obispo [*oh*-BEES-*poh*]
archbishop, arzobispo [*ahr-thoh*-BEES-*poh*]
(a) **bit,** (un) pedacito [*oon peh-dah*-THEE-*toh*]
(to) **bite,** morder [*mohr*-DEHR]
bitter, amargo, -a [*ah*-MAHR-*goh, -gah*]
bitterness, amargura [*ah-mahr*-GOO-*rah*]
★ **black,** negro, -a [NEH-*groh, -grah*]
blade, hoja [OH-*hah*]
blame, culpa [KOOL-*pah*]
blank, en blanco [*ehn* BLAHN-*koh*]
blanket, frazada [*frah*-THAH-*dah*]
(to) **bleed,** sangrar [*sahn*-GRAHR]
blessing, bendición [*behn-dee-th'*YOHN]
blind, ciego, -a [*th'*YEH-*goh, -gah*]

blister, ampolla [*ahm*-POH-*l'yah*]
block, cuadra [KWAH-*drah*]
four blocks from here, a cuatro cuadras de aquí [*ah* KWAH-*troh* KWAH-*drahs deh ah*-KEE]
blonde, rubio, -a [ROO-*b'yoh, -b'yah*]
blood, sangre (f) [SAHN-*greh*]
blouse, blusa [BLOO-*sah*]
blow, golpe (m) [GOHL-*peh*]
(to) **blow,** soplar [*soh*-PLAHR]
★ **blue,** azul [*ah*-THOOL]
board (lumber), tabla [TAH-*blah*]
boarding-house, casa de huéspedes [KAH-*sah deh* WEHS-*peh-dehs*]
boat, barco [BAHR-*koh*]
body, cuerpo [KWEHR-*poh*]
(to) **boil,** hervir [*ehr*-VEER]
bold, audaz [*ow*-DAHTH]
Bolivia, Bolivia [*boh*-LEE-*v'yah*]
Bolivian, boliviano, -a [*boh-lee-v'*YAH-*noh, -nah*]
bomb, bomba [BOHM-*bah*]
bombardment, bombardeo [*bohm-bahr*-DEH-*oh*]
bond (financial), bono [BOH-*noh*]
bone, hueso [*oo*-EH-*soh*]
★ **book,** libro [LEE-*broh*]
bookstore, librería [*lee-breh*-REE-*ah*]
boot, bota [BOH-*tah*]
border, frontera [*frohn*-TEH-*rah*]
(to) **bore** (a hole), taladrar [*tah-lah*-DRAHR]
boring, aburrido, -a [*ah-boo*-RREE-*doh, -dah*]
(to) **be born,** nacer [*nah*-THEHR]

NOTE: *nacer* is actively used, not passively as in English.

Where were you born? ¿Dónde nació? [DOHN-*deh* NAH-*th'yoh?*]

(to) **borrow,** pedir [*peh*-DEER]

★ **both,** ambos, -bas; los (las) dos [AHM-*bohs, -bahs, lohs (lahs) dohs*]

(to) **bother,** molestar(se) [*moh-lehs*-TAHR-*seh*]

Don't bother! ¡No se moleste! [*noh seh moh*-LEHS-*teh*]

Don't bother me! ¡No me moleste! [*noh meh moh*-LEHS-*teh*]

bottle, botella [*boh*-TEH-*l'yah*]

bottle-opener, abridor de botellas [*ah-bree*-DOHR *deh boh* TEH-*l'yahs*]

bottom, fondo [FOHN-*doh*]

boundary, límite [LEE-*mee-teh*]

bow (ship), proa [PROH-*ah*]

bow (on dress), lazo [LAH-*thoh*]

bowl, tazón [*tah*-THOHN]

★ **box,** caja [KAH-*hah*]

boxing (sport), boxeo [*boh*-KSEH-*oh*]

★ **boy,** muchacho [*moo*-CHAH-*choh*]

bracelet, pulsera [*pool*-SEH-*rah*]

braid, trenza [TREHN-*thah*]

brain, cerebro [*theh*-REH-*broh*]

brake, freno [FREH-*noh*]

branch (tree), rama [RAH-*mah*]

branch (business), sucursal [*soo-koor*-SAHL]

brand, marca [MAHR-*kah*]

brandy, coñac [*koh-n'*YAHK]

brass, latón (m) [*lah*-TOHN]

brassiere, ajustador (m) [*ah-hoos-tah*-DOHR]

Brazil, Brasil (m) [*brah*-SEEL]

Brazilian, brasileño [*brah-see*-LEH-*n'yoh*]

brave, valiente [*vah-l'*YEHN-*teh*]

★ **bread,** pan (m) [*pahn*]

(to) **break,** romper [*rohm*-PEHR]

★ **breakfast,** desayuno [*deh-sah*-YOO-*noh*]

to have breakfast, desayunar(se) [*deh-sah-yoo*-NAHR-*(seh)*]

breast, pecho [PEH-*choh*]

(to) **breathe,** respirar [*rehs-pee*-RAHR]

breath, aliento [*ah-l'*YEHN-*toh*]

breeze, brisa [BREE-*sah*]
(to) **bribe,** sobornar [*soh-bohr*-NAHR]
brick, ladrillo [*lah*-DREE-*l'yoh*]
bride, novia [NOH-*v'yah*]
bridegroom, novio [NOH-*v'yoh*]
bridesmaid, dama de honor [DAH-*mah deh oh*-NOHR]
bridge, puente [PWEHN-*teh*]
brief, breve [BREH-*veh*]
bright (and) **brilliant,** brillante [*bree-l'*YAHN-*teh*]
★ (to) **bring,** traer [*trah*-EHR]
to bring about, lograr [*loh*-GRAHR]
to bring together, reunir [*reh-oo*-NEER]
to bring up, educar [*eh-doo*-KAHR]
★ **Bring me . . . ,** Tráigame . . . [TRY-*gah-meh*]
British, británico, -a [*bree*-TAH-*nee-koh, -kah*]
broad, amplio, -a [AHM-*pl'yoh, -pl'yah*]
broadcast, transmisión (f) [*trahns-mee-s'*YOHN]
(to) **broil,** asar sobre las ascuas o en parrillas [*ah*-SAHR SOH-*breh lahs* AHS-*kwahs oh ehn pahr*-REE-*l'yahs*]
broiled, a la parrilla [*ah lah pahr*-REE-*l'yah*]
broken, roto, -a [ROH-*toh, -tah*]
bronze, bronce (m) [BROHN-*theh*]
brook, arroyo [*ahr*-ROH-*yoh*]
broom, escoba [*ehs*-KOH-*bah*]
★ **brother,** hermano [*ehr*-MAH-*noh*]
brother-in-law, cuñado [*koo-n'*YAH-*doh*]
★ **brown,** castaño [*kahs*-TAH-*n'yoh*]
brush (hair), cepillo [*theh*-PEE-*l'yoh*]
brush (paint), brocha, pincel (m) [BROH-*chah*, PEEN-*thehl*]
brush (for clothes), cepillo para la ropa [*theh*-PEE-*l'yoh* PAH-*rah lah* ROH-*pah*]
brush (for teeth), cepillo de dientes [*theh*-PEE-*l'yoh deh d'*YEHN-*tehs*]
(to) **brush,** cepillar [*theh-pee-l'*YAHR]
buckle, hebilla [*eh*-BEE-*l'yah*]
budget, presupuesto [*preh-soo*-PWEHS-*toh*]
(to) **build,** construir [*kohns-troo*-EER]

building, edificio [*eh-dee-*FEE-*th'yoh*]
bulb (light), bombilla [*bohm-*BEE-*l'yah*]
bull, toro [TOH-*roh*]
bullfight, corrida de toros [*koh-*RREE-*dah deh* TOH-*rohs*]
bullfighter, torero [*toh-*REH-*roh*]
NOTE: *Not* toreador.
burden, carga [KAHR-*gah*]
(to) **burn,** quemar [*keh-*MAHR]
bureau, tocador (m) [*toh-kah-*DOHR]
(to) **burst,** reventar [*reh-vehn-*TAHR]
bus, autobús (m) [*ow-toh-*BOOS]
bush, arbusto [*ahr-*BOOS-*toh*]
business, negocio, -s, comercio [*neh-*GOH-*th'yoh, -s, koh-*MEHR-*th'yoh*]
to do business with, hacer negocios con [*ah-*THEHR *neh-*GOH-*th'yohs kohn*]
business man, hombre de negocios [OHM-*breh deh neh-*GOH-*th'yohs*]
busy, ocupado, -a [*oh-koo-*PAH-*doh, -dah*]
★ **but,** pero [PEH-*roh*]
butcher-shop, carnicería [*kahr-nee-theh-*REE-*ah*]
butter, mantequilla [*mahn-teh-*KEE-*l'yah*]
butterfly, mariposa [*mah-ree-*POH-*sah*]
button, botón (m) [*boh-*TOHN]
★ (to) **buy,** comprar [*kohm-*PRAHR]
buyer, comprador [*kohm-prah-*DOHR]
★ **by,** por, a, para [*pohr, ah,* PAH-*rah*]
by chance, por casualidad [*pohr kah-swah-lee-*DAHD]
by hand, a mano [*ah* MAH-*noh*]
by the way, a propósito [*ah proh-*POH-*see-toh*]
by then, para entonces [PAH-*rah ehn-*TOHN-*thehs*]

NOTE: Spanish uses the present participle alone for constructions where English often uses "by." Examples: "By reading"—*leyendo,* "by speaking"—*hablando.*

C

cab, taxi (m) [*tah*-KSEE]
cabbage, repollo [*reh*-POH-*l'yoh*]
cabaret, cabaret (m) [*kah-bah*-REHT]
cabinet, gabinete (m) [*gah-bee*-NEH-*teh*]
cable, cable (m) [KAH-*bleh*]
café, café (m) [*kah*-FEH]
cage, jaula [HOW-*lah*]
cake, torta [TOHR-*tah*]
calendar, calendario [*kah-lehn*-DAH-*r'yoh*]
calf, ternero [*tehr*-NEH-*roh*]
call, llamada [*l'yah*-MAH-*dah*]
  telephone call, llamada por teléfono [*l'yah*-MAH-*dah-pohr teh*-LEH-*foh-noh*]
★ (to) **call,** llamar [*l'yah*-MAHR]
  to call off, suspender [*soos-pehn*-DEHR]
  to call on, visitar [*vee-see*-TAHR]
  Call me at 6:30. Llámeme a las seis y media. [L'YAH-*meh-meh ah lahs* SEH-*ees ee* MEH-*d'yah*]
calm (adj), tranquilo, -a [*trahn*-KEE-*loh, -lah*]
  Calm down! ¡Tranquilícese! [*trahn-kee*-LEE-*theh-seh*]
camera, cámara [KAH-*mah-rah*]
camp, campamento [*kahm-pah*-MEHN-*toh*]
★ **can** (to be able), poder [*poh*-DEHR]
  I can, yo puedo [*yoh* PWEH-*doh*]
  Can you? ¿Puede Ud.? [PWEH-*deh oos*-TEHD]

NOTE: "Can" is expressed by the verb *poder* followed by the infinitive of the next verb: "Can you come?" *¿Puede Ud. venir?*

can, lata [LAH-*tah*]
  can opener, abrelatas (m) [*ah-breh*-LAH-*tahs*]

Canada, Canadá [*kah-nah-*DAH]
Canadian, canadiense [*kah-nah-d'*YEHN-*seh*]
canal, canal (m) [*kah-*NAHL]
(to) **cancel,** anular [*ah-noo-*LAHR]
candle, vela [VEH-*lah*]
candy, dulce (m) [DOOL-*theh*]
cane, bastón (m) [*bahs-*TOHN]
sugar-cane, caña de azúcar [KAH-*n'yah deh ah-*THOO-*kahr*]
cap, gorra [GOH-*rrah*]
capable, capaz [*kah-*PATH]
capacity, capacidad (f) [*kah-pah-thee-*DAHD]
capital (money), capital (m) [*kah-pee-*TAHL]
capital (city), capital (f) [*kah-pee-*TAHL]
captain, capitán (m) [*kah-pee-*TAHN]
car, automóvil (m) [*ow-toh-*MOH-*veel*]
street-car, tranvía (m) [*trahn-*VEE-*ah*]
card, tarjeta [*tahr-*HEH-*tah*]
calling card, tarjeta de visita [*tahr-*HEH-*tah deh vee-*SEE-*tah*]
playing cards, naipes (m) [NAH-*ee-pehs*]
cardinal, cardenal (m) [*kahr-deh-*NAHL]
care, cuidado [*kwee-*DAH-*doh*]
I don't care. No me importa. [*noh meh eem-*POHR-*tah*]
in care of, al cuidado de [*ahl kwee-*DAH-*doh deh*]
to take care of, cuidar de [*kwee-*DAHR *deh*]
Take care! ¡Tenga cuidado! [TEHN-*gah kwee-*DAH-*doh*]
career, carrera [*kahr-*REH-*rah*]
(to) **care for,** gustar (See note on "to like")
careful, cuidadoso, prudente; esmerado [*kwee-dah-*DOH-*soh, proo-*DEHN-*teh; ehs-meh-*RAH-*doh*]
★ **Be careful!** ¡Cuidado! [*kwee-*DAH-*doh*]
carefully, cuidadosamente [*kwee-dah-doh-sah-*MEHN-*teh*]
careless, descuidado, -a [*dehs-kwee-*DAH-*doh, -dah*]
Caribbean Sea, el mar Caribe [*ehl mahr kah-*REE-*beh*]
carpenter, carpintero [*kahr-peen-*TEH-*roh*]
carpet, alfombra [*ahl-*FOHM-*brah*]
(to) **carry,** llevar [*l'yeh-*VAHR]

case (matter), caso [KAH-*soh*]
case (box), caja [KAH-*hah*]
in that case, en ese caso [*ehn* EH-*seh* KAH-*soh*]
in any case, en todo caso [*ehn* TOH-*doh* KAH-*soh*]
cash, dinero efectivo [*dee*-NEH-*roh eh-fehk*-TEE-*voh*]
to pay cash, pagar al contado [*pah*-GAHR *ahl kohn*-TAH-*doh*]
(to) **cash,** cobrar [*koh*-BRAHR]
cashier, cajero [*kah*-HEH-*roh*]
castanets, castañuelas [*kahs-tah*-NWEH-*lahs*]
Castilian, castellano [*kahs-teh-l'*YAH-*noh*]

NOTE: The Spanish language, originally the dialect of Castilla, can be called either *castellano* or *español.*

castle, castillo [*kahs*-TEE-*l'yoh*]
★ **cat,** gato [GAH-*toh*]
catalog, catálogo [*kah*-TAH-*loh-goh*]
Catalonian, catalán, catalana [*kah-tah*-LAHN, *kah-tah*-LAH-*nah*]
(to) **catch,** coger [*koh*-HEHR]
to catch cold, coger catarro [*koh*-HEHR *kah*-TAH-*rroh*]
category, categoría [*kah-teh-goh*-REE-*ah*]
cathedral, catedral (f) [*kah-teh*-DRAHL]
Catholic, católico, -a [*kah*-TOH-*lee-koh, -kah*]
cattle, ganado [*gah*-NAH-*doh*]
cauliflower, coliflor (f) [*koh-lee*-FLOHR]
cause, causa [KOW-*sah*]
caution, precaución (f) [*preh-kow-th'*YOHN]
Caution! ¡Cuidado! [*kwee*-DAH-*doh*]
cavalry, caballería [*kah-bah-l'yeh*-REE-*ah*]
cave, cueva [KWEH-*vah*]
cavity, cavidad (f) [*kah-vee*-DAHD]
(to) **cease,** cesar [*theh*-SAHR]
ceiling, cielo raso [*th'*YEH-*loh* RAH-*soh*]
(to) **celebrate,** celebrar [*theh-leh*-BRAHR]

celery, apio [AH-*p'yoh*]
cellar, bodega [*boh*-DEH-*gah*]
cement, cemento [*theh*-MEHN-*toh*]
cent, centavo [*thehn*-TAH-*voh*]
center, centro [THEHN-*troh*]
central, central [*thehn*-TRAHL]
central-heating, calefacción central (f) [*kah-leh-fahk-th'*YOHN *thehn*-TRAHL]
century, siglo [SEE-*gloh*]
cereal, cereal (m) [*theh-reh*-AHL]
ceremony, ceremonia [*theh-reh*-MOH-*n'yah*]
certain, cierto [*th'*YEHR-*toh*]
certainly, ciertamente [*th'yehr-tah*-MEHN-*teh*]
certificate, certificado [*thehr-tee-fee*-KAH-*doh*]
(to) **certify,** certificar [*thehr-tee-fee*-KAHR]
chain, cadena [*kah*-DEH-*nah*]
★ **chair,** silla [SEE-*l'yah*]
chalk, tiza [TEE-*thah*]
champagne, champaña [*chahm*-PAH-*n'yah*]
champion, campeón (m) [*kahm-peh*-OHN]
chance, casualidad (f) [*kah-soo-ah-lee*-DAHD]
  by chance, por casualidad (f) [*pohr kah-soo-ah-lee*-DAHD]
  to take a chance, correr un albur [*kohr*-REHR *oon ahl*-BOOR]
change, cambio [KAHM-*b'yoh*]
change (money), suelto [SWEHL-*toh*]
(to) **change,** cambiar [*kahm-b'*YAHR]
channel, canal (m) [*kah*-NAHL]
chapel, capilla [*kah*-PEE-*l'yah*]
chapter, capítulo [*kah*-PEE-*too-loh*]
character, carácter (m) [*kah*-RAHK-*tehr*]
characteristic (adj), característico, -a [*kah-rahk-teh*-REES-*tee-koh, -kah*]
charcoal, carbón (m) [*kahr*-BOHN]
(to) **charge** (a battery), cargar [*kahr*-GAHR]
(to) **charge** (a customer), cobrar [*koh*-BRAHR]
charity, caridad (f) [*kah-ree*-DAHD]
charming, encantador, -a [*ehn-kahn-tah*-DOHR, -*rah*]

(to) **chat,** charlar [*chahr*-LAHR]
chauffeur, chofer (m) [*choh*-FEHR]
cheap, barato, -a [*bah*-RAH-*toh, -tah*]
cheaper, más barato [*mahs-bah*-RAH-*toh*]
(to) **cheat,** engañar, timar, trampear [*ehn-gah-n'*YAHR, *tee*-MAHR, *trahm-peh*-AHR]
check (bank), cheque (m) [CHEH-*keh*]
check (bill), cuenta [KWEHN-*tah*]
check (baggage), comprobante (m) [*kohm-proh*-BAHN-*teh*]
check (verification), comprobación (f) [*kohm-proh-bah-th'*YOHN]
(to) **check** (verify), comprobar, verificar [*kohm-pro*-BAHR, *veh-ree-fee*-KAHR]
(to) **check** (luggage), facturar [*fahk-too*-RAHR]
checking account, cuenta corriente [KWEHN-*tah koh-rr'*YEHN-*teh*]
cheek, mejilla [*meh*-HEE-*l'yah*]
cheerful, alegre [*ah*-LEH-*greh*]
cheese, queso [KEH-*soh*]
chemical, químico [KEE-*mee-koh*]
cherry, cereza [*theh*-REH-*thah*]
chest (of person), pecho [PEH-*choh*]
chest of drawers, cómoda [KOH-*moh-dah*]
chestnut, castaña [*kahs*-TAH-*n'yah*]
(to) **chew,** masticar [*mahs-tee*-KAHR]
chicken, pollo [POH-*l'yoh*]
chief (n) jefe (m) [HEH-*feh*]
chief (adj) principal [*preen-thee*-PAHL]
★ **child,** niño [NEE-*n'yoh*]
Chile, Chile [CHEE-*leh*]
Chilean, chileno, -a [*chee*-LEH-*noh, -nah*]
chilly, frío [FREE-*oh*]
chimney, chimenea [*chee-meh*-NEH-*ah*]
chin, mentón (m) [*mehn*-TOHN]
China, China [CHEE-*nah*]
Chinese, chino, -a [CHEE-*noh, -nah*]
chocolate, chocolate (m) [*choh-koh*-LAH-*teh*]
choice, elección (f) [*eh-lehk-th'*YOHN]

(to) **choose,** escoger [*ehs-koh-*HEHR]
chop, chuleta [*choo-*LEH-*tah*]
  lamb chop, chuleta de cordero [*choo-*LEH-*tah deh kohr-*DEH-*roh*]
  pork chop, chuleta de cerdo [*choo-*LEH-*tah deh* THEHR-*doh*]
Christian, cristiano, -a [*krees-t'*YAH-*noh, -nah*]
Christmas, Pascuas; Navidades [PAHS-*kwahs, nah-vee-*DAH-*dehs*]
  Merry Christmas! ¡Felices Pascuas! [*feh-*LEE-*thehs* PAHS-*kwahs*]

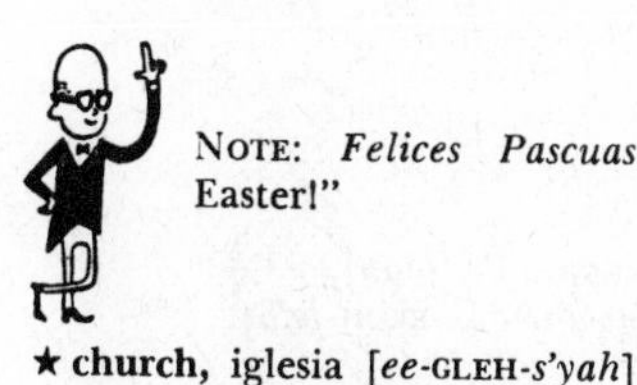

NOTE: *Felices Pascuas!* can also mean "Happy Easter!"

★ **church,** iglesia [*ee-*GLEH-*s'yah*]
cigar, tabaco [*tah-*BAH-*koh*]
cigarette, cigarrillo [*thee-gah-*RREE-*l'yoh*]
circle, círculo [THEER-*koo-loh*]
circulation, circulación (f) [*theer-koo-lah-th'*YOHN]
circus, circo [THEER-*koh*]
citizen, ciudadano, -a [*th'yoo-dah-*DAH-*noh, -nah*]
★ **city,** ciudad (f) [*th'yoo-*DAHD]
  city hall, ayuntamiento [*ah-yoon-tah-m'*YEHN-*toh*]
civilian, paisano, -a [*pah-ee-*SAH-*noh, -nah*]
civilization, civilización (f) [*thee-vee-lee-thah-th'*YOHN]
(to) **claim,** reclamar [*reh-klah-*MAHR]
clam, almeja [*ahl-*MEH-*hah*]
class, clase (f) [KLAH-*seh*]
★ **clean,** limpio, -a [LEEM-*p'yoh, -p'yah*]
(to) **clean,** limpiar [*leem-p'*YAHR]
cleaner's shop, tintorería [*teen-toh-reh-*REE-*ah*]
cleaning, aseo, limpieza [*ah-*SEH-*oh, leem-p'*YEH-*thah*]
cleaning woman, mujer para la limpieza [*moo-*HEHR PAH-*rah lah leem-p'*YEH-*thah*]

clear, claro, -a [KLAH-*roh, -rah*]
clerk, dependiente [*deh-pehn-d'*YEHN-*teh*]
clever, listo, -a [LEES-*toh, -tah*]
climate, clima (m) [KLEE-*mah*]
(to) **climb** (a tree), trepar [*treh*-PAHR]
(to) **climb** (a mountain), escalar [*ehs-kah*-LAHR]
clock, reloj [*reh*-LOHKH]

NOTE: Spanish has no equivalent for "o'clock.'
"It is four o'clock"—*Son las cuatro.*
"At eight o'clock"—*A las ocho.*

close (near), cerca [THEHR-*kah*]
★ (to) **close,** cerrar [*theh*-RRAHR]
★ **closed,** cerrado, -a [*theh*-RRAH-*doh, -dah*]
closet, guardarropa (m) [*gwahr-dah*-RROH-*pah*]
cloth, tela [TEH-*lah*]
clothes, ropa [ROH-*pah*]
  to put one's clothes on, vestir(se) [*vehs*-TEER-*seh*]
  to take one's clothes off, desvestir(se) [*dehs-vehs*-TEER-*seh*]
cloud, nube (f) [NOO-*beh*]
cloudy, nublado [*noo*-BLAH-*doh*]
  It's cloudy today, El tiempo está nublado hoy [*ehl t'*YEHM-*poh ehs*-TAH *noo*-BLAH-*doh oy*]
club (association), club (m) [*kloob*]
coal, carbón de piedra (m) [*kahr*-BOHN *deh p'*YEH-*drah*]
coast, costa [KOHS-*tah*]
coat (overcoat), abrigo [*ah*-BREE-*goh*]
coat (of a suit), saco [SAH-*koh*]
cocktail, coctel (m [*kohk*-TEHL]
cockfight, pelea de gallos [*peh*-LEH-*ah deh* GAH-*l'yohs*]
cocoa, cacao [*kah*-KAH-*oh*]
coconut, coco [KOH-*koh*]
coffee, café (m) [*kah*-FEH]
coffin, ataúd [*ah-tah*-OOD]

coin, moneda [*moh*-NEH-*dah*]
coincidence, coincidencia [*koh-een-thee*-DEHN-*th'yah*]
★ **cold,** frío [FREE-*oh*]
Are you cold? ¿Tiene frío? [*t'*YEH-*neh* FREE-*oh*]
to be cold, tener frío [*teh*-NEHR FREE-*oh*]
to catch a cold, resfriar(se) [*rehs-free*-AHR-*seh*]
collar, cuello [KWEH-*l'yoh*]
(to) **collect,** coleccionar [*koh-lehk-th'yoh*-NAHR]
college, universidad (f) [*oo-nee-vehr-see*-DAHD]
NOTE: *colegio* generally means "high school."
Colombia, Colombia [*koh*-LOHM-*b'yah*]
Colombian, colombiano, -a [*koh-lohm-b'*YAH-*noh, -nah*]
colonel, coronel (m) [*koh-roh*-NEHL]
colony, colonia [*koh*-LOH-*n'yah*]
color, color (m) [*koh*-LOHR]
column, columna [*koh*-LOOM-*nah*]
comb, peine (m) [PAY-*neh*]
(to) **comb,** peinar(se) [*pay*-NAHR-*(seh)*]
combination, combinación (f) [*kohm-bee-nah-th'*YOHN]
★ (to) **come,** venir [*veh*-NEER]
to come across, atravesar [*ah-trah-veh*-SAHR]
to come again (come back), volver [*vohl*-VEHR]
to come down, bajar [*bah*-HAHR]
to come for, venir por [*veh*-NEER *pohr*]
to come forward, avanzar [*ah-vahn*-THAHR]
Come here! ¡Venga aquí! [VEN-*gah ah*-KEE]
★ **Come in!,** ¡Entre! ¡Adelante! [EHN-*treh*] [*ah-deh*-LAHN-*teh*]
★ **Come on!** ¡Vamos! [VAH-*mohs*]
to come up, subir [*soo*-BEER]
comedy, comedia [*koh*-MEH-*d'yah*]
comfort, comodidad (f) [*koh-moh-dee*-DAHD]
(to) **comfort,** consolar [*kohn-soh*-LAHR]
comfortable, cómodo [KOH-*moh-doh*]
Are you comfortable? ¿Está Ud. cómodo? [*ehs*-TAH *oos*-TEHD KOH-*moh-doh*]
comma, coma [KOH-*mah*]
command, orden (f) [OHR-*dehn*]

(to) **command,** mandar [*mahn*-DAHR]
(to) **commence,** comenzar [*koh-mehn*-THAHR]
commentary, comentario [*koh-mehn*-TAH-*r'yoh*]
commercial, comercial [*koh-mehr-th'*YAHL]
commission, comisión (f) [*koh-mee-s'*YOHN]
committee, comité (m) [*koh-mee*-TEH]
common, común [*koh*-MOON]
(to) **communicate,** comunicar [*koh-moo-nee*-KAHR]
communication, comunicación (f) [*koh-moo-nee-kah-th'*YOHN]
communist, comunista (m and f) [*koh-moo*-NEES-*tah*]
companion, compañero, -a [*kohm-pah-n'*YEH-*roh, -rah*]
company, compañía [*kohm-pah-n'*YEE-*ah*]
(to) **compare,** comparar [*kohm-pah*-RAHR]
compartment, compartimiento [*kohm-pahr-tee-m'*YEHN-*toh*]
(to) **compel,** obligar [*oh-blee*-GAHR]
competent, competente [*kohm-peh*-TEHN-*teh*]
competition (contest), concurso [*kohn*-KOOR-*soh*]
(business), competencia [*kohm-peh*-TEHN-*th'yah*]
complaint, queja [KEH-*hah*]
complete, completo, -a [*kohm*-PLEH-*toh, -tah*]
completely, completamente [*kohm-pleh-tah*-MEHN-*teh*]
complexion (skin), cutis (m) [KOO-*tees*]
(to) **complicate,** complicar [*kohm-plee*-KAHR]
complicated, complicado, -a [*kohm-plee*-KAH-*doh, -dah*]
compliment, cumplido [*koom*-PLEE-*doh*]
(to) **compose,** componer [*kohm-poh*-NEHR]
composer, compositor, -a [*kohm-poh-see*-TOHR, *-ah*]
conceited, vanidoso, -a [*vah-nee*-DOH-*soh, -sah*]
(to) **concentrate,** concentrar [*kohn-then*-TRAHR]
concerning, sobre [SOH-*breh*]
concert, concierto [*kohn-th'*YEHR-*toh*]
(to) **condemn,** condenar [*kohn-deh*-NAHR]
(to) **condense,** condensar [*kohn-dehn*-SAHR]
condensed milk, leche condensada (f) [LEH-*cheh kohn-dehn*-SAH-*dah*]

condition, condición (f) [*kohn-dee-th'*YOHN]
  in good condition, en buen estado [*ehn bwehn ehs-*TAH-*doh*]
conduct, conducta [*kohn-*DOOK-*tah*]
(to) **conduct,** conducir [*kohn-doo-*THEER]
conductor (orchestra), director [*dee-rehk-*TOHR]
conductor (train), conductor [*kohn-dook-*TOHR]
(to) **confess,** confesar [*kohn-feh-*SAHR]
confession, confesión (f) [*kohn-feh-s'*YOHN]
confidential, confidencial [*kohn-fee-dehn-th'*YAHL]
(to) **confirm,** confirmar [*kohn-feer-*MAHR]
confusion, confusión (f) [*kohn-foo-s'*YOHN]
(to) **congratulate,** felicitar [*feh-lee-thee-*TAHR]
  congratulations! ¡felicitaciones! [*feh-lee-thee-tah-th'*YOH-*nehs*]
congress, congreso [*kohn-*GREH-*soh*]
connection, conexión (f) [*koh-nehk-s'*YOHN]
(to) **conquer,** conquistar [*kohn-kees-*TAHR]
conscientious, concienzudo, -a [*kohn-th'yehn-*THOO-*doh, -dah*]
conscious, consciente [*kohns-th'*YEHN-*teh*]
(to) **consent,** consentir [*kohn-sehn-*TEER]
consequence, consecuencia [*kohn-theh-*KWEHN-*th'yah*]
conservative, conservador [*kohn-sehr-vah-*DOHR]
(to) **consider,** considerar [*kohn-see-deh-*RAHR]
considerable, considerable [*kohn-see-deh-*RAH-*bleh*]
(to) **consist of,** consistir en [*kohn-sees-*TEER *ehn*]
consistent, consistente [*kohn-sees-*TEHN-*teh*]
constant, constante [*kohns-*TAHN-*teh*]
constitution, constitución (f) [*kohns-tee-too-th'*YOHN]
consul, cónsul (m) [KOHN-*sool*]
consulate, consulado [*kohn-soo-*LAH-*doh*]
(to) **consult,** consultar [*kohn-sool-*TAHR]
consumer, consumidor [*kohn-soo-mee-*DOHR]
contagious, contagioso, -a [*kohn-tah-h'*YOH-*soh, -sah*]
(to) **contain,** contener [*kohn-teh-*NEHR]
container, recipiente (m) [*reh-thee-p'*YEHN-*teh*]
contents (n), contenido [*kohn-teh-*NEE-*doh*]

continent, continente (m) [*kohn-tee*-NEHN-*teh*]
(to) **continue,** continuar [*kohn-tee*-NWAHR]
contract, contrato [*kohn*-TRAH-*toh*]
contractor, contratista (m), contratante (m) [*kohn-trah*-TEES-*tah, kohn-trah*-TAHN-*teh*]
contradiction, contradicción (f) [*kohn-trah-deek-th'*YOHN]
contrary, contrario, -a [*kohn*-TRAH-*r'yoh, -r'yah*]
on the contrary, al contrario [*ahl kohn*-TRAH-*r'yoh*]
(to) **contribute,** contribuir [*kohn-tree-boo*-EER]
control, control (m) [*kohn*-TROHL]
(to) **control,** controlar [*kohn-troh*-LAHR]
convenient, conveniente [*kohn-veh-n'*YEHN-*teh*]
convent, convento [*kohn*-VEHN-*toh*]
conversation, conversación (f) [*kohn-vehr-sah-th'*YOHN]
(to) **convince,** convencer [*kohn-vehn*-THEHR]
cook, cocinero, -a [*koh-thee*-NEH-*roh, -rah*]
(to) **cook,** cocinar [*koh-thee*-NAHR]
cooking, cocina [*koh*-THEE-*nah*]
NOTE: Also means kitchen.
cool, fresco, -a [FREHS-*koh, -kah*]
cooperation, cooperación (f) [*koh-oh-peh-rah-th'*YOHN]
copy, copia [KOH-*p'yah*]
coral, coral (m) [*koh*-RAHL]
cork, corcho [KOHR-*choh*]
corkscrew, sacacorchos (m) [SAH-*kah*-KOHR-*chohs*]
corn, maíz (m) [*mah*-EETH]
corner (of street), esquina [*ehs*-KEE-*nah*]
corner (of room), rincón (m) [*reen*-KOHN]
corporation, sociedad anónima (f) [*soh-th'yeh*-DAHD *ah*-NOH-*nee-mah*]
correct, correcto, -a [*koh*-RREHK-*toh, -tah*]
correction, corrección (f) [*koh-rrehk-th'*YOHN]
correspondence, correspondencia [*koh-rrehs-pohn*-DEHN-*th'yah*]
corridor, corredor (m) [*koh-rreh*-DOHR]
Costa Rica, Costa Rica [KOHS-*tah* REE-*kah*]
Costa Rican, costarricense [*kohs-tah-rree*-THEHN-*seh*]

cost (com), costo [KOHS-*toh*]
cost of living, coste de la vida (m) [KOHS-*teh deh lah* VEE-*dah*]
★ (to) **cost,** costar [*kohs*-TAHR]
How much does this cost? ¿Cuánto cuesta esto? [KWAHN-*toh* KWEHS-*tah* EHS-*toh*]
cotton, algodón (m) [*ahl-goh*-DOHN]
couch, sofá (m) [*soh*-FAH]
(to) **cough,** toser [*toh*-SEHR]
count (title), conde (m) [KOHN-*deh*]
(to) **count,** contar [*kohn*-TAHR]
countess, condesa [*kohn*-DEH-*sah*]
★ **country** (nation), país [*pah*-EES]
country (not city), campo [KAHM-*poh*]
country house, casa de campo [KAH-*sah deh* KAHM-*poh*]
couple, pareja [*pah*-REH-*hah*]
courage, valor (m) [*vah*-LOHR]
courageous, valiente, valeroso, -a [*vah-l'*YEHN-*teh, vah-leh*-ROH-*soh, -sah*]
course, curso [KOOR-*soh*]
court (law), tribunal [*tree-boo*-NAHL]
courtyard, patio [PAH-*t'yoh*]
cousin, primo, -a [PREE-*moh, -mah*]
cover, cubierta [*koo-b'*YEHR-*tah*]
(to) **cover,** cubrir [*koo*-BREER]
cow, vaca [VAH-*kah*]
coward, cobarde [*koh*-BAHR-*deh*]
cowboy, vaquero [*vah*-KEH-*roh*]
crab, cangrejo [*kahn*-GREH-*hoh*]
cradle, cuna [KOO-*nah*]
crash, estallido [*ehs-tah-l'*YEE-*doh*]
crawfish, langostino [*lahn-gohs*-TEE-*noh*]
crazy, loco, -a [LOH-*koh, -kah*]
cream, crema [KREH-*mah*]
(to) **create,** crear [*kreh*-AHR]
creation, creación (f) [*kreh-ah-th'*YOHN]
credit, crédito [KREH-*dee-toh*]

creditor, acreedor (m) [*ah-kreh-eh-*DOHR]
crew, tripulación (f) [*tree-poo-lah-th'*YOHN]
crime, crimen (m) [KREE-*mehn*]
crisis, crisis (f) [KREE-*sees*]
(to) **criticize,** criticar [*kree-tee-*KAHR]
crooked, encorvado, -a [*ehn-kohr-*VAH-*doh, -dah*]
crop, cosecha [*koh-*SEH-*chah*]
cross, cruz (f) [*krooth*]
(to) **cross,** cruzar [*kroo-*THAHR]
crossing, cruce (m) [KROO-*theh*]
crossroads, encrucijada [*ehn-kroo-thee-*HAH-*dah*]
crow, cuervo [KWEHR-*voh*]
crowd, gentío [*hehn-*TEE-*oh*]
crown, corona [*koh-*ROH-*nah*]
cruel, cruel [*krwehl*]
crumb, miga [MEE-*gah*]
cry, grito [GREE-*toh*]
(to) **cry,** llorar [*l'yoh-*RAHR]
crystal, cristal (m) [*krees-*TAHL]
Cuba, Cuba [KOO-*bah*]
Cuban, cubano, -a [*koo-*BAH-*noh, -nah*]
cucumber, pepino [*peh-*PEE-*noh*]
culture, cultura [*kool-*TOO-*rah*]
cup, taza [TAH-*thah*]
cure, cura [KOO-*rah*]
(to) **cure,** curar [*koo-*RAHR]
curiosity, curiosidad (f) [*koo-r'yoh-see-*DAHD]
curious, curioso, -a [*koo-r'*YOH-*soh; -sah*]
curl, rizo [REE-*thoh*]
currency, moneda corriente [*moh-*NEH-*dah koh-rr'*YEHN-*teh*]
current (n & adj), corriente [*koh-rr'*YEHN-*teh*] (feminine when used as noun)

NOTE: *corriente* or *crrte* refers to the present month in letters.

curtain, cortina [*kohr*-TEE-*nah*]
curve, curva [KOOR-*vah*]
  Dangerous curve, curva peligrosa [KOOR-*vah peh-lee*-GROH-*sah*]
cushion, cojín (m) [*koh*-HEEN]
custard, flan (m) [*flahn*]
custom, costumbre (f) [*kohs*-TOOM-*breh*]
customer, cliente [*klee*-EHN-*teh*]
customs or customs house, aduana [*ah*-DWAH-*nah*]
customs duties, derechos de aduana [*deh*-REH-*chohs deh ah*-DWAH-*nah*]
customs officer, aduanero [*ah-dwah*-NEH-*roh*]
cut (dress or cutting), corte (m) [KOHR-*teh*]
cut (wound), cortada [*kohr*-TAH-*dah*]
★ (to) **cut,** cortar [*kohr*-TAHR]
cylinder, cilindro [*thee*-LEEN-*droh*]
cypress, ciprés (m) [*thee*-PREHS]

D

daily, diario [*d'*YAH-*r'yoh*]
dairy, lechería [*leh-cheh*-REE-*ah*]
daisy, margarita [*mahr-gah*-REE-*tah*]
dam, represa [*reh*-PREH-*sah*]
damage, daño [DAH-*n'yoh*]
damaged, dañado, -a [*dah-n'*YAH-*doh, -dah*]
damp (adj), húmedo, *-a* [OO-*meh-doh, -dah*]
dance, baile (m) [BY-*leh*]
  May I have this dance? ¿Puede darme esta pieza? [PWEH-*deh dahr-meh* EHS-*tah p'*YEH-*thah*]
(to) **dance,** bailar [*by*-LAHR]
dancer, bailarín, bailarina [*by-lah*-REEN, *by-lah*-REE-*nah*]
★ **danger,** peligro [*peh*-LEE-*groh*]
  out of danger, fuera de peligro [FWEH-*rah deh peh*-LEE-*groh*]
★ **dangerous,** peligroso, -a [*peh-leh*-GROH-*soh, -sah*]
(to) **dare,** atrever(se) [*ah-treh*-VEHR-*(seh)*]

daring, atrevido, -a [*ah-treh-*VEE-*doh, -dah*]
dark (not light), oscuro, -a [*ohs-*KOO-*roh, -rah*]
(complexion), trigueño, -a [*tree-*GEH-*n'yoh, -n'yah*]
darkness, oscuridad (f) [*ohs-koo-ree-*DAHD]
date (appointment), compromiso [*kohm-proh-*MEE-*soh*]
date (day of month), fecha [FEH-*chah*]
date (fruit), dátil (m) [DAH-*teel*]
★ **daughter,** hija [EE-*hah*]
daughter-in-law, nuera [NWEH-*rah*]
dawn, amanecer (m) [*ah-mah-neh-*THEHR]
★ **day,** día (m) [DEE-*ah*]
all day long, todo el día [TOH-*doh ehl* DEE-*ah*]
day after tomorrow, pasado mañana [*pah-*SAH-*doh mah-n'*YAH-*nah*]
day before yesterday, anteayer [*ahn-teh-ah-*YEHR]
every day, todos los días [TOH-*dohs lohs* DEE-*ahs*]
the next day, el día siguiente [*ehl* DEE-*ah see-gh'*YEHN-*teh*]
twice a day, dos veces al día [*dohs* VEH-*thehs ahl* DEE-*ah*]
★ **dead,** muerto, -a [MWEHR-*toh, -tah*]
deaf, sordo, -a [SOHR-*doh, -dah*]
(to) **deal with,** tratar con [*trah-*TAHR *kohn*]
dealer, negociante (m) [*neh-goh-th'*YAHN-*teh*]
★ **dear** (endearment), querido, -a [*keh-*REE-*doh, -dah*]
dear (price), caro, -a [KAH-*roh, -rah*]
death, muerte (f) [MWEHR-*teh*]
debt, deuda [DEH-*oo-dah*]
deceased, difunto, -a [*dee-*FOON-*toh, -tah*]
(to) **deceive,** engañar [*ehn-gah-n'*YAHR]
December, diciembre [*dee-th'*YEHM-*breh*]
decent, decente [*deh-*THEHN-*teh*]
(to) **decide,** decidir [*deh-thee-*DEER]
decision, decisión (f) [*deh-thee-th'*YOHN]
deck (of ship), cubierta [*koo-b'*YEHR-*tah*]
declaration, declaración (f) [*deh-klah-rah-th'*YOHN]
(to) **decrease,** disminuir [*dees-mee-noo-*EER]
decree, decreto [*deh-*KREH-*toh*]
(to) **dedicate,** dedicar [*deh-dee-*KAHR]

deep, profundo, -a [*proh*-FOON-*doh, -dah*]
deer, venado [*veh*-NAH-*doh*]
(to) **defeat,** derrotar [*deh-rroh*-TAHR]
defect, defecto [*deh*-FEHK-*toh*]
(to) **defend,** defender [*deh-fehn*-DEHR]
defense, defensa [*deh*-FEHN-*sah*]
(to) **define,** definir [*deh-fee*-NEER]
definite, definido, -a [*deh-fee*-NEE-*doh, -dah*]
degree, grado [GRAH-*doh*]
delay, demora [*deh*-MOH-*rah*]
(to) **delay,** demorar [*deh-moh*-RAHR]
delegate, delegado, -a [*deh-leh*-GAH-*doh, -dah*]
delicate, delicado, -a [*deh-lee*-KAH-*doh, -dah*]
delicious, delicioso, -a [*deh-lee-th'*YOH-*soh, -sah*]
delighted, encantado, -a [*ehn-kahn*-TAH-*doh, -dah*]

NOTE: This can also be used to acknowledge an introduction.

delightful, encantador, -a [*ehn-kahn-tah*-DOHR, *-ah*]
(to) **deliver,** entregar [*ehn-treh*-GAHR]
delivery, entrega [*ehn*-TREH-*gah*]
(to) **demand,** reclamar [*reh-klah*-MAHR]
democracy, democracia [*deh-moh*-KRAH-*th'yah*]
democratic, democrático, -a [*deh-moh*-KRAH-*tee-koh, -kah*]
demonstration, demostración (f) [*deh-mohs-trah-th'*YOHN]
Denmark, Dinamarca [*dee-nah*-MAHR-*kah*]
dense, denso, -a [DEHN-*soh, -sah*]
dentist, dentista (m & f) [*dehn*-TEES-*tah*]
(to) **deny,** negar [*neh*-GAHR]
department, departamento [*deh-pahr-tah*-MEHN-*toh*]
department store, departamento comercial [*deh-pahr-tah* MEHN-*toh koh-mehr-th'*YAHL]
departure, partida [*pahr*-TEE-*dah*]
(to) **depend on,** contar con [*kohn*-TAHR *kohn*]
  that depends, eso depende [EH-*soh deh*-PEHN-*deh*]

deposit, depósito [*deh*-POH-*see-toh*]
to pay a deposit, pagar un depósito [*pah*-GAHR *oon deh*-POH-*see-toh*]
(to) **deposit,** depositar [*deh-poh-see*-TAHR]
depth, profundidad (f) [*proh-foon-dee*-DAHD]
deputy, diputado [*dee-poo*-TAH-*doh*]
(to) **descend,** descender [*dehs-thehn*-DEHR]
(to) **describe,** describir [*dehs-kree*-BEER]
description, descripción (f) [*dehs-kreep-th'*YOHN]
desert, desierto [*deh-s'*YEHR-*toh*]
(to) **deserve,** merecer [*meh-reh*-THEHR]
design, diseño [*dee*-SEH-*n'yoh*]
desire, deseo [*deh*-SEH-*oh*]
(to) **desire,** desear [*deh-seh*-AHR]
desk, escritorio [*ehs-kree*-TOH-*r'yoh*]
(to) **despair,** desesperar [*deh-sehs-peh*-RAHR]
desperate, desesperado, -a [*deh-sehs-peh*-RAH-*doh*, -*dah*]
★ **despite,** a pesar de [*ah peh*-SAHR *deh*]
dessert, postre (m) [POHS-*treh*]
destiny, destino [*dehs*-TEE-*noh*]
(to) **destroy,** destruir [*dehs-troo*-EER]
detail, detalle (m) [*deh*-TAH-*l'yeh*]
detective, detective (m) [*deh-tehk*-TEE-*veh*]
(to) **determine,** determinar [*deh-tehr-mee*-NAHR]
detour, desviación (f) [*dehs-v'yah-th'*YOHN]
(to) **develop,** desarrollar [*deh-sah-rroh-l'*YAHR]
development, desarrollo [*deh-sah*-RROH-*l'yoh*]
devil, diablo [*d'*YAH-*bloh*]
dialect, dialecto [*d'yah*-LEHK-*toh*]
dialogue, diálogo [*d'*YAH-*loh-goh*]
diamond, diamante (m) [*d'yah*-MAHN-*teh*]
diameter, diámetro [*d'*YAH-*meh-troh*]
dice, dados [DAH-*dohs*]
(to) **dictate,** dictar [*deek*-TAHR]
dictation, dictado [*deek*-TAH-*doh*]
dictionary, diccionario [*deek-th'yoh*-NAH-*r'yoh*]
(to) **die,** morir [*moh*-REER]

diet, dieta [*d'*YEH-*tah*]

to be on a diet, estar a dieta [*ehs*-TAHR *ah d'*YEH-*tah*]

difference, diferencia [*dee-feh*-REHN-*th'yah*]

It does not make any difference, No importa [*noh-eem*-POHR-*tah*]

What difference does it make? ¿Qué importa? [*keh-eem*-POHR-*tah*]

★ **different,** diferente [*dee-feh*-REHN-*teh*]

★ **difficult,** difícil [*dee*-FEE-*theel*]

difficulty, dificultad (f) [*dee-fee-kool*-TAHD]

(to) **dig,** cavar [*kah*-VAHR]

digestion, digestión (f) [*dee-hehs-t'*YOHN]

dignity, dignidad (f) [*deeg-nee*-DAHD]

(to) **diminish,** disminuir [*dees-mee-noo*-EER]

(to) **dine,** comer [*koh*-MEHR]

dining-car, coche comedor [KOH-*cheh koh-meh*-DOHR]

dining-room, comedor (m) [*koh-meh*-DOHR]

★ **dinner,** comida [*koh*-MEE-*dah*]

it is time for dinner, es hora de comer [*ehs*-OH-*rah deh koh*-MEHR]

dinner-jacket, smoking (m)

NOTE: See how English words have sometimes invaded Spanish.

diploma, diploma (m) [*dee*-PLOH-*mah*]

diplomat (and) **diplomatic,** diplomático, -a [*dee-ploh*-MAH-*tee-koh, -kah*]

direct (adj), directo, -a [*dee*-REHK-*toh, -tah*]

(to) **direct,** dirigir [*dee-ree*-HEER]

directly, directamente [*dee-rehk-tah*-MEHN-*teh*]

direction, dirección (f) [*dee-rehk-th'*YOHN]

NOTE: *Dirección* also means "address."

director, director (m) [*dee-rehk*-TOHR]

dirty, sucio, -a [soo-*th'yoh, -th'yah*]

disabled, incapacitado, -a [*een-kah-pah-thee*-TAH-*doh, -dah*]

disadvantage, desventaja [*dehs-vehn*-TAH-*hah*]

(to) **disagree,** no estar de acuerdo [*noh ehs*-TAHR *deh ah*-KWEHR-*doh*]

disagreeable, desagradable [*deh-sah-grah-*DAH-*bleh*]
(to) **disappear,** desaparecer [*deh-sah-pah-reh-*THEHR]
disappointed, decepcionado, -a [*deh-thehp-th'yoh-*NAH-*doh, -dah*]
(to) **disapprove,** desaprobar [*deh-sah-proh-*BAHR]
disaster, desastre (m) [*deh-*SAHS-*treh*]
(to) **discharge** (employes), despedir [*dehs-peh-*DEER]
discipline, disciplina [*dees-thee-*PLEE-*nah*]
(to) **discontinue,** descontinuar [*dehs-kohn-tee-noo-*AHR]
discount, descuento [*dehs-*KWEHN-*toh*]
(to) **discourage,** desanimar [*deh-sah-nee-*MAHR]
(to) **discover,** descubrir [*dehs-koo-*BREER]
discovery, descubrimiento [*dehs-koo-bree-m'*YEHN-*toh*]
discreet, discreto, -a [*dees-*KREH-*toh, -tah*]
(to) **discuss,** discutir [*dees-koo-*TEER]
discussion, discusión (f) [*dees-koo-s'*YOHN]
disease, enfermedad (f) [*ehn-fehr-meh-*DAHD]
disguise, disfraz (m) [*dees-*FRAHTH]
disgusted, disgustado, -a [*dees-goos-*TAH-*doh, -dah*]
dish, plato [PLAH-*toh*]
dishonest, no honrado [*noh ohn-*RAH-*doh*]
(to) **dislike,**

NOTE: To express "to dislike" you must use *gustar* with a negative, meaning that something displeases you. *No me gusta:* "I dislike it." *No le gusta bailar:* "He (or she) doesn't like to dance."

(to) **dismiss,** despedir [*dehs-peh-*DEER]
(to) **disobey,** desobedecer [*deh-soh-beh-deh-*THEHR]
disorder, desorden [*deh-*SOHR-*dehn*]
dispute, disputa [*dees-*POO-*tah*]
distance, distancia [*dees-*TAHN-*th'yah*]
(to) **dissolve,** disolver [*dee-sohl-*VEHR]
(to) **distinguish,** distinguir [*dees-teen-*GHEER]
distinguished, distinguido, -a [*dees-teen-*GHEE-*doh, -dah*]
(to) **distribute,** distribuir [*des-tree-boo-*EER]
distribution, distribución (f) [*dees-tree-boo-th'*YOHN]

district, distrito [*dees*-TREE-*toh*]
(to) **distrust,** desconfiar [*dehs-kohn-f'*YAHR]
(to) **disturb,** molestar [*moh-lehs*-TAHR]
ditch, zanja [THAHN-*hah*]
(to) **divide,** dividir [*dee-vee*-DEER]
division, división (f) [*dee-vee-s'*YOHN]
divine, divino, -a [*dee*-VEE-*noh, -nah*]
divorce, divorcio [*dee*-VOHR-*th'yoh*]
dizzy, desvanecido, -a [*dehs-vah-neh*-THEE-*doh, -dah*]
  to feel dizzy, tener vértigo [*teh*-NEHR VEHR-*tee-goh*]
★ (to) **do** (perform an action), hacer [*ah*-THEHR]
  How do you do? (state), ¿Cómo está Ud.? [KOH-*moh ehs*-TAH *oos*-TEHD]; (on being introduced), Mucho gusto [MOO-*choh* GOOS-*toh*]
  What can I do for you? ¿En qué puedo servirle? [*ehn keh* PWEH-*doh sehr*-VEER-*leh*]
  Do me the favor of . . . Hágame el favor de . . . [AH-*gah-meh ehl fah*-VOHR *deh*]

NOTE: "Do" is not used for asking questions as in English. To ask a question, simply invert the word order and raise your voice. "I am Spanish."—*Soy español.* "Am I Spanish?"—*¿Soy yo español?* The negative is not formed by "do not," as in English, but simply with the word *no.* "I understand."—*Yo comprendo.* "I don't understand."—*Yo no comprendo.*

dock, muelle (m) [MWEH-*l'yeh*]
doctor, doctor [*dohk*-TOHR]
document, documento [*doh-koo*-MEHN-*toh*]
★ **dog,** perro [PEH-*rroh*]
doll, muñeca [*moo-n'*YEH-*kah*]
dollar, dólar (m) [DOH-*lahr*]
dome, cúpula [KOO-*poo-lah*]
domestic, doméstico, -a [*doh*-MEHS-*tee-koh, -kah*]
Dominican, dominicano, -a [*doh-mee-nee*-KAH-*noh, -nah*]
done, hecho, -a [EH-*choh, -chah*]
donkey, burro, -a [BOO-*rroh, -rrah*]

★ **door,** puerta [PWEHR-*tah*]

Close the door, Cierre la puerta [*th'*YEH-*rreh lah* PWEHR-*tah*]

Open the door, Abra la puerta [AH-*brah lah* PWEHR-*tah*]

dose, dosis (f) [DOH-*sees*]

double, doble [DOH-*bleh*]

doubt, duda [DOO-*dah*]

(to) **doubt,** dudar [*doo*-DAHR]

doubtful, dudoso [*doo*-DOH-*soh*]

doubtless, sin duda [*seen* DOO-*dah*]

★ **down,** abajo [*ah*-BAH-*hoh*]

Down with . . . ! ¡Abajo con . . . ! [*ah*-BAH-*hoh kohn*]

to fall down, caer(se) [*kah*-EHR-*(seh)*]

to go down, bajar [*bah*-HAHR]

to lie down, acostar(se) [*ah-kohs*-TAHR-*(seh)*]

dowry, dote (f) [DOH-*teh*]

dozen, docena [*doh*-THEH-*nah*]

draft (of air), corriente de aire (f) [*koh-rr'*YEHN-*teh deh* EYE-*reh*]

draft (army), reclutamiento [*reh-kloo-tah-m'*YEHN-*toh*]

draft (money), giro [HEE-*roh*]

(to) **drag,** arrastrar [*ah-rrahs*-TRAHR]

drain, desagüe (m) [*deh*-SAH-*goo-eh*]

drama, drama (m) [DRAH-*mah*]

(to) **draw** (a picture), dibujar [*dee-boo*-HAHR]

(to) **draw** (a weapon), sacar [*sah*-KAHR]

drawer, gaveta [*gah*-VEH-*tah*]

dreadful, espantoso [*ehs-pahn*-TOH-*soh*]

dream, sueño [SWEH-*n'yoh*]

(to) **dream,** soñar [*soh-n'*YAHR]

★ **dress,** vestido [*vehs*-TEE-*doh*]

evening dress, vestido de noche [*vehs*-TEE-*doh deh* NOH-*cheh*]

(to get) **dressed,** vestir(se) [*vehs*-TEER-*(seh)*]

dressing-table, tocador (m) [*toh-kah*-DOHR]

dressmaker, modista [*moh*-DEES-*tah*]

(to) **drill** (oil), perforar [*pehr-foh*-RAHR]

drink, bebida [*beh*-BEE-*dah*]

★ (to) **drink,** beber [*beh*-BEHR], tomar [*toh*-MAHR]
drive (n), paseo en automóvil [*pah*-SEH-*oh ehn ow-toh*-MOH-*veel*]
(to) **drive** (a car), manejar [*mah-neh*-HAHR]
driver, chofer [*choh*-FEHR]
driving-license, licencia para manejar [*lee*-THEHN-*th'yah* PAH-*rah mah-neh*-HAHR]
drop, gota [GOH-*tah*]
(to) **drop,** gotear [*goh-teh*-AHR]
(to) **drown,** ahogar(se) [*ah-oh*-GAHR-(*seh*)]
drug, droga [DROH-*gah*]
druggist, farmacéutico [*fahr-mah*-THEH-*oo-tee-koh*]
drugstore, farmacia [*fahr*-MAH-*th'yah*]
drum, tambor (m) [*tahm*-BOHR]
drunk, borracho, -a [*boh*-RRAH-*choh, -chah*]
dry, seco, -a [SEH-*koh, -kah*]
(to) **dry,** secar [*seh*-KAHR]
(to) **dry clean,** limpiar en seco [*leem-p'*YAHR *ehn* SEH-*koh*]
duck, pato [PAH-*toh*]
due, debido [*deh*-BEE-*doh*]
due to, debido, -a [*deh*-BEE-*doh, -dah*]
to fall due, vencer [*vehn*-THEHR]
duchess, duquesa [*doo*-KEH-*sah*]
duke, duque (m) [DOO-*keh*]
dull, insulso, -a [*een*-SOOL-*soh, -sah*]
dumb, mudo, -a [MOO-*doh, -dah*]
★ **during,** durante [*doo*-RAHN-*teh*]
dust, polvo [POHL-*voh*]
Dutch, holandés, holandesa [*oh-lahn*-DEHS, *oh-lahn*-DEH *sah*]
duty, deber (m) [*deh*-BEHR]
to be on duty, estar de servicio [*ehs*-TAHR *deh sehr*-VEE-*th'yoh*]
duty-free, libre de derechos [LEE-*breh deh deh*-REH-*chohs*]
dye (n), tinte (m) [TEEN-*teh*]
(to) **dye,** teñir [*teh-n'*YEER]
dynamite, dinamita [*dee-nah*-MEE-*tah*]
dysentery, disentería [*dee-sehn-teh*-REE-*ah*]

E

★ **each,** cada [KAH-*dah*]
  each one, cada uno, -a [KAH-*dah* OO-*noh, -nah*]
  each time, cada vez [KAH-*dah veth*]
eager, ansioso, -a [*ahn-s'*YOH-*soh, -sah*]
eagle, águila [AH-*ghee-lah*]
ear, oído, oreja [*oh*-EE-*doh, oh*-REH-*hah*]

NOTE: the *oído* is the organ of hearing while *oreja* is what you see on the head.

earring, arete [*ah*-REH-*teh*]
early, temprano [*tehm*-PRAH-*noh*]
(to) **earn,** ganar [*gah*-NAHR]
★ **earth,** tierra [*t'*YEH-*rrah*]
earthquake, terremoto [*teh-rreh*-MOH-*toh*]
★ **east,** este (m) oriente [EHS-*teh, oh-r'*YEHN-*teh*]
  Far East, Oriente Lejano [*oh-r'*YEHN-*teh leh*-HAH-*noh*]
  Near East, Levante [*leh*-VAHN-*teh*]
Easter, Pascua Florida [PAHS-*kwah floh*-REE-*dah*]
easily, facilmente [*fah-theel*-MEHN-*teh*]
★ **easy,** fácil, simple [FAH-*theel,* SEEM-*pleh*]
  Take it easy! ¡Tenga calma! [TEHN-*gah* KAHL-*mah*]
  That's very easy! ¡Eso es muy fácil! [EH-*soh ehs mwee* FAH-*theel*]
★ (to) **eat,** comer [*koh*-MEHR]
economical, económico [*eh-koh*-NOH-*mee-koh*]
Ecuador, Ecuador (m) [*eh-kwah*-DOHR]
Ecuadorian, ecuatoriano, -a [*eh-kwah-toh-r'*YAH-*noh, -nah*]
edge, orilla [*oh*-REE-*l'yah*]
edition, edición (f) [*eh-dee-th'*YOHN]
editor, editor [*eh-dee*-TOHR]

education, educación (f) [*eh-doo-kah-th'*YOHN]
effect, efecto [*eh-*FEHK-*toh*]
effective, eficaz [*eh-fee-*KAHTH]
efficient, eficiente [*eh-fee-th'*YEHN-*teh*]
effort, esfuerzo [*ehs-f'*WEHR-*thoh*]
★ **egg,** huevo [WEH-*voh*]
fried eggs, huevos fritos [WEH-*vohs* FREE-*tohs*]
hard boiled eggs, huevos duros [WEH-*vohs* DOO-*rohs*]
scrambled eggs, huevos revueltos [WEH-*vohs reh-v'*WEHL-*tohs*]
soft boiled eggs, huevos pasados por agua [WEH-*vohs pah-*SAH-*dohs pohr* AH-*gwah*]
Egypt, Egipto [*eh-*HEEP-*toh*]
Egyptian, egipcio, -a [*eh-*HEEP-*th'yoh, -th'yah*]
★ **eight,** ocho [OH-*choh*]
eighth, octavo, -a [*ohk-*TAH-*voh, -vah*]
★ **eighteen,** dieciocho [*d'*YEHTH-*ee-*OH-*choh*]
★ **eighty,** ochenta [*oh-*CHEHN-*tah*]
either (one), cualquiera [*kwahl-k'*YEH-*rah*]
elbow, codo [KOH-*doh*]
elder, mayor [*mah-*YOHR]
elderly, de edad [*deh eh-*DAHD]
(to) **elect,** elegir [*eh-leh-*HEER]
electric, eléctrico, -a [*eh-*LEHK-*tree-koh, -kah*]
electricity, electricidad (f) [*eh-lehk-tree-thee-*DAHD]
elegant, elegante [*eh-leh-*GAHN-*teh*]
elementary, elemental [*eh-leh-mehn-*TAHL]
elephant, elefante (m) [*eh-leh-*FAHN-*teh*]
elevator, ascensor (m) [*ahs-thehn-*SOHR]
★ **eleven,** once [OHN-*theh*]
(to) **eliminate,** eliminar [*eh-lee-mee-*NAHR]
else, otro (or) más [OH-*troh, mahs*]
someone else, alguna otra persona [*ahl-*GOO-*nah* OH-*trah pehr-*SOH-*nah*]
somewhere else, en alguna otra parte [*ehn ahl-*GOO-*nah* OH-*trah* PAHR-*teh*]
Anything else? ¿Algo más? [AHL-*goh mahs*]
nothing else, nada más [NAH-*dah mahs*]

(to) **embark,** embarcar [*ehm-bahr-*KAHR]
embarrassed, abochornado, -a [*ah-boh-chohr-*NAH-*doh, -dah*]
embassy, embajada [*ehm-bah-*HAH-*dah*]
(to) **embrace,** abrazar [*ah-brah-*THAHR]
embroidery, bordado [*bohr-*DAH-*doh*]
emerald, esmeralda [*ehs-meh-*RAHL-*dah*]
emergency, emergencia [*eh-mehr-*HEHN-*th'yah*]
  In case of emergency, en caso de urgencia [*ehn* KAH-*soh deh oor-*HEHN-*th'yah*]
emotion, emoción (f) [*eh-moh-th'*YOHN]
emperor, emperador [*ehm-peh-rah-*DOHR]
emphasis, énfasis (f) [EHN-*fah-sees*]
employer, dueño, -a [*d'*WEH-*n'yoh, -n'yah*]
employment, empleo [*ehm-*PLEH-*oh*]
  employment agency, agencia de empleos [*ah-*HEHN-*th'yah deh ehm-*PLEH-*ohs*]
(to) **employ,** emplear [*ehm-pleh-*AHR]
★ **empty,** vacío, -a [*vah-*THEE-*oh, -ah*]
(to) **encourage,** animar [*ah-nee-*MAHR]
★ **end, ending,** fin (m) [*feen*]
(to) **end,** terminar [*tehr-mee-*NAHR]
(to) **endeavor,** intentar [*een-tehn-*TAHR]
(to) **endorse,** endosar [*ehn-doh-*SAHR]
enemy, enemigo, -a [*eh-neh-*MEE-*goh, -gah*]
energetic, enérgico, -a [*eh-*NEHR-*hee-koh, -kah*]
energy, energía [*eh-nehr-*HEE-*ah*]
engaged (busy), ocupado, -a [*oh-koo-*PAH-*doh, -dah*]
engaged (to be married), comprometido, -a [*kohm-proh-meh-*TEE-*doh, -dah*]
engine, motor (m) [*moh-*TOHR]
engineer, ingeniero [*een-heh-n'*YEH-*roh*]
England, Inglaterra [*een-glah-*TEH-*rrah*]
English, inglés, inglesa [*een-*GLEHS, *een-*GLEH-*sah*]
(to) **enjoy** (oneself), divertir(se) [*dee-vehr-*TEER-*seh*]
  Enjoy yourself! ¡Diviértase! [*dee-v'*YEHR-*tah-seh*]
(to) **enlarge,** aumentar [*ow-mehn-*TAHR]
(to) **enlist,** enrolar [*ehn-roh-*LAHR]
enormous, enorme [*eh-*NOHR-*meh*]

★ **enough,** bastante [*bahs*-TAHN-*teh*]
more than enough, más que suficiente [*mahs keh soo-fee th'*YEHN-*teh*]
That's enough, ¡Basta! [BAHS-*tah*]
(to) **enter,** entrar [*ehn*-TRAHR]
Do not enter! ¡No entre! [*noh* EHN-*treh*]
enterprise, empresa [*ehm*-PREH-*sah*]
(to) **entertain** (to amuse), divertir [*dee-vehr*-TEER]
(to) **entertain** (guests), recibir [*reh-thee*-BEER]
entertaining, divertido, -a [*dee-vehr*-TEE-*doh, -dah*]
enthusiasm, entusiasmo [*ehn-too-s'*YAHS-*moh*]
entire, entero, -a [*ehn*-TEH-*roh, -rah*]
entirely, enteramente [*ehn-teh-rah*-MEHN-*teh*]
entrance (entry), *entrada* [*ehn*-TRAH-*dah*]
envelope, sobre [SOH-*breh*]
envy, envidia [*ehn*-VEE-*d'yah*]
epoch, época [EH-*poh-kah*]
equal, igual [*ee*-GWAHL]
(to) **equal,** igualar [*ee-gwah*-LAHR]
equator, ecuador (m) [*eh-kwah*-DOHR]
equipment, equipo [*eh*-KEE-*poh*]
(to) **erase,** borrar [*boh*-RRAHR]
eraser, borrador (m) [*boh-rrah*-DOHR]
errand, diligencia [*dee-lee*-HEHN-*th'yah*]
error, error (m) [*eh*-RROHR]
(to) **escape,** escapar [*ehs-kah*-PAHR]
especially, especialmente [*ehs-peh-th'yahl*-MEHN-*teh*]
essence, esencia [*eh*-SEHN-*th'yah*]
essential, esencial [*eh-sehn-th'*YAHL]
(to) **establish,** establecer [*ehs-tah-bleh*-THEHR]
establishment, establecimiento [*ehs-tah-bleh-thee-m'*YEHN-*toh*]
estate (possessions), bienes (m) [*b'*YEH-*nehs*]
estate (land), propiedad [*proh-p'yeh*-DAHD]
(to) **esteem,** estimar [*ehs-tee*-MAHR]

NOTE: To write "dear friend" use *estimado amigo.*

estimate (of price), cálculo [KAHL-*koo-loh*]
eternal, eterno, -a [*eh*-TEHR-*noh, -nah*]

et cetera, etcétera [*eht*-THEH-*teh-rah*]
Europe, Europa [*eh-oo*-ROH-*pah*]
European, europeo, -a [*eh-oo-roh*-PEH-*oh, -ah*]
eve, víspera [VEES-*peh-rah*]
Christmas Eve, Nochebuena [NOH-*cheh-b'*WEH-*nah*]
★ **even** (adv), aun [*ah*-OON]
even I, hasta yo [AHS-*tah yoh*]
even so, aun así [*ah*-OON *ah*-SEE]
even then, aun entonces [*ah*-OON *ehn*-TOHN-*thehs*]
even though, aun cuando [*ah*-OON KWAHN-*doh*]
not even, ni siquiera [*nee see-k'*YEH-*rah*]
★ **evening,** tarde (f) noche (f) [TAHR-*deh,* NOH-*cheh*]

NOTE: *Tarde* is used both for afternoon and early evening. After dark, however, "evening" becomes *noche.*

Good evening! ¡Buenas noches! [BWEH-*nahs* NOH-*chehs*]
in the evening, por la noche [*pohr lah* NOH-*cheh*]
tomorrow evening, mañana por la noche [*mah-n'*YAH-*nah pohr lah* NOH-*cheh*]
yesterday evening, anoche [*ah*-NOH-*cheh*]
event, suceso [*soo*-THEH-*soh*]
in the event of, en caso de [*ehn* KAH-*soh deh*]
eventually, eventualmente [*eh-vehn-t'wahl*-MEHN-*teh*]
ever (at some time), alguna vez [*ahl*-GOO-*nah veth*]
as ever, como siempre [KOH-*moh s'*YEHM-*preh*]
for ever, para siempre [PAH-*rah s'*YEHM-*preh*]
★ **every,** cada, todo, -a [KAH-*dah,* TOH-*doh, -dah*]
every day, todos los días [TOH-*dohs lohs* DEE-*ahs*]
every other day, un día sí y un día no [*oon* DEE-*ah see ee oon* DEE-*ah noh*]
every time, cada vez [KAH-*dah veth*]
everybody, todo el mundo [TOH-*doh ehl* MOON-*doh*]
everything, todo [TOH-*doh*]

everywhere, por todas partes [*pohr* TOH-*dahs* PAHR-*tehs*]
evident, evidente [*eh-vee*-DEHN-*teh*]
evidently, evidentemente [*eh-vee-dehn-teh*-MEHN-*teh*]
exact, exacto, -a [*ehk*-SAHK-*toh, -tah*]
exactly, exactamente [*ehk*-SAHK-*tah*-MEHN-*teh*]
(to) **exaggerate,** exagerar [*ehk-sah-heh*-RAHR]
examination, examen (m) [*ehk*-SAH-*mehn*]
(to) **examine,** examinar [*ehk-sah-mee*-NAHR]
example, ejemplo [*eh*-HEHM-*ploh*]
(to) **exceed,** sobrepasar [*soh-breh-pah*-SAHR]
excellent, excelente [*ehk-seh*-LEHN-*teh*]
except, excepto [*ehk*-THEHP-*toh*]
exception, excepción [*ehk-thehp-th'*YOHN]
exceptional, excepcional [*ehk-thehp-th'yoh*-NAHL]
excess, exceso [*ehk*-THEH-*soh*]
(to) **exchange,** cambiar [*kahm-b'*YAHR]
in exchange for, a cambio de [*ah* KAHM-*b'yoh deh*]
excited, agitado, a- [*ah*-HEE-*tah-doh, -dah*]
Don't get excited! ¡No se agite! [*non seh ah*-HEE-*teh*]
exclusive, exclusivo, -a [*ehks-kloo*-SEE-*voh, -vah*]
excursion, excursión (f) [*ehks-koor-s'*YOHN]
excuse, excusa [*ehks*-KOO-*sah*]
(to) **excuse,** dispensar [*dees-pehn*-SAHR]
★ **Excuse me!** ¡Dispénseme! [*dees*-PEHN-*seh-meh*]
exercise, ejercicio [*eh-hehr*-THEE-*th'yoh*]
exhausted, agotado, -a [*ah-goh*-TAH-*doh, -dah*]
(to) **exhibit,** exhibir [*ehk-see*-BEER]
exhibition, exposición [*ehks-poh-see-th'*YOHN]
(to) **exist,** existir [*ehk-sees*-TEER]
existence, existencia [*ehk-sees*-TEHN-*th'yah*]
exit, salida [*sah*-LEE-*dah*]
(to) **expect,** esperar [*ehs-peh*-RAHR]
expedition, expedición (f) [*ehks-peh-dee-th'*YOHN]
expense, gasto [GAHS-*toh*]
expensive, costoso [*kohs*-TOH-*soh*]
experience, experiencia [*ehks-peh-r'*YEHN-*th'yah*]
experiment, experimento [*ehks-peh-ree*-MEHN-*toh*]
expert, experto [*ehks*-PEHR-*toh*]

(to) **explain,** explicar [*ehks-plee*-KAHR]

Please explain, ¡Sírvase explicar! [SEER-*vah-seh ehks-plee*-KAHR]

explanation, explicación (f) [*ehks-plee-kah-th'*YOHN]

(to) **explore,** explorar [*ehks-ploh*-RAHR]

explosion, explosión (f) [*ehks-ploh-s'*YOHN]

(to) **export,** exportar [*ehks-pohr*-TAHR]

export, exportación (f) [*ehks-pohr-tah-th'*YOHN]

express, expreso [*ehks*-PREH-*soh*]

by express, por expreso [*pohr ehks*-PREH-*soh*]

(to) **express,** expresar [*ehks-preh*-SAHR]

exquisite, exquisito, -a [*ehks-kee*-SEE-*toh, -tah*]

(to) **extend,** extender [*ehks-tehn*-DEHR]

extension, extent, extensión [*ehks-tehn-s'*YOHN]

to a certain extent, hasta cierto punto [AHS-*tah th'*YEHR-*toh* POON-*toh*]

exterior, exterior (m) [*ehks-teh-r'*YOHR]

external, externo, -a [*ehks*-TEHR-*noh, -nah*]

(to) **extinguish,** extinguir [*ehks-teen*-GHEER]

extra, extra [EHKS-*trah*]

(to) **extract** (a tooth), arrancar [*ah-rrahn*-KAHR]

extraordinary, extraordinario, -a [*ehks-trah-ohr-dee*-NAH-*r'yoh, -r'yah*]

extravagant (ridiculous), extravagante [*ehks-trah-vah*-GAHN-*teh*]

extravagant (with money), gastador [*gahs-tah*-DOHR]

extreme, extremo, -a [*ehks*-TREH-*moh, -mah*]

extremely, extremadamente [*ehks-treh-mah-dah*-MEHN-*teh*]

★ **eye,** ojo [OH-*hoh*]

eyebrow, ceja [THEH-*hah*]

eye doctor, oculista (m & f) [*oh-koo*-LEES-*tah*]

eyeglasses, gafas [GAH-*fahs*]

eyelash, pestaña [*pehs*-TAH-*n'yah*]

eyelid, párpado [PAHR-*pah-doh*]

eyesight, vista [VEES-*tah*]

F

fable, fábula [FAH-*boo-lah*]
fabric, tela [TEH-*lah*]
★ **face,** cara [KAH-*rah*]
fact, hecho [EH-*choh*]
  in fact, en realidad [*ehn reh-ah-lee*-DAHD]
factory, fábrica [FAH-*bree-kah*]
faculty, facultad [*fah-kool*-TAHD]
(to) **fail,** fracasar [*frah-kah*-SAHR]
(to) **faint,** desmayar(se) [*dehs-mah*-YAHR-*seh*]
fair (n), feria [FEH-*r'yah*]
fair (adj), justo, -a [HOOS-*toh, -tah*]
faith, fe [*feh*]
faithful, fiel [*f'yehl*]
(to) **fall,** caer [*kah*-EHR]
(to) **fall in love,** enamorarse [*ehn-ah-moh*-RAHR-*seh*]
fall, caída [*kah*-EE-*dah*]
fall (season), otoño [*oh*-TOH-*n'yoh*]
false, falso [FAHL-*soh*]
fame, fama [FAH-*mah*]
familiar, familiar [*fah-mee-l'*YAHR]
★ **family,** familia [*fah*-MEE-*l'yah*]
famous, famoso, -a [*fah*-MOH-*soh, -sah*]
fan (mechanical), ventilador [*vehn-tee-lah*-DOHR]
fan (in hand), abanico [*ah-bah*-NEE-*koh*]
fantastic, fantástico [*fahn*-TAHS-*tee-koh*]
★ **far,** lejos [LEH-*hohs*]
  How far? ¿A que distancia? [*ah keh dees*-TAHN-*th'yah*]
  far away, muy lejos [*mwee* LEH-*hohs*]
fare, tarifa [*tah*-REE-*fah*]
farewell, adiós [*ah-d'*YOHS]
farm, finca [FEEN-*kah*]
farmer, agricultor (m) [*ah-gree-kool*-TOHR]
farther, más lejos [*mahs* LEH-*hohs*]
fascinating, fascinante [*fahs-thee*-NAHN-*teh*]

fashion, moda [MOH-*dah*]
fashionable, de moda [*deh* MOH-*dah*]
fast, rápido, -a [RAH-*pee-doh, -dah*]
(to) **fasten,** fijar [*fee*-HAHR]
fat, gordo, -a [GOHR-*doh, -dah*]
fate, destino [*dehs*-TEE-*noh*]
★ **father,** padre [PAH-*dreh*]
father-in-law, suegro [SWEH-*groh*]
faucet, grifo [GREE-*foh*]
fault, culpa [KOOL-*pah*]
it's my fault, la culpa es mía [*lah* KOOL-*pah ehs* MEE-*ah*]
favor, favor [*fah*-VOHR]
fear, miedo [*m'*YEH-*doh*]
to fear, tener miedo de [*teh*-NEHR *m'*YEH-*doh deh*]
feather, pluma [PLOO-*mah*]
feature, rasgo [RAHS-*goh*]
February, febrero [*feh*-BREH-*roh*]
federal, federal [*feh-deh*-RAHL]
fee, honorarios (plural) [*oh-noh*-RAH-*r'yohs*]
(to) **feed,** dar de comer [*dahr deh koh*-MEHR]
★ (to) **feel,** sentir [*sehn*-TEER]
feeling, sentimiento [*sehn-tee-m'*YEHN-*toh*]
female, hembra [EHM-*brah*]
feminine, femenino, -a [*feh-meh*-NEE-*noh, -nah*]
fence, cerca [THEHR-*kah*]
fencing, esgrima [*ehs*-GREE-*mah*]
fender (auto), guardafango [*gwahr-dah*-FAHN-*goh*]
fertilizer, abono [*ah*-BOH-*noh*]
festival, fiesta [*f'*YEHS-*tah*]
(to) **fetch,** ir a buscar [*eer ah boos*-KAHR]
fever, fiebre (f) [*f'*YEH-*breh*]
★ **few,** pocos, -as [POH-*kohs, -kahs*]
★ **fewer,** menos [MEH-*nohs*]
fiancé, novio [NOH-*v'yoh*]
fiancée, novia [NOH-*v'yah*]
field, campo [KAHM-*poh*]
★ **fifteen,** quince [KEEN-*theh*]

fifth, quinto, -a [KEEN-*toh, -tah*]
★ **fifty,** cincuenta [*theen*-KWEHN-*tah*]
fig, higo [EE-*goh*]
(to) **fight,** pelear [*peh-leh*-AHR]
fight (n), pelea [*peh*-LEH-*ah*]
figure, figura [*fee*-GOO-*rah*]
file (tool), lima [LEE-*mah*]
file (records), archivo [*ahr*-CHEE-*voh*]
(to) **fill,** llenar [*l'yeh*-NAHR]
filling (teeth), empaste (m) [*ehm*-PAHS-*teh*]
film, película [*peh*-LEE-*koo-lah*]
filter, filtro [FEEL-*troh*]
final, final [*fee*-NAHL]
finally, finalmente [*fee-nahl*-MEHN-*teh*]
financial, financiero, -a [*fee-nahn-s'*YEH-*roh, -rah*]
★ (to) **find,** encontrar [*ehn-kohn*-TRAHR]
fine (good), excelente [*ehks-theh*-LEHN-*teh*]
fine (penalty), multa [MOOL-*tah*]
finger, dedo [DEH-*doh*]
★ (to) **finish,** terminar, acabar [*tehr-mee*-NAHR, *ah-kah* BAHR]
fire, fuego [FWEH-*goh*]
fireman, bombero [*bohm*-BEH-*roh*]
fireplace, chimenea [*chee-meh*-NEH-*ah*]
firm (adj), firme [FEER-*meh*]
firm (n), firma [FEER-*mah*]
★ **first,** primero, -a [*pree*-MEH-*roh, -rah*]
first aid, primeros auxilios [*pree*-MEH-*rohs ow-g'*ZEE-*l'yohs*]
first cousin, primo hermano [PREE-*moh ehr*-MAH-*noh*]
first name, nombre de pila [NOHM-*breh deh* PEE-*lah*]
★ **fish** (alive), pez (m) [*peth*]
(ready to eat), pescado [*pehs*-KAH-*doh*]
(to) **fish,** pescar [*pehs*-KAHR]
fisherman, pescador [*pehs-kah*-DOHR]
fishing, pesca [PEHS-*kah*]
fishing boat, barco de pesca [BAHR-*koh deh* PEHS-*kah*]
(to) **fit,** cuadrar [*kwah*-DRAHR]

(to) **fit** (for clothes), entallar [*ehn-tah-l'*YAHR]
★ **five,** cinco [THEEN-*koh*]
(to) **fix,** arreglar [*ah-rreh*-GLAHR]
fixed price, precio fijo [PREH-*th'yoh* FEE-*hoh*]
flag, bandera [*bahn*-DEH-*rah*]
flat, llano, -a [*l'*YAH-*noh, -nah*]
flame, llama [*l'*YAH-*mah*]
(to) **flatter,** lisonjear [*lee-sohn-heh*-AHR]
flatterer, lisonjero [*lee-sohn*-HEH-*roh*]
flavor, sabor [*sah*-BOHR]
flax, lino [LEE-*noh*]
flea, pulga [POOL-*gah*]
fleet, (n), flota [FLOH-*tah*]
flesh, carne [KAHR-*neh*]
flight, vuelo [VWEH-*loh*]
(to) **flirt,** coquetear [*koh-keh-teh*-AHR]
(to) **float,** flotar [*floh*-TAHR]
flood, inundación (f) [*ee-noon-dah-th'*YOHN]
floor, piso [PEE-*soh*]
flour, harina [*ah*-REE-*nah*]
(to) **flow,** fluir [*floo*-EER]
★ **flower,** flor (f) [*flohr*]
flowershop, florería [*floh-reh*-REE-*ah*]
fluently, corrientemente [*koh-rree-ehn-teh*-MEHN-*teh*]
flute, flauta [*flah*-OO-*tah*]
★ (to) **fly,** volar [*voh*-LAHR]
fly, mosca [MOHS-*kah*]
foam, espuma [*ehs*-POO-*mah*]
fog, neblina [*neh*-BLEE-*nah*]
(to) **follow,** seguir [*seh*-GHEER]
Follow me! ¡Sígame! [SEE-*gah-meh*]
(to) **fold,** doblar [*doh*-BLAHR]
food, comida [*koh*-MEE-*dah*]
fool, tonto [TOHN-*toh*]
★ **foot,** pie (m) [*p'yeh*]
foot (of animal or thing), pata [PAH-*tah*]

★ **for,** por, para [*pohr,* PAH-*rah*]
for example, por ejemplo [*pohr eh*-HEHM-*ploh*]
for me, for you, para mí, para Ud. [PAH-*rah mee,* PAH-*rah oos*-TEHD]
what for? ¿para qué? [PAH-*rah keh*]

NOTE: *Para* usually means "for" in the sense of "in order to" or to indicate destination.

(to) **forbid,** prohibir [*proh-ee*-BEER]
(to) **force,** forzar, obligar [*fohr*-THAHR, *oh-blee*-GAHR]
force (n), fuerza [*f'*WEHR-*thah*]
forehead, frente [FREHN-*teh*]
foreign (and) **foreigner,** extranjero, -a [*ehks-trahn*-HEH-*roh, -rah*]
foreign minister, ministro de relaciones exteriores [*mee*-NEES-*troh deh reh-lah-th'*YOH-*nehs ehks-teh-r'*YOH-*rehs*]
foreign office, ministerio de negocios extranjeros [*mee-nees*-TEH-*r'yoh deh neh*-GOH-*th'yos ehks-trahn*-HEH-*rohs*]
foreign policy, política exterior [*poh*-LEE-*tee-kah ehks-teh-r'*YOHR]
forest, selva [SEHL-*vah*]
(to) **forget,** olvidar [*ohl-vee*-DAHR]
(to) **forgive,** perdonar [*pehr-doh*-NAHR]
fork, tenedor (m) [*teh-neh*-DOHR]
form, forma [FOHR-*mah*]
(to) **form,** formar [*fohr*-MAHR]
formal, formal [*fohr*-MAHL]
formal dress, vestido de etiqueta [*vehs*-TEE-*doh deh eh-tee*-KEH-*tah*]
formality, formalidad (f) [*fohr-mah-lee*-DAHD]
former, anterior [*ahn-teh-r'*YOHR]

formerly, anteriormente [*ahn-teh-r'yohr*-MEHN-*teh*]
formula, fórmula [FOHR-*moo-lah*]
fort, fortaleza [*fohr-tah*-LEH-*thah*]
fortune, fortuna [*fohr*-TOO-*nah*]
fortunate, afortunado, -a; dichoso,- a [*ah-fohr-too*-NAH-*doh*, *-dah; dee*-CHOH-*soh, -sah*]
fortunately, afortunadamente [*ah-fohr-too-nah-dah*-MEHN-*teh*]
★ **forty,** cuarenta [*kwah*-REHN-*tah*]
forward, adelante [*ah-deh*-LAHN-*teh*]
(to) **found,** fundar [*foon*-DAHR]
foundation, fundación (f) [*foon-dah-th'*YOHN]
fountain, fuente (f) [FWEHN-*teh*]
fountain pen, pluma fuente [PLOO-*mah* FWEHN-*teh*]
★ **four,** cuatro [KWAH-*troh*]
★ **fourteen,** catorce [*kah*-TOHR-*theh*]
fourth, cuarto, -a [KWAHR-*toh, -tah*]
fox, zorra [THOH-*rrah*]
fracture, fractura [*frahk*-TOO-*rah*]
fragile, frágil [FRAH-*heel*]
fragrance, fragrancia [*frah*-GRAHN-*th'yah*]
frame, marco [MAHR-*koh*]
France, Francia [FRAHN-*th'yah*]
frank, franco [FRAHN-*koh*]
fraternity, fraternidad (f) [*frah-tehr-nee*-DAHD]
free, libre [LEE-*breh*]
freedom, libertad (f) [*lee-behr*-TAHD]
(to) **freeze,** helar [*eh*-LAHR]
freight, flete (m) [FLEH-*teh*]
French, francés, francesa [*frahn*-THEHS, *frahn*-THEH-*sah*]
Frenchman, francés [*frahn*-THEHS]
frequently, frecuentemente [*freh-kwehn-teh*-MEHN-*teh*]
fresh, fresco, -a [FREHS-*koh, -kah*]
Friday, viernes [*v'*YEHR-*nehs*]
fried, frito, -a [FREE-*toh, -tah*]
★ **friend,** amigo, -a [*ah*-MEE-*goh, -gah*]
friendship, amistad (f) [*ah-mees*-TAHD]
(to) **frighten,** asustar [*ah-soos*-TAHR]
frog, rana [RAH-*nah*]

★ **from,** de; desde [*deh,* DEHS-*deh*]
from far, desde lejos [*dehs-deh* LEH-*hohs*]
from now on, desde ahora en adelante [*dehs-deh ah*-OH-*rah ehn ah-deh*-LAHN-*teh*]
from where do you come? ¿de dónde es Ud.? [*deh* DOHN-*deh ehs oos*-TEHD]
front, frente (m) [FREHN-*teh*]
frozen, helado, -a [*eh*-LAH-*doh, -dah*]
(for food), congelado [*kohn-heh*-LAH-*doh, -ah*]
★ **fruit,** fruta [FROO-*tah*]
fruit salad, ensalada de frutas [*ehn-sah*-LAH-*dah deh* FROO-*tahs*]
fruit store, frutería [*froo-teh*-REE-*ah*]
(to) **fry,** freír [*freh*-EER]
frying pan, sartén (f) [*sahr*-TEHN]
fuel, combustible (m) [*kohm-boos*-TEE-*bleh*]
full, lleno, -a [*l'*YEH-*noh, -nah*]
fun, diversión [*dee-vehr-s'*YOHN]
funds, fondos [FOHN-*dohs*]
funeral, entierro [*ehn-t'*YEH-*rroh*]
funnel, embudo [*ehm*-BOO-*doh*]
funny, cómico, -a [KOH-*mee-koh, -kah*]
fur, piel [*p'yehl*]
fur coat, abrigo de pieles [*ah*-BREE-*goh deh p'*YEH-*lehs*]
(to) **furnish,** surtir, suministrar [*soor*-TEER, *soo-mee-nees*-TRAHR]
(to) **furnish** (a house), amueblar [*ah-mweh*-BLAHR]
furniture, muebles [MWEH-*blehs*]
further (distance), más lejos [*mahs* LEH-*hohs*]
(quantity), más [*mahs*]
furthermore, además [*ah-deh*-MAHS]
future, futuro, -a [*foo*-TOO-*roh, -rah*]
in the future, en lo futuro [*ehn loh foo*-TOO-*roh*]

G

(to) **gain,** ganar [*gah*-NAHR]
gallon, galón [*gah*-LOHN]

(to) **gamble,** jugar [*hoo*-GAHR]
gambling, juego [HWEH-*goh*]
game, juego [HWEH-*goh*]
gangplank, pasamano [*pah-sah*-MAH-*noh*]
garage, garaje (m) [*gah*-RAH-*heh*]
garbage, basura [*bah*-SOO-*rah*]
garden, jardín (m) [*hahr*-DEEN]
gardener, jardinero [*hahr-dee*-NEH-*roh*]
garlic, ajo [AH-*hoh*]
garter, liga [LEE-*gah*]
gas, gas (m) [*gahs*]
gasoline, gasolina [*gah-soh*-LEE-*nah*]
  gasoline station, puesto de gasolina [PWEHS-*toh deh gah-soh*-LEE-*nah*]
gate, puerta [PWEHR-*tah*]
(to) **gather,** recoger [*reh-koh*-HEHR]
gauge, indicador [*een-dee-kah*-DOHR]
gay, alegre [*ah*-LEH-*greh*]
gear, engranaje (m) [*ehn-grah*-NAH-*heh*]
gender, género [HEH-*neh-roh*]
general, general [*heh-neh*-RAHL]
general delivery, lista de correos [LEES-*tah deh koh*-RREH-*ohs*]
generally, generalmente [*heh-neh-rahl*-MEHN-*teh*]
generation, generación (f) [*heh-neh-rah-th'*YOHN]
generous, generoso, -a [*heh-neh*-ROH-*soh, -sah*]
gentle, suave [SWAH-*veh*]
★ **gentleman,** caballero [*kah-bah-l'*YEH-*roh*]
Gentlemen (for letter heading), muy señores nuestros [*mwee seh-n'*YOH-*rehs* NWEHS-*trohs*]
genuine, genuino, -a [*heh*-NWEE-*noh, -nah*]
geography, geografía [*heh-oh-grah*-FEE-*ah*]
geometry, geometría [*heh-oh-meh*-TREE-*ah*]
German, alemán, alemana [*ah-leh*-MAHN, *ah-leh*-MAH-*nah*]
Germany, Alemania [*ah-leh*-MAH-*n'yah*]
★ (to) **get** (obtain), conseguir [*kohn-seh*-GHEER]
(to) **get** (receive), recibir [*reh-thee*-BEER]

(to) **get** (become), llegar a ser [*l'yeh*-GAHR *ah sehr*]
to get back (return), volver, regresar [*vohl*-VEHR, *reh-greh*-SAHR]
to get down, bajar [*bah*-HAHR]
to get married, casarse [*kah*-SAHR-*seh*]
to get off, bajarse [*bah*-HAHR-*seh*]
to get in, entrar [*ehn*-TRAHR]
to get up, levantarse [*leh-vahn*-TAHR-*seh*]
to get to, llegar a [*l'yeh*-GAHR *ah*]
ghost, duende (m) [DWEHN-*deh*]
gift, regalo [*reh*-GAH-*loh*]
gigantic, gigantesco, -a [*hee-gahn*-TEHS-*koh, -kah*]
gin, ginebra [*hee*-NEH-*brah*]
★ **girl,** niña, muchacha [NEE-*n'yah, moo*-CHAH-*chah*]
★ (to) **give,** dar [*dahr*]
give me, déme [DEH-*meh*]
give him (her), déle [DEH-*leh*]
give us, dénos [DEH-*nohs*]
give them, déles [DEH-*lehs*]
to give a message, dar un recado [*dahr oon reh*-KAH-*doh*]
glad, contento, -a [*kohn*-TEHN-*toh, -tah*]
glass (material), vidrio [VEE-*dr'yoh*]
(for drinking), vaso [VAH-*soh*]
glasses, anteojos (m plural) [*ahn-teh*-OH-*hohs*]
glory, gloria [GLOH-*r'yah*]
glove, guante (m) [GWAHN-*teh*]
glue, cola [KOH-*lah*]
★ (to) **go,** ir [*eer*]
go away! ¡váyase! [VAH-*yah-seh*]
go on! ¡siga! [SEE-*gah*]
to go away, partir [*pahr*-TEER]
to go back, regresar [*reh-greh*-SAHR]
to go down, bajar [*bah*-HAHR]
to go in, entrar [*ehn*-TRAHR]
to go out, salir [*sah*-LEER]
to go to bed, acostarse [*ah-kohs*-TAHR-*seh*]
to go up, subir [*soo*-BEER]

goal, meta [MEH-*tah*]
★ **God,** Dios [*d'yohs*]
goddaughter, ahijada [*ah-ee-*HAH-*dah*]
godfather, padrino [*pah-*DREE-*noh*]
godmother, madrina [*mah-*DREE-*nah*]
godson, ahijado [*ah-ee-*HAH-*doh*]
gold, oro [OH-*roh*]
golden, de oro [*deh* OH-*roh*]
★ **good,** bueno, -a [BWEH-*noh, -nah*]
★ **good afternoon (evening),** buenas tardes [BWEH-*nahs* TAHR-*dehs*]
good luck! ¡buena suerte! [BWEH-*nah* SWEHR-*teh*]
★ **good morning,** buenos días [BWEH-*nohs* DEE-*ahs*]
★ **good night,** buenas noches [BWEH-*nahs* NOH-*chehs*]
goods, mercancía [*mehr-kahn-*THEE-*ah*]
★ **good-bye,** adiós [*ah-d'*YOHS]
goodlooking, guapo, -a [GWAH-*poh, -pah*]
goose, ganso [GAHN-*soh*]
gorgeous, suntuoso, -a [*soon-t'*WOH-*soh, -sah*]
gossip, chisme (m) [CHEES-*meh*]
gothic, gótico [GOH-*tee-koh*]
government, gobierno [*goh-b'*YEHR-*noh*]
governor, gobernador [*goh-behr-nah-*DOHR]
graceful, gracioso, -a [*grah-th'*YOH-*soh, -sah*]
grade, grado [GRAH-*doh*]
gradually, gradualmente [*grah-dwahl-*MEHN-*teh*]
graduation, graduación (f) [*grah-dwah-th'*YOHN]
grammar, gramática [*grah-*MAH-*tee-kah*]
grandchild, nieto, nieta [*n'*YEH-*toh, -tah*]
grandfather, abuelo [*ah-*BWEH-*loh*]
grandmother, abuela [*ah-*BWEH-*lah*]
grandparents, abuelos [*ah-*BWEH-*lohs*]
grandson, nieto [*n'*YEH-*toh*]
grape, uva [OO-*vah*]
grapefruit, toronja [*toh-*ROHN-*hah*]
grass, hierba [YEHR-*bah*]
grateful, agradecido, -a [*ah-grah-deh-*THEE-*doh, -dah*]
gratis, gratis [GRAH-*tees*]

grave (n), sepultura [*seh-pool-*TOO-*rah*]
grave (adj), grave [GRAH-*veh*]
gravy, salsa [SAHL-*sah*]
grease, grasa [GRAH-*sah*]
great, grande; gran (if used before the noun) [GRAHN-*deh, grahn*]
  a great deal, mucho, -a [MOO-*choh, -chah*]
  a great many, muchos, -as [MOO-*chohs, -chahs*]
Great Britain, Gran Bretaña [*grahn breh-*TAH-*n'yah*]
Greek, griego, -a [*gr'*YEH-*goh, -ah*]
Greece, Grecia [GREH-*th'yah*]
green, verde [VEHR-*deh*]
(to) **greet,** saludar [*sah-loo-*DAHR]
greetings, saludos [*sah-*LOO-*dohs*]
grey, gris [*grees*]
grocery, tienda de comestibles [*t'*YEHN-*dah deh koh-mehs-*TEE-*blehs*]
ground, tierra, suelo [*t'*YEH-*rrah,* SWEH-*loh*]
ground floor, piso bajo [PEE-*soh* BAH-*hoh*]
group, grupo [GROO-*poh*]
(to) **grow,** crecer [*kreh-*THEHR]
  to grow crops, cultivar [*kool-tee-*VAHR]
  to grow old, envejecer [*ehn-veh-heh-*THEHR]
  to grow (become), llegar a ser [*l'yeh-*GAHR *ah sehr*]
guarantee, garantía [*gah-rahn-*TEE-*ah*]
(to) **guarantee,** garantizar [*gah-rahn-tee-*THAHR]
guard, guardia [GWAHR-*d'yah*]
Guatemala, Guatemala [*gwah-teh-*MAH-*lah*]
Guatemalan, guatemalteco, -a [*gwah-teh-mahl-*TEH-*koh -kah*]
(to) **guess,** adivinar [*ah-dee-vee-*NAHR]
guest, invitado, -a [*een-vee-*TAH-*doh, -dah*]
guide, guía (m or f) [GHEE-*ah*]
guilty, culpable [*kool-*PAH-*bleh*]
guitar, guitarra [*ghee-*TAH-*rrah*]
gum (teeth), encía [*ehn-*THEE-*ah*]
gum (for chewing), chicle (m) [CHEE-*kleh*]
gun, fusil [*foo-*SEEL]

gymnasium, gimnasio [*heem*-NAH-*s'yoh*]
gypsy, gitano, -a [*hee*-TAH-*noh, -nah*]

H

habit, hábito, costumbre (f) [AH-*bee-toh, kohs*-TOOM *breh*]
hair, cabello, pelo [*kah*-BEH-*l'yoh,* PEH-*loh*]
hairbrush, cepillo para el pelo [*theh*-PEE-*l'yoh* PAH-*rah ehl* PEH-*loh*]
haircut, corte de pelo (m) [KOHR-*teh deh* PEH-*loh*]
hairdresser, peluquero [*peh-loo*-KEH-*roh*]
hair tonic, tónico para el cabello [TOH-*nee-koh* PAH-*rah ehl kah*-BEH-*l'yoh*]
half (n). mitad (f) [*mee*-TAHD]
(adj), medio, -a [MEH-*d'yoh, -d'yah*]
half past four, las cuatro y media [*lahs* KWAH-*troh ee* MEH-*d'yah*]
half way, medio camino [MEH-*d'yoh kah*-MEE-*noh*]
hall (passageway), pasillo [*pah*-SEE-*l'yoh*]
hall (entrance), vestíbulo [*vehs*-TEE-*boo-loh*]
halt! ¡alto! [AHL-*toh*]
★ **hand** (n), mano [MAH-*noh*]
handbag, cartera, bolso [*kahr*-TEH-*rah,* BOHL-*soh*]
handkerchief, pañuelo [*pah-n'yoo*-EH-*loh*]
handmade, hecho(-a) a mano [EH-*choh, (-chah) ah* MAH-*noh*]
handsewn, cosido(-a) a mano [*koh*-SEE-*doh, (-dah) ah* MAH-*noh*]
on the other hand, en cambio [*ehn* KAHM-*b'yoh*], por otra parte [*pohr* OH-*trah* PAHR-*teh*]
(to) **hand,** entregar [*ehn-treh*-GAHR]
handle (n), manejar [*mah-neh*-HAHR]
(to) **handle,** entregar [*ehn-treh*-GAHR]
(to) **hang,** colgar [*kohl*-GAHR]
hanger (clothes), percha [PEHR-*chah*]

★ (to) **happen,** pasar [*pah*-SAHR]
  what is happening? ¿qué pasa? [*keh* PAH-*sah*]
  when did it happen? ¿cuándo pasó? [KWAHN-*doh pah*-SOH]
★ **happy,** feliz [*feh*-LEETH]
  Happy New Year, Feliz Año Nuevo [*feh*-LEETH AH-*n'yoh* NWEH-*voh*]
  Happy Birthday! ¡Feliz Cumpleaños! [*feh*-LEETH *koom-pleh*-AH-*n'yohs*]
harbor, puerto [PWEHR-*toh*]
hard, duro, -a [DOO-*roh, -rah*]
  hardly, apenas [*ah*-PEH-*nahs*]
(to) **harm,** hacer daño [*ah*-THEHR DAH-*n'yoh*]
harmful, dañino [*dah-n'*YEE-*noh*]
harp, arpa [AHR-*pah*]
harvest, cosecha [*koh*-SEH-*chah*]
haste, prisa [PREE-*sah*]
hat, sombrero [*sohm*-BREH-*roh*]
(to) **hate,** odiar [*oh-d'*YAHR]
★ (to) **have,** tener [*teh*-NEHR]

NOTE: *tener* in the sense of possession but *haber* when used with other verbs as an auxiliary. Ex.: "I have money"—*Tengo dinero* [TEHN-*goh dee*-NEH-*roh*]. "I have missed the train"—*He perdido el tren* [*eh pehr*-DEE-*doh ehl trehn*].

(to) **have to,**
  NOTE: This expression is translated by *tener que* plus the infinitive of the following verb: "I have to go"—*tengo que ir.*
★ **he,** él [*ehl*]
★ **head** (body), cabeza [*kah*-BEH-*thah*]
head (chief), jefe [HEH-*feh*]
headache, dolor de cabeza [*doh*-LOHR *deh kah*-BEH-*thah*]
headquarters (army), estado mayor [*ehs*-TAH-*doh mah*-YOHR]
headquarters (business), oficina principal [*oh-fee*-THEE-*nah preen-thee*-PAHL]

★ **health,** salud (f) [*sah*-LOOD]

to be in good health, estar bien de salud [*ehs*-TAHR *b'yehn deh sah*-LOOD]

To your health! ¡A su salud! [*ah soo sah*-LOOD]

healthy, sano, -a [SAH-*noh, -nah*]

★ (to) **hear,** oir [*oh*-EER]

★ **heart,** corazón (m) [*koh-rah*-THOHN]

heart disease, enfermedad del corazón [*ehn-fehr-meh*-DAHD *dehl koh-rah*-THOHN]

by heart, de memoria [*deh meh*-MOH-*r'yah*]

heat, calor (m) [*kah*-LOHR]

(to) **heat,** calentar [*kah-lehn*-TAHR]

heating, calefacción [*kah-leh-fahk-th'*YOHN]

heaven, cielo [*th'*YEH-*loh*]

heavy, pesado, -a [*peh*-SAH-*doh, -dah*]

heavy industry, industria pesada [*een*-DOOS-*tr'yah peh*-SAH-*dah*]

Hebrew, hebreo, -a [*eh*-BREH-*oh, -ah*]

heel (foot), talón (m) [*tah*-LOHN]

(shoe), tacón (m) [*tah*-KOHN]

height, altura [*ahl*-TOO-*rah*]

heir, heredero [*eh-reh*-DEH-*roh*]

heiress, heredera [*eh-reh*-DEH-*rah*]

hell, infierno [*een-f'*YEHR-*noh*]

help, ayuda [*ah*-YOO-*dah*]

(to) **help,** ayudar [*ah-yoo*-DAHR]

★ **help!** socorro [*soh*-KOH-*rroh*]

helpful, útil [OO-*teel*]

hen, gallina [*gah-l'*YEE-*nah*]

★ **her** (as object), la, or a ella [*lah, ah* EH-*l'yah*]

(as possessive), su or de ella [*soo, deh* EH-*l'yah*]

★ **here,** aquí [*ah*-KEE]

come here, venga aquí [VEHN-*gah ah*-KEE]

Here it is. Aquí está. [*ah*-KEE *ehs*-TAH]

hero, héroe [EH-*roh-eh*]

hers, suyo, -a, el suyo, la suya [SOO-*yoh, -yah*]

herself, se (reflexive), ella misma [EH-*l'yah* MEES-*mah*] (see note on **himself**)

(to) **hesitate,** vacilar [*vah-thee-*LAHR]
(to) **hide,** esconder [*ehs-kohn-*DEHR]
high, alto, -a [AHL-*toh, -tah*]
high school, escuela secundaria [*ehs-*KWEH-*lah sen-koon-*DAH-*r'yah*]
high-school certificate, diploma de escuela secundaria [*dee-*PLOH-*mah deh ehs-*KWEH-*lah seh-koon-*DAH-*r'yah*]
highway, carretera [*kah-rreh-*TEH-*rah*]
hill, colina [*koh-*LEE-*nah*], cerro [THEH-*rroh*]
★ **him,** le, lo, a él [*leh, loh, ah, ehl*]
himself, él mismo [*ehl* MEES-*moh*]
NOTE: When used reflexively "himself" is expressed by *se.*
"He dresses himself"—*El se viste* [*ehl seh* VEES-*teh*]
(to) **hire** (rent), alquilar [*ahl-kee-*LAHR]
★ **his,** su, de él, suyo, suya (when used alone) [*soo, deh ehl,* SOO-*yoh,* SOO-*yah*]

NOTE: There is no difference between "his" or "her"; both are expressed by *su.* When it is necessary specify, *de él* or *de ella* is added to the noun.

history, historia [*ees-*TOH-*r'yah*]
hip, cadera [*kah-*DEH-*rah*]
(to) **hit,** pegar [*peh-*GAHR]
(to) **hold,** tener [*teh-*NEHR]
hole, agujero [*ah-goo-*HEH-*roh*]
holiday, día de fiesta [DEE-*ah deh f'*YEHS-*tah*]
Holland, Holanda [*oh-*LAHN-*dah*]
holy, santo, -a [SAHN-*toh, -tah*]
home, casa (m) [KAH-*sah*]
at home, en casa [*ehn* KAH-*sah*]
Make yourself at home! ¡Está en su casa! [*ehs-*TAH *ehn soo* KAH-*sah*]
homely, feo, -a [FEH-*oh, -ah*]
Honduras, Honduras [*ohn-*DOO-*rahs*]

Honduran, hondureño, -a [*ohn-doo*-REH-*n'yoh, -n'yah*]
honest, honrado, -a [*ohn*-RAH-*doh, -dah*]
honey (from bees), miel [*m'yehl*]
honey (endearment), querido, -a [*keh*-REE-*doh, -ah*]
honeymoon, luna de miel [LOO-*nah deh m'yehl*]
honor, honor (m) [*oh*-NOHR]
hook, gancho [GAHN-*choh*]
(for fishing), anzuelo [*ahn-th'*WEH-*loh*]
hope, esperanza [*ehs-peh*-RAHN-*thah*]
★ (to) **hope,** esperar [*ehs-peh*-RAHR]
horizon, horizonte [*oh-ree*-THOHN-*teh*]
horn (on a bull), cuerno [KWEHR-*noh*]
horn (on a car), bocina [*boh*-THEE-*nah*]
★ **horse,** caballo [*kah*-BAH-*l'yoh*]
horrible, horrible [*oh*-RREE-*bleh*]
hospital, hospital (m) [*ohs-pee*-TAHL]
hospitality, hospitalidad [*ohs-pee-tah-lee*-DAHD]
host, anfitrión (m) [*ahn-fee-tr'*YOHN]
hostess, anfitriona [*ahn-fee-tree*-OH-*nah*]
★ **hot,** caliente [*kah-l'*YEHN-*teh*]
hotel, hotel (m) [*oh*-TEHL]
hotel room, cuarto de hotel [KWAHR-*toh deh oh*-TEHL]
★ **hour,** hora [OH-*rah*]
hourly, por hora [*pohr* OH-*rah*]
★ **house,** casa [KAH-*sah*]
★ **how?** ¿cómo? [KOH-*moh*]
★ **How do you do?** ¿Cómo está Ud? [KOH-*moh ehs*-TAH *oos*-TEHD]
how far? ¿a qué distancia? [*ah keh dees*-TAHN-*th'yah*]
★ **how long?** (a time), ¿cuánto tiempo? [KWAHN-*toh t'*YEHM-*poh*]
★ **how many?** ¿cuántos? [KWAHN-*tohs*]
★ **how much?** ¿cuánto? [KWAHN-*toh*]
however, sin embargo [*seen ehm*-BAHR-*goh*]
human, humano, -a [*oo*-MAH-*noh, -nah*]
humid, húmedo, -a [OO-*meh-doh, -dah*]
humorous, humorístico, -a [*oo-moh*-REES-*tee-koh, -kah*]

humanity, humanidad (f) [*oo-mah-nee-*DAHD]
humble, humilde [*oo-*MEEL-*deh*]
★ **hundred,** cien, ciento (if used alone) [*th'yehn, th'*YEHN-*toh*]
Hungarian, húngaro, -a [OON-*gah-roh, -rah*]
Hungary, Hungría [*oon-*GRE-*ah*]
hunger, hambre [AHM-*breh*]
★ **to be hungry,** tener hambre [*teh-*NEHR AHM-*breh*]
I am hungry, tengo hambre [TEHN-*goh* AHM-*breh*]
Are you hungry? ¿Tiene hambre? [T'YEH-*neh* AHM-*breh*]
(to) **hunt,** cazar [*kah-*THAHR]
hunter, cazador [*kah-thah-*DOHR]
hunting, caza [KAH-*thah*]
hurricane, huracán (m) [*oo-rah-*KAHN]
(to) **hurry,** apresurar(se), darse prisa, afanarse [*ah-preh-soo-*RAHR-*seh,* DAHR-*seh* PREE-*sah, ah-fah-*NAHR-*seh*]
(to be) **in a hurry,** estar de prisa [*ehs-*TAHR *deh* PREE-*sah*]
★ **hurry up!** ¡dése prisa! [DEH-*seh* PREE-*sah*]
(to) **hurt** (somebody), herir [*eh-*REER]
(ache), doler [*doh-*LEHR]
husband, esposo, marido [*ehs-*POH-*soh, mah-*REE-*doh*]

I

★ **I,** yo [*yoh*]
ice, hielo [YEH-*loh*]
ice cream, helado [*eh-*LAH-*doh*]
idea, idea [*ee-*DEH-*ah*]
ideal, ideal [*ee-deh-*AHL]
identical, idéntico, -a [*ee-*DEHN-*tee-koh, -kah*]
identification papers, papeles de identidad [*pah-*PEH-*lehs deh ee-dehn-tee-*DAHD]
(to) **identify,** identificar [*ee-dehn-tee-fee-*KAHR]
idiot, idiota (m & f) [*ee-d'*YOH-*tah*]
★ **if,** si [*see*]
even if, aun si [*ah-*OON *see*]

ignorant, ignorante [*eeg-noh-*RAHN-*teh*]
★ **ill,** enfermo, -a [*ehn-*FEHR-*moh, -mah*]
illegal, ilegal [*ee-leh-*GAHL]
illegible, ilegible [*ee-leh-*HEE-*bleh*]
illness, enfermedad [*ehn-fehr-meh-*DAHD]
illustration, ilustración (f) [*ee-loos-trah-th'*YOHN]
imagination, imaginación (f) [*ee-mah-hee-nah-th'*YOHN]
(to) **imagine,** imaginar [*ee-mah-hee-*NAHR]
just imagine! ¡imagínese! [*ee-mah-*HEE-*neh-seh*]
(to) **imitate,** imitar [*ee-mee-*TAHR]
imitation, imitación (f) [*ee-mee-tah-th'*YOHN]
immediate, inmediato, -a [*een-meh-d'*YAH-*toh, -tah*]
immediately, inmediatamente [*een-meh-d'yah-tah-*MEHN-*teh*]
immense, inmenso, -a [*een-*MEHN-*soh, -sah*]
immigration, inmigración (f) [*een-mee-grah-th'*YOHN]
immoral, inmoral [*een-moh-*RAHL]
impatient, impaciente [*eem-pah-th'*YEHN-*teh*]
imperfect, imperfecto [*eem-pehr-*FEHK-*toh*]
implement, instrumento [*eens-troo-*MEHN-*toh*]
(to) **import,** importar [*eem-pohr-*TAHR]
important, importante [*eem-pohr-*TAHN-*teh*]
imported, importado [*eem-pohr-*TAH-*doh*]
impossible, imposible [*eem-poh-*SEE-*bleh*]
impression, impresión (f) [*eem-preh-s'*YOHN]
(to) **improve,** mejorar [*meh-hoh-*RAHR]
improvement, mejoramiento [*meh-hoh-rah-m'*YEHN-*toh*]
★ **in,** en, dentro de [*ehn,* DEHN-*troh deh*]
★ **in back of,** detrás de [*deh-*TRAHS-*deh*]
★ **in front of,** en frente de [*ehn* FREHN-*teh deh*]
in no way, de ninguna manera [*deh neen-*GOO-*nah mah-*NEH-*rah*]
in spite of, a pesar de [*ah peh-*SAHR *deh*]
in the evening, por la noche [*pohr lah* NOH-*cheh*]
Is Mr. Lopez in? ¿Está el Sr. López? [*ehs-*TAH *ehl seh-n'*YOHR LOH-*peth*]
★ **inside,** adentro [*ah-*DEHN-*troh*]

inch, pulgada [*pool*-GAH-*dah*]

NOTE: Inches are ordinarily not used. *Centímetro* is the local unit of measure. It takes 2.54 of these to make an inch.

incident, incidente (m) [*een-thee*-DEHN-*teh*]
incidentally, incidentalmente [*een-thee-dehn-tahl*-MEHN-*teh*]
inclination, inclinación (f) [*een-klee-nah-th'*YOHN]
included, incluído, -a [*een-kloo*-EE-*doh, -dah*]
income, ingresos (plural) [*een*-GREH-*sohs*]
income tax, impuesto sobre ingresos [*eem*-PWEHS-*toh* SOH-*breh een*-GREH-*sohs*]
incomparable, incomparable [*een-kohm-pah*-RAH-*bleh*]
incomplete, incompleto, -a [*een-kohm*-PLEH-*toh, -tah*]
inconvenience, molestia [*moh*-LEHS-*t'yah*]
It is no inconvenience, no es molestia [*noh ehs moh*-LEHS-*t'yah*]
(to) **inconvenience,** molestar [*moh-lehs*-TAHR]
incorrect, incorrecto, -a [*een-koh*-RREHK-*toh, -tah*]
increase (n), aumento [*ow*-MEHN-*toh*]
(to) **increase,** aumentar [*ow-mehn*-TAHR]
incredible, increíble [*een-kreh*-EE-*bleh*]
indecent, indecente [*een-deh*-THEHN-*teh*]
indeed, verdaderamente [*vehr-dah-deh-rah*-MEHN-*teh*]
yes, indeed! ¡claro que sí! [KLAH-*roh keh see*]
indefinite, indefinido, -a [*een-deh-fee*-NEE-*doh, -dah*]
independence, independencia [*een-deh-pehn*-DEHN-*th'yah*]
independent, independiente [*een-deh-pehn-d'*YEHN-*teh*]
index, índice [EEN-*dee-theh*]
India, India [EEN-*d'yah*]
Indian, indio, -a [EEN-*d'yoh, -d'yah*]
(to) **indicate,** indicar [*een-dee*-KAHR]
indigestion, indigestión (f) [*een-dee-hehs-t'*YOHN]

indirect, indirecto, -a [*een-dee-*REHK-*toh, -tah*]
indiscreet, indiscreto, -a [*een-dees-*KREH-*toh, -tah*]
individual (adj), individual [*een-dee-vee-*DWAHL]
indoors, adentro [*ah-*DEHN-*troh*]
indorsement, endoso [*ehn-*DOH-*soh*]
industrial, industrial [*een-doos-tr'*YAHL]
industry, industria [*een-*DOOS-*tr'yah*]
inefficient, ineficaz [*ee-neh-fee-*KAHTH]
infantry, infantería [*een-fahn-teh-*REE-*ah*]
infection, infección (f) [*een-fehk-th'*YOHN]
inferior, inferior [*een-feh-r'*YOHR]
infinitive, infinitivo [*een-fee-nee-*TEE-*voh*]
influence (n), influencia [*een-fl'*WEHN-*th'yah*]
information, información (f) [*een-fohr-mah-th'*YOHN]
informal, informal [*een-fohr-*MAHL]
NOTE: in the meaning "not serious, not reliable.
inhabitant, habitante [*ah-bee-*TAHN-*teh*]
(to) **inherit,** heredar [*eh-reh-*DAHR]
inheritance, herencia [*eh-*REHN-*th'yah*]
initial (n & adj), inicial [*ee-nee-th'*YAHL]
injection, inyección (f) [*een-yehk-th'*YOHN]
(to) **injure,** lesionar [*leh-s'yoh-*NAHR]
injured, lesionado, -a [*leh-s'yoh-*NAH-*doh, -dah*]
injury, lesión [*leh-s'*YOHN]
injustice, injusticia [*een-hoos-*TEE-*th'yah*]
ink, tinta [TEEN-*tah*]
innocent, inocente [*ee-noh-*THEHN-*teh*]
(to) **inquire,** preguntar [*preh-goon-*TAHR]
insane, loco, -a [LOH-*koh, -kah*]
insect, insecto [*een-*SEHK-*toh*]
inside (prep), dentro [DEHN-*troh*]
inside out, al revés [*ahl reh-*VEHS]
(to) **insist,** insistir [*een-sees-*TEER]
(to) **inspect,** inspeccionar [*eens-pehk-th'yoh-*NAHR]
inspection, inspección (f) [*eens-pehk-th'*YOHN]
inspector, inspector [*eens-pehk-*TOHR]
inspiration, inspiración [*eens-pee-rah-th'*YOHN]
(to) **install,** instalar [*eens-tah-*LAHR]
(for) **instance,** por ejemplo [*pohr eh-*HEHM-*ploh*]

★ **instead of,** en lugar de [*ehn loo*-GAHR *deh*]
institution, institución (f) [*eens-tee-too-th'*YOHN]
(to) **instruct,** instruir [*eens-troo*-EER]
instruction, instrucción (f) [*eens-trook-th'*YOHN]
instructor, instructor [*eens-trook*-TOHR]
instrument, instrumento [*eens-troo*-MEHN-*toh*]
insufficient, insuficiente [*een-soo-fee-th'*YEHN-*teh*]
insult, insulto [*een*-SOOL-*toh*]
insurance policy, poliza de seguro [*poh*-LEE-*thah deh seh*-GOO-*roh*]
(to) **insure,** asegurar [*ah-seh-goo*-RAHR]
intact, intacto, -a [*een*-TAHK-*toh, -tah*]
intelligent, inteligente [*een-teh-lee*-HEHN-*teh*]
(to) **intend,** intentar [*een-tehn*-TAHR]
intense, intenso, -a [*een*-TEHN-*soh, -sah*]
intention, intención (f) [*een-tehn-th'*YOHN]
interest, interés (m) [*een-teh*-REHS]
(to) **interest,** interesar [*een-teh-reh*-SAHR]
interested in, interesado en [*een-teh-reh*-SAH-*doh ehn*]
★ **interesting,** interesante [*een-teh-reh*-SAHN-*teh*]
interior, interior (m) [*een-teh-r'*YOHR]
intermission, entreacto [*ehn-treh*-AHK-*toh*]
internal, interno, -a [*een*-TEHR-*noh, -nah*]
international, internacional [*een-tehr-nah-th'yoh*-NAHL]
interpreter, intérprete [*een*-TEHR-*preh-teh*]
interview, entrevista [*ehn-treh*-VEES-*tah*]
★ **into,** dentro, en [DEHN-*troh, ehn*]
(to) **introduce** (people), presentar [*preh-sehn*-TAHR]
introduction, introducción (f) [*een-troh-dook-th'*YOHN]
invalid, inválido, -a [*een*-VAH-*lee-doh, -dah*]
invasion, invasión [*een-vah-s'*YOHN]
invention, invención (f), invento [*een-vehn-th'*YOHN, *een*-VEHN-*toh*]
inventor, inventor [*een-vehn*-TOHR]
(to) **invest** (money), invertir [*een-vehr*-TEER]
(to) **investigate,** investigar [*een-vehs-tee*-GAHR]
invisible, invisible [*een-vee*-SEE-*bleh*]
invitation, invitación (f) [*een-vee-tah-th'*YOHN]
(to) **invite,** invitar [*een-vee*-TAHR]

invoice, factura [*fahk*-TOO-*rah*]
iodine, yodo [YOH-*doh*]
Ireland, Irlanda [*eer*-LAHN-*dah*]
Irish, irlandés, -esa [*eer-lahn*-DEHS, -DEH-*sah*]
iron (metal), hierro [YEH-*rroh*]
iron (for ironing), plancha [PLAHN-*chah*]
(to) **iron,** planchar [*plahn*-CHAHR]
irrigation, irrigación [*ee-rree-gah-th'*YOHN]
irritation, irritación [*ee-rree-tah-th'*YOHN]
★ **is** (for general use), es (for position), está [*ehs, ehs*-TAH]
Where is it? ¿Donde está? [DOHN-*deh ehs*-TAH] (see Note on "to be")
★ **it** (subject),

NOTE: Spanish has no exact equivalent for "it." *El* or *ella* is sometimes used depending on the gender of the word referred to, but more often and *always* in impersonal expressions "it" is not translated at all.

It isn't so. No es verdad. [*noh ehs vehr*-DAHD]
It is late. Es tarde. [*ehs* TAHR-*deh*]
Is it raining? ¿Está lloviendo? [*ehs*-TAH *l'yoh-v'*YEHN-*doh*]
Where is the bird? ¿Dónde está el pájaro? [DOHN-*deh ehs*-TAH *ehl* PAH-*hah-roh*]
It is in the tree, (el) Está en el árbol [*ehs*-TAH *ehn ehl* AHR-*bohl*]
★ **it** (object of verb), lo (or) la [*loh, lah*]
Have you the book? ¿Tiene Ud. el libro? [*t'*YEH-*neh oos*-TEHD *ehl* LEE-*broh*]
Yes, I have it. Si, lo tengo. [*see loh* TEHN-*goh*]
Italian, italiano, -a [*ee-tah-l'*YAH-*noh, -nah*]
Italy, Italia [*ee*-TAH-*l'yah*]
(to) **itch,** picar [*pee*-KAHR]
itinerary, itinerario [*ee-tee-neh*-RAH-*r'yoh*]
its, su (plural: sus) [*soo, soos*]
ivory, marfil (m) [*mahr*-FEEL]

J

jacket, chaqueta [*chah*-KEH-*tah*]
jail, cárcel (f) [KAHR-*thehl*]
janitor, conserje (m) [*kohn*-SEHR-*heh*]
January, enero [*eh*-NEH-*roh*]
Japan, Japón (m) [*hah*-POHN]
Japanese, japonés, japonesa [*hah-poh*-NEHS, *hah-poh*-NEH *sah*]
jar, jarro [HAH-*rroh*]
jaw, quijada [*kee*-HAH-*dah*]
jealous, celoso, -a [*theh*-LOH-*soh, -sah*]
jelly, jalea [*hah*-LEH-*ah*]
Jew and **Jewish,** judío, -a [*hoo*-DEE-*oh, -ah*]
jewelry and **jewelry shop,** joyería [*hoh-yeh*-REE-*ah*]
job, empleo [*ehm*-PLEH-*oh*]
joke, chiste (m) [CHEES-*teh*]
(to) **joke,** bromear [*broh-meh*-AHR]
journalist, periodista [*peh-r'yoh*-DEES-*tah*]
journey, viaje (m) [*v'*YAH-*heh*]
joy, alegría [*ah-leh*-GREE-*ah*]
joyful, alegre [*ah*-LEH-*greh*]
judge, juez (m) [*hoo*-ETH]
(to) **judge,** juzgar [*hooth*-GAHR]
juice, jugo [HOO-*goh*]
July, julio [HOO-*l'yoh*]
(to) **jump,** saltar [*sahl*-TAHR]
June, junio [HOO-*n'yoh*]
jungle, selva [SEHL-*vah*]
jury, jurado [*hoo*-RAH-*doh*]
just (adj), justo, -a [HOOS-*toh, -tah*]
just (adv),

NOTE: "Just" as an adverb of time is expressed by the verb *acabar*.
"I have just come."—*Acabo de llegar*. "He has just left"—*Acaba de salir*.

just (*continued from page 71*)
just as, al momento que [*ahl moh*-MEHN-*toh keh*]
just now, ahora mismo [*ah*-OH-*rah* MEES-*moh*]
just as you please, como Ud. guste [KOH-*moh oos*-TEHD GOOS-*teh*]

K

(to) **keep,** guardar [*gwahr*-DAHR]
Keep out! ¡No entre! [*noh* EHN-*treh*]
Keep quiet! ¡Cállese, por favor! [KAH-*l'yeh-seh pohr fah*-VOHR]
key, llave (f) [*l'*YAH-*veh*]
(to) **kick,** patear [*pah-teh*-AHR]
kid (goat), cabritilla (*kah-bree*-TEE-*l'yah*]
kidney, riñón (m) [*ree-n'*YOHN]
(to) **kill,** matar [*mah*-TAHR]
kind, clase (f) [KLAH-*seh*]
kindness, bondad (f) [*bohn*-DAHD]
king, rey (m) [*ray*]
(to) **kiss,** besar [*beh*-SAHR]
kiss, beso [BEH-*soh*]
kitchen, cocina [*koh*-THEE-*nah*]
knee, rodilla [*roh*-DEE-*l'yah*]
★ **knife,** cuchillo [*koo*-CHEE-*l'yoh*]
(to) **knock** (at the door), tocar a la puerta [*toh*-KAHR *ah lah* PWEHR-*tah*]
knot, nudo [NOO-*doh*]
★ (to) **know,** saber, conocer [*sah*-BEHR, *koh-noh*-THEHR]
Do you know? ¿Sabe Ud.? [SAH-*beh oos*-TEHD]
Who knows? ¿Quién sabe? [*k'yehn* SAH-*beh*]

NOTE: "To know" in the sense of being acquainted with someone or something is translated by *conocer*. *¿Lo conoce Ud.?* "Do you know him?"

knowledge, conocimiento [*koh-noh-thee-m'*YEHN-*toh*]
known, conocido [*koh-noh-*THEE-*doh*]

L

label, etiqueta [*eh-tee-*KEH-*tah*]
laboratory, laboratorio [*lah-boh-rah-*TOH-*r'yoh*]
lace, encaje (m) [*ehn-*KAH-*heh*]
laborer, trabajador [*trah-bah-hah-*DOHR]
(to be) **lacking,** hacer falta [*ah-*THEHR FAHL-*tah*]
ladder, escalera [*ehs-kah-*LEH-*rah*]
lady, dama, señora [DAH-*mah, seh-n'*YOH-*rah*]
ladies' room, salón de señoras (m) [*sah-*LOHN *deh seh-n'*YOH-*rahs*]
lake, lago [LAH-*goh*]
lamb, cordero [*kohr-*DEH-*roh*]
lame, cojo, -a [KOH-*hoh, -hah*]
lamp, lámpara [LAHM-*pah-rah*]
land, tierra [*t'*YEH-*rrah*]
(to) **land** (for plane), aterrizar [*ah-teh-rree-*THAHR]
(for ship), atracar [*ah-trah-*KAHR]
landlady, dueña [DWEH-*n'yah*]
landlord, dueño [DWEH-*n'yoh*]

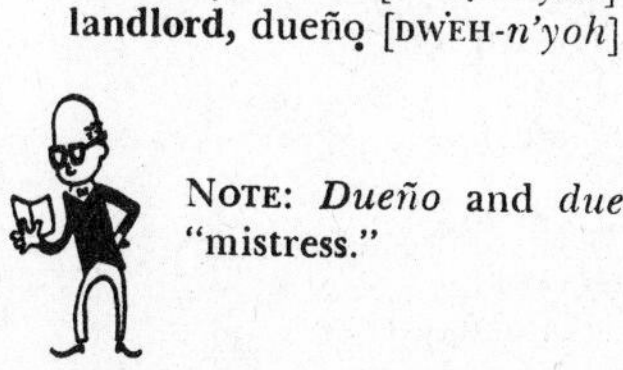

NOTE: *Dueño* and *dueña* also mean "master" and "mistress."

landowner, terrateniente (m) [*teh-rrah-teh-n'*YEHN-*teh*]
landscape, paisaje (m) [*pigh-*SAH-*heh*]
language, idioma (m) [*ee-d'*YOH-*mah*]
lantern, linterna [*leen-*TEHR-*nah*]
lard, manteca [*mahn-*TEH-*kah*]
★ **large,** grande [GRAHN-*deh*]

★ **last,** último, -a [OOL-*tee-moh, -mah*]
at last, al fin [*ahl feen*]
last night, anoche [*ah*-NOH-*cheh*]
last week, la semana pasada [*lah seh*-MAH-*nah pah*-SAH-*dah*]
(to) **last,** durar [*doo*-RAHR]
★ **late,** tarde (f) [TAHR-*deh*]
(to be) **late** (to arrive late), llegar tarde [*l'yeh*-GAHR TAHR-*deh*]
lately, últimamente [OOL-*tee-mah*-MEHN-*teh*]
lateness, tardanza [*tahr*-DAHN-*thah*]
later, más tarde [*mahs* TAHR-*deh*]
latest, último [OOL-*tee-moh*]
Latin (n), latín (m) [*lah*-TEEN]
(adj), latino, -a [*lah*-TEE-*noh, -nah*]
(to) **laugh,** reir [*reh*-EER]
laugh and **laughter,** risa [REE-*sah*]
laundress, lavandera [*lah-vahn*-DEH-*rah*]
laundry, lavandería [*lah-vahn-deh*-REE-*ah*]
law, ley (f) [*lay*]
lawyer, abogado [*ah-boh*-GAH-*doh*]
(to) **lay,** poner [*poh*-NEHR]
lazy, perezoso, -a [*peh-reh*-THOH-*soh, -sah*]
lead (metal), plomo [PLOH-*moh*]
(to) **lead,** conducir [*kohn-doo*-THEER]
leader, líder [LEE-*dehr*]
leading, principal [*preen-thee*-PAHL]
leaf, hoja [OH-*hah*]
leak, escape (m) [*ehs*-KAH-*peh*]
(to) **lean,** inclinar [*een-klee*-NAHR]
(to) **learn,** aprender [*ah-prehn*-DEHR]
lease, arriendo [*ah-rr'*YEHN-*doh*]
least, mínimo, -a [MEE-*nee-moh, -mah*]
at least, al menos [*ahl* MEH-*nohs*]
not in the least, de ningún modo [*deh neen*-GOON MOH-*doh*]
the least possible, lo menos posible [*loh* MEH-*nohs poh*-SEE-*bleh*]

leather, cuero [KWEH-*roh*]
(to) **leave** (to go away], salir [*sah*-LEER]
(to) **leave** (to abandon), dejar [*deh*-HAHR]
lecture, conferencia [*kohn-feh*-REHN-*th'yah*]
lecturer, conferencista [*kohn-feh-rehn*-THEES-*tah*]
★ **left,** izquierdo, -a [*eeth-k'*YEHR-*doh, -dah*]
to the left, a la izquierda [*ah lah eeth*-K'YEHR-*dah*]
How much is left? ¿Cuánto queda? [KWAHN-*toh* KEH-*dah*]
leg (people), pierna [P'YEHR-*nah*]
leg (animals or furniture), pata [PAH-*tah*]
legal, legal [*leh*-GAHL]
legion, legión (f) [*leh-h'*YOHN]
leisure, ocio [OH-*thee-oh*]
lemon, limón (m) [*lee*-MOHN]
lemonade, limonada [*lee-moh*-NAH-*dah*]
(to) **lend,** prestar [*prehs*-TAHR]
length, largo [LAHR-*goh*]
★ **less,** menos [MEH-*nohs*]
more or less, más o menos [*mahs oh* MEH-*nohs*]
lesson, lección (f) [*lehk-th'*YOHN]
(to) **let** (permit], dejar [*deh*-HAHR]
(to) **let** (to rent), alquilar [*ahl-kee*-LAHR]
to let alone, dejar tranquilo [*deh*-HAHR *trahn*-KEE-*loh*]
let's see, vamos a ver [VAH-*mohs ah vehr*]
room to let, se alquila un cuarto [*seh ahl*-KEE-*lah oon*-KWAHR-*toh*]
★ **letter** (mail), carta [KAHR-*tah*]
(alphabet), letra [LEH-*trah*]
letter of introduction, carta de presentación [KAHR-*tah deh preh-sehn-tah-th'*YOHN]
letter-box, buzón (m) [*boo*-THOHN]
lettuce, lechuga [*leh*-CHOO-*gah*]
level, nivel (m) [*nee*-VEHL]
liar, mentiroso, -a [*mehn-tee*-ROH-*soh, -sah*]
liberal, liberal [*lee-beh*-RAHL]
liberty, libertad (f) [*lee-behr*-TAHD]
library, biblioteca [*bee-blee-oh*-TEH-*kah*]

license, licencia [*lee*-THEHN-*th'yah*]
lie (n), mentira [*mehn*-TEE-*rah*]
(to) **lie,** mentir [*mehn*-TEER]
(to) **lie down,** acostarse [*ah-kohs*-TAHR-*seh*]
lieutenant, teniente (m) [*teh-n'*YEHN-*teh*]
life, vida [VEE-*dah*]
life insurance, seguro de vida [*seh*-GOO-*roh deh* VEE-*dah*]
lifeboat, salvavidas (m) [*sahl-vah*-VEE-*dahs*]
(to) **lift,** levantar [*leh-vahn*-TAHR]
light (n), luz (f) [*looth*]
light (not heavy) (adj), ligero, -a [*lee*-HEH-*roh, -rah*]
light (not dark), claro, -a [KLAH-*roh, -rah*]
(to) **light,** encender [*ehn-thehn*-DEHR]
lighter (cigarette), encendedor [*ehn-thehn-deh*-DOHR]
light house, faro [FAH-*roh*]
lightning, relámpago [*reh*-LAHM-*pah-goh*]
likable, simpático, -a [*seem*-PAH-*tee-koh, -kah*]
★ **like,** parecido, -a [*pah-reh*-THEE-*doh, -dah*]
★ (to) **like, gustar** [*goos*-TAHR]

NOTE: *Gustar* really means to please. So to express your liking, you must say something "pleases" you. Ex: "I like music."—*La música me gusta.* "Do you like it?"—*¿Le gusta?*

I don't like it, No me gusta [*noh meh* GOOS-*tah*]
Would you like? ¿Le gustaría? [*leh goos-tah*-REE-*ah*]
likely, probable [*proh*-BAH-*bleh*]
likewise, igualmente [*ee-gwahl*-MEHN-*teh*]
lily, lirio [LEE-*r'yoh*]
limit, límite (m) [LEE-*mee-teh*]
linen, hilo [EE-*loh*]
liner (ship), vapor (m) [*vah*-POHR]
lining, forro [FOH-*rroh*]
lingerie, ropa interior [ROH-*pah een-teh-r'*YOHR]
lion, león (m) [*leh*-OHN]
lip, labio [LAH-*b'yoh*]

lipstick, lápiz de labios [LAH-*peeth deh* LAH-*b'yohs*]
liquid (adj), líquido, -a [LEE-*kee-doh, -dah*]
liquor, licor (m) [*lee*-KOHR]
list, lista [LEES-*tah*]
(to) **listen,** escuchar [*ehs-koo*-CHAHR]
literally, literalmente [*lee-teh-rahl*-MEHN-*teh*]
literature, literatura [*lee-teh-rah*-TOO-*rah*]
★ **little** (adj), pequeño, -a [*peh*-KEH-*n'yoh, -n'yah*]
★ **little** (adv), poco [POH-*koh*]
  a little bit, un poquito [*oon poh*-KEE-*toh*]
  little by little, poco a poco [POH-*koh ah* POH-*koh*]
  very little, muy poco [*mwee* POH-*koh*]
★ (to) **live,** vivir [*vee*-VEER]
live (adj), vivo, -a [VEE-*voh, -vah*]
liver, hígado [EE-*gah-doh*]
living room, sala [SAH-*lah*]
(to) **load,** cargar [*kahr*-GAHR]
loan, préstamo [PREHS-*tah-moh*]
lobby, vestíbulo [*vehs*-TEE-*boo-loh*]
lobster, langosta [*lahn*-GOHS-*tah*]
local, local [*loh*-KAHL]
located, ubicado, -a [*oo-bee*-KAH-*doh, -dah*]
location, localidad (f) [*loh-kah-lee*-DAHD]
(to) **lock up,** cerrar [*theh*-RRAHR]
locomotive, locomotora [*loh-koh-moh*-TOH-*rah*]
logical, lógico, -a [LOH-*hee-koh, -kah*]
lonely, solitario, -a [*soh-lee*-TAH-*r'yoh, -r'yah*]
★ **long,** largo, -a [LAHR-*goh, -gah*]
longer (for measure), más largo [*mahs* LAHR-*goh*]
  (for time), más tiempo [*mahs t'*YEHM-*poh*]
  a long time, mucho tiempo [MOO-*choh t'*YEHM-*poh*]
  how long? ¿cuánto tiempo? [KWAHN-*toh t'*YEHM-*poh*]
  long ago, hace mucho tiempo [AH-*theh* MOO-*choh t'*YEHM-*poh*]
★ (to) **look,** mirar [*mee*-RAHR]
★ **look!** ¡mire! [MEE-*reh*]
★ **look out!** ¡cuidado! [*kwee*-DAH-*doh*]

loose, flojo, -a [FLOH-*hoh, -hah*]
(to) **loosen,** aflojar [*ah-floh*-HAHR]
(to) **lose,** perder [*pehr*-DEHR]
loss, pérdida [PEHR-*dee-dah*]
★ **lost,** perdido, -a [*pehr*-DEE-*doh, -dah*]
lot (real estate), terreno [*teh*-RREH-*noh*]
lot (a great deal), mucho [MOO-*choh*]
loud, ruidoso, -a [*rwee*-DOH-*soh, -sah*]
loudspeaker, altoparlante [*ahl-toh-pahr*-LAHN-*teh*]
★ (to) **love,** amar, querer [*ah*-MAHR, *keh*-REHR]

NOTE: *Querer,* which also means "to want" is the word most frequently used for "to love."

love, amor (m) [*ah*-MOHR]
lovely, bello, -a [BEH-*l'yoh, -l'yah*]
lover, amante (m, f), [*ah*-MAHN-*teh*]
low, bajo, -a [BAH-*hoh, -hah*]
loyal, leal [*leh*-AHL]
(to) **lubricate,** lubricar [*loo-bree*-KAHR]
luck, suerte (f) [SWEHR-*teh*]
(to be) **lucky,** tener suerte [*teh*-NEHR SWEHR-*teh*]
lunatic, lunático, -a [*loo*-NAH-*tee-koh, -kah*]
★ **lunch,** almuerzo [*ahl*-MWEHR-*thoh*]
(to) **have lunch,** almorzar [*ahl-mohr*-THAHR]
lung, pulmón (m) [*pool*-MOHN]
luxurious, lujoso, -a [*loo*-HOH-*soh, -sah*]
luggage, equipaje (m) [*eh-kee*-PAH-*heh*]

M

machine, máquina (f) [MAH-*kee-nah*]
machinery, maquinaria [*mah-kee*-NAH-*r'yah*]
mad (insane), loco, -a [LOH-*koh, -kah*]

machine gun, ametralladora [*ah-meh-trah-l'yah-*DOH-*rah*]
madam, señora [*seh-n'*YOH-*rah*]
made, hecho, -a [EH-*choh, -chah*]

NOTE: To indicate what something is made of, use *de. Una mesa de madera:* "A table made of wood."

magazine, revista [*reh-*VEES-*tah*]
magic, mágico, -a [MAH-*hee-koh, -kah*]
magnificent, magnífico, -a [*mahg-*NEE-*fee-koh, -kah*]
maid, criada [*kr'*YAH-*dah*]
mail, correo [*koh-*RREH-*oh*]
  mail box, buzón [*boo-*THOHN]
  mailman, cartero [*kahr-*TEH-*roh*]
(to) **mail,** enviar por correo [*ehn-v'*YAHR *pohr koh-*RREH-*oh*]
main, principal [*preen-thee-*PAHL]
  main office, oficina principal [*oh-fee-*THEE-*nah preen-thee-*PAHL]
  main street, calle principal [KAH-*l'yeh preen-thee-*PAHL]
mainly, principalmente [*preen-thee-pahl-*MEHN-*teh*]
(to) **maintain,** mantener [*mahn-teh-*NEHR]
majesty, majestad [*mah-hehs-*TAHD]
major, mayor [*mah-*YOHR]
majority, mayoría [*mah-yoh-*REE-*ah*]
★ (to) **make,** hacer [*ah-*THEHR]
  to make a mistake, equivocarse [*eh-kee-voh-*KAHR-*seh*]
  to make a speech, dar una conferéncia [*dahr* OO-*nah kohn-feh-*REHN-*th'yah*]
  to make fun of, burlar(se) de [*boor-*LAHR-*seh deh*]
  to make ready, preparar [*preh-pah-*RAHR]
  to make sure, asegurar [*ah-seh-goo-*RAHR]
  to make up one's mind, decidir(se) [*deh-thee-*DEER-*(seh)*]
  to make use of, servir(se) [*sehr-*VEER-*(seh)*]
malaria, paludismo [*pah-loo-*DEES-*moh*]
malicious, malicioso, -a [*mah-lee-th'*YOH-*soh, -sah*]

male, macho [MAH-*choh*]
★ **man,** hombre [OHM-*breh*]
young man, joven [HOH-*vehn*]
(to) **manage,** administrar [*ahd-mee-nees*-TRAHR]
manager, administrador [*ahd-mee-nees-trah*-DOHR]
manicure, manicura [*mah-nee*-KOO-*rah*]
manner, manera [*mah*-NEH-*rah*]
manners, modales (m) [*moh*-DAH-*lehs*]
mansion, mansión [*mahn-s'*YOHN]
(to) **manufacture,** fabricar [*fah-bree*-KAHR]
manufacturer, fabricante (m) [*fah-bree*-KAHN-*teh*]
manuscript, manuscrito [*mah-noos*-KREE-*toh*]
★ **many,** muchos, -as [MOO-*chohs, -chahs*]
how many? cuántos, -as? [KWAHN-*tohs, -tahs*]
too many, demasiados, -as [*deh-mah-s'*YAH-*dohs, -dahs*]
very many, muchísimos, -as [*moo*-CHEE-*see-mohs, -mahs*]
map, mapa (m) [MAH-*pah*]
marble, mármol (m) [MAHR-*mohl*]
(to) **march,** marchar [*mahr*-CHAHR]
March, marzo [MAHR-*thoh*]
(to) **mark,** marcar [*mahr*-KAHR]
mark, marca [MAHR-*kah*]
market, mercado; plaza [*mehr*-KAH-*doh;* PLAH-*thah*]
marriage, matrimonio [*mah-tree*-MOH-*n'yoh*]
married, casado, -a [*kah*-SAH-*doh, -dah*]
(to) **get married,** casar(se) [*kah*-SAHR-*seh*]
marvellous, maravilloso, -a [*mah-rah-vee-l'*YOH-*soh, -sah*]
mask, máscara [MAHS-*kah-rah*]
mass (church), misa [MEE-*sah*]
mass (quantity), masa [MAH-*sah*]
mass production, producción en serie [*proh-dook-th'*YOHN *ehn* SEH-*r'yeh*]
massage, masaje (m) [*mah*-SAH-*heh*]
mast, mástil (m) [MAHS-*teel*]
master, maestro [*mah*-EHS-*troh*]
masterpiece, obra maestra [OH-*brah mah*-EHS-*trah*]
match (cigarette), fósforo [FOHS-*foh-roh*]
(sport), partido [*pahr*-TEE-*doh*]
matching, haciendo juego [*ah-th'*YEHN-*doh* HWEH-*goh*]

material, material (m) [*mah-teh-r'*YAHL]
mathematics, matemáticas [*mah-teh-*MAH-*tee-kahs*]
matter, materia [*mah-*TEH-*r'yah*]
★ **What's the matter?** ¿Qué pasa? [*keh* PAH-*sah*]
It doesn't matter, no importa [*noh eem-*POHR-*tah*]
What's the matter with you? (with him, with her) ¿Qué le pasa? [*keh leh* PAH-*sah*]
mattress, colchón [*kohl-*CHOHN]
May, mayo [MAH-*yoh*]
★ **may,** poder [*poh-*DEHR]

NOTE: No exact equivalent, though generally expressed by *poder* "to be able."

It may be, Puede ser [PWEH-*deh sehr*]
May I come in? ¿Puedo entrar? [PWEH-*doh ehn-*TRAHR]
★ **maybe,** tal vez [*tahl veth*]
mayor, alcalde [*ahl-*KAHL-*deh*]
★ **me,** me [*meh*]
to me, a mí [*ah mee*]
with me, conmigo [*kohn* MEE-*goh*]
meal, comida [*koh-*MEE-*dah*]
(to) **mean,** significar [*seeg-nee-fee-*KAHR]
What does it mean? (also) **What do you mean?** ¿Qué quiere decir? [*keh k'*YEH-*reh deh-*THEER]
by all means, de todos modos [*deh* TOH-*dohs* MOH-*dohs*]
by means of, por medio de [*pohr* MEH-*d'yoh deh*]
by no means, de ningún modo [*deh neen-*GOON MOH-*doh*]
meantime (meanwhile), mientras tanto [*m'*YEHN-*trahs* TAHN-*toh*]
measles, sarampión (m) [*sah-rahm-p'*YOHN]
measure, medida [*meh-*DEE-*dah*]
(to) **measure,** medir [*meh-*DEER]
★ **meat,** carne (f) [KAHR-*neh*]
mechanic (and) **mechanical,** mecánico, -a [*meh-*KAH-*nee-koh, -kah*]

medal, medalla [*meh*-DAH-*l'yah*]
medical, médico [MEH-*dee-koh*]
medical school, escuela de medicina [*ehs*-KWEH-*lah deh meh-dee*-THEE-*nah*]
medicine, medicina [*meh-dee*-THEE-*nah*]
Mediterranean (n), Mediterráneo [*meh-dee-teh*-RRAH-*neh-oh*]
medium (adj), medio, -a [MEH-*d'yoh, -d'yah*]
(to) **meet** (encounter), encontrar [*ehn-kohn*-TRAHR]
(become acquainted), conocer [*koh-noh*-THEHR]
Delighted to meet you! ¡encantado de conocerle! [*ehn-kahn*-TAH-*doh deh koh-noh*-THEHR-*leh*]
meeting, reunión (f) [*reh-oo-n'*YOHN]
melody, melodía [*meh-loh*-DEE-*ah*]
melon, melón (m) [*meh*-LOHN]
melt, derretir(se) [*deh-rreh*-TEER-*seh*]
member, miembro [*m'*YEHM-*broh*]
memory, memoria [*meh*-MOH-*r'yah*]
(to) **mend,** remendar [*reh-mehn*-DAHR]
mental, mental [*mehn*-TAHL]
(to) **mention,** mencionar [*mehn-th'yoh*-NAHR]
menu, lista de platos [LEES-*tah deh* PLAH-*tohs*]
merchandise, mercancía [*mehr-kahn*-THEE-*ah*]
merchant, comerciante [*koh-mehr-th'*YAHN-*teh*]
mere, mero, -a [MEH-*roh, -rah*]
merit, mérito [MEH-*ree-toh*]
merry, alegre [*ah*-LEH-*greh*]
message, mensaje (m) [*mehn*-SAH-*heh*]
messenger, mensajero [*mehn-sah*-HEH-*roh*]
metal (n), metal (m [*meh*-TAHL]
meter, metro [MEH-*troh*]
metric system, sistema métrico [*sees*-TEH-*mah* MEH-*tree-koh*]

NOTE: see table at back of book for complete measure equivalents.

method, método [MEH-*toh-doh*]
Mexico, México [MEH-*hee-koh*]
Mexican, mexicano, -a [*meh-hee*-KAH-*noh, -nah*]
middle (n), medio [MEH-*d'yoh*]
middle (adj), del medio [*dehl* MEH-*d'yoh*]
midnight, medianoche [MEH-*d'yah* NOH-*cheh*]
midway, mitad del camino [*mee*-TAHD *dehl kah*-MEE-*noh*]
might (v),

NOTE: No exact equivalent; use conditional of *poder.*

I might, yo podría [*yoh poh*-DREE-*ah*]
mild, suave [SWAH-*veh*]
mile, milla [MEE-*l'yah*]

NOTE: Spanish-speaking countries use *kilómetros,* approximately ⅝ of a mile.

military, militar [*mee-lee*-TAHR]
military service, servicio militar [*sehr*-VEE-*th'yoh mee-lee*-TAHR]
★ **milk,** leche [LEH-*cheh*]
million, millón (m) [*mee-l'*YOHN]
millionaire, millonario, -a [*mee-l'yoh*-NAH-*r'yoh, -r'yah*]
mind, mente (f) [MEHN-*teh*]
mine (pro), mío, mía, míos, mías [MEE-*oh,* MEE-*ah,* MEE-*ohs,* MEE-*ahs*]

NOTE: The articles are used with these pronouns as follows to convey a special meaning:

This book is mine, Éste libro es mío [*ehs-teh* LEE-*broh ehs* MEE-*oh*]
Which is mine? ¿Cuál es el mío? [*kwahl ehs ehl* MEE-*oh*]
Which are mine? ¿Cuáles son los míos? [KWAH-*lehs sohn lohs* MEE-*ohs*]
mine (n), mina [MEE-*nah*]
mineral, mineral [*mee-neh*-RAHL]
minimum (n), mínimo [MEE-*nee-moh*]
minister, ministro [*mee*-NEES-*troh*]
mink, visón (m) [*vee*-SOHN]
minor (of age), menor de edad [*meh*-NOHR *deh eh*-DAHD]
minus, menos [MEH-*nohs*]

minute, minuto [*mee*-NOO-*toh*]

Wait a minute! ¡Espere un minuto! [*ehs*-PEH-*reh oon mee*-NOO-*toh*]

mirror, espejo [*ehs*-PEH-*hoh*]

miserable, miserable [*mee-seh*-RAH-*bleh*]

misery, miseria [*mee*-SEH-*r'yah*]

★ **Miss,** señorita [*seh-n'yoh*-REE-*tah*]

NOTE: abbreviated to Srta.

(to) **miss** (someone), echar de menos a [*eh*-CHAHR *deh* MEH-*nohs ah*]

(to) **miss** (lose), perder [*pehr*-DEHR]

mission, misión (f) [*mee-s'*YOHN]

missionary, misionero [*mee-s'yoh*-NEH-*roh*]

mistake, equivocación (f) [*eh-kee-voh-kah-th'*YOHN]

(to be) **mistaken,** estar equivocado, -a [*ehs*-TAHR *eh-kee-voh*-KAH-*doh, -dah*]

(to) **mistrust,** desconfiar [*dehs-kohn-f'*YAHR]

misunderstanding, malentendido [*mahl-ehn-tehn*-DEE-*doh*]

mixed, mezclado, -a [*meth*-KLAH-*doh, -dah*]

(to) **mix,** mezclar [*meth*-KLAHR]

model, modelo [*moh*-DEH-*loh*]

modern, moderno, -a [*moh*-DEHR-*noh, -nah*]

modest, modesto, -a [*moh*-DEHS-*toh, -tah*]

modesty, modestia [*moh*-DEHS-*t'yah*]

(to) **modify,** modificar [*moh-dee-fee*-KAHR]

moment, momento [*moh*-MEHN-*toh*]

monarch, monarca [*moh*-NAHR-*kah*]

monarchy, monarquía [*moh-nahr*-KEE-*ah*]

monastery, monasterio [*moh-nahs*-TEH-*r'yoh*]

★ **Monday,** lunes [LOO-*nehs*]

★ **money,** dinero [*dee*-NEH-*roh*]

monk, monje [MOHN-*heh*]

monkey, mono, -a [MOH-*noh, -nah*]

monotonous, monótono [*moh*-NOH-*toh-noh*]

★ **month,** mes [*mehs*]

monthly, mensual [*mehn*-SWAHL]

monument, monumento [*moh-noo*-MEHN-*toh*]

mood (feelings), humor [*oo*-MOHR]
in a bad mood, de mal humor [*deh mahl oo*-MOHR]
in a good mood, de buen humor [*deh bwehn oo*-MOHR]
★ **moon,** luna [LOO-*nah*]
moonlight, luz de la luna [*looth deh lah* LOO-*nah*]
moral, moral [*moh*-RAHL]
more, más [*mahs*]
more or less, más o menos [*mahs oh* MEH-*nohs*]
moreover, además [*ah-deh*-MAHS]
once more, una vez más [OO-*nah vehth mahs*]
★ **morning,** mañana [*mah-n'*YAH-*nah*]
★ **Good morning!** ¡Buenos días! [BWEH-*nohs* DEE-*ahs*]
(in the) **morning,** por la mañana [*pohr lah mah-n'*YAH-*nah*]
mortgage, hipoteca [*ee-poh*-TEH-*kah*]
mosquito, mosquito [*mohs*-KEE-*toh*]
mosquito net, mosquitero [*mohs-kee*-TEH-*roh*]
most,
most of . . ., la mayor parte de [*lah mah*-YOHR PAHR-*teh deh*]
NOTE: *más* is preceded by the definite article to form the superlative. "The most beautiful girl," *la más hermosa muchacha;* "the most beautiful picture," *el más hermoso cuadro.*
★ **mother,** madre (f) [MAH-*dreh*]
mother-in-law, suegra [SWEH-*grah*]
motherhood, maternidad [*mah-tehr-nee*-DAHD]
motion, moción [*moh-th'*YOHN]
motive, motivo [*moh*-TEE-*voh*]
motor, motor (m) [*moh*-TOHR]
motorcycle, motocicleta [*moh-toh-thee*-KLEH-*tah*]
(to) **mount,** montar [*mohn*-TAHR]
mountain, montaña [*mohn*-TAH-*n'yah*]
mountain range, sierra [*s'*YEH-*rrah*]
(in) **mourning,** de luto [*deh* LOO-*toh*]
mouse, ratón (m) [*rah*-TOHN]
★ **mouth,** boca [BOH-*kah*]

(to) **move** (change dwelling), mudar(se) [*moo*-DAHR-*seh*]
(motion), mover [*moh*-VEHR]
(to) **move** (motion), mover [*moh*-VEHR]
movies, cine (m) [THEE-*neh*]
Mr., señor [*seh-n'*YOHR] (abbreviation is *Sr.*)
Mrs., señora [*seh-n'*YOH-*rah*] (abbreviation is *Sra.*)
★ **much,** mucho [MOO-*choh*]
as much as, tanto como [TAHN-*toh* KOH-*moh*]
★ **how much?** ¿cuánto? [KWAHN-*toh*]
too much, demasiado [*deh-mah-s'*YAH-*doh*]
very much, muchísimo [*moo*-CHEE-*see-moh*]
mud, fango [FAHN-*goh*]
mule, mulo, -a [MOO-*loh, -lah*]
(to) **murder,** asesinar [*ah-seh-see*-NAHR]
murderer, asesino, -a [*ah-seh*-SEE-*noh, -nah*]
muscle, músculo [MOOS-*koo-loh*]
museum, museo [*moo*-SEH-*oh*]
mushroom, seta [SEH-*tah*]
music, música [MOO-*see-kah*]
musical, musical [*moo-see*-KAHL]
musician, músico [MOO-*see-koh*]
must,

NOTE: To be translated by forms of *deber* or *tener que* followed by the infinitive of the next verb.

I must go, Tengo que ir [TEHN-*goh keh eer*]
You must come, Ud. debe venir [*oos*-TEHD DEH-*beh veh*-NEER]
mustache, bigote [*bee*-GOH-*teh*]
mustard, mostaza [*mohs*-TAH-*thah*]
mutual, mutuo, -a [MOO-*twoh, -twah*]
★ **my,** mi, mis (plural) [*mee, mees*]
myself, yo mismo, -a [*yoh* MEES-*moh, -mah*]
NOTE: Used reflexively "myself" is rendered *me.*

I dress myself, Yo me visto [*yoh meh* VEES-*toh*]
mysterious, misterioso, -a [*mees-teh-r'*YOH-*soh, -sah*]
mystery, misterio [*mees*-TEH-*r'yoh*]

N

nail (on finger), uña [oo-*n'yah*]
(for hammer), clavo [KLAH-*voh*]
naked, desnudo, -a [*dehs*-NOO-*doh, -dah*]
★ **name,** nombre [NOHM-*breh*]
first name, nombre de pila [NOHM-*breh deh* PEE-*lah*]
last name, apellido [*ah-peh-l'*YEE-*doh*]
What is your name? ¿Cómo se llama Ud? [KOH-*moh seh l'*YAH-*mah oos*-TEHD]
NOTE: Compare the following English first names with their Spanish equivalents:
Charles, Carlos [KAHR-*lohs*]
Elisabeth, Isabel [*ee-sah*-BEHL]
Frank, Francisco [*frahn*-THEES-*koh*]
George, Jorge [HOHR-*heh*]
James, Jaime [HIGH-*meh*]
Jane, Juanita [*hoo-ah*-NEE-*tah*]
John, Juan [*hoo*-AHN]
Joseph, José [*hoh*-SEH]
Louise, Luisa [LWEE-*sah*]
Margaret, Margarita [*mahr-gah*-REE-*tah*]
Mary, María [*mah*-REE-*ah*]
Michael, Miguel [*mee*-GHEHL]
Paul, Pablo [PAH-*bloh*]
Peter, Pedro [PEH-*droh*]
Robert, Roberto [*roh*-BEHR-*toh*]
Stephen, Esteban [*ehs*-TEH-*bahn*]
William, Guillermo [*ghee-l'*YEHR-*moh*]
namely, a saber [*ah sah*-BEHR]
nap, siesta [*s'*YEHS-*tah*]
napkin, servilleta [*sehr-vee-l'*YEH-*tah*]
narrator, narrador [*nah-rrah*-DOHR]

narrow, estrecho, -a [*ehs*-TREH-*choh, -chah*]
nation, nación (f) [*nah-th'*YOHN]
national, nacional [*nah-th'yoh*-NAHL]
nationality, nacionalidad (f) [*nah-th'yoh-nah-lee*-DAHD]
native, nativo, -a [*nah*-TEE-*voh, -vah*]
  native land, patria [PAH-*tr'yah*]
natural, natural [*nah-too*-RAHL]
naturally, naturalmente [*nah-too-rahl*-MEHN-*teh*]
nature, naturaleza [*nah-too-rah*-LEH-*thah*]
naughty, travieso, -a [*trah-v'*YEH-*soh, -sah*]
navy, marina [*mah*-REE-*nah*]
★ **near, nearby,** cerca [THEHR-*kah*]
  Which is nearer? ¿Cuál está más cerca? [*kwahl ehs*-TAH *mahs* THEHR-*kah*]
nearly, casi [KAH-*see*]
neat, pulcro, -a [POOL-*kroh, -krah*]
★ **necessary,** necesario, -a [*neh-theh*-SAH-*r'yoh, -r'yah*]
neck, cuello [KWEH-*l'yoh*]
  necklace, collar (m) [*koh-l'*YAHR]
  necktie, corbata [*kohr*-BAH-*tah*]
(to) **need,** necesitar [*neh-theh-see*-TAHR]
needle, aguja [*ah*-GOO-*hah*]
negative, negativo, -a [*neh-gah*-TEE-*voh, -vah*]
(to) **neglect,** descuidar [*dehs-kwee*-DAHR]
Negro, negro, -a [NEH-*groh, -grah*]
neighbor, vecino, -a [*veh*-THEE-*noh, -nah*]
neighborhood, vecindario [*veh-theen*-DAH-*r'yoh*]
neither, ninguno, -a [*neen*-GOO-*noh, -nah*]
    NOTE: *Ninguno* drops the *o* before a masculine singular noun. *No tenemos ningun libro:* "We have no book."
  neither one, ninguno de los dos [*neen*-GOO-*noh deh lohs dohs*]
  neither . . . nor, ni . . . ni [*nee . . . nee*]
    NOTE: Use *ni* for both "neither" and "nor."
  Neither you nor I, Ni usted ni yo [*nee oos*-TEHD *nee yoh*]
nephew, sobrino [*soh*-BREE-*noh*]
nerves, nervios [NEHR-*v'yohs*]
  What a nerve! ¡Qué descaro! [*keh dehs*-KAH-*roh*]

nervous, nervioso, -a [*nehr-v'*YOH-*soh, -sah*]
nest, nido [NEE-*doh*]
net (for fisherman), red (f) [*rehd*]
net (for hair), redecilla [*reh-deh*-THEE-*l'yah*]
neutral, neutral [*neh-oo*-TRAHL]
never, nunca [NOON-*kah*]
  never mind! ¡no importa! [*noh eem*-POHR-*tah*]
nevertheless, sin embargo [*seen ehm*-BAHR-*goh*]
★ **new,** nuevo, -a [NWEH-*voh, -vah*]
  Happy New Year! ¡Feliz Año Nuevo! [*feh*-LEETH AH-*n'yoh* NWEH-*voh*]
news, noticias [*noh*-TEE-*th'yahs*]
newspaper, periódico [*peh-r'*YOH-*dee-koh*]
newsstand, puesto de periódicos [PWEHS-*toh deh peh-r'*YOH-*dee-kohs*]
next, próximo [PROH-*ksee-moh*]
  next time, la próxima vez [*lah* PROH-*ksee-mah vehth*]
  next to, al lado de [*ahl* LAH-*doh deh*]
  next week, la semana próxima [*lah seh*-MAH-*nah* PROH-*ksee-mah*]
nice (pleasing), simpático, -a [*seem*-PAH-*tee-koh, -kah*]
niece, sobrina [*soh*-BREE-*nah*]
★ **night,** noche (f) [NOH-*cheh*]
★ **Good night!** ¡Buenas noches! [BWEH-*nahs* NOH-*chehs*]
  last night, anoche [*ah*-NOH-*cheh*]
  nightclub, cabaret (m) [*kah-bah*-REHT]
  nightgown, camisa de dormir [*kah*-MEE-*sah deh dohr*-MEER]
★ **nine,** nueve [NWEH-*veh*]
★ **nineteen,** diecinueve [*d'*YEHTH-*ee*-NWEH-*veh*]
★ **ninety,** noventa [*noh*-VEHN-*tah*]
ninth, noveno, -a [*noh*-VEH-*noh, -nah*]
★ **no** (adv), no [*noh*]
no (adj), ningún, ninguna [*neen*-GOON, *neen*-GOO-*nah*]
  by no means, de ningún modo [*deh neen*-GOON MOH-*doh*]
  it's no good, no vale [*noh* VAH-*leh*]
  no fooling, sin broma [*seen* BROH-*mah*]
  no longer, ya no [*yah noh*]
  no more, no más [*noh mahs*]

★ **nobody,** nadie [NAH-*d'yeh*]
noise, ruido [RWEE-*doh*]
noisy, ruidoso, -a [*rwee*-DOH-*soh, -sah*]
none (persons), nadie [NAH-*d'yeh*]
(things), nada [NAH-*dah*]
There is none, No hay [*noh eye*]
nonsense, disparate [*dees-pah*-RAH-*teh*]
noon, mediodía [*meh-d'yoh*-DEE-*ah*]
nor, ni [*nee*]
normal, normal [*nohr*-MAHL]
north, norte [NOHR-*teh*]
North America, América del Norte [*ah*-MEH-*ree-kah dehl* NOHR-*teh*]
northeast, nordeste [*nohr*-DEHS-*teh*]
northwest, noroeste [*nohr-oh*-EHS-*teh*]
Norway, Noruega [*noh*-RWEH-*gah*]
Norwegian, noruego, -a [*noh-r'*WEH-*goh, -gah*]
★ **nose,** nariz [*nah*-REETH]
★ **not,** no [*noh*]
not at all, de ningún modo [*deh neen*-GOON MOH-*doh*]
not even, ni siquiera [*nee see-k'*YEH-*rah*]
not one, ni uno [*nee* OO-*noh*]

NOTE: For other negative uses of "not" see note on "do."

note, nota [NOH-*tah*]
(to) **note,** notar [*noh*-TAHR]
notebook, librito de apuntes [*lee*-BREE-*toh deh ah*-POON-*tehs*]
★ **nothing,** nada [NAH-*dah*]
nothing new, nada de nuevo [NAH-*dah deh* NWEH-*voh*]
nothing special, nada de particular [NAH-*dah deh pahr-tee-koo*-LAHR]
notice (n), aviso [*ah*-VEE-*soh*]

(to) **notice,** notar [*noh*-TAHR]
(to) **notify,** notificar [*noh-tee-fee*-KAHR]
noun, substantivo [*soobs-tahn*-TEE-*voh*]
novel, novela [*noh*-VEH-*lah*]
novelty, novedad [*noh-veh*-DAHD]
November, noviembre [*noh-v'*YEHM-*breh*]
★ **now,** ahora [*ah*-OH-*rah*]
  from now on, desde ahora en adelante [DEHS-*deh ah*-OH-*rah ehn ah-deh*-LAHN-*teh*]
  now and then, de vez en cuando [*deh vehth ehn* KWAHN-*doh*]
  until now, hasta ahora [AHS-*tah ah*-OH-*rah*]
nowadays, hoy día [*oy* DEE-*ah*]
nowhere, en ninguna parte [*ehn neen*-GOO-*nah* PAHR-*teh*]
number, número [NOO-*meh-roh*]
(to) **number,** numerar [*noo-meh*-RAHR]
numerous, numeroso, -a [*noo-meh*-ROH-*soh, -sah*]
nun, monja [MOHN-*hah*]
nurse, enfermera [*ehn-fehr*-MEH-*rah*]
nurse (for children), niñera [*nee-n'*YEH-*rah*]
nut (for eating), nuez (f) [*nwehth*]
nut (for a screw), tuerca [TWEHR-*kah*]
nylon, nilón (m) [*nee*-LOHN]

O

oak, roble (m) [ROH-*bleh*]
obedient, obediente [*oh-beh-d'*YEHN-*teh*]
(to) **obey,** obedecer [*oh-beh-deh*-THEHR]
object, objeto [*ohb*-HEH-*toh*]
objection, objeción [*ohb-heh-th'*YOHN]
obligation, obligación (f) [*oh-blee-gah-th'*YOHN]
obligatory, obligatorio, -a [*oh-blee-gah*-TOH-*r'yoh, -r'yah*]
(to) **oblige** (force), obligar [*oh-blee*-GAHR]
  (much) **obliged,** muy agradecido, -a [*mwee ah-grah-deh*-THEE-*doh, -dah*]
(to) **observe,** observar [*ohb-sehr*-VAHR]

observation, observación [*ohb-sehr-vah-th'*YOHN]
obstacle, obstáculo [*ohbs-*TAH-*koo-loh*]
(to) **obtain,** obtener [*ohb-teh-*NEHR]
obvious, obvio, -a [OHB-*v'yoh, -v'yah*]
occasion, ocasión (f) [*oh-kah-s'*YOHN]
occasionally, de vez en cuando [*deh vehth ehn·*KWAHN-*doh*]
occupation, ocupación (f) [*oh-koo-pah-th'*YOHN]
occupied, ocupado, -a [*oh-koo-*PAH-*doh, -dah*]
(to) **occupy,** ocupar [*oh-koo-*PAHR]
(to) **occur,** ocurrir [*oh-koo-*RREER]
occurrence, suceso [*soo-*THEH-*soh*]
ocean, océano [*oh-*THEH-*ah-noh*]
o'clock,

NOTE: No such word in Spanish. To say "1 o'clock," "2 o'clock," etc., say *a la una, a las dos,* etc. [*ah lah oo-nah; ah lahs dohs*].

October, octubre [*ohk-*TOO-*breh*]
odd (uneven), impar [EEM-*pahr*]
odd (unusual), raro, -a [RAH-*roh, -rah*]
odor, olor (m) [*oh-*LOHR]
★ **of,** de (or) del [*deh, dehl*]

NOTE: Remember always to use *de* for the possessive; never say "John's car" but always "the car of John"—*El automóvil de Juan.* The professor's hat—*El sombrero del professor.*

of course, por supuesto [*pohr soo-*PWEHS-*toh*]
off,

NOTE: No equivalent word exists. For words like "take off," "get off," "put off" look under the verb involved.

(to) **offend,** ofender [*oh-fehn-*DEHR]
offensive, ofensivo, -a [*oh-fehn-*SEE-*voh, -vah*]
offer (n), oferta [*oh-*FEHR-*tah*]
(to) **offer,** ofrecer [*oh-freh-*THEHR]
office, oficina [*oh-fee-*THEE-*nah*]

officer, oficial [*oh-fee-th'*YAHL]
★ **often,** a menudo [*ah meh-*NOO-*doh*]
oil (lubricant), aceite [*ah-*THEH-*ee-teh*]
(combustion), petróleo [*peh-*TROH-*leh-oh*]
oil field, campo de petróleo [KAHM-*poh deh peh-*TROH-*leh-oh*]
oil painting, óleo [OH-*leh-oh*]
oil well, pozo de petróleo [POH-*thoh deh peh-*TROH-*leh-oh*]
olive oil, aceite de oliva [*ah-*THEH-*ee-teh deh oh-*LEE-*vah*]
O.K. (coll), está bien [*ehs-*TAH *b'yehn*]
★ **old,** viejo, -a [*v'*YEH-*hoh, -hah*]
How old are you? ¿Cuántos años tiene? [KWAHN-*tohs* AH-*n'yohs t'*YEH-*neh*]
old age, vejez [*veh-*HEHTH]
olive, oliva [*oh-*LEE-*vah*]
omelet, tortilla de huevos [*tohr-*TEE-*l'yah deh* WEH-*vohs*]
omission, omisión (f) [*oh-mee-s'*YOHN]
★ **on,** en (or) encima de [*ehn, ehn-*THEE-*mah deh*]
on duty, de servicio [*deh sehr-*VEE-*th'yoh*]
on foot, a pie [*ah p'yeh*]
on my part, por mi parte [*pohr mee* PAHR-*teh*]
on purpose, adrede [*ah-*DREH-*deh*]
on the contrary, por el contrario [*pohr ehl kohn-*TRAH-*r'yoh*]
on the right, a la derecha [*ah lah deh-*REH-*chah*]
on time, a tiempo [*ah t'*YEHM-*poh*]
once, una vez [OO-*nah vehth*]
at once, en seguida [*ehn seh-*GHEE-*dah*]
once more, una vez más [OO-*nah vehth mahs*]
★ **one,** un, uno, una [*oon,* OO-*noh,* OO-*nah*]
one way (ticket), de ida [*deh* EE-*dah*]
one way (street), una sola vía [OO-*nah* SOH-*lah* VEE-*ah*]
★ **only** (adv), solamente [*soh-lah-*MEHN-*teh*]
only (adj), único, -a [OO-*nee-koh, -kah*]
open (adj), abierto, -a [*ah-b'*YEHR-*toh, -tah*]
★ (to) **open,** abrir [*ah-*BREER]
opening, apertura [*ah-pehr-*TOO-*rah*]

opera, ópera [OH-*peh-rah*]
(to) **operate** (a vehicle), manejar [*mah-neh*-HAHR]
(medical), operar [*oh-peh*-RAHR]
operation, operación (f) [*oh-peh-rah-th'*YOHN]
operator, operador, -a [*oh-peh-rah*-DOHR, -DOH-*rah*]
opinion, opinión (f) [*oh-pee-n'*YOHN]
opportunity, ocasión (f) [*oh-kah-s'*YOHN]
opposite, opuesto, -a [*oh*-PWEHS-*toh, -tah*]
optimist (and) **optimistic,** optimista (m & f) [*ohp-tee*-MEES-*tah*]
optional, optativo, -a [*ohp-tah*-TEE-*voh, -vah*]
or, o (*u* if the following word begins with "o") [*oh, oo*]
orange, naranja [*nah*-RAHN-*hah*]
orange juice, jugo de naranja [HOO-*goh deh nah*-RAHN-*hah*]
orchard, huerto [WEHR-*toh*]
orchestra, orquesta [*ohr*-KEHS-*tah*]
orchid, orquídea [*ohr*-KEE-*deh-ah*]
order (arrangement), orden (m) [OHR-*dehn*]
order (command), orden (f) [OHR-*dehn*]
(to) **order** (someone), mandar [MAHN-*dahr*]
(something), pedir [*peh*-DEER]
ordinary, ordinario, -a [*ohr-dee*-NAH-*r'yoh, -r'yah*]
ordinarily, ordinariamente [*ohr-dee-nah-r'yah*-MEHN-*teh*]
organization, organización [*ohr-gah-nee-thah-th'*YOHN]
oriental, oriental [*oh-r'yehn*-TAHL]
original, original [*oh-ree-hee*-NAHL]
originally, originalmente [*oh-ree-hee-nahl*-MEHN-*teh*]
ornament, ornamento [*ohr-nah*-MEHN-*toh*]
orphan, huérfano, -a [WEHR-*fah-noh, -nah*]
★ **other,** otro, -a [OH-*troh, -trah*]
on the other hand, por otra parte [*pohr* OH-*trah* PAHR-*teh*]
otherwise, de otro modo [*deh* OH-*troh* MOH-*doh*]
ought,
Note: Use appropriate conditional of *deber* with the infinitive of the following verb.

We ought to do it, Nosotros deberíamos hacerlo [*noh*-SOH-*trohs deh-beh*-REE-*ah-mohs ah*-THEHR-*loh*]

You ought to go, Usted debería ir [*oos*-TEHD *deh-beh*-REE-*ah eer*]

★ **our** (when object possessed is singular), nuestro, -a [NWEHS-*troh, -trah*]

our (when object possessed is plural) nuestros, -tras [NWEHS-*trohs, -trahs*]

ours (singular), el nuestro, la nuestra [*ehl* NWEHS-*troh, lah* NWEHS-*trah*]

ours (plural), los nuestros, las nuestras [*lohs* NWEHS-*trohs, lahs* NWEHS-*trahs*]

★ **out,** fuera [FWEH-*rah*]

out of order, descompuesto, -a [*dehs-kohm*-PWEHS-*toh, -tah*]

outdoors, al aire libre [*ahl* EYE-*reh* LEE-*breh*]

outside (prep), afuera [*ah*-FWEH-*rah*]

outside (adj), exterior [*ehks-teh-r'*YOHR]

outstanding, sobresaliente [SOH-*breh-sah-l'*YEHN-*teh*]

oven, horno [OHR-*noh*]

over (prep), sobre [SOH-*breh*]

(finished), acabado, -a [*ah-kah*-BAH-*doh, -dah*]

overboard, al agua [*ahl* AH-*gwah*]

overcoat, sobretodo [*soh-breh*-TOH-*doh*]

(to) **overcome,** vencer [*vehn*-THEHR]

overhead, arriba [*ah*-RREE-*bah*]

overseas, ultramar [*ool-trah*-MAHR]

oversight, descuido [*dehs*-KWEE-*doh*]

(to) **overturn,** volcar [*vohl*-KAHR]

(to) **owe,** deber [*deh*-BEHR]

How much do I owe you? ¿Cuánto le debo? [KWAHN-*toh leh* DEH-*boh*]

owing to, debido a [*deh*-BEE-*doh ah*]

own, propio, -a [PROH-*p'yoh, -p'yah*]

(to) **own,** poseer [*poh-seh*-EHR]

owner, dueño, -a [DWEH-*n'yoh, -n'yah*]

ox, buey (m) [*bway*]

oyster, ostra [OHS-*trah*]
oxygen, oxígeno [*oh*-KSEE-*heh-noh*]

P

Pacific (Ocean), Pacífico [*pah*-THEE-*fee-koh*]
pack (of cigarettes), caja de cigarrillos [KAH-*hah deh thee-gah*-RREE-*l'yohs*]
pack (of cards), juego de naipes [WEH-*goh deh* NIGH-*pehs*]
(to) **pack,** empaquetar [*ehm-pah-keh*-TAHR]
package, paquete [*pah*-KEH-*teh*]
packing, embalaje [*ehm-bah*-LAH-*heh*]
page, página [PAH-*hee-nah*]
paid, pagado, -a [*pah*-GAH-*doh, -dah*]
pail, cubo [KOO-*boh*]
pain, dolor [*doh*-LOHR]
painful, doloroso, -a [*doh-loh*-ROH-*soh, -sah*]
(to) **paint,** pintar [*peen*-TAHR]
painter, pintor [*peen*-TOHR]
painting, pintura [*peen*-TOO-*rah*]
pair, par [*pahr*]
pajamas, pijama (m) [*pee*-HAH-*mah*]
palace, palacio [*pah*-LAH-*th'yoh*]
pale, pálido, -a [PAH-*lee-doh, -dah*]
palm, palma [PAHL-*mah*]
palm tree, palmera [*pahl*-MEH-*rah*]
Panamá, Panamá [*pah-nah*-MAH]
Panamanian, panameño, -a [*pah-nah*-MEH-*n'yoh, -n'yah*]
pants, pantalones [*pahn-tah*-LOH-*nehs*]
paper, papel (m) [*pah*-PEHL]
  toilet paper, papel higiénico [*pah*-PEHL *ee-h'*YEH-*nee-koh*]
  writing paper, papel de escribir [*pah*-PEHL *deh ehs-kree*-BEER]
parade, desfile [*dehs*-FEE-*leh*]
parachute, paracaídas [PAH-*rah-kah*-EE-*dahs*]
paradise, paraíso [*pah-rah*-EE-*soh*]

paragraph, párrafo [PAH-*rrah-foh*]
Paraguay, Paraguay [*pah-rah-g'*WHY]
Paraguayan, paraguayo, -a [*pah-rah*-GWAH-*yoh, -yah*]
parallel, paralelo [*pah-rah*-LEH-*loh*]
paralyzed, paralizado, -a [*pah-rah-lee*-THAH-*doh, -dah*]
parcel, paquete [*pah*-KEH-*teh*]
pardon (n), perdón [*pehr*-DOHN]
(to) **pardon,** perdonar [*pehr-doh*-NAHR]
  pardon me, perdóneme, dispénseme [*pehr*-DOH-*neh-meh, dees*-PEHN-*seh-meh*]
parents, padres [PAH-*drehs*]
  NOTE: *Parientes* means relatives, not father and mother only.
park, parque [PAHR-*keh*]
(to) **park,** estacionar [*ehs-tah-th'yoh*-NAHR]
  no parking! se prohibe estacionar [*seh proh*-EE-*beh ehs-tah-th'yoh*-NAHR]
parlor, sala [SAH-*lah*]
parrot, cotorra [*koh*-TOH-*rrah*]
parsley, perejil (m) [*peh-reh*-HEEL]
part, parte (f) [PAHR-*teh*]
part (of a machine), pieza [*p'*YEH-*thah*]
part (in a play), papel [*pah*-PEHL]
partially, parcialmente [*pahr-th'yahl*-MEHN-*teh*]
(to) **participate,** participar [*pahr-tee-thee*-PAHR]
particular, particular [*pahr-tee-koo*-LAHR]
particularly, particularmente [*pahr-tee-koo-lahr*-MEHN-*teh*]
partly, en parte [*ehn* PAHR-*teh*]
partner (business), socio [SOH-*th'yoh*]
party (entertainment), fiesta [*f'*YEHS-*tah*]
  (political), partido [*pahr*-TEE-*doh*]
pass (permit), pase (m) [PAH-*seh*]
pass (mountain), paso [PAH-*soh*]
(to) **pass,** pasar [*pah*-SAHR]
passage, pasaje (m) [*pah*-SAH-*heh*]
passenger, pasajero, -a [*pah-sah*-HEH-*roh, -rah*]
passion, pasión (f) [*pah-s'*YOHN]
passionate, apasionado, -a [*ah-pah-s'yoh*-NAH-*doh, -dah*]

passive, pasivo, -a [*pah*-SEE-*voh, -vah*]
passport, pasaporte (m) [*pah-sah*-POHR-*teh*]
★ **past,** pasado, -a [*pah*-SAH-*doh, -dah*]
pastry and **pastry shop,** pastelería [*pahs-teh-leh*-REE-*ah*]
path, sendero [*sehn*-DEH-*roh*]
patience, paciencia [*pah-th'*YEHN-*th'yah*]
patient (n & adj), paciente [*pah-th'*YEHN-*teh*]
patriotic, patriótico, -a [*pah-tr'*YOH-*tee-koh, -kah*]
pattern (dress), patrón [*pah*-TROHN]
pavement, pavimento [*pah-vee*-MEHN-*toh*]
paw, pata [PAH-*tah*]
(to) **pawn,** empeñar [*ehm-peh-n'*YAHR]
pawnshop, casa de empeños [KAH-*sah deh ehm*-PEH-*n'yohs*]
paid, pagado, -a [*pah*-GAH-*doh, -dah*]
★ (to) **pay,** pagar [*pah*-GAHR]
(to) **pay a compliment,** hacer un cumplido [*ah*-THEHR *oon koom*-PLEE-*doh*]
(to) **pay by instalments,** pagar a plazos [*pah*-GAHR *ah* PLAH-*thohs*]
(to) **pay cash,** pagar al contado [*pah*-GAHR *ahl kohn*-TAH-*doh*]
payment (or) **pay,** pago [PAH-*goh*]
pea, guisante (m), chícharo [*ghee*-SAHN-*teh,* CHEE-*chah-roh*]

NOTE: The translation of "pea" and of some other vegetables and fruits varies from place to place. "Peas" are frequently called *petits pois* which is not Spanish at all, but French.

★ **peace,** paz (f) [*pahth*]
peaceful, pacífico, -a [*pah*-THEE-*fee-koh, -kah*]
peach, melocotón (m) [*meh-loh-koh*-TOHN]
peak, cima [THEE-*mah*]
peanut, cacahuete (m) [*kah-kah*-WEH-*teh*]
pear, pera [PEH-*rah*]
pearl, perla [PEHR-*lah*]
pearl necklace, collar de perlas [*koh-l'*YAHR *deh* PEHR-*lahs*]

peasant, campesino, -a [*kahm-peh-*SEE-*noh, -nah*]
peculiar, peculiar [*peh-koo-l'*YAHR]
pedestrian, transeunte [*trahn-seh-*OON-*teh*]
(to) **peel** (foods), pelar [*peh-*LAHR]
pen, pluma [PLOO-*mah*]
penalty, pena [PEH-*nah*]
pencil, lápiz (m) [LAH-*peeth*]
peninsula, península [*peh-*NEEN-*soo-lah*]
penny, centavo [*thehn-*TAH-*voh*] See currency table at end of dictionary.
pepper (black), pimienta [*pee-m'*YEHN-*tah*]
pepper (green), pimiento [*pee-m'*YEHN-*toh*]
peppermint, menta [MEHN-*tah*]
per, por [*pohr*]
(to) **perceive,** percibir [*pehr-thee-*BEER]
per cent, por ciento [*pohr th'*YEHN-*toh*]
perfect, perfecto, -a [*pehr-*FEHK-*toh, -tah*]
perfection, perfección (f) [*pehr-fehk-th'*YOHN]
performance (theater), función [*foon-th'*YOHN]
performance (of machine), funcionamiento [*foon-th'yoh nah-m'*YEHN-*toh*]
perfume, perfume (m) [*pehr-*FOO-*meh*]
perhaps, quizás [*kee-*THAHS]
period (of time), período [*peh-*REE-*oh-doh*]
period (of a sentence), punto [POON-*toh*]
permanent, permanente [*pehr-mah-*NEHN-*teh*]
permanent wave, ondulación permanente [*ohn-doo-lah th'*YOHN *pehr-mah-*NEHN-*teh*]
permanently, permanentemente [*pehr-mah-nehn-teh-*MEHN *teh*]
permission, permiso [*pehr-*MEE-*soh*]
(to) **permit,** permitir [*pehr-mee-*TEER]
Persian, persa [PEHR-*sah*]
(to) **persist,** persistir [*pehr-sees-*TEER]
person, persona [*pehr-*SOH-*nah*]
personal, personal [*pehr-soh-*NAHL]
personally, personalmente [*pehr-soh-nahl-*MEHN-*teh*]
personality, personalidad (f) [*pehr-soh-nah-lee-*DAHD]

personnel, personal (m) [*pehr-soh*-NAHL]
perspiration, transpiración (f) [*trahns-pee-rah-th'*YOHN]
(to) **persuade,** persuadir [*pehr-swah*-DEER]
pertaining to, relativo, -a [*reh-lah*-TEE-*voh, -vah*]
Peru, Perú [*peh*-ROO]
Peruvian, peruano, -a [*peh*-RWAH-*noh, -nah*]
pessimist (and) **pessimistic,** pesimista (m & f) [*peh-see*-MEES-*tah*]
petition, petición [*peh-tee-th'*YOHN]
petroleum, petróleo [*peh*-TROH-*leh-oh*]
petticoat, enaguas [*eh*-NAH-*gwahs*]
pharmacy, farmacia [*fahr-mah*-THEE-*ah*]
phase, fase (f) [FAH-*seh*]
Philippine Islands, Islas Filipinas [EES-*lahs fee-lee*-PEE-*nahs*]
Philippine, filipino, -a [*fee-lee*-PEE-*noh, -nah*]
philosopher, filósofo, -a [*fee*-LOH-*soh-foh, -fah*]
philosophy, filosofía [*fee-loh-soh*-FEE-*ah*]
phone, teléfono [*teh*-LEH-*foh-noh*]
  by phone, por teléfono [*pohr teh*-LEH-*foh-noh*]
(to) **phone,** telefonear [*teh-leh-foh-neh*-AHR]
phonograph, fonógrafo [*foh*-NOH-*grah-foh*]
photograph, fotografía [*foh-toh-grah*-FEE-*ah*]
photographer, fotógrafo [*foh*-TOH-*grah-foh*]
(to) **take a photograph,** tomar una fotografía [*toh*-MAHR OO-*nah foh-toh-grah*-FEE-*ah*]
physical, físico, -a [FEE-*see-koh, -kah*]
physician, médico [MEH-*dee-koh*]
physics, física [FEE-*see-kah*]
pianist, pianista (m & f) [*p'yah*-NEES-*tah*]
piano, piano [*p'*YAH-*noh*]
(to) **pick up,** recoger [*reh-koh*-HEHR]
picture, cuadro [KWAH-*droh*]
picturesque, pintoresco, -a [*peen-toh*-REHS-*koh, -kah*]
pie, pastel [PAHS-*tehl*]
piece, pedazo [*peh*-DAH-*thoh*]
pier, muelle [MWEH-*l'yeh*]
pig, puerco, -a [PWEHR-*koh, -kah*]

pigeon, pichón (m) [*pee*-CHOHN]
pile, pila [PEE-*lah*]
pill, píldora [PEEL-*doh-rah*]
pillow, almohada [*ahl-moh*-AH-*dah*]
pilot, piloto [*pee*-LOH-*toh*]
pin, alfiler (m) [*ahl-fee*-LEHR]
(to) **pinch,** pellizcar [*peh-l'yeeth*-KAHR]
pine, pino [PEE-*noh*]
pineapple, piña [PEE-*n'yah*]
pink, rosado, -a [*roh*-SAH-*doh, -dah*]
pint,

NOTE: Approximately a *litro* [LEE-*troh*], but see metric table at back of book.

pipe (for smoking), pipa [PEE-*pah*]
(for water), tubo [TOO-*boh*]
pistol, pistola [*pees*-TOH-*lah*]
pity, lástima [LAHS-*tee-mah*]
What a pity! ¡Qué lástima! [*keh* LAHS-*tee-mah*]
★ **place,** lugar [*loo*-GAHR]
in place of, en lugar de [*ehn loo*-GAHR *deh*]
to take place, tener lugar [*teh*-NEHR *loo*-GAHR]
(to) **place,** poner [*poh*-NEHR]
plain (flat land), llano [*l'*YAH-*noh*]
plain (simple), sencillo, -a [*sehn*-THEE-*l'yoh, -yah*]
plan (idea), plan (m) [*plahn*]
plan (map or sketch), plano [PLAH-*noh*]
(to) **plan,** proyectar [*proh-yehk*-TAHR]
planet, planeta (m) [*plah*-NEH-*tah*]
plant, planta [PLAHN-*tah*]
(to) **plant,** plantar [*plahn*-TAHR]
plaster, yeso [YEH-*soh*]
plastic, plástico, -a [PLAHS-*tee-koh, -kah*]
plate (dish), plato [PLAH-*toh*]
platform, plataforma [*plah-tah*-FOHR-*mah*]

(to) **play** (a game), jugar [*hoo*-GAHR]
(to) **play** (an instrument), tocar [*toh*-KAHR]
play (theater), obra de teatro [OH-*brah deh teh*-AH-*troh*]
pleasant, agradable [*ah-grah*-DAH-*bleh*]
★ **please!** ¡Por favor! [*pohr fah*-VOHR]

NOTE: *Sirvase* (SEER-vah-seh) also means "please" and combined with the infinitive of the verb, makes a complete and polite sentence.

Please bring me, Sírvase traerme [SEER-*vah-seh trah*-EHR-*meh*]
Please come in, Sírvase entrar [SEER-*vah-seh ehn*-TRAHR]
★ (to) **please,** agradar [*ah-grah*-DAHR]
Does it please you? ¿Le agrada? [*leh ah*-GRAH-*dah*]
Pleased to meet you! ¡Mucho gusto en conocerle! [MOO-*choh* GOOS-*toh ehn koh-noh*-THEHR-*leh*]
pleasure, placer [*plah*-THEHR]
pleasure trip, viaje de placer [*v'*YAH-*heh deh plah*-THEHR]
the pleasure is mine, el placer es mío [*ehl plah*-THEHR *ehs* MEE-*oh*]
with much pleasure, con mucho gusto [*kohn* MOO-*choh* GOOS-*toh*]
plenty (of), mucho, -a [MOO-*choh, -chah*]
plow (n), arado [*ah*-RAH-*doh*]
plug (electric), enchufe [*ehn*-CHOO-*feh*]
plum, ciruela [*thee*-RWEH-*lah*]
plumber, plomero [*ploh*-MEH-*roh*]
plural, plural [*ploo*-RAHL]
plus, más [*mahs*]
pneumonia, pulmonía [*pool-moh*-NEE-*ah*]
pocket, bolsillo [*bohl*-SEE-*l'yoh*]
pocketbook, cartera [*kahr*-TEH-*rah*]
poem, poema [*poh*-EH-*mah*]
poet, poeta (m & f) [*poh*-EH-*tah*]

poetry, poesía [*poh-eh*-SEE-*ah*]
point (abstract), punto [POON-*toh*]
point (land, pins, knives), punta [POON-*tah*]
(to) **point out,** indicar [*een-dee*-KAHR]
Please point it out, Sírvase indicarlo [SEER-*vah-seh een-dee*-KAHR-*loh*]
poison, veneno [*veh*-NEH-*noh*]
poisonous, venenoso, -a [*veh-neh*-NOH-*soh, -sah*]
Poland, Polonia [*poh*-LOH-*n'yah*]
polar, polar [*poh*-LAHR]
pole, poste [POHS-*teh*]
police, policía [*poh-lee*-THEE-*ah*]
police station, cuartel de policía [KWAHR-*tehl deh poh lee*-THEE-*ah*]
policeman, policía (m) [*poh-lee*-THEE-*ah*]
policy (government), política [*poh*-LEE-*tee-kah*]
policy (insurance), poliza [*poh*-LEE-*thah*]
Polish, polaco, -ca [*poh*-LAH-*koh, -kah*]
(to) **polish** (furniture), pulir [*poo*-LEER]
(to) **polish** (shoes), lustrar [*loos*-TRAHR]
polite, cortés (m & f) [*kohr*-TEHS]
political (and) **politician,** político [*poh*-LEE-*tee-koh*]
politics, política [*poh*-LEE-*tee-kah*]
pool (for swimming), piscina [*pees*-THEE-*nah*]
poor, pobre [POH-*breh*]
Pope, papa [PAH-*pah*]
poppy, amapola [*ah*-MAH-*poh-lah*]
popular, popular [*poh-poo*-LAHR]
popularity, popularidad (f) [*poh-poo-lah-ree*-DAHD]
population, población (f) [*poh-blah-th'*YOHN]
pork, puerco, -a [PWEHR-*koh, -kah*]
portable, portátil [*pohr*-TAH-*teel*]
porter (for baggage), maletero [*mah-leh*-TEH-*roh*]
portrait, retrato [*reh*-TRAH-*toh*]
Portugal, Portugal [*pohr-too*-GAHL]
Portuguese, portugués, portuguesa [*pohr-too*-GHEHS, -GHEH-*sah*]
position, posición (f) [*poh-see-th'*YOHN]

positive, positivo, -a [*poh-see*-TEE-*voh, -vah*]
(to) **possess,** poseer [*poh-seh*-EHR]
possibility, posibilidad [*poh-see-bee-lee*-DAHD]
possible, posible [*poh*-SEE-*bleh*]
as soon as possible, tan pronto como sea posible [*tahn* PROHN-*toh* KOH-*moh* SEH-*ah poh*-SEE-*bleh*]
possibly, posiblemente [*poh-see-bleh*-MEHN-*teh*]
post, poste [POHS-*teh*]
post office, correo [*koh*-RREH-*oh*]
post office box, apartado postal [*ah-pahr*-TAH-*doh pohs* TAHL]
postage, franqueo [*frahn*-KEH-*oh*]
postage stamp, sello [SEH-*l'yoh*]
postcard, tarjeta postal [*tahr*-HEH-*tah pohs*-TAHL]
postpone, aplazar [*ah-plah*-THAHR]
pot, olla [OH-*l'yah*]
potato (in Spain), patata [*pah*-TAH-*tah*]
(in Latin America), papa [PAH-*pah*]
pound, libra [LEE-*brah*]
NOTE: In Spanish countries *kilos* are used. See metric measures at end of book.
(to) **pour,** verter [*vehr*-TEHR]
(to) **pour** (rain), llover a cántaros [*l'yoh*-VEHR *ah* KAHN-*tah-rohs*]
powder, polvo [POHL-*voh*]
power, fuerza [FWEHR-*thah*]
horse power, caballos de fuerza [*kah*-BAH-*l'yohs deh* FWEHR-*thah*]
power of attorney, poder [*poh*-DEHR]
powerful, poderoso, -a [*poh-deh*-ROH-*soh, -sah*]
practical, práctico [PRAHK-*tee-koh*]
(to) **practice,** practicar [*prahk-tee*-KAHR]
(to) **praise,** elogiar [*eh-loh-h'*YAHR]
(to) **pray,** rezar [*reh*-THAHR]
prayer, oración (f) [*oh-rah-th'*YOHN]
(to) **precede,** preceder [*preh-theh*-DEHR]
precious, precioso, -a [*preh-th'*YOH-*soh, -sah*]
precise, preciso, -a [*preh*-THEE-*soh, -sah*]

precisely, precisamente [*preh-thee-sah-*MEHN-*teh*]
preface, prefacio [*preh-*FAH-*th'yoh*]
(to) **prefer,** preferir [*preh-feh-*REER]
preferable, preferible [*preh-feh-*REE-*bleh*]
preference, preferencia [*preh-feh-*REHN-*th'yah*]
pregnant, encinta [*ehn-*THEEN-*tah*]
prejudice, prejuicio [*preh-h'*WEE-*th'yoh*]
preparation, preparación (f) [*preh-pah-rah-th'*YOHN]
(to) **prepare,** preparar [*preh-pah-*RAHR]
prescription, receta [*reh-*THEH-*tah*]
presence, presencia [*preh-*SEHN-*th'yah*]
present, presente [*preh-*SEHN-*teh*]
  at present, por el momento [*pohr ehl moh-*MEHN-*toh*]
present (n), regalo [*reh-*GAH-*loh*]
(to) **present,** presentar [*preh-sehn-*TAHR]
(to) **preserve,** preservar [*preh-sehr-*VAHR]
president, presidente [*preh-see-*DEHN-*teh*]
(to) **press** (clothes), planchar [*plahn-*CHAHR]
(to) **press** (to squeeze), apretar [*ah-preh-*TAHR]
pressure, presión [*preh-s'*YOHN]
prestige, prestigio [*prehs-*TEE-*h'yoh*]
pretence, pretexto [*preh-*TEHKS-*toh*]
(to) **pretend,** fingir [*feen-*HEER]
★ **pretty** (adj), bonito, -a (or) lindo, -a [*boh-*NEE-*toh, -tah,* LEEN-*doh, -dah*]
(to) **prevent,** prevenir [*preh-veh-*NEER]
previous, previo, -a [PREH-*v'yoh, -v'yah*]
★ **price,** precio [PREH-*th'yoh*]
  price list, lista de precios [LEES-*tah deh* PREH-*th'yohs*]
pride, orgullo [*ohr-*GOO-*l'yoh*]
priest, sacerdote (m) [*sah-thehr-*DOH-*teh*]
prince, príncipe (m) [PREEN-*thee-peh*]
princess, princesa [*preen-*THEH-*sah*]
principal (adj), principal [*preen-thee-*PAHL]
principle (moral base), principio [*preen-*THEE-*p'yoh*]
principally, principalmente [*preen-thee-pahl-*MEHN-*teh*]
(to) **print,** imprimir [*eem-pree-*MEER]

printed matter, impresos [*eem*-PREH-*sohs*]
printer, impresor [*eem-preh*-SOHR]
prior, anterior [*ahn-teh-r'*YOHR]
prison, prisión (f) [*pree-s'*YOHN]
prisoner, prisionero, -a [*pree-s'yoh*-NEH-*roh, -rah*]
private, privado, -a [*pree*-VAH-*doh, -dah*]
privilege, privilegio [*pree-vee*-LEH-*h'yoh*]
prize, premio [PREH-*m'yoh*]
pro (in favor of), pro [*proh*]
probable, probable [*proh*-BAH-*bleh*]
probably, probablemente [*proh-bah-bleh*-MEHN-*teh*]
problem, problema (m) [*proh*-BLEH-*mah*]
procedure (or) **process,** procedimiento [*proh-theh-dee-m'*YEHN-*toh*]
(to) **produce,** producir [*proh-doo*-THEER]
product, producto [*proh*-DOOK-*toh*]
production, producción (f) [*proh-dook-th'*YOHN]
profession, profesión (f) [*proh-feh-s'*YOHN]
professor, profesor [*proh-feh*-SOHR]
profile, perfil (m) [*pehr*-FEEL]
profit, beneficio [*beh-neh*-FEE-*th'yoh*]
program, programa (m) [*proh*-GRAH-*mah*]
progress, progreso [*proh*-GREH-*soh*]
(to) **progress,** progresar [*proh-greh*-SAHR]
progressive, progresivo, -a, progresista (m & f) [*proh-greh*-SEE-*voh, -vah; proh-greh*-SEES-*tah*]
prohibited, prohibido [*proh-ee*-BEE-*doh*]
(to) **prohibit,** prohibir [*proh-ee*-BEER]
project, proyecto [*proh*-YEHK-*toh*]
prominent, prominente [*proh-mee*-NEHN-*teh*]
promise, promesa [*proh*-MEH-*sah*]
(to) **promise,** prometer [*proh-meh*-TEHR]
promotion, promoción (f) [*proh-moh-th'*YOHN]
prompt, pronto [PROHN-*toh*]
pronoun, pronombre (m) [*proh*-NOHM-*breh*]
pronunciation, pronunciación (f) [*proh-noon-th'yah-th'*YOHN]

(to) **pronounce,** pronunciar [*proh-noon-th'*YAHR]

How do you pronounce? ¿Cómo se pronuncia? [KOH-*moh seh proh-*NOON-*th'yah*]

proof, prueba [PRWEH-*bah*]

propaganda, propaganda [*proh-pah-*GAHN-*dah*]

propeller, hélice (f) [EH-*lee-theh*]

proper, propio [PROH-*p'yoh*]

property, propiedad (f) [*proh-p'yeh-*DAHD]

proportion, proporción (f) [*proh-pohr-th'*YOHN]

proposal, propuesta [*proh-*PWEHS-*tah*]

proprietor, propietario [*proh-p'yeh-*TAH-*r'yoh*]

prosperity, prosperidad (f) [*prohs-peh-ree-*DAHD]

prosperous, próspero, -a [PROHS-*peh-roh, -rah*]

(to) **protect,** proteger [*proh-teh-*HEHR]

protection, protección (f) [*proh-tehk-th'*YOHN]

(to) **protest,** protestar [*proh-tehs-*TAHR]

Protestant, protestante [*proh-tehs-*TAHN-*teh*]

proud, orgulloso, -a [*ohr-goo-l'yoh-soh, -sah*]

(to) **prove,** probar [*proh-*BAHR]

proverb, proverbio [*proh-*VEHR-*b'yoh*]

provided that, con tal que [*kohn tahl keh*]

province, provincia [*proh-*VEEN-*th'yah*]

provincial, provincial, provinciano [*proh-veen-th'*YAHL. *proh-veen-th'*YAH-*noh*]

provisions, provisiones (f) [*proh-vee-s'*YOH-*nehs*]

prune, ciruela [*thee-r'*WEH-*lah*]

psychiatrist, psiquiatra (m & f) [*psee-k'*YAH-*trah*]

psychological, psicológico, -a [*psee-koh-*LOH-*hee-koh, -kah*]

public, público, -a [POO-*blee-koh, -kah*]

publication, publicación [*poo-blee-kah-th'*YOHN]

publicity, publicidad [*poo-blee-thee-*DAHD]

(to) **publish,** publicar [*poo-blee-*KAHR]

Puerto Rico, Puerto Rico [PWEHR-*toh* REE-*koh*]

Puerto Rican, puertorriqueño, -a [*pwehr-toh-rree-*KEH-*n'yoh, -n'yah*]

(to) **pull,** halar [*ah-*LAHR]

(to) **pull out,** sacar [*sah-*KAHR]

pulse (n), pulso [POOL-*soh*]

pump, bomba [BOHM-*bah*]
pumpkin, calabaza [*kah-lah*-BAH-*thah*]
punctual, puntual [*poon-t'*WAHL]
punishment, castigo [*kahs*-TEE-*goh*]
(to) **punish,** castigar [*kahs-tee*-GAHR]
pupil (student), discípulo, -a [*dees*-THEE-*poo-loh, -lah*]
purchase (n), compra [KOHM-*prah*]
(to) **purchase,** comprar [*kohm*-PRAHR]
pure, puro, -a [POO-*roh, -rah*]

NOTE: Smokers should know that *puro* as a noun means a "cigar."

purple, morado, -a [*moh*-RAH-*doh, -dah*]
purpose, propósito [*proh*-POH-*see-toh*]
  on purpose, adrede [*ah*-DREH-*deh*]
purse, bolsa [BOHL-*sah*]
(to) **pursue,** perseguir [*pehr-seh*-GHEER]
(to) **push,** empujar [*ehm-poo*-HAHR]
★ (to) **put,** poner [*poh*-NEHR]
  to put off, aplazar [*ah-plah*-THAHR]
  to put on (a light), encender [*ehn-thehn*-DEHR]
  to put on (clothes), poner(se) [*poh*-NEHR-*seh*]
  to put out (a light), apagar [*ah-pah*-GAHR]
puzzled, perplejo, -a [*pehr*-PLEH-*hoh, -hah*]
pyramid, pirámide (f) [*pee*-RAH-*mee-deh*]

Q

qualification, calificación [*kah-lee-fee-kah-th'*YOHN]
quality (for things), calidad (f) [*kah-lee*-DAHD]
  (for character), cualidad (f) [*kwah-lee*-DAHD]
quantity, cantidad (f) [*kahn-tee*-DAHD]

quarrel, riña [REE-*n'yah*]
quart (or) **quarter,** quarto [KWAHR-*toh*] (See metric table at end of book for equivalent Spanish measure.)
quarter hour, cuarto de hora [KWAHR-*toh deh* OH-*rah*]
queen, reina [RAY-*nah*]
queer, raro, -a [RAH-*roh, -rah*]
How queer! ¡Qué raro! [*keh* RAH-*roh*]
question (query), pregunta [*preh*-GOON-*tah*]
question mark, signo de interrogación [SEEG-*noh deh een-teh-rroh-gah-th'*YOHN]
questionnaire, cuestionario [*kwehs-t'yoh*-NAH-*r'yoh*]
★ **quick,** rápido [RAH-*pee-doh*]
quickly, pronto [PROHN-*toh*]
★ **quiet,** tranquilo [*trahn*-KEE-*loh*]
be quiet! (to one person), ¡cállese! [KAH-*l'yeh-seh*]
(to several persons), ¡cállense! [KAH-*l'yehn-seh*]
quinine, quinina [*kee*-NEE-*nah*]
quite, bastante [*bahs*-TAHN-*teh*]
quotation (business), cotización (f) [*koh-tee*-THAH-*th'*YOHN]
(literary), citación (f) [*thee-tah-th'*YOHN]
(to) **quote,** citar [*thee*-TAHR]

R

rabbit, conejo, -a [*koh*-NEH-*hoh, -hah*]
race (human), raza [RAH-*thah*]
race (contest), carrera [*kah*-RREH-*rah*]
race (horse race), carrera de caballos [*kah*-RREH-*rah deh kah*-BAH-*l'yohs*]
radiator, radiador (m) [*rah-d'yah*-DOHR]
radio, radio (f) [RAH-*d'yoh*]
radio station, emisora de radio [*eh-mee*-SOH-*rah deh* RAH-*d'yoh*]
radish, rábano [RAH-*bah-noh*]
rag, trapo [TRAH-*poh*]
railroad (or) **railway,** ferrocarril [*feh-rroh-kah*-RREEL]

railroad car, vagón (m) [*vah*-GOHN]
railway crossing, paso a nivel [PAH-*soh ah* NEE-*vehl*]
rain (n), lluvia [*l'*YOO-*v'yah*]
(to) **rain,** llover [*l'yoh*-VEHR]
it is raining, llueve or está lloviendo [*l'yoo*-EH-*veh,* or *ehs*-TAH *l'yoh-v'*YEHN-*doh*]
rainbow, arco iris (m) [AHR-*koh* EE-*rees*]
raincoat, impermeable [*eem-pehr-meh*-AH-*bleh*]
(to) **raise** (to lift), levantar [*leh-vahn*-TAHR]
(to) **raise** (children or animals), criar [*kree*-AHR]
(to) **raise** (prices), aumentar [*ow-mehn*-TAHR]
raisin, pasa [PAH-*sah*]
range (extension), alcance (m) [*ahl*-KAHN-*theh*]
rank, rango [RAHN-*goh*]
rapid, rápido, -a [RAH-*pee-doh, -dah*]
rapidly, rápidamente [*rah-pee-dah*-MEHN-*teh*]
rare (unusual), raro, -a [RAH-*roh, -rah*]
rare (for meats), poco asado, -a [POH-*koh ah*-SAH-*doh, -dah*]
rarely, rara vez [RAH-*rah vehth*]
raspberry, frambuesa [*frahm*-BWEH-*sah*]
rat, rata [RAH-*tah*]
rate, tarifa [*tah*-REE-*fah*]
at the rate of, a razón de [*ah-rah*-THOHN *deh*]
rather, más bien [*mahs b'*YEHN]
I would rather . . . Me gustaría más [*meh goos-tah*-REE-*ah mahs*]
Would you (he, she) rather . . . Le gustaría más [*leh goos-tah*-REE-*ah mahs*]
raw, crudo, -a [KROO-*doh, -dah*]
raw material, materia prima [*mah*-TEH-*r'yah* PREE-*mah*]
rayon, rayón (m) [*rah*-YOHN]
razor, navaja de afeitar [*nah*-VAH-*hah deh ah-fay*-TAHR]
electric razor, maquinilla de afeitar [*mah-kee*-NEEL-*yah deh ah-fay*-TAHR]
razor blade, hoja de afeitar [OH-*hah deh ah-fay*-TAHR]
(to) **reach,** alcanzar [*ahl-kahn*-THAHR]
reaction, reacción (f) [*reh-ahk-th'*YOHN]

★ (to) **read,** leer [*leh*-EHR]
reading (n), lectura [*lehk*-TOO-*rah*]
★ **ready,** listo, -a [LEES-*toh, -tah*]

NOTE: "Are you ready?" and "Is he (she or it) ready?" can all be expressed by "*¿Está listo?*" [*ehs*-TAH LEES-*toh,* LEES-*tah*]

real, verdadero, -a [*vehr-dah*-DEH-*roh, -rah*]
real estate, bienes raíces [*b'*YEH-*nehs rah*-EE-*thehs*]
(to) **realize,** dar(se) cuenta [DAHR-*seh* KWEHN-*tah*]
really, verdaderamente [*vehr-dah*-DEH-*rah*-MEHN-*teh*]
rear (adj), trasero, -a [*trah*-SEH-*roh, -rah*]
reason, razón (f) [*rah*-THOHN]
reasonable, razonable [*rah-thoh*-NAH-*bleh*]
rebel, rebelde (m) [*reh*-BEHL-*deh*]
receipt, recibo [*reh*-THEE-*boh*]
  to acknowledge receipt, acusar recibo [*ah-koo*-SAHR *reh*-THEE-*boh*]
★ (to) **receive,** recibir [*reh-thee*-BEER]
recent, reciente [*reh-th'*YEHN-*teh*]
recently, recientemente [*reh-th'yehn-teh*-MEHN-*teh*]
reception, recepción (f) [*reh-thehp-th'*YOHN]
recipe, receta [*reh*-THEH-*tah*]
(to) **recognize,** reconocer [*reh-koh-noh*-THEHR]
(to) **recommend,** recomendar [*reh-koh-mehn*-DAHR]
recommendation, recomendación (f) [*reh-koh-mehn-dah-th'*YOHN]
record (phonograph), disco [DEES-*koh*]
record (police), archivo [*ahr*-CHEE-*voh*]
record (school), expediente [*ehks-peh-d'*YEHN-*teh*]
record (sports), record [REH-*kohrd*]
(to) **recover** (from illness), recuperar [*reh-koo-peh*-RAHR]
recovery, restablecimiento [*rehs-tah-bleh-thee-m'*YEHN-*toh*]
recreation, recreo [*reh*-KREH-*oh*]

★ **red,** rojo, -a [ROH-*hoh, -hah*]
  Red Cross, cruz roja [*krooth* ROH-*hah*]
  red wine, vino tinto [VEE-*noh* TEEN-*toh*]
(to) **reduce,** reducir [*reh-doo*-THEER]
reduction, reducción (f) [*reh-dook-th'*YOHN]
reef, arrecife (m) [*ah-rreh*-THEE-*feh*]
(to) **refer,** referir [*reh-feh*-REER]
referee, árbitro [AHR-*bee-troh*]
reference, referencia [*reh-feh*-REHN-*th'yah*]
(in) **reference to,** respecto de [*rehs*-PEHK-*toh deh*]
refined (adj), refinado, -a [*reh-fee*-NAH-*doh, -dah*]
refinery, refinería [*reh-fee-neh*-REE-*ah*]
reflection (mind), reflexión [*reh-flehk-s'*YOHN]
  (light), reflejo [*reh*-FLEH-*hoh*]
reform (n), reforma [*reh*-FOHR-*mah*]
(to) **refresh,** refrescar [*reh-frehs*-KAHR]
refreshing, refrescante [*reh-frehs*-KAHN-*teh*]
refreshments, refrescos [*reh*-FREHS-*kohs*]
refrigerator, refrigerador [*reh-free-heh-rah*-DOHR]
refugee, refugiado, -a [*reh-foo-h'*YAH-*doh, -dah*]
(to) **refund,** reembolsar [*reh-ehm-bohl*-SAHR]
(to) **refuse,** rehusar [*reh-oo*-SAHR]
(to) **regain,** recobrar [*reh-koh*-BRAHR]
regards, recuerdos [*reh*-KWEHR-*dohs*]
  kind regards, sinceros recuerdos [*seen*-THEH-*rohs reh*-KWEHR-*dohs*]
  in regard to, con respecto a [*kohn rehs*-PEHK-*toh ah*]
regardless, a pesar de [*ah-peh*-SAHR *deh*]
regime, régimen [REH-*hee-mehn*]
regiment, regimiento [*reh-hee-m'*YEHN-*toh*]
region, región (f) [*reh-h'*YOHN]
register, registro [*reh*-HEES-*troh*]
(to) **register,** inscribir [*een-skree*-BEER]
  registered letter, carta certificada [KAHR-*tah thehr-tee-fee*-KAH-*dah*]
(to) **regret,** sentir [*sehn*-TEER]
regular, regular [*reh-goo*-LAHR]

regulation, regulación (f) [*reh-goo-lah-th'*YOHN]
rehearsal, ensayo [*ehn*-SAH-*yoh*]
rein, rienda [*r'*YEHN-*dah*]
(to) **be related,** ser pariente (de) [*sehr pah-r'*YEHN-*teh deh*]
relative (adj), relativo, -a [*reh-lah*-TEE-*voh, -vah*]
relationship, parentesco [*pah-rehn*-TEHS-*koh*]
relatively, relativamente [*reh-lah-tee-vah*-MEHN-*teh*]
relatives, parientes [*pah-r'*YEHN-*tehs*]
(to) **release,** soltar [*sohl*-TAHR]
reliable, de confianza [*deh kohn-f'*YAHN-*thah*]
relief (from discomfort), alivio [*ah*-LEE-*v'yoh*]
relief (aid), socorro [*soh*-KOH-*rroh*]
religion, religión (f) [*reh-lee-h'*YOHN]
religious, religioso, -a [*reh-lee-h'*YOH-*soh, -sah*]
(to) **remain,** quedar(se) [*keh*-DAHR-*seh*]
remainder, el resto [*ehl* REHS-*toh*]
remark, observación (f) [*ohb-sehr-vah-th'*YOHN]
(to) **remark,** observar [*ohb-sehr*-VAHR]
remarkable, notable [*noh*-TAH-*bleh*]
remedy, remedio [*reh*-MEH-*d'yoh*]
★ (to) **remember,** recordar [*reh-kohr*-DAHR]
Do you remember? ¿Recuerda Ud? [*reh*-KWEHR-*dah oos*-TEHD]
(to) **remind,** recordar [*reh-kohr*-DAHR]
(to) **remit,** remitir [*reh-mee*-TEER]
remittance, remesa [*reh*-MEH-*sah*]
remote, remoto, -a [*reh*-MOH-*toh, -tah*]
(to) **remove,** quitar [*kee*-TAHR]
(to) **renew,** renovar.[*reh-noh*-VAHR]
rent, alquiler (m) [*ahl-kee*-LEHR]
for rent, de alquiler [*deh ahl-kee*-LEHR]
(to) **rent,** alquilar [*ahl-kee*-LAHR].
repair, reparación (f) [*reh-pah-rah-th'*YOHN]
(to) **repair,** componer [*kohm-poh*-NEHR]
(to) **repeat,** repetir [*reh-peh*-TEER]
Please repeat! ¡Sírvase repetir! [SEER-*vah-seh reh-peh*-TEER]

(to) **replace,** reemplazar [*reh-ehm-plah-*THAHR]
reply (n), respuesta [*rehs-*PWEHS-*tah*]
(to) **report,** reportar [*reh-pohr-*TAHR]
reporter, reportero [*reh-pohr-*TEH-*roh*]
(to) **represent,** representar [*reh-preh-sehn-*TAHR]
representative, representante [*reh-preh-sehn-*TAHN-*teh*]
reproduction, reproducción (f) [*reh-proh-dook-th'*YOHN]
republic, república [*reh-*POO-*blee-kah*]
reputation, reputación (f) [*reh-poo-tah-th'*YOHN]
(to) **request,** solicitar [*soh-lee-thee-*TAHR]
(to) **require,** requerir [*reh-keh-*REER]
(to) **rescue,** salvar [*sahl-*VAHR]
research, investigación (f) [*een-vehs-tee-gah-th'*YOHN]
(to) **resemble,** parecer(se) a [*pah-reh-*THEHR-*seh ah*]
resemblance, parecido [*pah-reh-*THEE-*doh*]
resentment, resentimiento [*reh-sehn-tee-m'*YEHN-*toh*]
reservation, reservación (f) [*reh-sehr-vah-th'*YOHN]
residence, residencia [*reh-see-*DEHN-*th'yah*]
resident, residente (m & f) [*reh-see-*DEHN-*teh*]
(to) **resign,** renunciar [*reh-noon-th'*YAHR]
(to) **resist,** resistir [*reh-sees-*TEER]
resolution, resolución [*reh-soh-loo-th'*YOHN]
(to) **resolve,** resolver [*reh-sohl-*VEHR]
respect, respecto [*rehs-*PEHK-*toh*]
  in respect to, con respecto a [*kohn rehs-*PEHK-*toh ah*]
(to) **respect,** respetar [*rehs-peh-*TAHR]
respectable, respetable [*rehs-peh-*TAH-*bleh*]
respectful, respetuoso, -a [*rehs-peh-t'*WOH-*soh, -sah*]
respective, respectivo, -a [*rehs-pehk-*TEE-*voh, -vah*]
responsible, responsable [*rehs-pohn-*SAH-*bleh*]
rest, descanso [*dehs-*KAHN-*soh*]
(to) **rest,** descansar [*dehs-kahn-*SAHR]
restaurant, restaurante (m) [*rehs-tow-*RAHN-*teh*]
result, resultado [*reh-sool-*TAH-*doh*]
(to) **resume,** reanudar [*reh-ah-noo-*DAHR]
retail, al detalle [*ahl deh-*TAH-*l'yeh*]
(to) **retain,** retener [*reh-teh-*NEHR]
(to) **retire,** retirarse [*reh-tee-*RAHR-*seh*]

★ (to) **return,** volver [*vohl*-VEHR]
When will he (she) return? ¿Cuándo volverá [KWAHN-*doh vohl-veh*-RAH?] (Also applicable for "you" and "she.")
revenge, venganza [*vehn*-GAHN-*thah*]
review, revista [*reh*-VEES-*tah*]
to revise, revisar [*reh-vee*-SAHR]
(to) **revolve,** girar [*hee*-RAHR]
revolver, revólver (m) [*reh*-VOHL-*vehr*]
revolution, revolución (f) [*reh-voh-loo-th'*YOHN]
reward, recompensa [*reh-kohm*-PEHN-*sah*]
(to) **reward,** recompensar [*reh-kohm-pehn*-SAHR]
rheumatism, reumatismo [*reh-oo-mah*-TEEZ-*moh*]
rhythm, ritmo [REET-*moh*]
rib, costilla [*kohs*-TEE-*l'yah*]
ribbon, cinta [THEEN-*tah*]
rice, arroz (m) [*ah*-RROTH]
★ **rich,** rico, -a [REE-*koh, -kah*]
to get rid of, deshacer(se) de [*dehs-ah*-THEHR-*seh deh*]
ride, paseo [*pah*-SEH-*oh*]
NOTE: *Paseo* also means a "walk."
(to) **ride,** pasear [*pah-seh*-AHR]
(to) **ride a horse,** montar a caballo [*mohn*-TAHR *ah kah* BAHL-*yoh*]
ridiculous, ridículo, -a [*ree*-DEE-*koo-loh, -lah*]
rifle, rifle (m) [REE-*fleh*]
right (n), derecho [*deh*-REH-*choh*]
★ **right** (adj, not left), derecho, -a [*deh*-REH-*choh, -chah*]
(adj, not wrong), correcto, -a [*koh*-RREHK-*toh, -tah*]
★ **all right,** está bien [*ehs*-TAH *b'yehn*]
★ **right away,** ahora mismo [*ah*-OH-*rah* MEES-*moh*]
right here, aquí mismo [*ah*-KEE MEES-*moh*]
to the right, a la derecha [*ah lah deh*-REH-*chah*]
(to) **be right,** tener razón [*teh*-NEHR *rah*-THOHN]
ring (for finger), anillo [*ah*-NEE-*l'yoh*]
(to) **ring,** sonar [*soh*-NAHR]
riot (n), motín (m) [*moh*-TEEN]
ripe, maduro, -a [*mah*-DOO-*roh, -rah*]
(to) **rise,** levantarse [*leh-vahn*-TAHR-*seh*]

risk, riesgo [*r'*YEHS-*goh*]
rival, rival [*ree*-VAHL]
★ **river,** río [REE-*oh*]
★ **road,** camino [*kah*-MEE-*noh*]
(to) **roast,** asar [*ah*-SAHR]
roasted, asado, -a [*ah*-SAH-*doh, -dah*]
(to) **rob,** robar [*roh*-BAHR]
robber, ladrón, -a [*lah*-DROHN, *-nah*]
rock, roca [ROH-*kah*]
Roman, romano, -a [*roh*-MAH-*noh, -nah*]
romantic, romántico, -a [*roh*-MAHN-*tee-koh, -kah*]
roof, techo [TEH-*choh*]
★ **room** (house), cuarto [KWAHR-*toh*]
room (space), lugar [*loo*-GAHR]
There's no room, No hay lugar [*noh I loo*-GAHR]
rooster, gallo [GAH-*l'yoh*]
root, raíz (f) [*rah*-EETH]
rope, soga [SOH-*gah*]
rose, rosa [ROH-*sah*]
rouge, colorete (m) [*koh-loh*-REH-*teh*]
rough, áspero, -a [AHS-*peh-roh, -rah*]
round, redondo, -a [*reh*-DOHN-*doh, -dah*]
round trip, viaje de ida y vuelta [*v'*YAH-*heh deh* EE-*dah ee v'*WEHL-*tah*]
route, ruta [ROO-*tah*]
routine (n), rutina [*roo*-TEE-*nah*]
(adj), rutinario, -a [*roo-tee*-NAH-*r'yoh, -r'yah*]
row (of chairs), fila [FEE-*lah*]
(to) **row,** remar [*reh*-MAHR]
(to) **rub,** frotar [*froh*-TAHR]
rubber, caucho (or) goma [KOW-*choh,* GOH-*mah*]
ruby, rubí (m) [*roo*-BEE]
rude, grosero, -a [*groh*-SEH-*roh, -rah*]
rudeness, grosería [*groh-seh*-REE-*ah*]
ruin, ruina [RWEE-*nah*]
ruler (for measuring), regla [REH-*glah*]
(to) **rule,** gobernar [*goh-behr*-NAHR]

rum, ron (m) [*rohn*]
rumor, rumor [*roo*-MOHR]
(to) **run,** correr [*koh*-RREHR]
  to run into, chocar con [*choh*-KAHR *kohn*]
  to run over, atropellar [*ah-troh-peh-l'yahr*]
running water, agua corriente [AH-*gwah koh-rr'*YEHN-*teh*]
Russia, Rusia [ROO-*s'yah*]
Russian, ruso, -a [ROO-*soh, -sah*]
rust, herrumbre (f) [*eh*-RROOM-*breh*]

S

sack, saco [SAH-*koh*]
★ **sad,** triste [TREES-*teh*]
saddle, montura [*mohn*-TOO-*rah*]
sadness, tristeza [*tres*-TEH-*thah*]
safe (n), caja fuerte [KAH-*hah* FWEHR-*teh*]
safe (adj), salvo, -a [SAHL-*voh, -vah*]
  safe and sound, sano, -a, y salvo, -a [SAH-*noh, -nah, ee* SAHL-*voh, -vah*]
  safe conduct, salvo conducto [SAHL-*voh kohn*-DOOK-*toh*]
safety, seguridad (f) [*seh-goo-ree*-DAHD]
said, dicho [DEE-*choh*]
sail, vela [VEH-*lah*]
  sailboat, buque de vela [BOO-*keh deh* VEH-*lah*]
(to) **sail,** navegar [*nah-veh*-GAHR]
  When does the ship sail? ¿Cuándo sale el barco? [KWAHN-*doh* SAH-*leh ehl* BAHR-*koh*]
sailor, marinero [*mah-ree*-NEH-*roh*]
saint, santo, -a [SAHN-*toh, -tah*]
sake,
    NOTE: No exact equivalent exists. For more common expressions observe:
  for Heaven's sake, por el amor del cielo [*pohr ehl ah*-MOHR *dehl th'*YEH-*loh*]
  for your sake, por su bien [*pohr soo b'yehn*]

salad, ensalada [*ehn-sah*-LAH-*dah*]
salary, sueldo [*s'*WEHL-*doh*]
sale, venta [VEHN-*tah*]
  for sale, de venta [*deh* VEHN-*tah*]
salesclerk, dependiente [*deh-pehn-d'*YEHN-*teh*]
salmon, salmón (m) [*sahl*-MOHN]
salt, sal (f) [*sahl*]
salty, salado, -a [*sah*-LAH-*doh, -dah*]
Salvador, El Salvador [*ehl sahl-vah*-DOHR]
Salvadorian, salvadoreño, -a [*sahl-vah-doh*-REH-*n'yoh, -n'yah*]
(to) **salute,** saludar [*sah-loo*-DAHR]
  NOTE: The word "to greet" and the military "to salute" is expressed by the one word *saludar (sah-loo*-DAHR).
★ **same,** mismo, -a [MEES-*moh, -mah*]
  It's all the same to me, lo mismo me da [*loh* MEES-*moh meh dah*]
sample, muestra [MWEHS-*trah*]
sand, arena [*ah*-REH-*nah*]
sane, cuerdo, -a [KWEHR-*doh, -dah*]
sandwich, emparedado [*ehm-pah-reh*-DAH-*doh*]
sanatorium, sanatorio [*sah-nah*-TOH-*r'yoh*]
sanitary, sanitario, -a [*sah-nee*-TAH-*r'yoh, -r'yah*]
sapphire, zafiro [*thah*-FEE-*roh*]
sarcastic, sarcástico, -a [*sahr*-KAHS-*tee-koh, -kah*]
satin, satín [*sah*-TEEN]
satisfaction, satisfacción (f) [*sah-tees-fahk-th'*YOHN]
satisfactory, satisfactorio, -a [*sah-tees fahk*-TOH-*r'yoh -r'yah*]
satisfied, satisfecho, -a [*sah-tees*-FEH-*choh, -chah*]
(to) **satisfy,** satisfacer [*sah-tees-fah*-THEHR]
★ **Saturday,** sábado [SAH-*bah-doh*]
sauce, salsa [SAHL-*sah*]
saucer, platillo [*plah*-TEE-*l'yoh*]
sausage, salchicha [*sahl*-CHEE-*chah*]
savage, salvaje [*sahl*-VAH-*heh*]

(to) **save** (money), ahorrar [*ah-oh*-RRAHR]
(to) **save** (life), salvar [*sahl*-VAHR]
savings account, cuenta de ahorros [KWEHN-*tah deh ah*-OH-*rrohs*]
saw (tool), sierra [*s'*YEH-*rrah*]
(to) **say,** decir [*deh*-THEER]
scale (for weighing), balanza [*bah*-LAHN-*thah*]
(music etc.), escala [*ehs*-KAH-*lah*]
scandal, escándalo [*ehs*-KAHN-*dah-loh*]
scar, cicatriz (f) [*thee-kah*-TREETH]
scarce, escaso, -a [*ehs*-KAH-*soh, -sah*]
scarcely, apenas [*ah*-PEH-*nahs*]
(to) **scare,** asustar [*ah-soos*-TAHR]
scarf, bufanda [*boo*-FAHN-*dah*]
scarlate, escarlata [*ehs-kahr*-LAH-*tah*]
scarlet fever, escarlatina [*ehs-kahr-lah*-TEE-*nah*]
scene, escena [*ehs*-THEH-*nah*]
scenery, paisaje (m) [*pie*-SAH-*heh*]
schedule, horario [*oh*-RAH-*r'yoh*]
★ **school,** escuela [*ehs*-KWEH-*lah*]
school mate, compañero de colegio [*kohm-pah-n'*YEH-*roh deh koh*-LEH-*h'yoh*]
school teacher, maestro(a) de escuela [*mah*-EHS-*troh deh ehs*-KWEH-*lah*]
science, ciencia [*th'*YEHN-*th'yah*]
scientist (or) **scientific,** científico, -a [*th'yehn*-TEE-*fee-koh -kah*]
scissors, tijeras [*tee*-HEH-*rahs*]
(to) **scold,** regañar [*reh-gah-n'*YAHR]
Scotch, escocés, escocesa [*ehs-koh*-THEHS, *-sah*]
Scotland, Escocia [*ehs*-KOH-*th'yah*]
(to) **scratch,** rascar [*rahs*-KAHR]
scream, gritar [*gree*-TAHR]
screen (movies), pantalla [*pahn*-TAH-*l'yah*]
(for windows), alambrado [*ah-lahm*-BRAH-*doh*]
screw, tornillo [*tohr*-NEE-*l'yoh*]
screwdriver, destornillador [*dehs-tohr-nee-l'yah*-DOHR]

sculpture, escultura [*ehs-kool-*TOO-*rah*]
★ **sea,** mar (m or f) [*mahr*]
seal (animal), foca [FOH-*kah*]
seal (for document), sello [SEH-*l'yoh*]
(to) **seal,** sellar [*seh-l'*YAHR]
seam, costura [*kohs-*TOO-*rah*]
search (n), búsqueda [BOOS-*keh-dah*]
(to) **search for,** buscar [*boos-*KAHR]
(to) **search,** registrar [*reh-hees-*TRAHR]
season, estación (f) [*ehs-tah-th'*YOHN]
(to) **season,** sazonar [*sah-thoh-*NAHR]
seat, asiento [*ah-s'*YEHN-*toh*]
Have a seat, please! ¡Tome asiento, por favor! [TOH-*meh ah-s'*YEHN-*toh pohr fah-*VOHR]
seated, sentado, -a [*sehn-*TAH-*doh, -dah*]
second (of minute), segundo [*seh-*GOON-*doh*]
second (adj), segundo, -a [*seh-*GOON-*doh, -dah*]
secret, secreto [*seh-*KREH-*toh*]
secretary, secretario, -a [*seh-kreh-*TAH-*r'yoh, -r'yah*]
section, sección (f) [*sehk-th'*YOHN]
secure, seguro, -a [*seh-*GOO-*roh, -rah*]
(to) **secure** (to make secure), asegurar [*ah-seh-goo-*RAHR]
(to obtain), conseguir [*kohn-seh-*GHEER]
★ (to) **see,** ver [*vehr*]
Let me see, déjeme ver [DEH-*heh-meh vehr*]
Let's see, vamos a ver [VAH-*mohs ah vehr*]
seed, semilla [*seh-*MEE-*l'yah*]
(to) **seek,** buscar [*boos-*KAHR]
(to) **seem,** parecer [*pah-reh-*THEHR]
How does it seem to you? ¿Qué le parece? [*keh leh pah-*REH-*theh*]
It seems to me that . . . Me parece que . . . [*meh pah-*REH-*theh-keh . . .*]
seen, visto [VEES-*toh*]
(to) **seize,** agarrar [*ah-gah-*RRAHR]
seldom, rara vez [RAH-*rah vehth*]
(to) **select,** seleccionar [*seh-lehk-th'yoh-*NAHR]

self, mismo, -a [MEES-*moh, -mah*]

NOTE: Mismo is added to the noun or pronoun:

I myself, yo mismo [*yoh* MEES-*moh*]

Otherwise "self" is understood from the reflexive pronouns *me, te, se* or *nos.*

I wash myself, yo me lavo [*yoh meh* LAH-*voh*]

selfish, egoísta [*eh-goh*-EES-*tah*]

★ (to) **sell,** vender [*vehn*-DEHR]

senate, senado [*seh*-NAH-*doh*]

senator, senador [*seh-nah*-DOHR]

★ (to) **send,** enviar [*ehn-v'*YAHR]

to send for, mandar a buscar [*mahn*-DAHR *ah boos*-KAHR]

sender, remitente [*reh-mee*-TEHN-*teh*]

sense, sentido [*sehn*-TEE-*doh*]

common sense, sentido común [*sehn*-TEE-*doh koh*-MOON]

sensible, sensato, -a [*sehn*-SAH-*toh, -tah*]

sensitive, sensible [*sehn*-SEE-*bleh*]

sentence (speech), frase (f) [FRAH-*seh*]

sentimental, sentimental [*sehn-tee-mehn*-TAHL]

(to) **separate,** separar [*seh-pah*-RAHR]

separate (adj), separado, -a [*seh-pah*-RAH-*doh, -dah*]

separately, por separado [*pohr seh-pah*-RAH-*doh*]

separation, separación [*seh-pah-rah-th'*YOHN]

September, septiembre [*sehp-t'*YEHM-*breh*]

sergeant, sargento [*sahr*-HEHN-*toh*]

series, serie (f) [SEH-*r'yeh*]

serious, serio, -a [SEH-*r'yoh, -r'yah*]

seriously, seriamente [*seh-r'yah* MEHN-*teh*]

servant, sirviente, -a [*seer-v'*YEHN-*teh, -tah*]

(to) **serve,** servir [*sehr*-VEER]

service, servicio [*sehr*-VEE-*th'yoh*]

at your service, a sus órdenes [*ah-soos* OHR-*deh-nehs*]

set (n), juego [*h'*WEH-*goh*]

(to) **set,** poner [*poh*-NEHR]

(to) **set a watch,** poner un reloj en hora [*poh*-NEHR *oon reh*-LOH *ehn* OH-*rah*]

(to) **settle** (for accounts), arreglar [*ah-rreh*-GLAHR]

(to) **settle** (a country), colonizar [*koh-loh-nee*-THAHR]

★ **seven,** siete [*s'*YEH-*teh*]
★ **seventeen,** diecisiete [*d'*YEHTH-*ee-s'*YEH-*teh*]
seventh, séptimo, -a [SEHP-*tee-moh, -mah*]
★ **seventy,** setenta [*seh*-TEHN-*tah*]
several, varios, -as [VAH-*r'yohs, -r'yahs*]
severe, severo, -a [*seh*-VEH-*roh, -rah*]
(to) **sew,** coser [*koh*-SEHR]
sewing machine, máquina de coser [MAH-*kee-nah deh koh*-SEHR]
sex, sexo [SEHK-*soh*]
shade (and) **shadow,** sombra [SOHM-*brah*]

NOTE: One Spanish word may frequently serve for two English ones.

(to) **shake,** sacudir [*sah-koo*-DEER]
(to) **shake hands,** dar la mano [*dahr lah* MAH-*noh*]
★ **shall** (will),

NOTE: Since no such word exists in Spanish, you must use the future tense. This is formed by adding the letter *é* to the infinitive for the pronoun *yo* and *á, emos* and *án* for the other persons. Therefore if the word "to go" is *ir,* the future will be: *Yo iré Ud.* (*él, ella*) *irá, nosotros iremos, Uds.* (*ellos, ellas*), *irán.*

shame, vergüenza [*vehr*-GWEHN-*thah*]
shameful, vergonzoso, -a [*vehr-gohn*-THOH-*soh, -sah*]
shameless, sinvergüenza [*seen-vehr*-GWEHN-*thah*]

NOTE: One of the most widely used epithets in Spanish, but not generally so disparaging as when used in English.

shampoo, champú (m) [*chahm*-POO]
shape, forma [FOHR-*mah*]
(to) **shape,** formar [*fohr*-MAHR]
share (a part), parte (f) [PAHR-*teh*]
(stock), acción (f) [*ahk-th'*YOHN]
(to) **share,** compartir [*kohm-pahr*-TEER]
shark, tiburón (m) [*tee-boo*-ROHN]
sharp, agudo, -a [*ah*-GOO-*doh, -dah*]

(to) **shave,** afeitar [*ah-fey*-TAHR]
shaving brush, brocha de afeitar [BROH-*chah deh ah-fey*-TAHR]
shaving cream, crema de afeitar [KREH-*mah deh ah-fey*-TAHR]
shawl, mantón (m) [*mahn*-TOHN]
★ **she,** ella [EH-*l'yah*]
sheep, oveja [*oh*-VEH-*hah*]
sheet (on bed), sábana [SAH-*bah-nah*]
(paper), hoja [OH-*hah*]
shelf, estante [*ehs*-TAHN-*teh*]
shell (sea), concha [KOHN-*chah*]
shell (egg), cáscara [KAHS-*kah-rah*]
shell (gun), proyectil [*proh-yehk*-TEEL]
shelter, refugio [*reh*-FOO-*h'yoh*]
shepherd, pastor [*pahs*-TOHR]
sherry (wine), vino de Jerez [VEE-*noh deh heh*-REHTH]
(to) **shift,** cambiar [*kahm-b'*YAHR]
(to) **shine** (sun), brillar [*bree-l'*YAHR]
(to) **shine** (shoes), lustrar [*loos*-TRAHR]
★ **ship,** barco [BAHR-*koh*]
(to) **ship,** despachar [*dehs-pah*-CHAHR]
shipment, envío [*ehn*-VEE-*oh*]
shipwreck, naufragio [*now*-FRAH-*h'yoh*]
★ **shirt,** camisa [*kah*-MEE-*sah*]
(to) **shiver,** tiritar [*tee-ree*-TAHR]
shock, choque [CHOH-*keh*]
★ **shoe,** zapato [*thah*-PAH-*toh*]
shoe laces, cordones de zapatos [*kohr*-DOH-*nehs deh thah* PAH-*tohs*]
shoe shine boy, limpiabotas [LEEM-*p'yah* BOH-*tahs*]
shoe store, zapatería [*thah-pah-teh*-REE-*ah*]
shoemaker, zapatero [*thah-pah*-TEH-*roh*]
(to) **shoot** (to fire), disparar [*dees-pah*-RAHR]
(to) **shoot** (to execute), fusilar [*foo-see*-LAHR]
★ **shop,** tienda [*t'*YEHN-*dah*]
shop window, vidriera [*vee-dr'*YEH-*rah*]
(to) **shop,** ir de compras [*eer deh* KOHM-*prahs*]

shore, orilla [*oh*-REE-*l'yah*]
short (not long), corto, -a [KOHR-*toh, -tah*]
(not tall), bajo, -a [BAH-*hoh, -hah*]
short cut, atajo [*ah*-TAH-*hoh*]
shortsighted, corto de vista [KOHR-*toh deh* VEES-*tah*]
in a short time, en poco tiempo [*ehn* POH-*koh t'*YEHM-*poh*]
shot, disparo [*dees*-PAH-*roh*]
should,

NOTE: No exact equivalent in Spanish. "Should" in the sense of obligation is rendered by the conditional forms of *deber.* (e.g.) *debería, deberíamos, deberían.*

We should go. Nosotros deberíamos ir. [*noh*-SOH-*trohs deh-beh*-REE-*ah-mohs eer*]
You should see it. Usted debería verlo. [*oos*-TEHD *deh-beh*-REE-*ah* VEHR-*loh*]
shoulder, hombro [OHM-*broh*]
(to) **shout,** gritar [GREE-*tahr*]
shovel, pala [PAH-*lah*]
show (theater), función (f) [*foon-th'*YOHN]
show (exhibition), exposición (f) [*ehks-poh-see-th'*YOHN]
(to) **show,** mostrar [*mohs*-TRAHR]
show me! ¡muéstreme! [MWEHS-*treh-meh*]
shower (bath), ducha [DOO-*chah*]
shrimp, camarón (m) [*kah-mah*-ROHN]
(to) **shrink,** encoger(se) [*ehn-koh*-HEHR-*seh*]
★ (to) **shut,** cerrar [*theh*-RRAHR]
★ **shut,** cerrado, -a [*theh*-RRAH-*doh, -dah*]
shutter, persiana [*pehr-s'*YAH-*nah*]
shy, tímido, -a [TEE-*mee-doh, -dah*]
★ **sick,** enfermo, -a [*ehn*-FEHR-*moh, -mah*]
sickness, enfermedad (f) [*ehn-fehr-meh*-DAHD]
side, lado [LAH-*doh*]
wrong side out, al revés [*ahl reh*-VEHS]

sidewalk, acera [*ah*-THEH-*rah*]
sight, vista [VEES-*tah*]
sign, signo [SEEG-*noh*]
(written sign), letrero [*leh*-TREH-*roh*]
(to) **sign,** firmar [*feer*-MAHR]
(to) **signal,** hacer señas [*ah*-THEHR SEH-*n'yahs*]
signature, firma [FEER-*mah*]
significance, significación (f) [*seeg-nee-fee-kah-th'*YOHN]
silence, silencio [*see*-LEHN-*th'yoh*]
silent, silencioso, -a [*see-lehn-th'*YOH-*soh, -sah*]
silently, silenciosamente [*see-lehn-th'yoh-sah*-MEHN-*teh*]
silk, seda [SEH-*dah*]
silly, tonto, -a [TOHN-*toh, -tah*]
silver, plata [PLAH-*tah*]
similar, parecido, -a [*pah-reh*-THEE-*doh, -dah*]
simple, simple [SEEM-*pleh*]
simply, simplemente [*seem-pleh*-MEHN-*teh*]
sin, pecado [*peh*-KAH-*doh*]
★ **since** (adv), desde [DEHS-*deh*]
since (conj), puesto que [PWEHS-*toh keh*]
since when? ¿desde cuándo? [DEHS-*deh* KWAHN-*doh*]
sincere, sincero, -a [*seen*-THEH-*roh, -rah*]
sincerely yours,

NOTE: The lengthy equivalent: *De usted muy atento y seguro servidor* is usually shortened to: *De Ud. muy atto y S.S.* [*deh oos*-TEHD *mwee ah*-TEHN-*toh ee seh*-GOO-*roh sehr-vee*-DOHR].

(to) **sing,** cantar [*kahn*-TAHR]
singer, cantante (m & f) [*kahn*-TAHN-*teh*]
single (alone), solo, -a [SOH-*loh, -ah*]
(not married), soltero [*sohl*-TEH-*roh*]
not a single one, ni uno solo [*nee* OO-*noh* SOH-*loh*]
(to) **sink,** hundir [*oon*-DEER]

★ **Sir,** señor, caballero [*seh-n'*YOHR, *kah-bah-l'*YEH-*roh*]
Note: In correspondence "Dear Sir" is translated *Muy señor mío* or *Muy señor nuestro.*
★ **sister,** hermana [*ehr*-MAH-*nah*]
sister-in-law, cuñada [*koo-n'*YAH-*dah*]
(to) **sit** (or) (to) **sit down,** sentarse [*sehn*-TAHR-*seh*]
Sit down, please! ¡Siéntese, por favor! [S'YEHN-*teh-seh pohr fah*-VOHR]
situated, situado, -a [*see*-TWAH-*doh, -dah*]
situation, situación (f) [*see-twah-th'*YOHN]
★ **six,** seis [SEH-*ees*]
★ **sixteen,** dieciséis (*d'*YEHTH-*ee*-SEH-*ees*]
sixth, sexto, -a [SEHKS-*toh, -tah*]
★ **sixty,** sesenta [*seh*-SEHN-*tah*]
size, tamaño [*tah*-MAH-*n'yoh*]
size (for clothes), talla [TAH-*l'yah*]
(to) **skate,** patinar [*pah-tee*-NAHR]
skeleton, esqueleto [*ehs-keh*-LEH-*toh*]
(to) **ski,** esquiar [*ehs-kee*-AHR]
skill, destreza [*dehs*-TREH-*thah*]
skilful, diestro, -a [*d'*YEHS-*troh, -trah*]
skin, piel (f) [*p'yehl*]
skirt, falda [FAHL-*dah*]
★ **sky,** cielo [*th'*YEH-*loh*]
skyscraper, rascacielos [*rahs-kah-th'*YEH-*lohs*]
slave, esclavo [*ehs*-KLAH-*voh*]
★ (to) **sleep,** dormir [*dohr*-MEER]
to be asleep, (estar) dormido [*ehs*-TAHR *dohr*-MEE-*doh*]
to be sleepy, tener sueño [*teh*-NEHR SWEH-*n'yoh*]
sleeping car, coche dormitorio [KOH-*cheh dohr-mee*-TOH *r'yoh*]
sleeve, manga [MAHN-*gah*]
slender, esbelto, -a [*ehs*-BEHL-*toh, -tah*]
slice, tajada [*tah*-HAH-*dah*]
slight, ligero, -a [*lee*-HEH-*roh, -rah*]
slightly, ligeramente [*lee-heh-rah*-MEHN-*teh*]
slip (fall), resbalón (m) [*rehs-bah*-LOHN]
(lingerie), combinación (f) [*kohm-bee-nah-th'*YOHN]

(to) **slip,** resbalar [*rehs-bah*-LAHR]
slippery, resbaloso, -a [*rehs-bah*-LOH-*soh, -sah*]
slippers, zapatillas [*thah-pah*-TEE-*l'yahs*]
★ **slow,** despacioso, -a [*dehs-pah-th'*YOH-*soh, -sah*]
slowly, despacio [*dehs*-PAH-*th'yoh*]
★ **small,** pequeño, -a [*peh*-KEH-*n'yoh, -n'yah*]
smaller, más pequeño, -a [*mahs peh*-KEH-*n'yoh, -n'yah*]
small change, dinero suelto [*dee*-NEH-*roh* SWEHL-*toh*]
smart (quick-witted), listo, -a [LEES-*toh, -tah*]
(to) **smash,** aplastar [*ah-plahs*-TAHR]
smell (n), olor (m) [*oh*-LOHR]
(to) **smell,** oler [*oh*-LEHR]
smile (n), sonrisa [*sohn*-REE-*sah*]
(to) **smile,** sonreir [*sohn-reh*-EER]
smoke (n), humo [OO-*moh*]
(to) **smoke** (tobacco), fumar [*foo*-MAHR]
smooth, liso, -a [LEE-*soh, -sah*]
snail, caracol (m) [*kah-rah*-KOHL].
snake, culebra [*koo*-LEH-*brah*]
(to) **sneeze,** estornudar [*ehs-tohr-noo*-DAHR]
(to) **snore,** roncar [*rohn*-KAHR]
★ **snow,** nieve (f) [*n'*YEH-*veh*]
(to) **snow,** nevar [*neh*-VAHR]
snow storm, tempestad de nieve (f) [*tehm-pehs*-TAHD *deh n'*YEH-*veh*]
★ **so,** así [*ah*-SEE]
and so forth, Y así por el estilo [*ee ah*-SEE *pohr ehl ehs*-TEE-*loh*]
I don't think so. Creo que no. [KREH-*oh keh noh*]
I hope so! ¡ojalá! [*oh-hah*-LAH]
I think so. Creo que sí. [KREH-*oh keh see*]
Is that so? ¿De veras? [*deh* VEH-*rahs*]
Just so, así mismo [*ah*-SEE MEES-*moh*]
Mr. So and So. El Sr. Fulano de Tal [*ehl seh-n'*YOHR *foo* LAH-*noh deh tahl*]
so far, hasta aquí [AHS-*tah ah*-KEE]
so so, así, así [*ah*-SEE *ah*-SEE]
so that, de manera que [*deh mah*-NEH-*rah keh*]

soap, jabón (m) [*hah*-BOHN]
sober, sobrio, -a [SOH-*br'yoh, -br'yah*]
social, social [*soh-th'*YAHL]
socialist, socialista (m & f) [*soh-th'yah*-LEES-*tah*]
society, sociedad (f) [*soh-th'yeh*-DAHD]
sock, calcetín (m) [*kahl-theh*-TEEN]
soda water, agua gaseosa [AH-*gwah gah-seh*-OH-*sah*]
sofa, sofá (m) [*soh*-FAH]
soft, blando, -a (or) suave [BLAHN-*doh, -dah,* SWAH-*veh*]
softness, suavidad (f) [*swah-vee*-DAHD]
soiled, sucio, -a [SOO-*th'yoh, -th'yah*]
soldier, soldado [*sohl*-DAH-*doh*]
sole (of shoe), suela [SWEH-*lah*]
sole (fish), lenguado [*lehn*-GWAH-*doh*]
sole (adj) (only one), único [OO-*nee-koh*]
solid, sólido, -a [SOH-*lee-doh, -dah*]
(to) **solve,** resolver [*reh-sohl*-VEHR]
★ **some** (adj), algún, alguna [*ahl*-GOON, *ahl*-GOO-*nah*]
(adv), algo de [AHL-*goh deh*]
Give me some. Déme un poco [DEH-*meh oon* POH-*koh*]
★ **somebody,** alguien [*ahl-g'*YEHN]
★ **something,** algo; alguna cosa [AHL-*goh; ahl*-GOO-*nah* KOH-*sah*]
some one (of others), alguno, -a [*ahl*-GOO-*noh, -nah*]
★ **sometimes,** algunas veces [*ahl*-GOO-*nahs* VEH-*thehs*]
somewhat, un poco [*oon* POH-*koh*]
somewhere, en alguna parte [*ehn ahl*-GOO-*nah* PAHR-*teh*]
somewhere else, en alguna otra parte [*ehn ahl*-GOO-*nah* OH-*trah* PAHR-*teh*]
★ **son,** hijo [EE-*hoh*]
son-in-law, yerno [YEHR-*noh*]
song, canción (f) [*kahn-th'*YOHN]
★ **soon,** pronto [PROHN-*toh*]
as soon as, tan pronto como [*tahn* PROHN-*toh* KOH-*moh*]
How soon? ¿Cuándo? [KWAHN-*doh*]
sooner or later, tarde o temprano [TAHR-*deh oh tehm*-PRAH-*noh*]
sore (adj), adolorido, -a [*ah-doh-loh*-REE-*doh, -dah*]

sore throat, dolor de garganta (m) [*doh*-LOHR DEH *gahr*-GAHN-*tah*]
sorrow, pena [PEH-*nah*]
sorrowful, triste [TREES-*teh*]
★ (to be) **sorry,** sentir [*sehn*-TEER]
I am very sorry. Lo siento mucho. [*loh s'*YEHN-*toh* MOO-*choh*]
sort, clase (f) [KLAH-*seh*]
soul, alma [AHL-*mah*]
sound (n), sonido [*soh*-NEE-*doh*]
(to) **sound,** sonar [*soh*-NAHR]
soup, sopa [SOH-*pah*]
sour, agrio, -a [AH-*gr'yoh, -gr'yah*]
south, sur (or) sud [*soor, sood*]
South America, América del Sur [*ah*-MEH-*ree-kah dehl soor*] (or) Suramérica [*soor-ah*-MEH-*ree-kah*]
South American, suramericano, -a [*soor-ah-meh-ree*-KAH-*noh, -nah*]
souvenir, recuerdo [*reh*-KWEHR-*doh*]
(to) **sow,** sembrar [*sehm*-BRAHR]
space, espacio [*ehs*-PAH-*th'yoh*]
spacious, espacioso, -a [*ehs-pah-th'*YOH-*soh, -sah*]
Spain, España [*ehs*-PAH-*n'yah*]
Spaniard or **Spanish,** español, -a [*ehs-pah-n'*YOHL, *-n'*YOH-*lah*]
★ **Spanish** (language), castellano (or) español [*kahs-teh-l'*YAH-*noh, ehs-pah-n'*YOHL]
Spanish American, hispanoamericano, -a [*ees*-PAH-*noh-ah-meh-ree*-KAH-*noh, -nah*]
spare parts, piezas de repuesto [*p'*YEH-*thahs deh reh* PWEHS-*toh*]
spare tire, neumático de repuesto [*neh-oo*-MAH-*tee-koh deh reh*-PWEHS-*toh*]
spark, chispa [CHEES-*pah*]
spark plug, bujía [*boo*-HEE-*ah*]
sparrow, gorrión (m) [*goh-rr'*YOHN]
★ (to) **speak,** hablar [*ah*-BLAHR]

Do you speak English? ¿Habla Ud. inglés? [AH-*blah oos*-TEHD *een*-GLEHS]

special, especial [*ehs-peh-th'*YAHL]

specially, especialmente [*ehs-peh-th'yahl*-MEHN-*teh*]

specialist, especialista (m & f) [*ehs-peh-th'yah*-LEES-*tah*]

specialty, especialidad (f) [*ehs-peh-th'yah-lee*-DAHD]

specification, especificación (f) [*ehs-peh-thee-fee-kah-th'*YOHN]

spectacle, espectáculo [*ehs-pehk*-TAH-*koo-loh*]

spectator, espectador, -a [*ehs-pehk-tah*-DOHR, *-rah*]

speech, discurso [*dees*-KOOR-*soh*]

speed, velocidad (f) [*veh-loh-thee*-DAHD]

full speed ahead, a toda velocidad [*ah*-TOH-*dah veh-loh-thee*-DAHD]

speed limit, límite de velocidad [LEE-*mee-teh deh veh-loh-thee*-DAHD]

speedy, veloz, rápido [*veh*-LOHTH, RAH-*pee-doh*]

(to) **spell,** deletrear [*deh-leh-treh*-AHR]

How is it spelled? ¿Cómo se deletrea? [KOH-*moh seh deh-leh*-TREH-*ah*]

(to) **spend** (money), gastar [*gahs*-TAHR]

(time), pasar [*pah*-SAHR]

spider, araña [*ah*-RAH-*n'yah*]

spinach, espinaca [*ehs-pee*-NAH-*kah*]

spine, columna vertebral [*koh*-LOOM-*nah vehr-teh*-BRAHL]

spiral, espiral [*ehs-pee*-RAHL]

spirit, espiritu (m) [*ehs*-PEE-*ree-too*]

spiritual, espiritual [*ehs-pee-ree*-TWAHL]

(to) **spit,** escupir [*ehs-koo*-PEER]

(in) **spite of,** a pesar de [*ah peh*-SAHR *deh*]

splendid, espléndido, -a [*ehs*-PLEHN-*dee-doh, -dah*]

(to) **split,** rajar [*rah*-HAHR]

(to) **spoil,** estropear [*ehs-troh-peh*-AHR]

sponge, esponja [*ehs*-POHN-*hah*]

sponsor, patrocinador, -a [*pah-troh-thee-nah*-DOHR, *-rah*]

★ **spoon,** cuchara [*koo*-CHAH-*rah*]

a teaspoonful, una cucharadita [OO-*nah koo-chah-rah*-DEE-*tah*]

tea spoon, cucharita [*koo-chah-*REE-*tah*]
sport, deporte (m) [*deh-*POHR-*teh*]
spot (place), lugar (m) [*loo-*GAHR]
spot (ink, etc.), mancha [MAHN-*chah*]
(to) **sprain,** torcer(se) [*tohr-*THEHR-*seh*]
(to) **spray,** rociar [*roh-th'*YAHR]
(to) **spread,** extender [*ehks-tehn-*DEHR]
★ **spring** (season), primavera [*pree-mah-*VEH-*rah*]
spring (in watches, etc.), resorte [*reh-*SOHR-*teh*]
spy, espía (m & f) [*ehs-*PEE-*ah*]
squad, escuadra [*ehs-*KWAH-*drah*]
square (adj), cuadrado, -a [*kwah-*DRAH-*doh, -dah*]
square (of a city), plaza [PLAH-*thah*]
squash, calabaza [*kah-lah-*BAH-*thah*]
(to) **squeeze** (fruit), exprimir [*ehks-pree-*MEER]
squirrel, ardilla [*ahr-*DEE-*l'yah*]
(to) **stab,** apuñalar [*ah-poo-n'yah-*LAHR]
stadium, estadio [*ehs-*TAH-*d'yoh*]
stage (theater), escenario [*ehs-theh-*NAH-*r'yoh*]
stain, mancha [MAHN-*chah*]
stairs (and) **staircase,** escalera [*ehs-kah-*LEH-*rah*]
stamp (in Spain), sello [SEH-*l'yoh*]
(in some other countries), estampilla [*ehs-tahm-*PEE-*l'yah*]
stand (m), puesto [PWEHS-*toh*]
(to) **stand,** estar de pie [*ehs-*TAHR *deh p'yeh*]
standing, de pie [*deh-p'yeh*]
(to) **stand up,** levantarse [*leh-vahn-*TAHR-*seh*]
standard (adj), corriente [*koh-rr'*YEHN-*teh*]
standpoint, punto de vista [POON-*toh deh* VEES-*tah*]
star, estrella [*ehs-*TREH-*l'yah*]
starboard, estribor [*ehs-tree-*BOHR]
starch, almidón (m) [*ahl-mee-*DOHN]
start (n), principio [*preen-*THEE-*p'yoh*]
★ (to) **start,** empezar [*ehm-peh-*THAHR]
starter (of a car], botón de arranque [*boh-*TOHN *deh ah-*RRAHN-*keh*]
(to) **starve,** morir de hambre [*moh-*REER *deh* AHM-*breh*] (lit: "to die of hunger")

statement (of fact), declaración (f) [*deh-klah-rah-th'*YOHN]
statement (of account), estado de cuenta [*ehs-*TAH-*doh deh* KWEHN-*tah*]
stateroom, camarote (m) [*kah-mah-*ROH-*teh*]
statesman, estadista [*ehs-tah-*DEES-*tah*]
station, estación (f) [*ehs-tah-th'*YOHN]
railway station, estación de ferrocarril [*ehs-tah-th'*YOHN *deh feh-rroh-kah-*RREEL]
statue, estatua [*ehs-*TAH-*twah*]
★ (to) **stay,** quedar(se) [*keh-*DAHR-*seh*]
At what hotel are you staying? ¿En qué hotel se hospeda? [*ehn keh* OH-*tehl seh ohs-*PEH-*dah*]
Stay here! ¡Quédese aquí! [KEH-*deh-seh ah-*KEE]
steady, firme [FEER-*meh*]
steak, biftec (or) filete [*beef-*TEHK or *fee-*LEH-*teh*]
(to) **steal,** robar [*roh-*BAHR]
steam, vapor [*vah-*POHR] (also can mean "steamship")
steamship line, línea de vapores [LEE-*neh-ah deh vah-*POH-*rehs*]
steel, acero [*ah-*THEH-*roh*]
steep, empinado, -a [*ehm-pee-*NAH-*doh, -dah*]
steering wheel, volante (m) [*voh-*LAHN-*teh*]
stenographer, taquígrafo, -a [*tah-*KEE-*grah-foh, -fah*]
step, paso [PAH-*soh*]
step-father, padrastro [*pah-*DRAHS-*troh*]
step-mother, madrastra [*mah-*DRAHS-*trah*]
(to) **step,** dar un paso [*dahr oon* PAH-*soh*]
(to) **step on,** pisar [*pee-*SAHR]
sterilized, esterilizado, -a [*ehs-teh-ree-lee-*THAH-*doh, -dah*]
stern (boat), popa [POH-*pah*]
stern (adj), severo, -a [*seh-*VEH-*roh, -rah*]
stew (food), guisado [*ghee-*SAH-*doh*]
steward, -ess, camarero, -a [*kah-mah-*REH-*roh, -rah*]
stick, palo [PAH-*loh*]
(to) **stick** (to fasten), fijar [*fee-*HAHR]
(to) **stick** (to glue), pegar [*peh-*GAHR]
stiff, tieso, -a [*t'*YEH-*soh, -sah*]

still (adj), tranquilo, -a [*trahn*-KEE-*loh, -lah*]
★ **still** (adv), todavía [*toh-dah*-VEE-*ah*]
still (however), sin embargo [*seen ehm*-BAHR-*goh*]
stimulant, estimulante [*ehs-tee-moo*-LAHN-*teh*]
sting, picadura [*pee-kah*-DOO-*rah*]
(to) **sting,** picar [*pee*-KAHR]
(to) **stir,** revolver [*reh-vohl*-VEHR]
stirrup, estribo [*ehs*-TREE-*boh*]
stock (share), acción (f) [*ahk-th'*YOHN]
stock (of merchandise), existencias [*ehk-sees*-TEHN *th'yahs*]
stock broker, corredor de bolsa [*koh-rreh*-DOHR *deh* BOHL-*sah*]
stock exchange, bolsa [BOHL-*sah*]
stocking, media [MEH-*d'yah*]
stolen, robado, -a [*roh*-BAH-*doh, -dah*]
stomach, estómago [*ehs*-TOH-*mah-goh*]
stomach-ache, dolor de estómago [*doh*-LOHR *deh ehs*-TOH-*mah-goh*]
stone, piedra [*p'*YEH-*drah*]
stop, parada [*pah*-RAH-*dah*]
★ (to) **stop,** parar [*pah*-RAHR]
Stop! (Halt!), ¡alto! [AHL-*toh*]
Stop here! ¡Pare aquí! [PAH-*reh ah*-KEE]
Stop that! ¡Deje eso! [DEH-*heh* EH-*soh*]
storage, almacenaje [*ahl-mah-theh*-NAH-*heh*]
★ **store,** tienda [*t'*YEHN-*dah*]
department store, almacenes (m, plural) [*ahl-mah*-THEH-*nehs*]
stork, cigüeña [*thee*-GWEH-*n'yah*]
storm, tormenta [*tohr*-MEHN-*tah*]
story (tale), cuento [KWEHN-*toh*]
story (floor), piso [PEE-*soh*]
stove, estufa [*ehs*-TOO-*fah*]
straight, recto, -a [REHK-*toh, -tah*]
straight ahead, derecho [*deh*-REH-*choh*]
strange, extraño, -a [*ehks*-TRAH-*n'yoh, -n'yah*]

stranger, extranjero, -a [*ehks-trahn*-HEH-*roh, -rah*]

NOTE: *extranjero* also means "foreign" and "foreigner."

strap, correa [*koh*-RREH-*ah*]
straw, paja [PAH-*hah*]
strawberry, fresa [FREH-*sah*]
stream, arroyo [*ah*-RROH-*yoh*]
★ **street,** calle (f) [KAH-*l'yeh*]
  streetcar, tranvía (m) [*trahn*-VEE-*ah*]
strength, fuerza [FWEHR-*thah*]
(to) **strengthen,** fortalecer [*fohr-tah-leh*-THEHR]
strict, estricto, -a [*ehs*-TREEK-*toh, -tah*]
strictly, estrictamente [*ehs-treek-tah*-MEHN-*teh*]
strike (n), huelga [WEHL-*gah*]
(to) **strike** (hit), pegar [*peh*-GAHR]
stripe, raya [RAH-*yah*]
strong, fuerte [FWEHR-*teh*]
structure, construcción (f) [*kohns-trook-th'*YOHN]
struggle (n), lucha [LOO-*chah*]
(to) **struggle,** luchar [*loo*-CHAHR]
stubborn, terco, -a [TEHR-*koh, -kah*]
student, estudiante [*ehs-too-d'*YAHN-*teh*]
study (n), estudio [*ehs*-TOO-*d'yoh*]
★ (to) **study,** estudiar [*ehs-too-d'*YAHR]
stuff (n),

NOTE: No exact equivalent. The nearest is *cosa:* "thing."

stupid, estúpido, -a [*ehs*-TOO-*pee-doh, -dah*]
style, estilo [*ehs*-TEE-*loh*]
subject, sujeto [*soo*-HEH-*toh*]

submarine, submarino [*soob-mah-*REE-*noh*]
(to) **submit,** someter [*soh-meh-*TEHR]
subsequently, subsecuentemente [*soob-seh-kwehn-teh-*MEHN-*teh*]
substantial, substancioso, -a [*soobs-tahn-th'*YOH-*soh, -sah*]
substitute (n), substituto, -a [*soobs-tee-*TOO-*toh, -tah*]
substitution, substitución [*soobs-tee-too-th'*YOHN]
subtraction, substracción [*soobs-trahk-th'*YOHN]
suburbs, afueras [*ah-*FWEH-*rahs*]
subway, metro [MEH-*troh*]
(to) **succeed in,** tener éxito en [*teh-*NEHR EHK-*see-toh ehn*]
success, éxito [EHK-*see-toh*]
successive, sucesivo, -a [*soo-theh-*SEE-*voh, -vah*]
successor, sucesor [*soo-theh-*SOHR]
such, tal [*tahl*]
Such is life, Así es la vida [*ah-*SEE *ehs lah* VEE-*dah*]
There is no such person, No hay tal persona [*noh I tahl pehr-*SOH-*nah*]
sudden, repentino [*reh-pehn-*TEE-*noh*]
suddenly, de repente [*deh reh-*PEHN-*teh*]
(to) **suffer,** sufrir [*soo-*FREER]
(to) **suffice,** bastar [*bahs-*TAHR]
sufficient, suficiente [*soo-fee-th'*YEHN-*teh*]
★ **sugar,** azúcar (m) [*ah-*THOO-*kahr*]
sugar bowl, azucarero, -a [*ah-thoo-kah-*REH-*roh, -rah*]
sugar cane, caña de azúcar [KAH-*n'yah deh ah-*THOO *kahr*]
(to) **suggest,** sugerir [*soo-heh-*REER]
suggestion, sugerencia [*soo-heh-*REHN-*th'yah*]
suicide (m), suicidio [*swee-*THEE-*d'yoh*]
(to) **commit suicide,** suicidar(se) [*swee-thee-*DAHR-*seh*]
★ **suit** (clothes), traje [TRAH-*heh*]
suit (court), juicio [HWEE-*th'yoh*]
(to) **suit,** convenir [*kohn-veh-*NEER]
suitable, conveniente [*kohn-veh-n'*YEHN-*teh*]
suitcase, maleta [*mah-*LEH-*tah*]
sum, suma [SOO-*mah*]
summary, sumario [*soo-*MAH-*r'yoh*]

★ **summer,** verano [*veh*-RAH-*noh*]
summit, cima [THEE-*mah*]
summons, citación [*thee-tah-th'*YOHN]
★ **sun,** sol (m) [*sohl*]
sunburn, quemadura de sol [*keh-mah*-DOO-*rah deh sohl*]
sunburned, tostado, -a [*tohs*-TAH-*doh, -dah*]
sunrise, salida del sol [*sah*-LEE-*dah dehl sohl*]
sunset, puesta del sol [PWEHS-*tah dehl sohl*]
★ **Sunday,** domingo [*doh*-MEEN-*goh*]
superb, soberbio, -a [*soh*-BEHR-*b'yoh, -b'yah*]
superfluous, supérfluo, -a [*soo*-PEHR-*floo-oh, -ah*]
superficial, superficial [*soo-pehr-fee-th'*YAHL]
superintendent, superintendente [*soo-pehr-een-tehn*-DEHN-*teh*]
superior, superior [*soo-peh-r'*YOHR]
superiority, superioridad (f) [*soo-peh-r'yoh-ree*-DAHD]
superstitious, supersticioso, -a [*soo-pehr-stee-th'*YOH-*soh, -sah*]
★ **supper,** cena [THEH-*nah*]
(to) **have supper,** cenar [*theh*-NAHR]
supply (n), provisión (f) [*proh-vee-s'*YOHN]
(to) **supply,** suministrar [*soo-mee-nees*-TRAHR]
(to) **support,** sostener [*sohs-teh*-NEHR]
(to) **suppose,** suponer [*soo-poh*-NEHR]
supreme, supremo, -a [*soo*-PREH-*moh, -mah*]
★ **sure,** seguro, -a [*seh*-GOO-*roh, -rah*]
Are you sure? ¿Está seguro? [*ehs*-TAH *seh*-GOO-*roh?*]

NOTE: This construction can also be used for "he," "she" (*segura*) and "it."

surely, seguramente [*seh-goo-rah*-MEHN-*teh*]
surface, superficie (f) [*soo-pehr*-FEE-*th'yeh*]
surgeon, cirujano [*thee-roo*-HAH-*noh*]
surprise, sorpresa [*sohr*-PREH-*sah*]

(to) **surprise,** sorprender [*sohr-prehn*-DEHR]
(to be) **surprised at,** sorprenderse de [*sohr-prehn*-DEHR-*seh deh*]
surprising, sorprendente [*sohr-prehn*-DEHN-*teh*]
(to) **surrender,** rendir(se) [*rehn*-DEER-*seh*]
(to) **surround,** rodear [*roh-deh*-AHR]
surroundings, alrededores (m plural) [*ahl-reh-deh*-DOH-*rehs*]
survivor, sobreviviente [*soh-breh-vee-v'*YEHN-*teh*]
(to) **suspect,** sospechar [*sohs-peh*-CHAHR]
suspicion, sospecha [*sohs*-PEH-*chah*]
suspicious, sospechoso, -a [*sohs-peh*-CHOH-*soh, -sah*]
swallow, golondrina [*goh-lohn*-DREE-*nah*]
(to) **swallow,** tragar [*trah*-GAHR]
swan, cisne (m) [THEES-*neh*]
(to) **swear,** jurar [*hoo*-RAHR]
sweat, sudor [*soo*-DOHR]
Sweden, Suecia [SWEH-*th'yah*]
Swedish, sueco, -a [SWEH-*koh, -kah*]
(to) **sweep,** barrer [*bah*-RREHR]
★ **sweet,** dulce [DOOL-*theh*]
sweet potato, batata [*bah*-TAH-*tah*]
sweetheart, novio, -a [NOH-*v'yoh, -v'yah*]
(to) **swell,** hinchar [*een*-CHAHR]
(to) **swim,** nadar [*nah*-DAHR]
swimmer, nadador, -a [*nah-dah*-DOHR, *-rah*]
swimming pool, piscina [*pees*-THEE-*nah*]
swing (n), columpio [*koh*-LOOM-*p'yoh*]
switch (electric), llave eléctrica [*l'*YAH-*veh eh*-LEHK-*tree-kah*]
Switzerland, Suiza [SWEE-*thah*]
sword, espada [*ehs*-PAH-*dah*]
syllable, sílaba [SEE-*lah-bah*]
sympathy, compasión [*kohm-pah-s'*YOHN]
my deepest sympathy, mi sentido pésame [*mee sehn*-TEE-*doh* PEH-*sah-meh*]
symphony, sinfonía [*seen-foh*-NEE-*ah*]
system, sistema [*sees*-TEH-*mah*]
systematic, sistemático, -a [*sees-teh*-MAH-*tee-koh, -kah*]

T

★ **table,** mesa [MEH-*sah*]
to set the table, poner la mesa [*poh*-NEHR *lah* MEHS-*ah*]
tablecloth, mantel (m) [*mahn*-TEHL]
tact, tacto [TAHK-*toh*]
tack, tachuela [*tah*-CHWEH-*lan*]
tail, cola [KOH-*lah*]
tailor, sastre (m) [SAHS-*treh*]
tailor shop, sastrería [*sahs-treh*-REE-*ah*]
★ (to) **take,** tomar [*toh*-MAHR]
take it, tómelo [TOH-*meh-loh*]
to take advantage of, aprovecharse de [*ah-proh-veh*-CHAHR-*seh deh*]
to take away, quitar [*kee*-TAHR]
to take care of, cuidar(se) de [*kwee*-DAHR-*(seh) deh*]
to take down, bajar [*bah*-HAHR]
to take leave, despedirse [*dehs-peh*-DEER-*seh*]
to take notice, notar [*noh*-TAHR]
to take off, quitar(se) [*keeh*-TAHR-*(seh)*]
to take the opportunity, aprovechar la oportunidad [*ah-proh-veh*-CHAHR *lah oh-pohr-too-nee*-DAHD]
to take out, sacar [*sah*-KAHR]
to take place, tener lugar [*teh*-NEHR *loo*-GAHR]
to take a walk, dar un paseo [*dahr oon pah*-SEH-*oh*]
(to) **take** (carry), llevar [*l'yeh*-VAHR]
talent, talento [*tah*-LEHN-*toh*]
talented, talentoso, -a [*tah-lehn*-TOH-*soh, -sah*]
talk (n), conversación (f) [*kohn-vehr-sah-th'*YOHN]
★ (to) **talk,** conversar [*kohn-vehr*-SAHR]
tall, alto, -a [AHL-*toh, -tah*]
tame, manso, -a [MAHN-*soh, -sah*]
tank, tanque (m) [TAHN-*keh*]
tape, cinta [THEEN-*tah*]
target, blanco [BLAHN-*koh*]
tariff, tarifa [*tah*-REE-*fah*]

taste, gusto [GOOS-*toh*]
  this tastes good ¡esto sabe bien! [EHS-*toh* SAH-*beh b'yehn*]
tax, impuesto [*eem*-PWEHS-*toh*]
taxi, taxi (m) [TAHK-*see*]
★ **tea,** té (m) [*teh*]
★ (to) **teach,** enseñar [*ehn-seh-n'*YAHR]
teacher, maestro, -a [*mah*-EHS-*troh, -ah*]
teaching, enseñanza [*ehn-seh-n'*YAHN-*thah*]
team, equipo [*eh*-KEE-*poh*]
teardrop, lágrima [LAH-*gree-mah*]
(to) **tear,** rasgar [*rahs*-GAHR]
technical, técnico, -a [TEHK-*nee-koh, -kah*]
teeth, dientes (m) [*d'*YEHN-*tehs*]
telegram, telegrama (m) [*teh-leh*-GRAH-*mah*]
telephone, teléphono [*teh*-LEH-*phoh-noh*]
  telephone book, guía telefónica [GHEE-*ah teh-leh*-FOH-*nee-kah*]
  telephone call, llamada telefónica [*l'yah*-MAH-*dah teh-leh*-FOH-*nee-kah*]
  telephone operator, telefonista [*teh-leh-foh*-NEES-*tah*]
(to) **telephone,** telefonear [*teh-leh-foh-neh*-AHR]
television, televisión (f) [*teh-leh-vee-s'*YOHN]
★ (to) **tell,** decir [*deh*-THEER]
  tell me, dígame [DEE-*gah-meh*]
  tell him (or her), dígale [DEE-*gah-leh*]
  don't tell him, no le diga [*noh leh* DEE-*gah*]
temple, templo [TEHM-*ploh*]
temporary, temporario, -a [*tehm-poh*-RAH-*r'yoh, -r'yah*]
temptation, tentación (f) [*tehn-tah-th'*YOHN]
★ **ten,** diez [*d'yehth*]
tenant, inquilino [*een-kee*-LEE-*noh*]
tendency, tendencia [*tehn*-DEHN-*th'yah*]
tender, tierno, -a [*t'*YEHR-*noh, -nah*]
tenderloin, filete (m) [*fee*-LEH-*teh*]
tennis, tenis (m) [TEH-*nees*]
tent, tienda [*t'*YEHN-*dah*]
tenth, décimo, -a [DEH-*thee-moh, -mah*]
term (and) **terminal,** término [TEHR-*mee-noh*]

terrace, terraza [*teh*-RRAH-*thah*]
terrible, terrible [*teh*-RREE-*bleh*]
terribly, terriblemente [*teh-rree-bleh*-MEHN-*teh*]
territory, territorio [*teh-rree*-TOH-*r'yoh*]
terror, terror (m) [*teh*-RROHR]
test, prueba [*proo*-EH-*bah*]
(to) **test,** probar [*proh*-BAHR]
text, texto [TEHKS-*toh*]
textile (n), tejido [*teh*-HEE-*doh*]
★ **than,** que [*keh*]
(to) **thank,** agradecer or dar las gracias a [*ah-grah-deh*-THEHR or *dahr lahs* GRAH-*th'yahs ah*]
★ **thank you,** gracias [GRAH-*th'yahs*]
thank you very much, muchas gracias [MOO-*chahs* GRAH-*th'yahs*]
thankful, agradecido, -a [*ah-grah*-DEH-*thee-doh, -dah*]
★ **that** (conj), que [*keh*]
★ **that** (demonstrative adj), ese, esa, aquel, aquella [EH-*seh*, EH-*sah, ah*-KEHL, *ah*-KEH-*l'yah*]
that (demonstrative pron), ése, ésa, aquél, aquélla [EH-*seh*, EH-*sah, ah*-KEHL, *ah*-KEH-*l'yah*]

NOTE: There are two words for "that." *Ese* signifies a "that" not so far away from the speaker as *aquel*. When the gender of "that" is not known it is translated as *eso*. *¿que es eso?* "what is that?"

that which, lo que [*loh keh*]
★ **the** (singular), el, la (plural) los, las [*ehl, lah, lohs, lahs*]
theater, teatro [*teh*-AH-*troh*]
theft, robo [ROH-*boh*]
★ **their,** su, sus [*soo, soos*]
NOTE: *Su* or *sus* agrees in number with the object possessed. "Their book" *Su libro* "Their books" *Sus libros*.
theirs, suyo, suya, de ellos, de ellas [soo-*yoh, -ah, deh*-EH-*l'yohs, deh*-EH-*l'yahs*]

★ **them,** los, las, or les (use before verb) [*lohs, lahs, lehs*]
(to) **them,** les [*lehs*]
themselves, ellos mismos, ellas mismas [EH-*l'yohs* MEES-*mohs,* EH-*l'yahs* MEES-*mahs*]
NOTE: Used reflexively "themselves" is rendered *se.*
They dress themselves, Ellos se visten [EH-*l'yohs seh* VEES-*tehn*]

★ **then,** entonces [*ehn*-TOHN-*thehs*]
now and then, de vez en cuando [*deh vehth ehn* KWAHN-*doh*]
theory, teoría [*teh-oh*-REE-*ah*]

★ **there,** ahí, allí, allá [*ah*-EE, *ah-l'*YEE, *ah-l'*YAH]
NOTE: There are three words for "there." *Ahí* signifies a "there" not so far away from the speaker as *allí* and *allá.*

★ there **is** (or) **there are,** hay [*eye*]

IMPORTANT NOTE: This is the key word for you to learn in Spanish; it means "is there?" "are there?" "there is," "there are" according to the context.

therefore, por eso [*pohr*-EH-*soh*]
thermometer, termómetro [*tehr*-MOH-*meh-troh*]

★ **these** (adj), estos, estas [EHS-*tohs,* EHS-*tahs*]
(pron), éstos, éstas [EHS-*tohs,* EHS-*tahs*]

★ **they,** ellos, ellas [EH-*l'yohs,* EH-*l'yahs*]
thick (for liquids), espeso, -a [*ehs*-PEH-*soh, -sah*]
thick (for solids), grueso, -a [GRWEH-*soh, -sah*]
thief, ladrón, ladrona [*lah*-DROHN, *lah*-DROH-*nah*]
thin, delgado, -a [*dehl*-GAH-*doh, -dah*]

★ **thing,** cosa [KOH-*sah*]

★ (to) **think,** pensar [*pehn*-SAHR]
Don't you think so? ¿No cree Ud.? [*noh* KREH-*eh oos*-TEHD]
I don't think so, Creo que no [KREH-*oh keh noh*]
NOTE: When belief is implied *creer* is preferred.

third, tercero [*tehr*-THEH-*roh*]
thirst, sed (f) [*sehd*]
★ (to be) **thirsty,** tener sed [*teh*-NEHR *sehd*]
★ **thirteen,** trece [TREH-*theh*]
★ **thirty,** treinta [TRAIN-*tah*]
★ **this** (adj), este, esta [EHS-*teh,* EHS-*tah*]
(pron), éste, ésta [EHS-*teh,* EHS-*tah*]
(neuter pron), esto [EHS-*toh*]
What is this? ¿Qué es esto? [KEH *ehs* EHS-*toh*]
thorn, espina [*ehs*-PEE-*nah*]
thoroughly, completamente [*kohm-pleh-tah*-MEHN-*teh*]
those (adj), esos, esas, aquellos, aquellas [EH-*sohs,* EH-*sahs, ah*-KEH-*l'yohs, ah*-KEH-*l'yahs*]
(pron), ésos, ésas, aquéllos, aquéllas [EH-*sohs,* EH-*sahs, ah*-KEH-*l'yohs, ah*-KEH-*l'yahs*]

NOTE: There are two words for "those": *esos* signifies a "those" not so far away from the speaker as *aquellos.*

though, aunque (AWN-*keh*]
thought, pensamiento [*pehn-sah-m'*YEHN-*toh*]
thoughtful (kind), atento, -a [*ah*-TEHN-*toh, -tah*]
thoughtless, desconsiderado, -a [*dehs-kohn-see-deh*-RAH-*doh, -dah*]
★ **thousand,** mil [*meel*]
thread, hilo [EE-*loh*]
threat, amenaza [*ah-meh*-NAH-*thah*]
(to) **threaten,** amenazar [*ah-meh-nah*-THAHR]
★ **three,** tres [*trehs*]
thrifty, ahorrativo, -a [*ah-oh-rrah*-TEE-*voh, -vah*]
thrilling, emocionante [*eh-moh-th'yoh*-NAHN-*teh*]
throat, garganta [*gahr*-GAHN-*tah*]
(to have a sore) **throat,** tener dolor de garganta [*teh*-NEHR-*doh*-LOHR-*deh gahr*-GAHN-*tah*]
throne, trono [TROH-*noh*]

through (adv), a través de [*ah trah*-VEHS-*deh*]
through (finished), terminado, -a [*tehr-mee*-NAH-*doh, -dah*]
throughout, por todo [*pohr*-TOH-*doh*]
(to) **throw, throw away,** tirar [*tee*-RAHR]
thumb, pulgar (m) [*pool*-GAHR]
thunder, trueno [TRWEH-*noh*]
★ **Thursday,** jueves [HWEH-*vehs*]
thus, así [*ah*-SEE]
ticket (for trains), billete (m) [*bee-l'*YEH-*teh*]
(for shows), entrada [*ehn*-TRAH-*dah*]
ticket window, taquilla [*tah*-KEE-*l'yah*]
(round trip) **ticket,** billete de ida y vuelta [*bee-l'*YEH-*teh deh* EE-*dah ee* VWEHL-*tah*]
tide, marea [*mah*-REH-*ah*]
tie (necktie), corbata [*kohr*-BAH-*tah*]
tiger, tigre (m) [TEE-*greh*]
tight, apretado, -a [*ah-preh*-TAH-*doh, -dah*]
(to) **tighten,** apretar [*ah-preh*-TAHR]
tile, teja [TEH-*hah*]
till (adv), hasta [AHS-*tah*]
★ **time** (extent), tiempo [*t'*YEHM-*poh*]
time (occasion), vez [*vehth*]
What time is it? ¿Qué hora es? [*keh* OH-*rah ehs*]
At what time? ¿A qué hora? [*ah keh* OH-*rah*]
Have a good time! Diviértase [*dee-v'*YEHR-*tah-seh*]
At times, A veces [*ah* VEH-*thehs*]
How much time ago? ¿Cuánto tiempo hace? [KWAHN-*toh t'*YEHM-*poh* AH-*theh*]
tip (of money), propina [*proh*-PEE-*nah*]
tip (end), punta [POON-*tah*]
timid, tímido, -a [TEE-*mee-doh, -dah*]
tire (of a car), llanta or neumáutico [*l'*YAHN-*tah, neh-oo* MAH-*tee-koh*]
★ **tired,** cansado, -a [*kahn*-SAH-*doh, -dah*]
tiresome, aburrido, -a [*ah-boo*-RREE-*doh, -dah*]
tissue paper, papel de seda [*pah*-PEHL *deh* SEH-*dah*]
title, títúlo [TEE-*too-loh*]

★ **to,** a [*ah*]
toast (for breakfast), tostada [*tohs*-TAH-*dah*]
toast (to one's health), brindis (m) [BREEN-*dees*]
tobacco, tabaco [*tah*-BAH-*koh*]
★ **today,** hoy [*oy*]
from today on, desde hoy en adelante [DEHS-*deh oy ehn ah-deh*-LAHN-*teh*]
toe, dedo [DEH-*doh*]
NOTE: Since "toe" and "finger" both are *dedo* you must say *dedo del pie* or *dedo de la mano* when necessary to differentiate between them.
★ **together,** juntos, -as [HOON-*tohs, -tahs*]
toilet, excusado [*eks-koo*-SAH-*doh*]
(to) **tolerate,** tolerar [*toh-leh*-RAHR]
tomato, tomate (m) [*toh*-MAH-*teh*]
tomato juice, jugo de tomate [HOO-*goh deh toh*-MAH-*teh*]
tomb, tumba [TOOM-*bah*]
tomorrow, mañana [*mah-n'*YAH-*nah*]
tomorrow morning, mañana por la mañana [*mah-n'*YAH-*nah pohr lah mah-n'*YAH-*nah*]
ton, tonelada [*toh-neh*-LAH-*dah*]
tone, tono [TOH-*noh*]
tongue, lengua [LEHN-*gwah*]
★ **tonight,** esta noche [EHS-*tah* NOH-*cheh*]
★ **too** (too much or too many), demasiado, -a [*deh-mah-s'*YAH-*doh, -dah*]
★ **too** (also), también [*tahm-b'*YEHN]
tool, herramienta [*eh-rrah-m'*YEHN-*tah*]
tooth (front), diente (m) [*d'*YEHN-*teh*]
(back), muela [MWEH-*lah*]
toothache, dolor de muelas [*doh*-LOHR *deh* MWEH-*lahs*]
toothbrush, cepillo de dientes [*theh*-PEE-*l'yoh deh d'*YEHN-*tehs*]
top (cover), tapa [TAH-*pah*]
top (high point), cumbre [KOOM-*breh*]
on top of, encima de [*ehn*-THEE-*mah deh*]
topic, tópico [TOH-*pee-koh*]
toreador, torero (NEVER toreador) [*toh*-REH-*roh*]

torn, roto, -a [ROH-*toh, -tah*]
total, total [*toh*-TAHL]
(to) **touch,** tocar [*toh*-KAHR]
touching, conmovedor, -a [*kohn-moh-veh*-DOHR, *-rah*]
tough, duro, -a [DOO-*roh, -rah*]
tour, jira [HEE-*rah*]
tourist, turista (m or f) [*too*-REES-*tah*]
★ **toward,** hacia [AH-*th'yah*]
towel, toalla [*toh*-AH-*l'yah*]
tower, torre (f) [TOH-*rreh*]
★ **town,** pueblo [PWEH-*bloh*]
townhall, ayuntamiento [*ah-yoon-tah-m'*YEHN-*toh*]
toy, juguete (m) [*hoo*-GHEH-*teh*]
trace, rastro [RAHS-*troh*]
track, vía [VEE-*ah*]
trade, comercio [*koh*-MEHR-*th'yoh*]
trade mark, marca de fábrica [MAHR-*kah deh* FAH-*bree kah*]
tradition, tradición (f) [*trah-dee-th'*YOHN]
traditional, tradicional [*trah-dee-th'yoh*-NAHL]
traffic (automobile), tránsito [TRAHN-*see-toh*]
tragedy, tragedia [*trah*-HEH-*d'yah*]
tragic, trágico, -a [TRAH-*hee-koh, -kah*]
train, tren (m) [*trehn*]
training, entrenamiento [*ehn-treh-nah-m'*YEHN-*toh*]
traitor or **treacherous,** traidor, -a [*trah-ee*-DOHR, *-rah*]
(to) **transfer,** trasladar [*trahs-lah*-DAHR]
(to) **transform,** transformar [*trahns-fohr*-MAHR]
(in) **transit,** de tránsito [*deh* TRAHN-*see-toh*]
(to) **translate,** traducir [*trah-doo*-THEER]
translation, traducción (f) [*trah-dook-th'*YOHN]
translator, traductor, -a [*trah-dook*-TOHR, *-rah*]
transmission, transmisión (f) [*trahns-mee-s'*YOHN]
(to) **transmit,** transmitir [*trahns-mee*-TEER]
transportation, transportación (f) [*trahns-pohr-tah-th'*YOHN]
trap, trampa [TRAHM-*pah*]
(to) **travel,** viajar [*v'yah*-HAHR]
traveler, viajero, -a [*v'yah*-HEH-*roh, -rah*]

travel agency, agencia de viajes [*ah*-HEHN-*th'yah deh v'*YAH-*hehs*]
tray, bandeja [*bahn*-DEH-*hah*]
treasure, tesoro [*teh*-SOH-*roh*]
treasurer, tesorero, -a [*teh-soh*-REH-*roh, -rah*]
treasury, tesorería [*teh-soh-reh*-REE-*ah*]
(to) **treat,** tratar [*trah*-TAHR]

NOTE: Remember that *tratar de* means "to try."

treatment, tratamiento [*trah-tah-m'*YEHN-*toh*]
treaty, tratado [*trah*-TAH-*doh*]
★ **tree,** árbol (m) [AHR-*bohl*]
(to) **tremble,** temblar [*tehm*-BLAHR]
tremendous, tremendo, -a [*treh*-MEHN-*doh, -dah*]
trial (legal), juicio [HWEE-*th'yoh*]
trial (test), prueba [PRWEH-*bah*]
triangle, triángulo [*tree*-AHN-*goo-loh*]
tribe, tribu (f) [TREE-*boo*]
trick, engaño [*ehn*-GAH-*n'yoh*]
★ **trip,** viaje (m) [*v'*YAH-*heh*]
triple, triple [TREE-*pleh*]
triumphant, triunfante [*tree-oon*-FAHN-*teh*]
trivial, trivial [*tree-v'*YAHL]
trolley car, tranvía (m) [*trahn*-VEE-*ah*]
troop, tropa [TROH-*pah*]
tropical, tropical [*troh-pee*-KAHL]
trouble, molestia [*moh*-LEHS-*t'yah*]
It is no trouble! ¡No es molestia! [*noh ehs moh*-LEHS-*t'yah*]
(to) **trouble,** molestar [*moh-lehs*-TAHR]
Don't trouble yourself! ¡No se moleste! [*noh seh moh*-LEHS-*teh*]
trousers, pantalones (m plural) [*pahn-tah*-LOH-*nehs*]
trout, trucha [TROO-*chah*]

truck, camión (m) [*kah-m'*YOHN]
★ **true,** verdadero, -a [*vehr-dah*-DEH-*roh, -rah*]
  Is it true? ¿Es verdad? [*ehs vehr*-DAHD]
trunk, baúl (m) [*bah*-OOL]
(to) **trust** (in), confiar (en) [*kohn-f'*YAHR-*(ehn)*]
truth, verdad [*vehr*-DAHD]
(to) **try,** tratar de [*trah*-TAHR-*deh*]
(to) **try on,** probarse [*proh*-BAHR-*seh*]
tube, tubo [TOO-*boh*]
tuberculosis, tuberculosis (f) [*too-behr-koo*-LOH-*sees*]
★ **Tuesday,** martes (m) [MAHR-*tehs*]
tugboat, remolcador (m) [*reh-mohl-kah*-DOHR]
tulip, tulipán (m) [*too-lee*-PAHN]
tune (for singing), tonada [*toh*-NAH-*dah*]
tunnel, túnel (m) [TOO-*nehl*]
Turkey, Turquía [*toor*-KEE-*ah*]
turkey (for eating), pavo [PAH-*voh*]
Turkish, turco, -a [TOOR-*koh, -kah*]
turn (in order), turno [TOOR-*noh*]
turn (of a road), viraje (m) [*vee*-RAH-*heh*]
(to) **turn,** virar [*vee*-RAHR]
  to turn around, dar vuelta [*dahr* VWEHL-*tah*]
  turn off (light), apagar [*ah-pah*-GHAHR]
  turn on (light), encender [*ehn-thehn*-DEHR]
turtle, tortuga [*tohr*-TOO-*ghah*]
★ **twelve,** doce [DOH-*theh*]
★ **twenty,** veinte [VAIN-*teh*]
twice, dos veces [*dohs*-VEH-*thehs*]
twin, gemelos [*heh*-MEH-*lohs*]
★ **two,** dos [*dohs*]
(the) **two,** los dos [*lohs-dohs*], las dos [*lahs-dohs*]
(to) **twist,** torcer [*tohr*-THEHR]
type, tipo [TEE-*poh*]
(to) **typewrite,** escribir a máquina [*ehs-kree*-BEER *ah* MAH-*kee-nah*]
typical, típico, -a [TEE-*pee-koh, -kah*]
tyranny, tiranía [*tee-rah*-NEE-*ah*]
typist, mecanógrafo, -a [*meh-kah*-NOH-*grah-foh, -fah*]

U

ugly, feo, -a [FEH-*oh, -ah*]
umbrella, paraguas (m) [*pah-rah*-GWAHS]
(to be) **unable,**

NOTE: Use appropriate forms of *poder* preceded by *no:* "I am unable to come." *No puedo venir.*

uncle, tío [TEE-*oh*]
unbearable, insoportable [*een-soh-pohr*-TAH-*bleh*]
uncertain, incierto, -a [*een-th'*YEHR-*toh, -tah*]
uncomfortable, incómodo, -a [*een*-KOH-*moh-doh, -dah*]
unconscious, inconsciente [*een-kohns-th'*YEHN-*teh*]
★ **under** (or) **underneath,** debajo de [*deh*-BAH-*hoh deh*]
underground, subterráneo, -a [*soob-teh*-RRAH-*neh-oh, -ah*]
★ (to) **understand,** comprender [*kohm-prehn*-DEHR]
Do you understand? ¿Comprende Ud.? [*kohm*-PREHN-*deh oos*-TEHD]
It is understood. Está comprendido. [*ehs*-TAH *kohm-prehn*-DEE-*doh*]
(to) **undertake,** emprender [*ehm-prehn*-DEHR]
undertaking, empresa [*ehm*-PREH-*sah*]
underwear, ropa interior [ROH-*pah een-teh-r'*YOHR]
(to) **undress,** desvestirse [*dehs-vehs*-TEER-*seh*]
uneasy, intranquilo, -a [*een-trahn*-KEE-*loh, -lah*]
unemployed, desempleado, -a [*deh-sehm-pleh*-AH-*doh, -dah*]
unequal, desigual [*deh-see*-GWAHL]
unexpected, inesperado, -a [*ee-nehs-peh*-RAH-*doh, -dah*]
unfair, injusto, -a [*een*-HOOS-*toh, -tah*]
unfaithful, infiel (m, f) [*een-f'*YEHL]
unfavorable, desfavorable [*dehs-fah-voh*-RAH-*bleh*]
unforeseen, imprevisto, -a [*eem-preh*-VEES-*toh, -tah*]

unforgettable, inolvidable [*ee-nohl-vee*-DAH-*bleh*]
unfortunate, desgraciado, -a [*dehs-grah-th'*YAH-*doh, -dah*]
unfortunately, desgraciadamente [*dehs-grah-th'yah-dah-*MEHN-*teh*]
ungrateful, malagradecido, -a [*mah-lah-grah-deh*-THEE-*doh, -dah*]
unhappy, infeliz [*een-feh*-LEETH]
unhealthy, malsano, -a [*mahl*-SAH-*noh, -nah*]
uniform, uniforme (m) [*oo-nee*-FOHR-*meh*]
unimportant, sin importancia [*seen eem-pohr*-TAHN-*th'yah*]
union, unión (f) [*oo-n'*YOHN]
unit, unidad (f) [*oo-nee*-DAHD]
(to) **unite,** unir [*oo*-NEER]
United States, (los) Estados Unidos [(*lohs*) *ehs*-TAH-*dohs oo-*NEE-*dohs*]

NOTE: The U.S.A. generally referred to as *Los Estados Unidos del Norte.* Venezuela, México and Brazil are also "United States."

universal, universal [*oo-nee-vehr*-SAHL]
universe, universo [*oo-nee*-VEHR-*soh*]
university, universidad (f) [*oo-nee-vehr-see*-DAHD]
unjust, injusto, -a [*een*-HOOS-*toh, -tah*]
unknown, desconocido, -a [*dehs-koh-noh*-THEE-*doh, -dah*]
unlawful, ilegal [*ee-leh*-GHAHL]
unless, a menos que [*ah* MEH-*nohs keh*]
(to) **unload,** descargar [*dehs-kahr*-GHAHR]
unlucky, desafortunado, -a [*deh-sah-fohr-too*-NAH-*doh, -dah*]
(to) **unpack,** desempaquetar [*deh-sehm-pah-keh*-TAHR]
unpleasant, desagradable [*deh-sah-grah*-DAH-*bleh*]
unsafe, peligroso, -a [*peh-lee*-GROH-*soh, -sah*]
★ **until,** hasta [AHS-*tah*]
untrue, falso, -a [FAHL-*soh, -sah*]
unusual, excepcional [*ehks-thehp-th'yoh*-NAHL]

(to be) **unwilling,**

NOTE: No equivalent word. Use appropriate forms of *querer* preceded by *no.*

up, arriba [*ah*-RREE-*bah*]

to get up, levantarse [*leh-vahn*-TAHR-*seh*]

to go down, bajar [*bah*-HAHR]

to go up, subir [*soo*-BEER]

up hill, cuesta arriba [KWEHS-*tah-ah*-RREE-*bah*]

up to now, hasta ahora [AHS-*tah-ah*-OH-*rah*]

upon, sobre [SOH-*breh*]

upper, superior [*soo-peh-r'*YOHR]

upper floor, piso de arriba [PEE-*soh-deh-ah*-RREE-*bah*]

(to) **upset,** trastornar [*trahs-tohr*-NAHR]

upside down, al revés [*ahl reh*-VEHS]

upstairs, arriba [*ah*-RREE-*bah*]

urgent, urgente [*oor*-HEHN-*teh*]

Uruguay, Uruguay [*oo-roo*-GWAHY]

Uruguayan, uruguayo, -a [*oo-roo*-GWAH-*yoh, -yah*]

us, nos [*nohs*]

to us, nos (or) a nosotros [*nohs, ah noh*-SOH-*trohs*]

use, uso [OO-*soh*]

★ (to) **use,** usar [*oo*-SAHR]

to be used (to), estar acostumbrado, -a [*ehs*-TAHR *ah-kohs*-TOOM-*brah-doh, -dah*]

What is this used for? ¿Para que sirve esto? [PAH-*rah keh* SEER-*veh* EHS-*toh*]

useful, útil [OO-*teel*]

useless, inútil [*ee*-NOO-*teel*]

usher, acomodador, -a [*ah-koh-moh-dah*-DOHR, -*rah*]

usual, usual [*oo*-SWAHL]

usually, generalmente [*heh-neh-rahl*-MEHN-*teh*]

V

vacant, vacante [*vah*-KAHN-*teh*]

vacation, vacaciones (f, plural) [*vah-kah-th'*YOH-*nehs*]

vaccination, vacuna [*vah*-KOO-*nah*]
vacuum cleaner, aspiradora [*ahs-pee-rah*-DOH-*rah*]
vain, vanidoso, -a [*vah-nee*-DOH-*soh, -sah*]
in vain, en vano [*ehn* VAH-*noh*]
valley, valle (m) [VAH-*l'yeh*]
valuable, valioso, -a [*vah-l'*YOH-*soh, -sah*]
value, valor [*vah*-LOHR]
valve, válvula [VAHL-*voo-lah*]
vanilla, vainilla [*vy*-NEE-*l'yah*]
variety, variedad (f) [*vah-r'yeh*-DAHD]
various, varios, -as [VAH-*r'yohs, -r'yahs*]
(to) **vary,** variar [*vah-r'*YAHR]
vast, vasto, -a [VAHS-*toh, -tah*]
veal, ternera [*tehr*-NEH-*rah*]
vegetables, verduras [*vehr*-DOO-*rahs*]
vehicle, vehículo [*veh*-EE-*koo-loh*]
veil, velo [VEH-*loh*]
vein, vena [VEH-*nah*]
velvet, terciopelo [*tehr-th'yoh*-PEH-*loh*]
verb, verbo [VEHR-*boh*]
verse, verso [VEHR-*soh*]
vertical, vertical [*vehr-tee*-KAHL]
★ **very,** muy [*mwee*]
very much, mucho, -a [MOO-*choh, -chah*]
very well, muy bien [*mwee b'*YEHN]
vest, chaleco [*chah*-LEH-*koh*]
veterinary, veterinario [*veh-teh-ree*-NAH-*r'yoh*]
vice, vicio [VEE-*th'yoh*]
vice-president, vice-presidente [VEE-*theh-preh-see*-DEHN-*teh*]
vicinity, vecindad (f) [*veh-theen*-DAHD]
victim, víctima (f) [VEEK-*tee-mah*]
victory, victoria [*veek*-TOH-*r'yah*]
view, vista [VEES-*tah*]
vigorous, vigoroso, -a [*vee-ghoh*-ROH-*soh, -sah*]
village, pueblecito (or) aldea [*pweh-bleh*-THEE-*toh, ahl*-DEH-*ah*]
vinegar, vinagre (m) [*vee*-NAH-*greh*]

vineyard, viña [VEE-*n'yah*]
violence, violencia [*v'yoh*-LEHN-*th'yah*]
violet, violeta [*v'yoh*-LEH-*tah*]
violin, violín (m) [*v'yoh*-LEEN]
virgin, virgen (f) [VEER-*hehn*]
virtue, virtud (f) [*veer*-TOOD]
virtuous, virtuoso, -a [*veer*-TWOH-*soh, -sah*]
visa, visa [VEE-*sah*]
visible, visible [*vee*-SEE-*bleh*]
visit, visita [*vee*-SEE-*tah*]
(to) **visit,** visitar [*vee-see*-TAHR]
  to pay a visit to, hacer una visita [*ah*-THEHR OO-*nah vee*-SEE-*tah*]
visitor, visitante [*vee-see*-TAHN-*teh*]
vitamin, vitamina [*vee-tah*-MEE-*nah*]
voice, voz (f) [*voth*]
volcano, volcán (m) [*vohl*-KAHN]
volt, voltio [VOHL-*t'yoh*]
volume, volumen (m) [*voh*-LOO-*mehn*]
voluntary (and) **volunteer,** voluntario, -a [*voh-loon*-TAH *r'yoh, -r'yah*]
vote, voto [VOH-*toh*]
(to) **vote,** votar [*voh*-TAHR]
voyage, viaje (m) [*v'*YAH-*heh*]
vulgar, vulgar [*vool*-GHAHR]
vulture, buitre (m) [BWEE-*treh*]

W

wages, sueldo [SWEHL-*doh*]
wagon, carreta [*kah*-RREH-*tah*]
waist, cintura [*theen*-TOO-*rah*]
★ (to) **wait,** esperar [*ehs-peh*-RAHR]
  wait a moment! ¡espere un momento! [*ehs*-PEH-*reh oon moh*-MEHN-*toh*]
  wait for me here! ¡espéreme aquí! [*ehs*-PEH-*reh-meh ah*-KEE]

waiter, camarero [*kah-mah*-REH-*roh*]
waiting room, sala de espera [SAH-*lah deh ehs*-PEH-*rah*]
waitress, camarera [*kah-mah*-REH-*rah*]
★ (to) **wake** (up), despertar(se) [*dehs-pehr*-TAHR-(*seh*)]
★ (to) **walk,** caminar [*kah-mee*-NAHR]
to take a walk, dar un paseo [*dahr oon pah*-SEH-*oh*]
walk, paseo [*pah*-SEH-*oh*]
wall, pared (f) [*pah*-REHD]
wallet, portamonedas (m) [*pohr-tah-moh*-NEH-*dahs*]
walnut, nogal (m) [*noh*-GAHL]
waltz, vals (m) [*vahls*]
★ (to) **want,** querer [*keh*-REHR]

NOTE: When used with another verb the second verb remains in the infinitive form. "Do you want to go?" *¿Quiere Ud. ir?*

★ **war,** guerra [GHEH-*rrah*]
warehouse, almacén (m) [*ahl-mah*-THEHN]
warm, tibio, -a [TEE-*b'yoh, -b'yah*]
(to) **warm** (up), calentar [*kah-lehn*-TAHR]
(to) **warn,** advertir [*ahd-vehr*-TEER]
warning (n), aviso [*ah*-VEE-*soh*]
warship, buque (m) de guerra [BOO-*keh deh* GHEH-*rrah*]
★ **was,** era, estaba [EH-*rah, ehs*-TAH-*bah*]
NOTE: For general use "I was"—*Yo era.* "He or she was"—*El or ella era.* For position, "I was"—*Yo estaba.* "He or she was"—*El* or *ella estaba.*
★ (there) **was,** había [*ah-b'*YAH]
(to) **wash,** lavar [*lah*-VAHR]
wash basin, lavabo [*lah*-VAH-*boh*]
washing machine, máquina de lavar [MAH-*kee-nah deh lah*-VAHR]
wasp, avispa [*ah*-VEES-*pah*]
(to) **waste,** malgastar [*mahl-gahs*-TAHR]
wastebasket, cesto de papeles [THEHS-*toh deh pah*-PEH-*lehs*]

watch, reloj (m) [*reh*-LOH]
  pocket watch, reloj de bolsillo [*reh*-LOH *deh bohl*-SEE-*l'yoh*]
  watchmaker, relojero [*reh-loh*-HEH-*roh*]
  wrist watch, reloj pulsera [*reh*-LOH *pool*-SEH-*rah*]
(to) **watch,** observar [*ohb-sehr*-VAHR]
★ **watch out!** ¡cuidado! [*kwee*-DAH-*doh*]
★ **watchman,** guardia (m) [GWAHR-*d'yah*]
★ **water,** agua [AH-*gwah*]
  fresh water, agua dulce [AH-*gwah* DOOL-*theh*]
  mineral water, agua mineral [AH-*gwah mee-neh*-RAHL]
  running water, agua corriente [AH-*gwah-koh-rr'*YEHN-*teh*]
waterfall, cascada [*kahs*-KAH-*dah*]
watermelon, melón de agua [*meh*-LOHN *deh* AH-*gwah*]
waterproof, impermeable [*eem-pehr-meh*-AH-*bleh*]
wave (electric, hair, etc.), onda [OHN-*dah*]
  (sea), ola [OH-*lah*]
  short wave, onda corta [OHN-*dah* KOHR-*tah*]
(to) **wave,** ondear; hacer señas [*ohn-deh*-AHR; *ah*-THEHR SEH-*n'yahs*]
wax, cera [THEH-*rah*]
★ **way** (manner), modo, manera [MOH-*doh, mah*-NEH-*rah*]
  (road), camino [*kah*-MEE-*noh*]
  anyway, de todas maneras [*deh* TOH-*dahs mah*-NEH-*rahs*]
  by the way, a propósito [*ah-proh*-POH-*see-toh*]
  in no way, de ninguna manera [*deh neen*-GOO-*nah mah*-NEH-*rah*]
  in this way, de esta manera [*deh* EHS-*tah mah*-NEH-*rah*]
  Which is the way to Taxco? ¿Cómo se va a Taxco? [KOH-*moh seh vah ah* TAHKS-*koh*]
★ **we,** nosotros, -as [*noh*-SOH-*trohs, -trahs*]
weak, débil [DEH-*beel*]
weakness, debilidad (f) [*deh-bee-lee*-DAHD]
wealth, riqueza [*ree*-KEH-*thah*]
wealthy, rico, -a [REE-*koh, -kah*]
weapon, arma [AHR-*mah*]
(to) **wear,** usar [*oo*-SAHR]

weather, tiempo [*t'*YEHM-*poh*]

How is the weather? ¿Cómo está el tiempo? [KOH-*moh ehs*-TAH *ehl t'*YEHM-*poh*]

web, telaraña [*teh-lah*-RAH-*n'yah*]

wedding, boda [BOH-*dah*]

Wednesday, miércoles (m) [*m'*YEHR-*koh-lehs*]

★ **week,** semana [*seh*-MAH-*nah*]

last week, la semana pasada [*lah seh*-MAH-*nah pah*-SAH-*dah*]

next week, la semana próxima [*lah seh*-MAH-*nah* PROHK-*see-mah*]

week end, fin (m) de semana [*feen deh seh*-MAH-*nah*]

(to) **weep,** llorar [*l'yoh*-RAHR]

weight, peso [PEH-*soh*]

(to) **weigh,** pesar [*peh*-SAHR]

welcome, bienvenido, -a [*b'yehn-veh*-NEE-*doh, -dah*]

(to) **welcome,** dar la bienvenida [*dahr lah b'yehn-veh*-NEE-*dah*]

★ (you are) **welcome,** de nada [*deh* NAH-*dah*]

well (n), pozo [POH-*zoh*]

★ **well** (adv), bien [*b'yehn*]

(to be) **well,** (estar) bien [(*ehs*-TAHR) *b'yehn*]

well bred, bien educado, -a [*b'yehn-eh-doo*-KAH-*doh, -dah*]

well known, muy conocido, -a [*mwee koh-noh*-THEE-*doh, -dah*]

well off, acomodado, -a [*ah-koh-moh*-DAH-*doh, -dah*]

★ **very well!** ¡Está bien! [*ehs*-TAH-*b'yehn*]

well (interjc)! ¡Bueno! [BWEH-*noh*]

well . . . (as hesitation), pues . . . [*pwehs*]

★ **were,** for nosotros: éramos or estábamos (EH-*rah-mohs* or *ehs*-TAH-*bah-mohs*]

for Uds., ellos, ellas: eran or estaban [EH-*rahn* or *ehs*-TAH-*bahn*]

SEE: **Is and are.**

★ (there) **were,** había [*ah*-BEE-*ah*]

★ **west,** oeste [*oh*-EHS-*teh*]

western, occidental [*ohk-thee-dehn*-TAHL]

West Indies, las Antillas [*lahs-ahn*-TEE-*l'yahs*]

wet, mojado, -a [*moh*-HAH-*doh, -dah*]
(to) **get wet,** mojar(se) [*moh*-HAHR-(*seh*)]
whale, ballena [*bah-l'*YEH-*nah*]
★ **what,** que [*keh*]
What a pity! ¡Qué lástima! [*keh* LAHS-*tee-mah*]
What else? ¿Qué más? [*keh mahs*]
What for? ¿Para qué? [PAH-*rah keh*]
What is the matter? ¿Qué pasa? [*keh*-PAH-*sah*]
whatever, cualquiera [*kwahl-k'*YEH-*rah*]
NOTE: Drop the *a* when you use it before a noun.
whatever you wish, lo que usted quiera [*loh keh oos*-TEHD *k'*YEH-*rah*]
wheat, trigo [TREE-*goh*]
wheel, rueda [RWEH-*dah*]
steering wheel, volante [*voh*-LAHN-*teh*]
when, cuando [KWAHN-*doh*]
since when, desde cuando [DEHS-*deh* KWAHN-*doh*]
When will you (he) (she) return? ¿Cuándo regresará? [KWAHN-*doh reh-greh-sah*-RAH]
★ **where,** donde [DOHN-*deh*]
Where is it (he) (she)? ¿Dónde está? [DOHN-*deh ehs*-TAH]
wherever, dondequiera [DOHN-*deh-k'*YEH-*rah*]
whether, si [*see*]
★ **which** (of several), cual [*kwahl*]
(relative pronoun), que [*keh*]
while (conj), mientras [*m'*YEHN-*trahs*]
(a short) **while ago,** hace poco tiempo [AH-*theh* POH-*koh t'*YEHM-*poh*]
whip, látigo [LAH-*tee-goh*]
whipped cream, crema batida [KREH-*mah bah*-TEE-*dah*]
(to) **whisper,** susurrar [*soo-soo*-RRAR]
whistle (n) (noise), silbido [*seel*-BEE-*doh*]
whistle (n) (instrument), silbato [*seel*-BAH-*toh*]
★ **white,** blanco, -a [BLAHN-*koh, -kah*]
★ **who,** quien [*k'yehn*], quienes (plural) [*k'*YEH-*nehs*]
whoever, quienquiera [*k'yehn-k'*YEH-*rah*]
whole, entero, -a [*ehn*-TEH-*roh, -rah*]
wholesale, al por mayor [*ahl pohr mah*-YOHR]

★ **whom,** a quien; a quienes [*ah-k'yehn; ah-k'*YEH-*nehs*]
whose (interrogative), ¿de quién? [*deh-k'*YEHN], plural ¿de quiénes? [*deh-k'*YEH-*nehs*]
(relative), cuyo, -a [KOO-*yoh, -yah*], plural cuyos, -as [KOO-*yohs, -yahs*]
★ **why?** ¿por qué? [*pohr*-KEH]
why not? ¿por qué no? [*pohr*-KEH-*noh*]
wide, ancho, -a [AHN-*choh, -ah*]
widow, viuda [*v'*YOO-*dah*]
widower, viudo [*v'*YOO-*doh*]
width, anchura [*ahn*-CHOO-*rah*]
★ **wife,** esposa [*ehs*-POH-*sah*]
wild, salvaje [*sahl*-VAH-*heh*]
★ **will** (to express future) (See note on "shall")
will (testament), testamento [*tehs-tah*-MEHN-*toh*]
will (for polite requests),
NOTE: Use forms of *querer*. "Will you have a cigarette? *¿Quiere Ud. un cigarrillo?*
willing, dispuesto, -a [*dees*-PWEHS-*toh, -tah*]
willingly, de buena gana [*deh* BWEH-*nah* GAH-*nah*]
(to) **win,** ganar [*gah*-NAHR]
wind, viento [*v'*YEHN-*toh*]
(to) **wind a watch,** dar cuerda a un reloj [*dahr* KWEHR-*dah ah oon reh*-LOH]
windmill, molino de viento [*moh*-LEE-*noh deh v'*YEHN-*toh*]
window, ventana [*vehn*-TAH-*nah*]
(to be) **windy,** hacer viento [*ah*-THEHR *v'*YEHN-*toh*]
wine, vino [VEE-*noh*]
red wine, vino tinto [VEE-*noh* TEEN-*toh*]
white wine, vino blanco [VEE-*noh* BLAHN-*koh*]
wing, ala [AH-*lah*]
NOTE: Although *ala* is a feminine word, it uses the article *el* in the singular.
winner, vencedor [*vehn-theh*-DOHR]
winter, invierno [*een-v'*YEHR-*noh*]
wire (metal), alambre (m) [*ah*-LAHM-*breh*]
(to) **wire** (telegram), telegrafiar [*teh-leh-grah-f'*YAHR]

wisdom, sabiduría [*sah-bee-doo-*REE-*ah*]
wise, sabio, -a [SAH-*b'yoh, -b'yah*]
wish, deseo [*deh-*SEH-*oh*]
(to) **wish,** desear [*deh-seh-*AHR]
  What do you wish? ¿Qué desea Ud.? [*keh deh-*SEH-*ah oos-*TEHD]
wit, ingenio [*een-*HEH-*n'yoh*]
witch, bruja [BROO-*hah*]
★ **with,** con [*kohn*]
(to) **withdraw,** retirar [*reh-tee-*RAHR]
within, dentro de [DEHN-*troh-deh*]
★ **without,** sin [*seen*]
witness, testigo [*tehs-*TEE-*goh*]
(to) **witness,** presenciar [*preh-sehn-th'*YAHR]
witty, gracioso, -a [*grah-th'*YOH-*soh, -sah*]
wolf, lobo [LOH-*boh*]
★ **woman,** mujer [*moo-*HEHR]
(to) **wonder,** preguntarse [*preh-goon-*TAHR-*seh*]
wonderful, maravilloso, -a [*mah-rah-vee-l'*YOH-*soh, -ah*]
wonderfully, maravillosamente [*mah-rah-vee-l'yoh-sah-*MEHN-*teh*]
★ **wood,** madera [*mah-*DEH-*rah*]
wooden, de madera [*deh-mah-*DEH-*rah*]
woods, bosque (m) [BOHS-*keh*]
wool, lana [LAH-*nah*]
woolen, de lana [*deh-*LAH-*nah*]
word, palabra [*pah-*LAH-*brah*]
work, trabajo [*trah-*BAH-*hoh*]
  work of art, obra de arte [OH-*brah deh* AHR-*teh*]
★ (to) **work,** trabajar [*trah-bah-*HAHR]
  This isn't working. Esto no funciona [EHS-*toh noh foon-th'*YOH-*nah*]
  Where do you work? ¿Dónde trabaja? [DOHN-*deh trah-*BAH-*hah*] (Also applicable for "he" and "she")
worker, obrero [*oh-*BREH-*roh*]
★ **world,** mundo [MOON-*doh*]
world war, guerra mundial [GHEH-*rrah moon-d'*YAHL]
worm, gusano [*goo-*SAH-*noh*]

worn out (for objects), gastado, -a [*gahs*-TAH-*doh, -dah*]
(for persons), agotado, -a [*ah-goh*-TAH-*doh, -dah*]
worry, preocupación (f) [*preh-oh-koo-pah-th'*YOHN]
(to) **worry,** preocuparse [*preh-oh-koo*-PAHR-*seh*]
worried, preocupado, -a [*preh-oh-koo*-PAH-*doh, -dah*]
don't worry! ¡No se preocupe! [*noh seh preh-oh*-KOO-*peh*]
worse, peor [*peh*-OHR]
worse than, peor que [*peh*-OHR *ken*]
worst, el peor, la peor [*ehl-peh*-OHR, *lah peh*-OHR]
lo peor (unspecified gender) [*loh peh*-OHR]
worth, valor (m) [*vah*-LOHR]
How much is this worth? ¿Cuánto vale esto? [KWAHN-*toh* VAH-*leh*-EHS-*toh*]
worthy, digno, -a [DEEG-*noh, -nah*]
★ **would,**

NOTE: To say "I would," "he would," "she would," "you would," add *ía* to the infinitive of the verb in question. For "we would" add *íamos* and for "they would", "you would" add *ían*. Ex.: "I would go"—*yo iría*. "We would eat"—*Nosotros comeríamos.*

wounded, herido, -a [*eh*-REE-*doh, -dah*]
(to) **wrap up,** envolver [*ehn-vohl*-VEHR]
wrench (tool), llave inglesa [*l'*YAH-*veh een*-GLEH-*sah*]
wrestling, lucha libre [LOO-*chah* LEE-*breh*]
wrinkle, arruga [*ah*-RROO-*gah*]
wrist, muñeca [*moo-n'*YEH-*kah*]
NOTE: *Muñeca* also means "doll."
★ (to) **write,** escribir [*ehs-kree*-BEER]
writer, escritor [*ehs-kree*-TOHR]
writing, escritura [*ehs-kree*-TOO-*rah*]
in writing, por escrito [*pohr-ehs*-KREE-*toh*]
writing paper, papel de escribir [*pah*-PEHL *deh ehs-kree* BEER]
wrong, equivocado, -a [*eh-kee-voh*-KAH-*doh, -dah*]
(to) **be wrong,** estar equivocado, -a [*ehs*-TAHR *eh-kee-voh*-KAH-*doh, -dah*]

Y

yard (measure), yarda [YAHR-*dah*]

NOTE: The *metro,* approximately 40 inches, is usually employed as the unit of measure in Spanish countries. See metric table at rear of book.

(to) **yawn,** bostezar [*bohs-teh*-THAHR]

yacht, yate (m) [YAH-*teh*]

★ **year,** año [AH-*n'yoh*]

last year, el año pasado [*ehl* AH-*n'yoh pah*-SAH-*doh*]

next year, el año próximo [*ehl* AH-*n'yoh* PROHK-*see-moh*]

yearly (adv), anualmente [*ah-noo-ahl*-MEHN-*teh*]

(to) **yell,** gritar [*gree*-TAHR]

★ **yellow,** amarillo, -a [*ah-mah*-REE-*l'yoh, -l'yah*]

★ **yes,** sí [*see*]

yes indeed! ¡ya lo creo! [*yah loh* KREH-*oh*]

★ **yesterday,** ayer [*ah*-YEHR]

yesterday evening, anoche [*ah*-NOH-*cheh*]

the day before yesterday, anteayer [*ahn-teh-ah*-YEHR]

★ **not yet,** todavía no [*toh-dah*-VEE-*ah noh*]

yet (however), sin embargo [*seen ehm*-BAHR-*goh*]

★ **you** (formal and polite form), usted (Ud.) [*oos*-TEHD], plural ustedes (Uds.) [*oos*-TEH-*dehs*]

NOTE: If used as an object as in "I see you" or "I give the money to you," use *le.* These two sentences are translated *Yo le veo* and *Yo le doy el dinero.* For plural use *les* in the same fashion. Direct and indirect object forms are *te.* Plural forms are *vosotros* for the subject and *os* for the object.

you (familiar), tú [*too*]

NOTE: Use the familiar *tú* only when speaking to close friends or relatives. The object and possessive forms are *te* and *tú* respectively. The plural of *tú* is *vosotros.*

★ **young,** joven [HOH-*vehn*]
  the young man, el joven [*ehl* HOH-*vehn*]
  the young woman, la joven [*lah* HOH-*vehn*]
your (formal and polite form), su [*soo*], plural sus [*soos*]
your (familiar), tu [*too*], plural tus [*toos*]
yours (formal and polite form), suyo, -a [*soo-yoh, -ah*]
yours (familiar form), tuyo, -a [TOO-*yoh, -ah*]
Very truly yours (correspondence), de Ud. muy atto. y S. S. [*deh oos*-TEHD *mooy ah*-TEHN-*toh ee seh*-GOO-*roh sehr-vee*-DOHR]
yourself (formal), Usted mismo, -a [*oos*-TEHD MEES-*moh, mah*]
  (See note on "myself")
yourself (familiar), tú mismo, -a [*too*-MEES-*moh, -mah*]
  (See note on "myself")
yourselves (formal), Ustedes mismos, -as [*oos*-TEH-*dehs* MEES-*mohs, -mahs*]
  (See note on "myself")
yourselves (familiar), vosotros, -as mismos, -as [*voh*-SOH-*trohs, -ahs* MEES-*mohs, -mahs*]
  (See note on "myself")
youth, juventud (f) [*hoo-vehn*-TOOD]

Z

zebra, cebra [THEH-*brah*]
zero, cero [THEH-*roh*]
zipper, cremallera [*kreh-mah-l'*YEH-*rah*]
zone, zona [THOH-*nah*]
zoo, jardín (m) zoológico [*hahr*-DEEN *thoh-oh*-LOH-*hee-koh*]

A

★ a [*ah*] to; at

NOTE: For expressing time or indicating location *à* is used: *a las cuatro:* "at four o'clock." *Llegamos a la estación:* "We are arriving at the station." *A* is also used before a proper noun or person when it is the direct object. *Veo a Roberto:* "I see Robert."

abajo [*ah*-BAH-*hoh*] down; below
abandonado, -a [*ah-bahn-doh*-NAH-*doh, -dah*] abandoned
abandonar [*ah-bahn-doh*-NAHR] to abandon
abanico [*ah-bah*-NEE-*koh*] fan
abastecer [*ah-bahs-teh*-THEHR] to supply
abeja [*ah*-BEH-*hah*] bee
abierto, -a [*ah-b'*YEHR-*toh, -tah*] open
abochornado, -a [*ah-boh-chohr*-NAH-*doh, -dah*] embarrassed
abogado [*ah-boh*-GAH-*doh*] lawyer
aborrecer [*ah-boh-rre*-THEHR] to despise
abrazar [*ah-brah*-THAHR] to embrace
abrazo [*ah*-BRAH-*thoh*] embrace (n)
abreviatura [*ah-breh-v'yah*-TOO-*rah*] abbreviation
abridor [*ah-bree*-DOHR] opener (n)
abrigo [*ah*-BREE-*goh*] overcoat
  abrigo de pieles [*ah*-BREE-*goh deh p'*YEH-*lehs*] fur coa.
abril [*ah*-BREEL] April
★ **abrir** [*ah*-BREER] to open
abrochar [*ah-broh*-CHAHR] to fasten
absolutamente [*ahb-soh-loo-tah*-MEHN-*teh*] absolutely
absoluto, -a [*ahb-soh*-LOO-*toh, -tah*] absolute

absurdo, -a [*ahb*-SOOR-*doh, -dah*] absurd
abuelo, -a [*ah*-BWEH-*loh, -lah*] grandfather, grandmother
abundancia [*ah-boon*-DAHN-*th'yah*] abundance
abundante [*ah-boon*-DAHN-*teh*] abundant
aburrido, -a [*ah-boo*-RREE-*doh,- dah*] boring
aburrir [*ah-boo*-RREER] to bore
abuso [*ah*-BOO-*soh*] abuse (n)
★ **acá** [*ah*-KAH] here
acabado [*ah-kah*-BAH-*doh*] finished
acabar [*ah-kah*-BAHR] to finish
academia [*ah-kah*-DEH-*m'yah*] academy
acariciar [*ah-kah-ree-th'*YAHR] to caress
acaso [*ah*-KAH-*soh*] perhaps
  por si acaso [*pohr see ah*-KAH-*soh*] (just) in case
accidente (m) [*ak-thee*-DEHN-*teh*] accident
acción (f) [*ahk-th'*YOHN] action
aceite (m) [*ah*-THAY-*teh*] oil
aceituna [*ah-thay*-TOO-*nah*] olive
acelerar [*ah-theh-leh*-RAHR] to accelerate
acento [*ah*-THEHN-*toh*] accent
aceptar [*ah-thehp*-TAHR] to accept
acera [*ah*-THEH-*rah*] sidewalk
★ **acerca (de)** [*ah*-THEHR-*kah (deh)*] about
acercar(se) [*ah-thehr*-KAHR-*(seh)*] to approach
acero [*ah*-THEH-*roh*] steel
ácido (n and adj) [AH-*thee-doh*] acid
aclarar [*ah-klah*-RAHR] to clarify
acogida [*ah-koh*-HEE-*dah*] reception
acomodador, -a [*ah-koh-moh-dah*-DOHR, *-rah*] usher (in a theater)
acomodar [*ah-koh-moh*-DAHR] to arrange
acompañar [*ah-kohm-pah-n'*YAHR] to accompany
aconsejar [*ah-kohn-seh*-HAHR] to advise
acontecer [*ah-kohn-teh*-THEHR] to happen
acontecimiento [*ah-kohn-teh-thee-m'*YEHN-*toh*] event
acordar [*ah-kohr*-DAHR] to agree or to remind
acordar(se) de [*ah-kohr*-DAHR-*(seh) deh*] to remember
acostar(se) [*ah-kohs*-TAHR-*(seh)*] to go to bed

acostumbrado, -a [*ah-kohs-toom*-BRAH-*doh, -dah*] accustomed
acostumbrar [*ah-kohs-toom*-BRAHR] to accustom or to be accustomed
acreedor, -a [*ah-kreh-eh*-DOHR, *-rah*] creditor
acta [AHK-*tah*] deed (legal)
activo, -a [*ahk*-TEE-*voh, -vah*] active
acto [AHK-*toh*] act
actor [*ahk*-TOHR] actor
actriz (f) [*ahk*-TREETH] actress
actual [*ahk*-TWAHL] present

NOTE: *Actual* never has the meaning of the English "real" or "actual."

actualidad (f) [*ahk-twah-lee*-DAHD] present time
actualmente [*ahk-twahl*-MEHN-*teh*] at present
actuar [*ahk*-TWAHR] to act (theater)
acuarela [*ah-kwah*-REH-*lah*] water-color (painting)
acudir [*ah-koo*-DEER] to attend
acuerdo [*ah*-KWEHR-*doh*] agreement
acusar [*ah-koo*-SAHR] to accuse; to acknowledge (receipt of a letter)
adecuado, -a [*ah-deh*-KWAH-*doh, -dah*] adequate
adelantado, -a [*ah-deh-lahn*-TAH-*doh, -dah*] advanced
adelantar [*ah-deh-lahn*-TAHR] to advance
adelantar(se) [*ah-deh-lahn*-TAHR-*(seh)*] to be in advance
★ **¡adelante!** [*ah-deh*-LAHN-*teh*] Forward! Come in!
adelgazar [*ah-dehl-gah*-THAHR] to become thin
además [*ah-deh*-MAHS] moreover, besides
adentro [*ah*-DEHN-*troh*] inside
adición (f) [*ah-dee-th'*YOHN] addition
adicional [*ah-dee-th'yoh*-NAHL] additional
★ **adiós** [*ah-d'*YOHS] goodbye
adivinar [*ah-dee-vee*-NAHR] to guess
adjetivo [*ahd-heh*-TEE-*voh*] adjective

adjunto, -a [*ahd*-HOON-*toh, -tah*] enclosed
administración (f) [*ahd-mee-nees-trah-th'*YOHN] administration
administrador, -a [*ahd-mee-nees-trah*-DOHR, *-rah*] administrator
admiración (f) [*ahd-mee-rah-th'*YOHN] admiration
admirador, -a [*ahd-mee-rah*-DOHR, *-rah*] admirer
admirar [*ahd-mee*-RAHR] to admire
admisión (f) [*ahd-mee-s'*YOHN] admission
admitir [*ahd-mee*-TEER] to admit; to accept
★ **¿adónde?** [*ah*-DOHN-*deh*] where? where to?
adorable [*ah-doh*-RAH-*bleh*] adorable
adornar [*ah-dohr*-NAHR] to adorn
adquirir [*ahd-kee*-REER] to acquire
adrede [*ah*-DREH-*deh*] on purpose
aduana [*ah*-DWAH-*nah*] customs house
adulto, -a [*ah*-DOOL-*toh, -tah*] adult
adverbio [*ahd*-VEHR-*byoh*] adverb
advertencia [*ahd-vehr*-TEHN-*th'yah*] warning
advertir [*ahd-vehr*-TEER] to warn
aéreo [*ah*-EH-*reh-oh*] (pertaining to air)
  por correo aéreo [*pohr koh*-RREH-*oh ah*-EH-*reh-oh*] by airmail
aeroplano [*ah-eh-roh*-PLAH-*noh*] airplane
afectar [*ah-fehk*-TAHR] to affect
afecto [*ah*-FEHK-*toh*] affection
afeitada [*ah-fay*-TAH-*dah*] shave
afeitar(se) [*ah-fay*-TAHR-*(seh)*] to shave oneself
aficionado, -a [*ah-fee-th'yoh*-NAH-*doh, -dah*]
  NOTE: No exact equivalent in English; it means "fond of" or in the case of sports etc., a "fan."
afiliar(se) [*ah-fee-l'*YAHR-*(seh)*] to become affiliated with
afirmar [*ah-feer*-MAHR] to affirm
afligir [*ah-flee*-HEER] to afflict
aflojar [*ah-floh*-HAHR] to loosen
afortunadamente [*ah-fohr-too-nah-dah*-MEHN-*teh*] fortunately
afortunado, -a [*ah-fohr-too*-NAH-*doh, -dah*] fortunate

afuera (prep) [*ah*-FWEH-*rah*] outside
afueras (n) (f plural) [*ah*-FWEH-*rahs*] surroundings (of a town)
agarrar [*ah-gah*-RRAHR] to grasp
agencia [*ah*-HEHN-*th'yah*] (agency)
agente [*ah*-HEHN-*teh*] agent
ágil [AH-*heel*] agile
agitación (f) [*ah-hee-tah-th'*YOHN] agitation, excitement
agitar [*ah-hee*-TAHR] to stir; to shake up
agosto [*ah*-GOHS-*toh*] August; harvest time
agotar [*ah-goh*-TAHR] to exhaust
agradable [*ah-grah*-DAH-*bleh*] agreeable
agradar [*ah-grah*-DAHR] to please

NOTE: To express liking for something, use *agradar* with the indirect object. *Me agrada*—"I like it."

agradecer [*ah-grah-deh*-THEHR] to thank (for)
Se lo agradezco mucho [*seh loh ah-grah*-DETH-*koh moo-choh*] thank you very much for it
agradecido, -a [*ah-grah-deh*-THEE-*doh, -dah*] grateful
agradecimiento [*ah-grah-deh-thee-m'*YEHN-*toh*] gratitude
agrado [*ah*-GRAH-*doh*] pleasure
agregado, -a [*ah-greh*-GAH-*doh, -dah*] attached
agregar [*ah-greh*-GAHR] to add (to)
agresivo, -a [*ah-greh*-SEE-*voh, -vah*] aggressive
agricultor (m) [*ah-gree-kool*-TOHR] farmer
agricultura [*ah-gree-kool*-TOO-*rah*] agriculture
agrio, -a [AH-*gr'yoh, -ah*] sour
★ **agua** [AH-*gwah*] water
agua corriente [AH-*gwah koh*-RR'YEHN-*teh*] running water
agua dulce [AH-*gwah* DOOL-*theh*] fresh water
agua tibia [AH-*gwah* TEE-*b'yah*] warm water
aguacate (m) [*ah-gwah*-KAH-*teh*] alligator pear (avocado)
aguacero [*ah-gwah*-THEH-*roh*] heavy shower

aguantar [*ah-gwahn*-TAHR] to endure
aguardar [*ah-gwahr*-DAHR] to wait (for)
aguardiente [*ah-gwahr-d'*YEHN-*teh*] brandy
agudo, -a [*ah*-GOO-*doh, -dah*] sharp
águila [AH-*ghee-lah*] eagle
aguja [*ah*-GOO-*hah*] needle
agujero [*ah-goo*-HEH-*roh*] hole
★ **ahí** [*ah*-EE] there
por ahí [*pohr ah*-EE] over there
ahijado, -a [*ah-ee*-HAH-*doh, -dah*] godson, goddaughter
ahogar(se) [*ah-oh*-GAHR-*(seh)*] to drown
★ **ahora** [*ah*-OH-*rah*] now
ahora mismo [*ah*-OH-*rah* MEES-*moh*] right now
por ahora [*pohr ah*-OH-*rah*] for the present
ahorrar [*ah-oh*-RRAHR] to save (economy)
ahorros (m plural) [*ah*-OH-*rrohs*] savings
★ **aire** (m) [EYE-*reh*] air
al aire libre [*ahl* EYE-*reh* LEE-*breh*] in the open air
aislar [*eyes*-LAHR] to isolate
ajedrez (m) [*ah-heh*-DRETH] chess
ajeno, -a [*ah*-HEH-*noh, -ah*] (pertaining to another person or place, *En tierra ajena*—"In another land")
ají (m) [*ah*-HEE] hot pepper
ajo [AH-*hoh*] garlic
ajustar [*ah-hoos*-TAHR] to adjust
★ **al** [*ahl*] (contraction of *a* and *el*, "to" and "the")

NOTE: When *al* precedes an infinitive, it can mean "when." *Al llegar yo a casa.* "When I arrived home."

ala [AH-*lah*] wing
NOTE: Although *ala* is feminine, the masculine article *el* is used in the singular for euphony.
alabar [*ah-lah*-BAHR] to praise
alacrán (m) [*ah-lah*-KRAHN] scorpion

alambre (m) [*ah*-LAHM-*breh*] wire
alameda [*ah-lah*-MEH-*dah*] public walk
alargar [*ah-lahr*-GAHR] to extend
alarma [*ah*-LAHR-*mah*] alarm
albañil (m) [*ahl-bah-n'*YEEL] mason
albaricoque (m) [*ahl-bah-ree*-KOH-*keh*] apricot
albóndiga [*ahl*-BOHN-*dee-gah*] meat ball
alboroto [*ahl-boh*-ROH-*toh*] disturbance
alcalde (m) [*ahl*-KAHL-*deh*] mayor
alcance (m) [*ahl*-KAHN-*theh*] reach
alcanzar [*ahl-kahn*-THAHR] to reach
alcoba [*ahl*-KOH-*bah*] bedroom
alcohol (m) [*ahl-koh*-OHL] alcohol
aldea [*ahl*-DEH-*ah*] village
alegrar(se) [*ah-leh*-GRAHR-*(seh)*] to be glad
  me alegro mucho que [*meh ah*-LEH-*groh* MOO-*choh keh*] I am very glad that
alegre [*ah*-LEH-*greh*] joyful, gay
alegría [*ah-leh*-GREE-*ah*] joy
alejar(se) [*ah-leh*-HAHR-*(seh)*] to go away
Alemania [*ah-leh*-MAH-*n'yah*] Germany
alemán, -na [*ah-leh*-MAHN, *-nah*] German
alérgico, -a [*ah*-LEHR-*hee-koh, -kah*] allergic
alfabeto [*ahl-fah*-BEH-*toh*] alphabet
alfiler (m) [*ahl-fee*-LEHR] pin
alfombra [*ahl*-FOHM-*brah*] rug
álgebra [AHL-*heh-brah*] algebra
★ **algo** [AHL-*goh*] something
  algo más [AHL-*goh mahs*] something more
  algo que hacer [AHL-*goh keh ah*-THEHR] something to do
algodón (m) [*ahl-goh*-DOHN] cotton
alguien [AHL-*g'yehn*] somebody, someone, anybody, anyone
alguno, -a [*ahl*-GOO-*noh, -nah*] some, someone
  NOTE: *Alguno* drops the *o* before a masculine singular noun. *algún hombre:* "some man."
  alguna cosa [*ahl*-GOO-*nah* KOH-*sah*] something
  algunas veces [*ahl*-GOO-*nahs* VEH-*thehs*] sometimes
alhaja [*ahl*-AH-*hah*] jewel

aliado, -a [*ahl'*YAH-*doh, -dah*] allied
aliento [*ah-l'*YEHN-*toh*] breath
alimento [*ah-lee-*MEHN-*toh*] food, nutriment
alistar [*ah-lees-*TAHR] to enlist
aliviar [*ah-lee-v'*YAHR] to relieve
alivio [*ah-*LEE-*v'yoh*] relief
★ **allá** [*ahl-l'*YAH] there
por allá [*pohr ah-l'*YAH] there
★ **allí** [*ah-l'*YEE] over there
alma [AHL-*mah*] soul

NOTE: Although *alma* is feminine, the masculine article *el* is used in the singular for harmony.

almacén (m) [*ahl-mah-*THEHN] warehouse
almacenes (m plural) [*ahl-mah-*THEH-*nehs*] department store
almeja [*ahl-*MEH-*hah*] clam
almendra [*ahl-*MEHN-*drah*] almond
almíbar (m) [*ahl-*MEE-*bahr*] sirup
almidón (m) [*ahl-mee-*DOHN] starch
almirante (m) [*ahl-mee-*RAHN-*teh*] admiral
almohada [*ahl-moh-*AH-*dah*] pillow
almorzar [*ahl-mohr-*THAHR] to have lunch
almuerzo [*ahl-*MWEHR-*thoh*] lunch
alquilar [*ahl-kee-*LAHR] to rent
se alquila [*seh ahl-*KEE-*lah*] for rent
alquiler (m) [*ahl-kee-*LEHR] rent
de alquiler [*deh ahl-kee-*LEHR] for rent
alrededor [*ahl-reh-deh-*DOHR] around
altamar [*ahl-tah-*MAHR] high seas
altar (m) [*ahl-*TAHR] altar
alterar [*ahl-teh-*RAHR] to alter
alto, -a [AHL-*toh, -tah*] high or tall
¡Alto! [AHL-*toh*] Halt!

altoparlante [*ahl-toh-pahr-*LAHN-*teh*] loudspeaker
altura [*ahl-*TOO-*rah*] height
alumbrar [*ah-loom-*BRAHR] to light up
aluminio [*ah-loo-*MEE-*n'yoh*] aluminum
alumno, -a [*ah-*LOOM-*noh, -nah*] pupil
alzar [*ahl-*THAHR] to raise
amabilidad (f) [*ah-mah-bee-lee-*DAHD] kindness
amable [*ah-*MAH-*bleh*] kind
amado, -a [*ah-*MAH-*doh, -dah*] beloved
amanecer (m) [*ah-mah-neh-*THEHR] (n and v) dawn
amante [*ah-*MAHN-*teh*] lover
amapola [*ah-mah-*POH-*lah*] poppy
★ **amar** [*ah-*MAHR] to love
NOTE: *Amar* means "to love" in a rather lofty sense. The usual word is *querer*.
amargar [*ah-mahr-*GAHR] to make bitter
amargo, -a [*ah-*MAHR-*goh, -gah*] bitter
amargura [*ah-mahr-*GOO-*rah*] bitterness
amarillo, -a [*ah-mah-*REE-*l'yoh, -l'yah*] yellow
amarrar [*ah-mah-*RRAHR] to tie
ambición (f) [*ahm-bee-th'*YOHN] ambition
ambiente (m) [*ahm-b'*YEHN-*teh*]
ambos, -as [AHM-*bohs, -bahs*] both
ambulancia [*ahm-boo-*LAHN-*th'yah*] ambulance
amenazar [*ah-meh-nah-*THAHR] to threaten
ameno, -a [*ah-*MEH-*noh, -nah*] pleasant
ametralladora [*ah-meh-trah-l'yah-*DOH-*rah*] machine gun
★ **amigo, -a** [*ah-*MEE-*goh, -gah*] friend
amistad (f) [*ah-mees-*TAHD] friendship
★ **amor** (m) [*ah-*MOHR] love
amor mío [*ah-*MOHR MEE-*oh*] my love
amoroso, -a [*ah-moh-*ROH-*soh, -sah*] affectionate
ampliar [*ahm-plee-*AHR] to enlarge
análisis (m) [*ah-*NAH-*lee-sees*] analysis
anatomía [*ah-nah-toh-*MEE-*ah*] anatomy
anciano, -a [*ahn-th'*YAH-*noh, -nah*] old man, old woman
ancla (f) [AHN-*klah*] **anchor**

ancho, -a [AHN-*choh, -chah*] wide
andar [*ahn*-DAHR] to walk

NOTE: When applied to mechanisms *andar* means "to run." *Mi reloj no anda:* "My watch isn't running."

andar a pie [*ahn*-DAHR *ah p'yeh*] to go on foot
anfitrión, anfitriona [*ahn-fee-tree*-OHN, *ahn-fee-tree*-OH-*nah*] host, hostess
ángel (m) [AHN-*hehl*] angel
angosto, -a [*ahn*-GOHS-*toh, -tah*] narrow
ángulo [AHN-*goo-loh*] angle
angustia [*ahn*-GOOS-*t'yah*] anguish
anhelar [*ahn-eh*-LAHR] to desire
anhelo [*ahn*-EH-*loh*] desire
animal [*ah-nee*-MAHL] animal
animar [*ah-nee*-MAHR] to encourage
aniversario [*ah-nee-vehr*-SAH-*r'yoh*] anniversary
★ **anoche** [*ah*-NOH-*cheh*] last night
anochecer (n) (m) [*ah-noh-cheh*-THEHR] dusk
(v) to grow dark
anotar [*ah-noh*-TAHR] to take note of
ansiar [*ahn-s'*YAHR] to long for
ansioso, -a [*ahn-s'*YOH-*soh, -sah*] anxious
ante [AHN-*teh*] in the presence of
ante todo [AHN-*teh* TOH-*doh*] above all
anteanoche [AHN-*teh-ah*-NOH-*cheh*] night before last
anteayer [AHN-*teh-ah-y'*EHR] the day before yesterday
(de) antemano [*deh ahn-teh*-MAH-*noh*] in advance
anteojos (m, plural) [*ahn-teh*-OH-*hohs*] eyeglasses
antepasado [*ahn-teh-pah*-SAH-*doh*] ancestor
anterior [*ahn-teh-r'*YOHR] former
anteriormente [*ahn-teh-r'yohr*-MEHN-*teh*] formerly
★ **antes** [AHN-*tehs*] before
cuanto antes [KWAHN-*toh* AHN-*tehs*] as soon as possible

antiguo, -a [*ahn*-TEE-*gwoh, -gwah*] ancient
Antillas [*ahn*-TEE-*l'yahs*] Antilles (West Indies)
antipático, -a [*ahn-tee*-PAH-*tee-koh, -kah*] unpleasant
anual [*ah*-NWAHL] annual, yearly
anular [*ah-noo*-LAHR] to cancel
anunciar [*ah-noon-th'*YAHR] to announce
anuncio [*ah*-NOON-*th'yoh*] announcement
anzuelo [*ahn*-THWEH-*loh*] fish hook
añadir [*ah-n'yah*-DEER] to add to
★ **año** [AH-*n'yoh*] year
  el año pasado [*ehl* AH-*n'yoh pah*-SAH-*doh*] last year
  el año que viene [*ehl* AH-*n'yoh keh v'*YEH-*neh*] the coming year
apagar [*ah-pah*-GAHR] to put out (the light), to extinguish
aparador (m) [*ah-pah-rah*-DOHR] cupboard
aparato [*ah-pah*-RAH-*toh*] apparatus
aparecer [*ah-pah-reh*-THEHR] to appear
aparente [*ah-pah*-REHN-*teh*] apparent
  aparentemente [*ah-pah-rehn-teh*-MEHN-*teh*] apparently
apariencia [*ah-pah-r'*YEHN-*th'yah*] appearance
apartado [*ah-pahr*-TAH-*doh*] post office box
apartamiento [*ah-pahr-tah-m'*YEHN-*toh*] apartment
apartar [*ah-pahr*-TAHR] to separate
aparte [*ah*-PAHR-*teh*] aside
apasionadamente [*ah-pah-s'yoh-nah-dah*-MEHN-*teh*] passionately
apasionado, -a [*ah-pah-s'yoh*-NAH-*doh, -dah*] passionate
apearse [*ah-peh*-AHR-*seh*] to get out or off (a vehicle or horse)
apellido [*ah-peh-l'*YEE-*doh*] family name
apenas [*ah*-PEH-*nahs*] scarcely
apéndice [*ah*-PEHN-*dee-theh*] appendix
apertura [*ah-pehr*-TOO-*rah*] opening
apetito [*ah-peh*-TEE-*toh*] appetite
apio [AH-*p'yoh*] celery
aplaudir [*ah-plaw*-DEER] to applaud
aplazar [*ah-plah*-THAHR] to postpone
aplicado, -a [*ah-plee*-KAH-*doh, -dah*] industrious

apoderado [*ah-poh-deh-*RAH-*doh*] attorney
apoderar(se) de [*ah-poh-deh-*RAHR-*(seh)-deh*] to take possession of
apostar [*ah-pohs-*TAHR] to bet
apoyar [*ah-poh-*YAHR] to support
apoyo [*ah-*POH-*yoh*] support
apreciar [*ah-preh-th'*YAHR] to appreciate
aprecio [*ah-*PREH-*th'yoh*] regard
aprender [*ah-prehn-*DEHR] to learn
apretado, -a [*ah-preh-*TAH-*doh, -dah*] tight
apretar [*ah-preh-*TAHR] to tighten
apretón de manos [*ah-preh-*TOHN *deh* MAH-*nohs*] handshake
aprisa [*ah-*PREE-*sah*] quickly
aprobar [*ah-proh-*BAHR] to approve
apropiado, -a [*ah-proh-p'*YAH-*doh, -dah*] appropriate
aprovechar or **aprovechar(se) de** [*ah-proh-veh-*CHAHR, *ah-proh-veh-*CHAHR-*(seh) deh*] to take advantage of
aproximadamente [*ah-prohk-see-mah-dah-*MEHN-*teh*] approximately
aproximado, -a [*ah-prohk-see-*MAH-*doh, -dah*] approximate
apuesta [*ah-*PWEHS-*tah*] bet
apuntar [*ah-poon-*TAHR] to aim, to point out
apunte (m) [*ah-*POON-*teh*] memorandum
apurar(se) [*ah-poo-*RAHR-*seh*] to hurry or to worry
  ¡Apúrese! [*ah-*POO-*reh-seh*] Hurry up!
★ **aquel (aquella)** [*ah-*KEHL, *ah-*KEH-*l'yah*] that (adj)
aquél (aquélla) [*ah-*KEHL, *ah-*KEH-*l'yah*] that one (pron)
aquellos, -as [*ah-*KEH-*l'yohs, -l'yahs*] those (adj)
aquéllos, -as [*ah-*KEH-*l'yohs, -l'yahs*] those (pron)
★ **aquí** [*ah-*KEE] here
  aquí está [*ah-*KEE *ehs-*TAH] here it is
árabe [AH-*rah-beh*] Arab
araña [*ah-*RAH-*n'yah*] spider
★ **árbol** (m) [AHR-*bohl*] tree
archivo [*ahr-*CHEE-*voh*] file (record)
arco [AHR-*koh*] arch

arder [*ahr*-DEHR] to burn
ardilla [*ahr*-DEE-*l'yah*] squirrel
arena [*ah*-REH-*nah*] sand
Argentina [*ahr-hehn*-TEE-*nah*] Argentina
argentino, -a [*ahr-hehn*-TEE-*noh, -nah*] Argentine
argumento [*ahr-goo*-MEHN-*toh*] plot

NOTE: "argument" is translated by *discusión* or *disputa.*

árido, -a [AH-*ree-doh, -dah*] arid
aristocracia [*ah-rees-toh*-KRAH-*th'yah*] aristocracy
aristocrático, -a [*ah-rees-toh*-KRAH-*tee-koh, -kah*] aristocratic
aritmética [*ah-reet*-MEH-*tee-kah*] arithmetic
arma [AHR-*mah*] arm (weapon)

NOTE: *Arma* is feminine but uses *el* in the singular for harmony.

armada [*ahr*-MAH-*dah*] navy
armar [*ahr*-MAHR] to arm
armario [*ahr*-MAH-*r'yoh*] wardrobe, closet
armonía [*ahr-moh*-NEE-*ah*] harmony
arpa [AHR-*pah*] harp

NOTE: *Arpa* is feminine but uses *el* in the singular for harmony.

arqueología [*ahr-keh-oh-loh*-HEE-*ah*] archæology
arquitecto [*ahr-kee*-TEHK-*toh*] architect
arquitectura [*ahr-kee-tehk*-TOO-*rah*] architecture
arrancar [*ah-rrahn*-KAHR] to pull out, tear off
arrastrar [*ah-rrahs*-TRAHR] to drag
arreglar [*ah-rreh*-GLAHR] to arrange
arrendar [*ah-rrehn*-DAHR] to rent, to lease
arrestar [*ah-rrehs*-TAHR] to arrest
arriba [*ah*-RREE-*bah*] up
por arriba [*pohr ah*-RREE-*bah*] above

arrodillar(se) [*ah-rroh-dee-l'*YAHR-*(seh)*] to kneel
arrojar [*ah-rroh*-HAHR] to throw
arroyo [*ah*-RROH-*yoh*] brook
★ **arroz** (m) [*ah*-RROTH] rice
arruga [*ah*-RROO-*gah*] wrinkle
arte (m) [AHR-*teh*] art
NOTE: *Arte* becomes feminine in the plural. *Bellas Artes*—"Fine Arts."
artículo [*ahr*-TEE-*koo-loh*] article
artificial [*ahr-tee-fee-th'*YAHL] artificial
artista (m and f) [*ahr*-TEES-*tah*] artist
artístico, -a [*ahr*-TEES-*tee-koh, -kah*] artistic
arzobispo [*ahr-thoh*-BEES-*poh*] archbishop
as (m) [*ahs*] ace
asado, -a [*ah*-SAH-*doh, -dah*] roasted
asalto [*ah*-SAHL-*toh*] assault
asamblea [*ah-sahm*-BLEH-*ah*] assembly
asar [*ah*-SAHR] to roast
ascender [*ahs-thehn*-DEHR] to go up
ascensor [*ahs-thehn*-SOHR] elevator
asegurar [*ah-seh-goo*-RAHR] to secure, to insure
asesino, -a [*ah-seh*-SEE-*noh, -nah*] murderer
★ **así** [*ah*-SEE] so, in this way, like this
así, así [*ah*-SEE, *ah*-SEE] so, so
asiento [*ah-s'*YEHN-*toh*] seat
asignatura [*ah-seek-nah*-TOO-*rah*] subject (of study)
asilo [*ah*-SEE-*loh*] asylum
asistir [*ah-sees*-TEER] to attend, to assist
asno [AHS-*noh*] ass
asomar(se) [*ah-soh*-MAHR-*(seh)*] to appear
asombro [*ah*-SOHM-*broh*] astonishment
aspecto [*ahs*-PEHK-*toh*] aspect
aspirina [*ahs-pee*-REE-*nah*] aspirin
astro [AHS-*troh*] star
asunto [*ah*-SOON-*toh*] subject
asustar [*ah-soos*-TAHR] to frighten
atacar [*ah-tah*-KAHR] to attack
atar [*ah*-TAHR] to tie

atención (f) [*ah-tehn-th'*YOHN] attention
atento, -a [*ah-*TEHN-*toh, -tah*] attentive, courteous

NOTE: *Atento* has a special use in business correspondence, *atenta carta* means "kind letter" while *atento y seguro servidor* is equivalent to "Very truly yours."

aterrizar [*ah-teh-rree-*THAHR] to land (airplane)
Atlántico [*ah-*TLAHN-*tee-koh*] Atlantic
atlético, -a [*ah-*TLEH-*tee-koh, -kah*] athletic
atmósfera [*aht-*MOHS-*feh-rah*] atmosphere
atómico, -a [*ah-*TOH-*mee-koh, -kah*] atomic
átomo [AH-*toh-moh*] atom
atracar [*ah-trah-*KAHR] to land (a ship)
atractivo, -a [*ah-trahk-*TEE-*voh, -ah*] attractive
atraer [*ah-trah-*EHR] to attract
atrás [*ah-*TRAHS] back, behind
atrasar [*ah-trah-*SAHR] to delay
atravesar [*ah-trah-veh-*SAHR] to cross
atrevido, -a [*ah-treh-*VEE-*doh, -dah*] daring
atribuir [*ah-tree-b'*WEER] to attribute
atropellar [*ah-troh-peh-l'*YAHR] to run over
atún (m) [*ah-*TOON] tuna fish
audición (f) [*ow-dee-th'*YOHN] audition
audiencia [*ow-d'*YEHN-*th'yah*] audience, hearing; audience chamber
aula [OW-*lah*] classroom
aumentar [*ow-mehn-*TAHR] to increase
aumento [*ow-*MEHN-*toh*] increase (n)
aun [*ah-*OON] even
aún [*ah-*OON] yet, still
aún no [*ah-*OON *noh*] not yet
aunque [*ah-*OON *keh*] although
ausencia [*ow-*SEHN-*th'yah*] absence
ausente [*ow-*SEHN-*teh*] absent
Austria [OWS-*tree-ah*] Austria

austríaco, -a [*ows-tr'*YAH-*koh, -kah*] Austrian
auténtico, -a [*ow*-TEHN-*tee-koh, -kah*] authentic
autobús [*ow-toh*-BOOS] bus
automóvil [*ow-toh*-MOH-*veel*] automobile
autor (m) **autora** [*ow*-TOHR, *ow*-TOH-*rah*] author, authoress
autorizar [*ow-toh-ree*-THAHR] to authorize
auxilio [*ow*-KSEE-*l'yoh*] help
avanzar [*ah-vahn*-THAHR] to advance
ave (f) [AH-*veh*] fowl
¡Ave María! [AH-*veh mah*-REE-*ah*] Good Heavens!
NOTE: This exclamation is derived from the first words of the *Ave-María,* literally "Hail Mary."
aventura [*ah-vehn*-TOO-*rah*] adventure
avergonzado, -a [*ah-vehr-gohn*-THAH-*doh, -dah*] ashamed
averiguar [*ah-veh-ree*-GWAHR] to find out
aviador, -a [*ah-v'yah*-DOHR, *-ah*] aviator
avión (m) [*ah-v'*YOHN] airplane
avisar [*ah-vee*-SAHR] to inform, to warn
aviso [*ah*-VEE-*soh*] notice
★ **ayer** [*ah*-YEHR] yesterday
ayuda [*ah*-YOO-*dah*] aid
ayudante [*ah-yoo*-DAHN-*teh*] assistant
ayudar [*ah-yoo*-DAHR] to aid
ayuntamiento [*ah-yoon-tah-m'*YEHN-*toh*] city hall
azote (m) [*ah*-THOH-*teh*] whip
azúcar (m and f) [*ah*-THOO-*kahr*] sugar
NOTE: *Azúcar* uses *el* in the singular for harmony
azucarera [*ah-thoo-kah*-REH-*rah*] sugar bowl
azucena [*ah-thoo*-THEH-*nah*] white lily
azufre (m) [*ah*-THOO-*freh*] sulphur
★ **azul** [*ah*-THOOL] blue
azulejo [*ah-thoo*-LEH-*hoh*] glazed tile

B

bacalao [*bah-kah*-LAH-*oh*] codfish
bahía [*bah*-EE-*ah*] bay

bachillerato [*bah-chee-l'yeh*-RAH-*toh*] (school degree equivalent to junior college diploma)
bailar [*by*-LAHR] to dance
bailarín, bailarina [*by-lah*-REEN, *by-lah*-REE-*nah*] dancer
baile (m) [BY-*leh*] dance
bajar [*bah*-HAHR] to go down, to get out (of a vehicle)
bajo, -a [BAH-*hoh, -ah*] low
bala [BAH-*lah*] bullet
balanza [*bah*-LAHN-*thah*] scales
balcón (m) [*bahl*-KOHN] balcony
ballena [*bah-l'*YEH-*nah*] whale
balneario [*bahl-neh*-AH-*r'yoh*] bathing resort
banana [*bah*-NAH-*nah*] banana
banco [BAHN-*koh*] bench, bank
banda [BAHN-*dah*] band
bandeja [*bahn*-DEH-*hah*] tray
bandera [*bahn*-DEH-*rah*] flag
bandido [*bahn*-DEE-*doh*] bandit
banquero [*bahn*-KEH-*roh*] banker
banquete (m) [*bahn*-KEH-*teh*] banquet
bañera [*bah-n'*YEH-*rah*] bathtub
baño [BAH-*n'yoh*] bath
barajas [*bah*-RAH-*hahs*] pack of cards
barato, -a [*bah*-RAH-*toh, -tah*] cheap
barba [BAHR-*bah*] chin, beard
barbaridad (f) [*bahr-bah-ree*-DAHD] nonsense or barbarity
  ¡Qué barbaridad! [*keh bahr-bah-ree*-DAHD] What nonsense! How terrible!
barbería [*bahr-beh*-REE-*ah*] barber shop
barbero [*bahr*-BEH-*roh*] barber
barco [BAHR-*koh*] boat, vessel, ship
barón, -esa [*bah*-ROHN, *bah-roh*-NEH-*sah*] baron, baroness
barra [BAH-*rrah*] bar
barrer [*bah*-RREHR] to seep
barril (m) [*bah*-RREEL] barrel
barrio [BAH-*rr'yoh*] city district or suburb
barro [BAH-*rroh*] mud

base (f) [BAH-*seh*] base
básico, -a [BAH-*see-koh, -kah*] basic
bastante [*bahs*-TAHN-*teh*] enough
bastar [*bahs*-TAHR] to be enough
  ¡Basta! [BAHS-*tah*] That is quite enough!
bastón (m) [*bahs*-TOHN] walking cane
basura [*bah*-SOO-*rah*] garbage
bata [BAH-*tah*] bath robe, dressing gown
batalla [*bah*-TAH-*l'yah*] battle
batallón [*bah-tah-l'*YOHN] batallion
batata [*bah*-TAH-*tah*] sweet potato
batir [*bah*-TEER] to beat
baúl (m) [*bah*-OOL] trunk
bautizar [*bah-oo-tee*-THAHR] to baptize
bautizo [*bah-oo*-TEE-*thoh*] baptism
beber [*beh*-BEHR] to drink
bebida [*be*-BEE-*dah*] drink
beca [BEH-*kah*] scholarship
becerro [*beh*-THEH-*rroh*] calf
belga (m & f) [BEHL-*gah*] Belgian
Bélgica [BEHL-*hee-kah*] Belgium
belleza [*beh-l'*YEH-*thah*] beauty
bello, -a [BE-*l'yoh, -l'yah*] beautiful
bendecir [*behn-deh*-THEER] to bless
  ¡Qué Dios te bendiga! [*keh* D'*yohs teh behn*-DEE-*gah*] May God bless you!
bendición (f) [*behn-dee-th'*YOHN] blessing
beneficio [*beh-neh*-FEE-*th'yoh*] benefit
berenjena [*beh-rehn*-HEH-*nah*] eggplant
berro [BEH-*rroh*] water cress
besar [*beh*-SAHR] to kiss
beso [BEH-*soh*] kiss
bestia [BEHS-*t'yah*] beast
betún (m) [*beh*-TOON] shoe polish
biberón (m) [*bee-beh*-ROHN] baby's bottle
Biblia [BEE-*bl'yah*] Bible
biblioteca [*bee-bl'yoh*-TEH-*kah*] library
bicicleta [*bee-thee*-KLEH-*tah*] bicycle

bien [*b'yehn*] well
  está bien [*ehs*-TAH *b'yehn*] all right
  muy bien [*mwee-b'yehn*] very well
bienestar [*b'yeh-nehs*-TAHR] well-being, comfort
bienvenido, -a [*b'yehn-veh*-NEE-*doh, -dah*] welcome (to a place)
  ¡Sea Ud. bienvenido! [SEH-*ah oos*-TEHD *b'yehn-veh*-NEE-*do*] You are welcome (here)!
biftec (m) [*beef*-TEHK] (also spelled bistec) beefsteak
bigote (m) [*bee*-GOH-*teh*] mustache
billete (m) [*bee-l'*YEH-*teh*] ticket
billete de banco [*bee-l'*YEH-*teh-deh*-BAHN-*koh*] bill
biografía [*b'yoh-grah*-FEE-*ah*] biography
biología [*b'yoh-loh*-HEE-*ah*] biology
bisabuelo, -a [*bee-sah*-BWEH-*loh, -lah*] great-grandfather, great-grandmother
bizcocho [*beeth*-KOH-*choh*] biscuit; sponge cake
biznieto, -a [*beeth-n'*YEH-*toh, -tah*] great-grandson, great-granddaughter
blanco, -a [BLAHN-*koh, -kah*] white
blando, -a [BLAHN-*doh, -dah*] soft
blusa [BLOO-*sah*] blouse
bobería [*boh-beh*-REE-*ah*] foolishness
bobo, -a [BOH-*boh, -bah*] foolish
boca [BOH-*kah*] mouth
bocadillo or **bocadito** [*boh-kah*-DEE-*l'yoh, boh-kah*-DEE-*toh*] canapé
bocado [*boh*-KAH-*doh*] morsel
bocina [*boh*-THEE-*nah*] horn (of an automobile)
boda [BOH-*dah*] wedding
bodega [*boh*-DEH-*gah*] cellar
  NOTE: In some countries *bodega* means "grocery store."
bofetada or **bofetón** [*boh-feh*-TAH-*dah, boh-feh*-TOHN] slap in the face
bolero [*boh*-LEH-*roh*] bolero (a dance)
boleto or **boleta** [*boh*-LEH-*toh*] admission ticket
bolívar [*boh*-LEE-*vahr*] bolívar

NOTE: Besides referring to the famous general this is also the monetary unit of Venezuela.

Bolivia [*boh*-LEE-*v'yah*] Bolivia
boliviano, -a [*boh-lee-v'yah-noh, -nah*] Bolivian
boliviano [*boh-lee-v'*YAH-*noh*] (The monetary unit of Bolivia)
bolsa [BOHL-*sah*] purse
bolsillo [*bohl*-SEE-*l'yoh*] pocket
bomba [BOHM-*bah*] pump
bomba atómica [BOHM-*bah ah*-TOH-*mee-kah*] atom bomb
bombardear [*bohm-bahr-deh*-AHR] to bombard
bombón (m) [*bohm*-BOHN] candy
bondad (f) [*bohn*-DAHD] kindness
tenga la bondad de... [TEHN-*gah lah bohn*-DAHD *deh*] would you be so kind as to
bondadoso, -a [*bohn-dah*-DOH-*soh, -sah*] kind, good
bonito, -a [*boh*-NEE-*toh, -tah*] pretty
bordado, -a [*bohr*-DAH-*doh, -dah*] embroidered
borde (m) [BOHR-*deh*] edge
(a) bordo [*ah*-BOHR-*doh*] on board
borracho, -a [*boh*-RRAH-*choh, -chah*] (adj) drunk or (as noun) drunkard
borrar [*boh*-RRAHR] to cross out
bosque (m) [BOHS-*keh*] wood, forest
bostezar [*bohs-teh*-THAHR] to yawn
bota [BOH-*tah*] boot
botar [*boh*-TAHR] to throw away
botica [*boh*-TEE-*kah*] drugstore
botella [*boh*-TEH-*l'yah*] bottle
botón [*boh*-TOHN] button
botones [*boh*-TOH-*nehs*] bellboy
boxeo [*bohk*-SEH-*oh*] boxing
Brasil [*brah*-SEEL] Brazil

brasileño, -a [*brah-see-leh-n'yoh, -n'yah*] Brazilian
bravo, -a [BRAH-*voh, -vah*] fierce
brazo [BRAH-*thoh*] arm
breve [BREH-*veh*] brief
brillante (adj) [*bree-l'*YAHN-*teh*] brilliant
(noun) diamond
brillar [*bree-l'*YAHR] to shine
brincar [*breen*-KAHR] to leap
brindar [*breen*-DAHR] to toast (someone)
brindis (m) [BREEN-*dees*] toast (to someone's health)
brisa [BREE-*sah*] breeze
brocha [BROH-*chah*] brush (for shaving or painting]
broche (m) [BROH-*cheh*] brooch
broma [BROH-*mah*] joke
en broma [*ehn* BROH-*mah*] as a joke
bronce (m) [BROHN-*theh*] bronze
bronquitis (f) [*brohn*-KEE-*tees*] bronchitis
bruja [BROO-*hah*] witch
brújula [BROO-*hoo-lah*] compass
brusco, -a [BROOS-*koh, -kah*] rude
brutal [*broo*-TAHL] brutal
bruto, -a [BROO-*toh, -tah*] brute, crude (for oil, minerals, etc.)
buen [*bwehn*] good

NOTE: *Buen* is the contraction of *bueno* when used before a masculine noun.

¡Buen viaje! [*bwehn v'*YAH-*heh*] Have a good trip!
buenaventura [*bweh-nah-vehn*-TOO-*rah*] fortune, good luck
★ **bueno, -a** [BWEH-*noh, -nah*] good, kind
★ **buenos días** [BWEH-*nohs d'yahs*] good morning
★ **buenas noches** [BWEH-*nahs* NOH-*chehs*] good evening and good night
★ **buenas tardes** [BWEH-*nahs* TAHR-*dehs*] good afternoon

buey (m) [*bway*] ox
buho [BOO-*oh*] owl
buitre [BWEE-*treh*] vulture
bujía [*boo*-HEE-*ah*] candle
bulto [BOOL-*toh*] package
buque (m) [BOO-*keh*] boat
burlar(se) [*boor*-LAHR-*seh*] to make fun of
burro [BOO-*rroh*] donkey
buscar [*boos*-KAHR] to seek, to look for
butaca [*boo*-TAH-*kah*] armchair, orchestra seat (in theater)
buzón (m) [*boo*-THOHN] letter box

C

caballero [*kah-bah-l'*YEH-*roh*] gentleman, knight
caballería [*kah-bah-l'yeh*-REE-*ah*] cavalry
Note: also means "chivalry."
★ **caballo** [*kah*-BAH-*l'yoh*] horse
cabaña [*kah*-BAH-*n'yah*] cabin
cabaret (m) [*kah-bah*-REHT] night club
cabello [*kah*-BEH-*l'yoh*] hair
caber [*kah*-BEHR] to fit into
cabeza [*kah*-BEH-*thah*] head
cable (m) [KAH-*bleh*] cable
cabo [KAH-*boh*] tip; corporal
al fin y al cabo [*ahl feen ee ahl* KAH-*boh*] after all
cabra [KAH-*brah*] goat
cacahuete (m) [*kah-kah*-WEH-*teh*] peanut
cacao [*kah*-KAH-*oh*] cocoa
★ **cada** [KAH-*dah*] every or each
cada vez [KAH-*dah veth*] every time
cadena [*kah*-DEH-*nah*] chain
cadera [*kah*-DEH-*rah*] hip
caer (or) **caer(se)** [*kah*-EHR-*(seh)*] to fall
café (m) [*kah*-FEH] coffee and café
caída [*kah*-EE-*dah*] fall (n)

★ **caja** [KAH-*hah*] box
  caja fuerte [KAH-*hah* FWEHR-*teh*] safe (n)
cajero [*kah*-HEH-*roh*] cashier
calabaza [*kah-lah*-BAH-*thah*] pumpkin
calamar (m) [*kah-lah*-MAHR] squid
calamidad (f) [*kah-lah-mee*-DAHD] calamity
calavera [*kah-lah*-VEH-*rah*] skull
calcetín (m) [*kahl-theh*-TEEN] sock
calcular [*kahl-koo*-LAHR] to calculate
caldo [KAHL-*doh*] broth
calendario [*kah-lehn*-DAH-*r'yoh*] calendar
calentador (m) [*kah-lehn-tah*-DOHR] heater
calentar [*kah-lehn*-TAHR] to warm
calidad (f) [*kah-lee*-DAHD] quality
cálido, -a [KAH-*lee-doh, -dah*] warm
caliente (m and f) [*kah-l'*YEHN-*teh*] hot
calma [KAHL-*mah*] calm
calmar [*kahl*-MAHR] to calm
  ¡cálmese Ud.! [KAHL-*meh-seh oos*-TEHD] Calm down!
★ **calor** (m) [*kah*-LOHR] heat
  Hace calor [AH-*theh kah*-LOHR] It is hot
calumniar [*kah-loom-n'*YAHR] to slander
caluroso, -a [*kah-loo*-ROH-*soh, -sah*] warm
calvo, -a [KAHL-*voh, -vah*] bald
calzado [*kahl*-THAH-*doh*] footwear
calzoncillos [*kahl-thohn*-THEE-*l'yohs*] underpants
callado, -a [*kah-l'*YAH-*doh, -dah*] quiet
callar [*kah-l'*YAHR] to keep silent
  ¡Cállese! [KAH-*l'yeh-seh*] Be quiet!
★ **calle** (f) [KAH-*l'yeh*] street
★ **cama** [KAH-*mah*] bed
camarera [*kah-mah*-REH-*rah*] chambermaid, waitress
camarero [*kah-mah*-REH-*roh*] waiter
camarón (m) [*kah-mah*-ROHN] shrimp
camarote (m) [*kah-mah*-ROH-*teh*] stateroom, cabin
cambiar [*kahm-b'*YAHR] to change
cambio [KAHM-*b'yoh*] change
  en cambio [*ehn* KAHM-*b'yoh*] on the other hand

camello [*kah*-MEH-*l'yoh*] camel
★ **caminar** [*kah-mee*-NAHR] to walk
camino [*kah*-MEE-*noh*] road
camión (m) [*kah-m'*YOHN] truck
camisa [*kah*-MEE-*sah*] shirt
camiseta [*kah-mee*-SEH-*tah*] undershirt
campamento [*kahm-pah*-MEHN-*toh*] camp
campana [*kahm*-PAH-*nah*] bell
campéon (m) [*kahm-peh*-OHN] champion
campesino, -a [*kahm-peh*-SEE-*noh, -ah*] rural inhabitant
campo [KAHM-*poh*] country, field
Canadá [*kah-nah*-DAH] Canada
canadiense (m and f) [*kah-nah-d'*YEHN-*seh*] Canadian
canal (m) [*kah*-NAHL] channel, canal
canario [*kah*-NAH-*r'yoh*] canary bird
canasta [*kah*-NAHS-*tah*] basket
cancelar [*kahn-theh*-LAHR] to cancel
canción (f) [*kahn-th'*YOHN] song
candidato, -a [*kahn-dee*-DAH-*toh, -ah*] candidate
canela [*kah*-NEH-*lah*] cinnamon
cangrejo [*kahn*-GREH-*hoh*] crab
canoa [*kah*-NOH-*ah*] canoe
cansado, -a [*kahn*-SAH-*doh, -dah*] tired
cansancio [*kahn*-SAHN-*th'yoh*] tiredness
cansar(se) [*kahn*-SAHR-*(seh)*] to get tired
cantante (m and f) [*kah*-TAHN-*teh*] singer
cantar [*kahn*-TAHR] to sing
cantidad (f) [*kahn-tee*-DAHD] quantity
cantina [*kahn*-TEE-*nah*] bar (for liquors)
caña de azúcar [KAH-*n'yah deh ah*-THOO-*kahr*] sugar cane
caña de pescar [KAH-*n'yah deh* PEHS-*kahr*] fishing pole
cañón (m) [*kah-n'*YOHN] cannon
capacidad (f) [*kah-pah-thee*-DAHD] capacity
capataz (m) [*kah-pah*-TATH] foreman
capaz [*kah*-PATH] capable
capilla [*kah*-PEE-*l'yah*] chapel
capital (m) [*kah-pee*-TAHL] capital (sum of money]
capital (f) [*kah-pee*-TAHL] capital (city)

capitán (m) [*kah-pee-*TAHN] captain
capitolio [*kah-pee-*TOH-*l'yoh*] capitol
capítulo [*kah-*PEE-*too-loh*] chapter
capricho [*kah-*PREE-*choh*] whim
★ **cara** [KAH-*rah*] face
caracol (m) [*kah-rah-*KOHL] snail
carácter (m) [*kah-*RAHK-*tehr*] character, firmness, nature
característico, -a [*kah-rahk-teh-*REES-*tee-koh, -kah*] characteristic
¡caramba! [*kah-*RAHM-*bah*]

NOTE: This word is used to convey a variety of meanings ranging from "well!" "you don't say!" to "heavens!"

carbón (m) [*kahr-*BOHN] coal, charcoal
cárcel (f) [KAHR-*thehl*] jail
carecer [*kah-reh-*THEHR] to lack
carga [KAHR-*gah*] load, cargo
cargar [*kahr-*GAHR] to load, to charge
  a cargo de [*ah* KAHR-*goh deh*] in charge of
caricia [*kah-*REE-*th'yah*] caress
caridad (f) [*kah-ree-*DAHD] charity (Also is widely used as a girl's name.)
cariño [*kah-*REE-*n'yoh*] fondness, affection
cariñoso, -a [*kah-ree-n'*YOH-*soh, -sah*] affectionate
carnaval (m) [*kahr-nah-*VAHL] carnival
carne (f) [KAHR-*neh*] meat, flesh
  de carne y hueso [*deh-*KAHR-*neh ee* WEH-*soh*] flesh and blood
carnero [*kahr-*NEH-*roh*] sheep
carnicería [*kahr-nee-theh-*REE-*ah*] butcher's shop
caro, -a [KAH-*roh, -rah*] expensive
carpintero [*kahr-peen-*TEH-*roh*] carpenter
carrera [*kah-*RREH-*rah*] race

carretera [*kah-rreh-*TEH*-rah*] highway
carro [KAH*-rroh*] cart

NOTE: *Carro* is widely used in Latin America for automobile, while *coche* is the preferred word in Spain.

carta [KAHR*-tah*] letter
  carta de crédito [KAHR*-tah deh* KREH*-dee-toh*] letter of credit
  carta de presentación [KAHR*-tah deh preh-sehn-tah-th'*YOHN] letter of introduction
cartera [*kahr-*TEH*-rah*] pocketbook
cartero [*kahr-*TEH*-roh*] postman
cartón (m) [*kahr-*TOHN] cardboard
casa [KAH*-sah*] house
casado, -a [*kah-*SAH*-doh, -dah*] married
casamiento [*kah-sah-m'*YEHN*-toh*] marriage
casar(se) con [*kah-*SAHR*(seh) kohn*] to get married (to)
cáscara [KAHS*-kah-rah*] peel, shell
★ **casi** [KAH*-see*] almost
casilla [*kah-*SEE*-l'yah*] ticket office
caso [KAH*-soh*] case
  en caso que [*ehn* KAH*-soh keh*] in case that
castaña [*kahs-*TAH*-n'yah*] chestnut
castañuelas [*kahs-tah-n'*WEH*-lahs*] castanets
★ **castellano** [*kahs-teh-l'*YAH*-noh*] Castilian

NOTE: *Castellano* is generally used to denote the Spanish language as it was originally the language of Castille.

castigar [*kahs-tee-*GAHR] to punish
castillo [*kahs-*TEE*-l'yoh*] castle

casualidad (f) [*kah-soo-ah-lee*-DAHD] chance, event
 por casualidad [*pohr kah-soo-ah-lee*-DAHD] by chance
catarro [*kah*-TAH-*rroh*] (head) cold
catástrofe (f) [*kah*-TAHS-*troh-feh*] catastrophe
catedral (f) [*kah-teh*-DRAHL] cathedral
categoría [*kah-teh-goh*-REE-*ah*] category
católico, -a [*kah*-TOH-*lee-koh, -kah*] catholic
★ **catorce** [*kah*-TOHR-*theh*] fourteen
causa [COW-*sah*] cause
cavar [*kah*-VAHR] to dig
caverna [*kah*-VEHR-*nah*] cave
cavidad (f) [*kah-vee*-DAHD] cavity
caza [KAH-*thah*] hunting
cazador [*kah-thah*-DOHR] hunter
cazar [*kah*-THAHR] to hunt (animals)
cazuela [*kah*-THWEH-*lah*] pot
cebolla [*theh*-BOH-*l'yah*] onion
cebra [THEH-*brah*] zebra
ceder [*theh*-DEHR] to yield
cédula de identidad [THEH-*doo-lah deh ee-dehn-tee*-DAHD] identity card
ceja [THEH-*hah*] eyebrow
celebración (f) [*theh-leh-brah-th'*YOHN] celebration
celebrar [*theh-leh*-BRAHR] to celebrate
célebre [THEH-*leh-breh*] famous
celoso, -a [*theh*-LOH-*soh, -sah*] jealous
cementerio [*theh-mehn*-TEH-*r'yoh*] cemetery
cemento [*theh*-MEHN-*toh*] cement
cena [THEH-*nah*] supper
cenar [*theh*-NAHR] to have supper
cenicero [*theh-nee*-THEH-*roh*] ash-tray
ceniza [*theh*-NEE-*thah*] ashes

NOTE: singular in Spanish although plural in English.

censurado, -a [*thehn-thoo*-RAH-*doh, -dah*] censored
centavo [*thehn*-TAH-*voh*] cent
centeno [*thehn*-TEH-*noh*] rye
centígrado [*thehn*-TEE-*grah-doh*] centigrade
centímetro [*then*-TEE-*meh-troh*] centimeter
céntimo [THEHN-*tee-moh*] cent
central [*thehn*-TRAHL] central
centro [THEHN-*troh*] center
cepillar [*theh-pee-l'*YAHR] to brush
cepillo [*theh*-PEE-*l'yoh*] brush
  cepillo de dientes [*theh*-PEE-*l'yoh deh d'*YEHN-*tehs*] tooth brush
  cepillo para el cabello [*theh*-PEE-*l'yoh* PAH-*rah ehl kah*-BEH-*l'yoh*] hair-brush
cera [THEH-*rah*] wax
★ **cerca** [THEHR-*kah*] near, close by
  está cerca [*ehs*-TAH THEHR-*kah*] It is near
  cercano, -a [*thehr*-KAH-*noh, -ah*] near by
cerdo [THEHR-*doh*] hog
cereal [*theh-reh*-AHL] cereal
cerebro [*theh*-REH-*broh*] brain
ceremonia [*theh-reh*-MOH-*n'yah*] ceremony
cereza [*theh*-REH-*thah*] cherry
★ **cero** [THEH-*roh*] zero
cerrado, -a [*theh*-RRAH-*doh, -ah*] closed
cerrar [*theh*-RRAHR] to close
cerro [THEH-*rroh*] hill
certeza [*thehr*-TEH-*thah*] certainty
certificado [*thehr-tee-fee*-KAH-*doh*] certificate
certificar [*thehr-tee-fee*-KAHR] to certify
cerveza [*thehr*-VEH-*thah*] beer
cesar [*theh*-SAHR] to cease
cesta [THEHS-*tah*] basket
cicatriz (f) [*thee-kah*-TREETH] scar
ciclón (m) [*thee*-KLOHN] cyclone
ciego, -a [*th'*YEH-*goh, -gah*] blind
cielo [*th'*YEH-*loh*] sky
★ **cien** [*th'*YEHN] one hundred

NOTE: *Cien* is used before nouns instead of *ciento*. Ex: *Cien hombres*—"One hundred men."

ciencia [*th'*YEHN-*th'yah*] science
ciento (n) [*th'*YEHN-*toh*] one hundred
ciertamente [*th'yehr-tah-*MEHN-*teh*] certainly
cierto, -a [*th'*YEHR-*toh, -tah*] certain
¿No es cierto? [*noh ehs th'*YEHR-*toh*] Isn't that so?
cigarro, cigarrillo [*thee-*GAH-*rroh, thee-gah-*RREE-*l'yoh*] cigarette
NOTE: Do not confuse *cigarro* with "cigar" which is translated by *puro* or *tabaco*.
cigüeña [*thee-*GWEH-*n'yah*] stork
cima [THEE-*mah*] peak
★ **cinco** [THEEN-*koh*] five
las cinco [*lahs* THEEN-*koh*] five o'clock
cincuenta [*theen-*KWEHN-*tah*] fifty
cine (m) [THEE-*neh*] moving picture, movies
cínico, -a [THEE-*nee-koh, -kah*] cynic
cinta [THEEN-*tah*] ribbon
cintura [*theen-*TOO-*rah*] waist
cinturón (m) [*theen-too-*ROHN] belt
circo [THEER-*koh*] circus
circular [*theer-koo-*LAHR] to circulate
circular (adj) (m, f) [*theer-koo-*LAHR] circular
circunstancia [*theer-koons-*TAHN-*th'yah*] circumstance
ciruela [*thee-*RWEH-*lah*] plum, prune
cirujano [*thee-roo-*HAH-*noh*] surgeon
cisne (m) [THEES-*neh*] swan
cita [THEE-*tah*] appointment, date
★ **ciudad** (f) [*th'yoo-*DAHD] city
ciudadano, -a [*th'yoo-dah-*DAH-*noh, -nah*] citizen
civil [*thee-*VEEL] civil
claridad (f) [*klah-ree-*DAHD] brightness, light

claro, -a [KLAH-*roh, -rah*] clear
  ¡Claro está! [KLAH-*roh ehs*-TAH] Certainly!
clase (f) [KLAH-*seh*] class
clásico, -a [KLAH-*see-koh, -kah*] classical, classic
clavel (m) [*klah*-VEHL] carnation
clavo [KLAH-*voh*] nail
cliente [*klee*-EHN-*teh*] customer
clientela [*klee-ehn*-TEH-*lah*] clientele
clima (m) [KLEE-*mah*] climate
clínica [KLEE-*nee-kah*] clinic
cobarde [*koh*-BAHR-*deh*] coward
cobrar [*koh*-BRAHR] to collect
cobre (m) [KOH-*breh*] copper
cocido (n) [*koh*-THEE-*doh*] a special dish of Spain
cocido, -a [*koh*-THEE-*doh, -dah*] cooked
cocina [*koh*-THEE-*nah*] kitchen
cocinar [*koh-thee*-NAHR] to cook
cocinero, -a [*koh-thee*-NEH-*roh, -rah*] cook
coctel (m) [*kohk*-TEHL] cocktail
coche (m) [KOH-*cheh*] coach, car
  coche cama [KOH-*cheh* KAH-*mah*] sleeping car
  coche comedor [KOH-*cheh koh-meh*-DOHR] dining car
codo [KOH-*doh*] elbow
coger [*koh*-HEHR] to catch, to take hold of
  ¡cójalo! [KOH-*hah-loh*] grab it!
cohete (m) [*koh*-EH-*teh*] firecracker
coincidencia [*koh-een-thee*-DEHN-*th'yah*] coincidence
cojín (m) [*koh*-HEEN] cushion
cojo, -a [KOH-*hoh, -hah*] lame
col (f) [*kohl*] cabbage
cola [KOH-*lah*] tail, glue
  hacer cola [*ah*-THEHR KOH-*lah*] to wait in line
colaborar [*koh-lah-boh*-RAHR] to collaborate
colar [*koh*-LAHR] to strain
colcha [KOHL-*chah*] bedspread
colchón (m) [*kohl*-CHOHN] mattress
colección (f) [*koh-lehk-th'*YOHN] collection

colegio [*koh*-LEH-*h'yoh*] school
  NOTE: Do not confuse with "college."
colgar [*kohl*-GAHR] to hang up
coliflor (f) [*koh-lee*-FLOHR] cauliflower
colina [*koh*-LEE-*nah*] hill
colmo [KOHL-*moh*] heap
  ¡Eso es el colmo! [EH-*soh ehs ehl* KOHL-*moh*] That is the limit!
colocar [*koh-loh*-KAHR] to place
Colombia [*koh*-LOHM-*b'yah*] Colombia
colombiano, -a [*koh-lohm-b'*YAH-*noh, -nah*] Colombian
colonia [*koh*-LOH-*n'yah*] colony
colonial [*koh-loh-n'*YAHL] colonial
color [*koh*-LOHR] color
colorado, -a [*koh-loh*-RAH-*doh, -dah*] red
colorete (m) [*koh-loh*-REH-*teh*] rouge
columna [*koh*-LOOM-*nah*] column
columpio [*koh*-LOOM-*p'yoh*] swing
collar [*koh-l'*YAHR] necklace
coma [KOH-*mah*] comma
comandante (m) [*koh-mahn*-DAHN-*teh*] major (military)
  NOTE: In some countries *mayor* is used.
combate (m) [*kohm*-BAH-*teh*] combat
combatir [*kohm-bah*-TEER] to combat
combinación (f) [*kohm-bee-nah-th'*YOHN] combination
combinar [*kohm-bee*-NAHR] to combine
combustible [*kohm-boos*-TEE-*bleh*] combustible
comedia [*koh*-MEH-*d'yah*] comedy
comedor (m) [*koh-meh*-DOHR] dining room
comentar [*koh-mehn*-TAHR] to comment
comenzar [*koh-mehn*-THAHR] to begin
★ **comer** [*koh*-MEHR] to eat
comercial [*koh-mehr-th'*YAHL] commercial
comercio [*koh*-MEHR-*th'yoh*] trade
cometer [*koh-meh*-TEHR] to commit
cómico, -a [KOH-*mee-koh, -kah*] comic
★ **comida** [*koh*-MEE-*dah*] food, dinner, meal
comienzo [*koh-m'*YEHN-*thoh*] beginning

comillas [*koh*-MEE-*l'yahs*] quotation marks
comisión (f) [*koh-mee-s'*YOHN] commission
comité (m) [*koh-mee*-TEH] committee
★ **como** [KOH-*moh*] how, as
★ **¿Cómo está Ud.?** [KOH-*moh ehs*-TAH *oos*-TEHD] How are you?
¡Como no! [KOH-*moh-noh*] Certainly!
comodidad (f) [*koh-moh-dee*-DAHD] comfort
cómodo, -a [KOH-*moh-doh, -dah*] comfortable
compadecer [*kohm-pah-deh*-THEHR] to pity
compañero, -a [*kohm-pah-n'*YEH-*roh, -rah*] companion
compañía [*kohm-pah*-N'YEE-*ah*] company
comparar [*kohm-pah*-RAHR] to compare
compensar [*kohm-pehn*-SAHR] to compensate
competencia [*kohm-peh*-TEHN-*th'yah*] competition
complacer [*kohm-plah*-THEHR] to please
complemento [*kohm-pleh*-MEHN-*toh*] complement
completar [*kohm-pleh*-TAHR] to complete
completo [*kohm*-PLEH-*toh*] complete
complicado, -a [*kohm-plee*-KAH-*doh, -dah*] complicated
componer [*kohm-poh*-NEHR] to repair
composición (f) [*kohm-poh-see-th'*YOHN] composition
compositor, -a [*kohm-poh-see*-TOHR, *-ah*] composer
compra [KOHM-*prah*] purchase
hacer compras [*ah*-THEHR KOHM-*prahs*] to shop
ir de compras [*eer deh* KOHM-*prahs*] to go shopping
★ **comprar** [*kohm*-PRAHR] to buy
★ **comprender** [*kohm-prehn*-DEHR] to understand
¿comprende Ud.? [*kohm*-PREHN-*deh oos*-TEHD] Do you understand?
comprobar [*kohm-proh*-BAHR] to verify
compromiso [*kohm-proh*-MEE-*soh*] engagement
común [*koh*-MOON] common
sentido común [*sehn*-TEE-*doh koh*-MOON] common sense
comunicación (f) [*koh-moo-nee-kah-th'*YOHN] communication
comunicar [*koh-moo-nee*-KAHR] to communicate
comunista [*koh-moo*-NEES-*tah*] (m and f) communist

★ **con** [*kohn*] with

con todo y eso [*kohn* TOH-*doh ee* EH-*soh*] however

conceder [*kohn-theh*-DEHR] to grant, to concede

concentración (f) [*kohn-thehn-trah-th'*YOHN] concentration

concentrar [*kohn-thehn*-TRAHR] to concentrate

concepción (f) [*kohn-thehp-th'*YOHN] conception (Also a girl's name)

concepto [*kohn*-THEHP-*toh*] concept

concerniente [*kohn-thehr-n'*YEHN-*teh*] concerning

conciencia [*kohn-th'*YEHN-*th'yah*] conscience

concienzudo, -a [*kohn-th'yehn*-THOO-*doh, -dah*] conscientious

concierto [*kohn-th'*YEHR-*toh*] concert

conciso, -a [*kohn*-THEE-*soh, -sah*] concise

concluir [*kohn-kloo*-EER] to conclude, to end

conclusión (f) [*kohn-kloo-s'*YOHN] conclusion, end

concretamente [*kohn-kreh-tah*-MEHN-*teh*] concretely

concreto (n and adj) [*kohn*-KREH-*toh*] concrete

concurrir [*kohn-koo*-RREER] to attend

concurso [*kohn*-KOOR-*soh*] contest

concha [KOHN-*chah*] shell

conde (m) [KOHN-*deh*] count

condecoración (f) [*kohn-deh-koh-rah-th'*YOHN] decoration

condenar [*kohn-deh*-NAHR] to condemn

condensar [*kohn-dehn*-SAHR] to condense

condesa [*kohn*-DEH-*sah*] countess

condición (f) [*kohn-dee-th'*YOHN] condition

condicional [*kohn-dee-th'yoh*-NAHL] conditional

condimento [*kohn-dee*-MEHN-*toh*] seasoning

cóndor (m) [KOHN-*dohr*] condor

conducir [*kohn-doo*-THEER] to drive (an automobile]

conducta [*kohn*-DOOK-*tah*] conduct, behavior

conductor (m) [*kohn-dook*-TOHR] conductor

conejo [*koh*-NEH-*hoh*] rabbit

conexión (f) [*kohn-nehk-s'*YOHN] connection

conferencia [*kohn-feh*-REHN-*th'yah*] conference, lecture

confesar [*kohn-feh*-SAHR] to confess

confesión (f) [*kohn-feh-s'*YOHN] confession

confianza [*kohn-f'*YAHN-*thah*] confidence
confiar (en) [*kohn-f'*YAHR *(ehn)*] to trust
confidencial [*kohn-fee-dehn-th'*YAHL] confidential
confirmar [*kohn-feer*-MAHR] to confirm
conflicto [*kohn*-FLEEK-*toh*] conflict
conforme [*kohn*-FOHR-*meh*] in agreement
confortar [*kohn-fohr*-TAHR] to comfort
confundir [*kohn-foon*-DEER] to confuse
confusión (f) [*kohn-foo-s'*YOHN] confusion
congelar [*kohn-heh*-LAHR] to freeze
congreso [*kohn*-GREH-*soh*] congress
conjunto [*kohn*-HOON-*toh*] (adj) joined, (n) group
conmigo [*kohn*-MEE-*goh*] with me
conocer [*koh-noh*-THEHR] to know

NOTE: *Conocer* means "to know" in the sense of "to be acquainted with." *Saber* means to know a fact.

conocido, -a [*koh-noh*-THEE-*doh, -dah*] (adj) acquainted
conque [KOHN-*keh*] so then
conquista [*kohn*-KEES-*tah*] conquest
conquistador [*kohn-kees-tah*-DOHR] conqueror
consciente [*kohns-th'*YEHN-*teh*] conscious
consecuencia [*kohn-seh*-KWEHN-*th'yah*] consequence
conseguir [*kohn-seh*-GHEER] to obtain, to get
consejo [*kohn*-SEH-*hoh*] advice
consentimiento [*kohn-sehn-tee-m'*YEHN-*toh*] consent
consentir [*kohn-sehn*-TEER] to allow
conserva [*kohn*-SEHR-*vah*] preserve, jam
conservador [*kohn-sehr-vah*-DOHR] conservative
conservar [*kohn-sehr*-VAHR] to conserve
considerable [*kohn-see-deh*-RAH-*bleh*] considerable
consideración (f) [*kohn-see-deh-rah-th'*YOHN] consideration
considerar [*kohn-see-deh*-RAHR] to consider
consigo [*kohn*-SEE-*goh*] with oneself, with himself, with herself

consistir (de) [*kohn-sees-*TEER *(deh)*] to consist (of)
consonnante (f) [*kohn-soh-*NAHN-*teh*] consonant
constancia [*kohns-*TAHN-*th'yah*] constancy (Also used as a girl's name)
constantemente [*kohns-tahn-teh-*MEHN-*teh*] constantly
constitución (f) [*kohns-tee-too-th'*YOHN] constitution
constituir [*kohns-tee-too-*EER] to constitute
construcción (f) [*kohns-trook-th'*YOHN] construction
construir [*kohns-troo-*EER] to build
consuelo [*kohn-*SWEH-*loh*] comfort, consolation (Also a girl's name)
cónsul (m) [KOHN-*sool*] consul
consulado [*kohn-soo-*LAH-*doh*] consulate
consultar [*kohn-sool-*TAHR] to consult
contabilidad (f) [*kohn-tah-bee-lee-*DAHD] bookkeeping
contacto [*kohn-*TAHK-*toh*] contact
(al) contado [*(ahl) kohn-*TAH-*doh*] cash
contar [*kohn-*TAHR] to count, or to relate
contener [*kohn-teh-*NEHR] to contain
contento, -a [*kohn-*TEHN-*toh, -tah*] glad, contented
contestación (f) [*kohn-tehs-tah-th'*YOHN] answer
contestar [*kohn-tehs-*TAHR] to answer
contigo [*kohn-*TEE-*goh*] with you (familiar form)
continente (m) [*kohn-tee-*NEHN-*teh*] continent
continuar [*kohn-tee-noo-*AHR] to continue
¡continúe! [*kohn-tee-*NOO-*eh*] continue! go on!
★ **contra** [KOHN-*trah*] against
contrabando [*kohn-trah-*BAHN-*doh*] contraband
contradecir [*kohn-trah-deh-*THEER] to contradict
contraer [*kohn-trah-*EHR] to contract
contrario, -a [*kohn-*TRAH-*r'yoh, -r'yah*] contrary
al contrario [*ahl kohn-*TRAH-*r'yoh*] on the contrary
contraste (m) [*kohn-*TRAHS-*teh*] contrast
contratiempo [*kohn-trah-t'*YEHM-*poh*] mishap
contrato [*kohn-*TRAH-*toh*] contract
contribución (f) [*kohn-tree-boo-th'*YOHN] contribution
controlar [*kohn-troh-*LAHR] to control
convencer [*kohn-vehn-*THEHR] to convince
conveniente [*kohn-veh-n'*YEHN-*teh*] convenient

convenir [*kohn-veh-*NEER] to agree
convengo [*kohn-*VEHN-*goh*] I agree
me conviene [*meh kohn-v'*YEH-*neh*] it suits me
convento [*kohn-*VEHN-*toh*] convent
conversación (f) [*kohn-vehr-sah-th'*YOHN] conversation
conversar [*kohn-vehr-*SAHR] to converse, talk
convertible [*kohn-vehr-*TEE-*bleh*] convertible
convertir [*kohn-vehr-*TEER] to convert
convidar [*kohn-vee-*DAHR] to invite
cooperación (f) [*ko-oh-peh-rah-th'*YOHN] cooperation
copa [KOH-*pah*] wine glass
NOTE: Do not confuse with "cup," which is *taza*.
copia [KOH-*p'yah*] copy
copiar [*koh-p'*YAHR] to copy
coquetear [*koh-keh-teh-*AHR] to flirt
coraje (m) [*koh-*RAH-*heh*] courage
corazón (m) [*koh-rah-*THOHN] heart
corbata [*kohr-*BAH-*tah*] necktie
corcho [KOHR-*choh*] cork
cordel (m) [*kohr-*DEHL] cord
cordero [*kohr-*DEH-*roh*] lamb
cordial [*kohr-d'*YAHL] cordial
cordialmente [*kohr-d'yahl-*MEHN-*teh*] cordially
cordillera [*kohr-dee-l'*YEH-*rah*] mountain range
coro [KOH-*roh*] chorus
corona [*koh-*ROH-*nah*] crown
coronel (m) [*koh-roh-*NEHL] colonel
correa [*koh-*RREH-*ah*] belt, leather strap
correctamente [*koh-rrehk-tah-*MEHN-*teh*] correctly
correcto, -a [*koh-*RREHK-*toh, -tah*] correct
corredor (m) [*koh-rreh-*DOHR] corridor
corregir [*koh-rreh-*HEER] to correct
correo [*koh-*RREH-*oh*] mail, post office
apartado de correos [*ah-pahr-*TAH-*doh deh koh-*RREH-*ohs*] post office box
lista de correos [LEES-*tah deh koh-*RREH-*ohs*] general delivery

★ **correr** [*koh*-RREHR] to run
correspondencia [*koh-rrehs-pohn*-DEHN-*th'yah*] correspondence
correspondiente [*koh-rrehs-pohn-d'*YEHN-*teh*] corresponding
corresponsal [*koh-rrehs-pohn*-SAHL] correspondent
corrida de toros [*koh*-RREE-*dah deh* TOH-*rohs*] bullfight
corriente (f) [*koh-rr'*YEHN-*teh*] current, average
de los corrientes [*deh lohs koh-rr'*YEHN-*tehs*] of this month and year
cortar [*kohr*-TAHR] to cut
corte (f) [KOHR-*teh*] court (legal or royal)
corte de pelo [KOHR-*teh deh* PEH-*loh*] haircut
cortés [*kohr*-TEHS] courteous, polite
cortesía [*kohr-teh*-SEE-*ah*] courtesy
cortina [*kohr*-TEE-*nah*] curtain
★ **corto, -a** [KOHR-*toh, -tah*] short
★ **cosa** [KOH-*sah*] thing
cosecha [*koh*-SEH-*chah*] harvest, crop
coser [*koh*-SEHR] to sew
cosmético [*kohs*-MEH-*tee-koh*] cosmetic
costa [KOHS-*tah*] coast, shore
Costa Rica [*kohs-tah* REE-*kah*] Costa Rica
costarricense [*kohs-tah-rree*-THEHN-*seh*] Costa Rican
costado [*kohs*-TAH-*doh*] side
★ **costar** [*kohs*-TAHR] to cost
costilla [*kohs*-TEE-*l'yah*] rib; chop
costo [KOHS-*toh*] cost
costoso, -a [*kohs*-TOH-*soh, -sah*] expensive
costumbre (f) [*kohs*-TOOM-*breh*] custom, habit
costura [*kohs*-TOO-*rah*] sewing
cotidiano, -a [*koh-tee-d'*YAH-*noh, -nah*] daily
cotizar [*koh-tee*-THAHR] to quote (prices)
cotorra [*koh*-TOH-*rrah*] parrot
crear [*kreh*-AHR] to create
crecer [*kreh*-THEHR] to grow

crecimiento [*kreh-thee-m'*YEHN-*toh*] growth
crédito [KREH-*dee-toh*] credit
★ **creer** [*kreh*-EHR] to believe
¡Creo que no! [KREH-*oh keh noh*] I think not!
¡Creo que sí! [KREH-*oh keh see*] I think so!
¡Ya lo creo! [*yah loh* KREH-*oh*] Certainly!
crema [KREH-*mah*] cream
criado, -a [*kree*-AH-*doh, -dah*] servant
criar [*kree*-AHR] to create; to bring up
criatura [*kree-ah*-TOO-*rah*] creature
NOTE: It is often used meaning "child."
crimen (m) [KREE-*mehn*] crime
criminal [*kree-mee*-NAHL] criminal
crisis (f) [KREE-*sees*] crisis
cristal [*krees*-TAHL] crystal
cristiano, -a [*krees-t'*YAH-*noh, -nah*] Christian
crítica [KREE-*tee-kah*] criticism
criticar [*kree-tee*-KAHR] to criticize
cruce (m) [KROO-*theh*] crossroad
crudo, -a [KROO-*doh, -dah*] crude, raw
cruel [*kroo*-EHL] cruel
cruz (f) [*krooth*] cross (also a girl's name)
cruzar [*kroo*-THAHR] to cross
cuaderno [*kwah*-DEHR-*noh*] notebook
cuadra [KWAH-*drah*] block
cuadrado, -a [*kwah*-DRAH-*doh, -dah*] square
cuadrilla [*kwah*-DREE-*l'yah*] bullfight team, group. work gang
cuadro [KWAH-*droh*] picture
★ **¿cual?** [*kwahl*] which (of several)
cualquier [*kwahl-k'*YEHR] any
NOTE: Always used before the noun.
cualquiera [*kwahl-k'*YEH-*rah*] whatever, whoever (Used after nouns)
★ **cuando** [KWAHN-*doh*] when
de vez en cuando [*deh vehth ehn* KWAHN-*doh*] occasionally

★ **¿cuánto? -a** [KWAHN-*toh, -tah*] how much?

¡Cuánto me alegro! [KWAHN-*toh meh ah*-LEH-*groh*] How happy I am!

¿cuántos? -as [KWAHN-*tohs,- tahs*] how many?

cuarenta [*kwah*-REHN-*tah*] forty

cuartel (m) [*kwahr*-TEHL] barracks

cuarto, -a [KWAHR-*toh, -tah*] fourth

★ **cuarto** [KWAHR-*toh*] room

★ **cuatro** [KWAH-*troh*] four

Son las cuatro [*sohn-lahs*-KWAH-*troh*] It is four o'clock

Cuba [KOO-*bah*] Cuba

cubano, -a [*koo*-BAH-*noh, -nah*] Cuban

cubierta [*koo-b'*YEHR-*tah*] deck (of ship), cover

cubierto, -a [*koo-b'*YEHR-*toh, -tah*] covered

cubo [KOO-*boh*] pail

cubrir [*koo*-BREER] to cover

cucaracha [*koo-kah*-RAH-*chah*] cockroach

cuchara [*koo*-CHAH-*rah*] spoon, soupspoon

cucharada [*koo-chah*-RAH-*dah*] spoonful

cucharadita [*koo-chah-rah*-DEE-*tah*] teaspoonful

cucharilla [*koo-chah*-REE-*l'yah*] teaspoon

cucharón (m) *koo-chah*-ROHN] ladle

cuchilla [*koo*-CHEE-*l'yah*] razor blade

★ **cuchillo** [*koo*-CHEE-*l'yoh*] knife

cuello [KWEH-*l'yoh*] neck

cuenta [KWEHN-*tah*] account, bill

cuenta corriente [KWEHN-*tah koh-rr'*YEHN-*teh*] current account

cuento [KWEHN-*toh*] story

cuerda [KWEHR-*dah*] cord, rope

cuerno [KWEHR-*noh*] horn

cuero [KWEH-*roh*] leather

cuerpo [KWEHR-*poh*] body

cuervo [KWEHR-*voh*] crow

cuesta (KWEHS-*tah*] hill

cuesta abajo [KWEHS-*tah ah*-BAH-*hoh*] down hill

cuesta arriba [KWEHS-*tah ah*-RREE-*bah*] uphill

cuestión (f) [*kwehs-t'*YOHN] question (under discussion)
NOTE: "Question" as in "to ask a question" is *pregunta.*
cueva [KWEH-*vah*] cave
cuidado [*kwee*-DAH-*doh*] care
¡cuidado! [*kwee*-DAH-*doh*] watch out!
cuidadoso, -a [*kwee-dah*-DOH-*soh, -sah*] careful
cuidar [*kwee*-DAHR] to take care of
culebra [*koo*-LEH-*brah*] snake
culpa [KOOL-*pah*] fault
culpable [*kool*-PAH-*bleh*] guilty
cultivar [*kool-tee*-VAHR] to cultivate
culto, -a [KOOL-*toh, -tah*] cultured
cultura [*kool*-TOO-*rah*] culture
cumpleaños (m) [*koom-pleh*-AH-*n'yohs*] birthday
¡Feliz cumpleaños! [*feh*-LEETH *koom-pleh*-AH-*n'yohs*] Happy birthday!
cumplido [*koom*-PLEE-*doh*] compliment
cumplir [*koom*-PLEER] to fulfill
cuna [KOO-*nah*] cradle, baby's bed
cuñado, -a [*koo-n'*YAH-*doh, -dah*] brother-in-law (sister-in-law)
cura (m) [KOO-*rah*] priest
curar [*koo*-RAHR] to cure
curioso, -a [*koo-r'*YOH-*soh, -sah*] curious
curso [KOOR-*soh*] course
curva [KOOR-*vah*] curve
cutis (m) [KOO-*tees*] complexion, facial skin
cuyo, -a [KOO-*yoh, -yah*] whose, of which

CH

chaleco [*chah*-LEH-*koh*] vest
chalet (m) [*chah*-LEHT] country house
champaña (*cham*-PAH-*n'yah*] champagne
champú (m) [*cham*-POO] shampoo
chapa [CHAH-*pah*] license plate
chaqueta [*chah*-KEH-*tah*] jacket, coat (of suit)

charla [CHAHR-*lah*] chat
charlar [*chahr*-LAHR] to chat, to converse
charro [CHAH-*rroh*] cowboy (of Mexico)
Checoeslovaquia [*chek-koh-ehs-loh*-VAH-*k'yah*] Czechoslovakia
checoeslovaco, -a [*cheh-koh-ehs-loh*-VAH-*koh, -kah*] Czechoslovak
cheque [CHEH-*keh*] check (on bank)
cheque de viajero [CHEH-*keh deh v'yah*-HEH-*roh*] travelers' check
★ **chico, -a** [CHEE-*koh, -kah*] small, little
chico, -a [CHEE-*koh, -kah*] (noun) boy (or) girl
chícharo [CHEE-*chah-roh*] pea
chicharrón (m) [*chih-chah*-RROHN] pork rind (a local specialty)
chiflado, -a [*chee*-FLAH-*doh, -dah*] crazy
Chile [CHEE-*leh*] Chile
chileno, -a [*chee*-LEH-*noh, -nah*] Chilean
chillar [*chee-l'*YAHR] to scream
chimenea [*chee-meh*-NEH-*ah*] chimney
China [CHEE-*nah*] China
chinche (f) [CHEEN-*cheh*] bedbug, thumb-tack
chinela [*chee*-NEH-*lah*] slipper
chino, -a [CHEE-*noh, -nah*] Chinese
chiquillo, -a [*chee*-KEE-*l'yoh, -l'yah*] little boy (little girl)
chiquito, -a [*chee*-KEE-*toh, -tah*] little
chisme (m) [CHEES-*meh*] gossip
chismoso, -a [*chees*-MOH-*soh, -sah*] a person given to gossip
chispa [CHEES-*pah*] spark
chiste (m) [CHEES-*teh*] joke
chivo, -a [CHEE-*voh, -vah*] kid (goat)
chocar [*choh*-KAHR] to collide
choclo [CHOH-*kloh*] ear of corn
chocolate (m) [*choh-koh*-LAH-*teh*] chocolate
chofer [*choh*-FEHR] chauffeur
choque [CHOH-*keh*] collision, shock
chorizo [*choh*-REE-*thoh*] sausage
choza [CHOH-*thah*] hut

chuleta [*choo*-LEH-*tah*] chop, cutlet
chupar [*choo*-PAHR] to suck, to sip

D

dama [DAH-*mah*] lady
dañado, -a [*dah-n'*YAH-*doh, -dah*] damaged
danés, -nesa [*dah*-NEHS, -NEH-*sah*] Danish
dañino, -a [*dah-n'*YEE-*noh, -nah*] harmful
daño [DAH-*n'yoh*] damage
★ **dar** [*dahr*] to give
dar de comer a [*dahr deh koh*-MEHR *ah*] to feed
dar a conocer [*dahr ah koh-noh*-THEHR] to make known
dar a luz [*dahr ah looth*] to give birth to
darse cuenta de [DAHR-*seh* KWEHN-*tah deh*] to realize something
darse prisa [DAHR-*seh* PREE-*sah*] to hurry
dátil (m) [DAH-*teel*] date
datos (plural) [DAH-*tohs*] information
★ **de** [*deh*] of, from

NOTE: *De* is also used to introduce a descriptive adjective or noun. *de pie*—"on foot," *de plata*—"(made) of silver," *de día*—"during the day."

★ **de nada** [*deh* NAH-*dah*] you are welcome
debajo [*deh*-BAH-*hoh*] underneath
★ **debajo de** [*deh*-BAH-*hoh deh*] under, beneath
deber (n) [*deh*-BEHR] duty
★ **deber** (verb) [*deh*-BEHR] to owe
NOTE: When followed by an infinitive of another verb, *deber* means "must," "have to."
debido, -a [*deh*-BEE-*doh, -dah*] owing to, on account to
débil [DEH-*beel*] weak
debilidad (f) [*deh-bee-lee*-DAHD] weakness

decente [*deh*-THEHN-*teh*] decent
decepción (f) [*deh-thehp-th'*YOHN] disappointment
decidir [*deh-thee*-DEER] to decide
décimo, -a [DEH-*thee-moh, -mah*] tenth
★ **decir** [*deh*-THEHR] to say, to tell
decisión (f) [*deh-thee-th'*YOHN] decision
declaración (f) [*deh-klah-rah-th'*YOHN] declaration
declarar [*deh-klah*-RAHR] to declare
decoración (f) [*deh-koh-rah-th'*YOHN] decoration
decorar [*deh-koh*-RAHR] to decorate
dedicar [*deh-dee*-KAHR] to dedicate
dedo [DEH-*doh*] finger or toe
deducir [*deh-doo*-THEER] to deduce, to infer
defecto [*deh*-FEHK-*toh*] defect
defender [*deh-fehn*-DEHR] to defend
defensa [*deh*-FEHN-*sah*] defense
defensor [*deh-fehn*-SOHR] defender
deficiente [*deh-fee-th'*YEHN-*teh*] deficient
definido, -a [*deh-fee*-NEE-*doh, -dah*] definite
degradar [*deh-grah*-DAHR] to degrade
★ **dejar** [*deh*-HAHR] to leave, to let, to allow
  déjeme pasar [DEH-*heh-meh pah*-SAHR] let me pass!
  déjeme ver [DEH-*heh-meh vehr*] let me see (it)
★ **del** [*dehl*] (contraction of *de* and *el*)
delantal (m) [*deh-lahn*-TAHL] apron
delante [*deh*-LAHN-*teh*] ahead, in front
  delante de [*deh*-LAHN-*teh deh*] in front of
delegado, -a [*deh-leh*-GAH-*doh, -dah*] delegate
deleite [*deh*-LAY-*teh*] delight
deletrear [*deh-leh-treh*-AHR] to spell
  ¿Cómo se deletrea? [KOH-*moh seh deh-leh*-TREH-*ah*] How is it spelled?
delgado, -a [*dehl*-GAH-*doh, -dah*] thin
delicadeza [*deh-lee-kah*-DEH-*thah*] delicacy
delicado, -a [*deh-lee*-KAH-*doh, -dah*] delicate
delincuente (m) [*deh-leen*-KWEHN-*teh*] delinquent
delirio [*deh*-LEE-*r'yoh*] delirium
demanda [*deh*-MAHN-*dah*] claim

demás [*deh*-MAHS] rest, other
los, las demás [*lohs, lahs deh*-MAHS] the others
demasiado, -a [*deh-mah-s'*YAH-*doh, -dah*] too much
demasiados, -as [*deh-mah-s'*YAH-*dohs, -dahs*] too many
¡deme! [DEH-*meh*] give me!
¡dele! [DEH-*leh*] give him! (or her)
democracia [*deh-moh*-KRAH-*th'yah*] democracy
demócrata [*deh*-MOH-*krah-tah*] democrat
demonio [*deh*-MOH-*n'yoh*] demon, devil
demora [*deh*-MOH-*rah*] delay
demorar [*deh-moh*-RAHR] to delay
demostrar [*deh-mos*-TRAHR] to demonstrate
denso, -a [DEHN-*soh,- sah*] dense, thick
dentista (f and m) [*dehn*-TEES-*tah*] dentist
★ **dentro** [DEHN-*troh*] inside, within
dentro de [DEHN-*troh deh*] inside of
dentro del año [DEHN-*troh dehl* AH-*n'yoh*] in the course of the year
dentro de poco [DEHN-*troh deh* POH-*koh*] shortly, presently
denunciar [*deh-noon-th'*YAHR] to denounce
departamento [*deh-pahr-tah*-MEHN-*toh*] department
depender [*deh-pehn*-DEHR] to depend
dependiente (m or f) [*deh-pehn-d'*YEHN-*teh*] salesman or saleswoman, clerk
deportar [*deh-pohr*-TAHR] to deport, to exile
deporte (m) [*deh*-POHR-*teh*] sport
depositar [*deh-poh-see*-TAHR] to deposit
depósito [*deh*-POH-*see-toh*] deposit
depresión (f) [*deh-preh-s'*YOHN] depression
deprimir [*deh-pree*-MEER] to depress
derechista (m and f) [*deh-reh*-CHEES-*tah*] rightist (politics)
derecho (n) [*deh*-REH-*choh*] law, right
★ **derecho, -a** [*deh*-REH-*choh, -chah*] right; straight
a la derecha [*ah lah deh*-REH-*chah*] to the right
¡derecho! [*deh*-REH-*choh*] straight ahead!
derramar [*deh-rrah*-MAHR] overflow, to spill
derretir [*deh-rreh*-TEER] to melt

derrota [*deh*-RROH-*tah*] defeat
derrotar [*deh-rroh*-TAHR] to defeat
desacuerdo [*deh-sah*-KWEHR-*doh*] disagreement
desafiar [*deh-sah-f'*YAHR] to challenge
desagradable [*deh-sah-grah*-DAH-*bleh*] disagreeable
desagradar [*deh-sah-grah*-DAHR] to displease
desagradecido, -a [*deh-sah-grah-deh*-THEE-*doh, -dah*] ungrateful
desalentar [*deh-sah*-LEHN-*tahr*] to discourage
desanimar [*deh-sah-nee*-MAHR] to discourage
desaparecer [*deh-sah-pah-reh*-THEHR] to disappear
desaprobar [*deh-sah-proh*-BAHR] to disapprove
desarreglar [*deh-sah-rreh*-GLAHR] to disarrange
desarrollado, -a [*deh-sah-rroh-l'*YAH-*doh, -dah*] developed
desarrollar [*deh-sah-rroh-l'*YAHR] to develop
desarrollo [*deh-sah*-RROH-*l'yoh*] development
desastre (m) [*deh*-SAHS-*treh*] disaster
desayunar(se) [*deh-sah-yoo*-NAHR-*(seh)*] to have breakfast
desayuno [*deh-sah*-YOO-*noh*] breakfast
descalzo, -a [*dehs*-KAHL-*thoh, -thah*] barefoot
descansar [*dehs-kahn*-SAHR] to rest
¡Que descanse! [*keh dehs*-KAHN-*seh*] Have a (good) rest!
descanso [*dehs*-KAHN-*soh*] rest
descargar [*dehs-kahr*-GAHR] to unload
descaro [*dehs*-KAH-*roh*] impudence, nerve
descender [*dehs-thehn*-DEHR] to descend
descendiente [*dehs-then-d'*YEHN-*teh*] descendant
descolgar [*dehs-kohl*-GAHR] to take down
descomponer [*dehs-kohm-poh*-NEHR] to disarrange, upset
descompuesto, -a [*dehs-kohm*-PWEHS-*toh, -tah*] out of orde
desconectar [*dehs-koh-nehk*-TAHR] to disconnect
desconfiado, -a [*dehs-kohn-f'*YAH-*doh, -dah*] distrustful
desconfiar de [*dehs-kohn-f'*YAHR-*deh*] to mistrust, to suspect
desconocido, -a [*dehs-koh-noh*-THEE-*doh, -dah*] unknown
desconsiderado, -a [*dehs-kohn-see-deh*-RAH-*doh, -dah*] inconsiderate, thoughtless
descontar [*dehs-kohn*-TAHR] to discount
descontento, -a [*dehs-kohn*-TEHN-*toh, -tah*] dissatisfied

descortés [*dehs-kohr*-TEHS] impolite, rude
descrédito [*dehs*-KREH-*dee-toh*] discredit
describir [*dehs-kree*-BEER] to describe
descripción (f) [*dehs-kreep-th'*YOHN] description
descubridor [*dehs-koo-bree*-DOHR] discoverer
descubrimiento [*dehs-koo-bree-m'*YEHN-*toh*] discovery
descubrir [*dehs-koo*-BREER] to discover
descuento [*dehs*-KWEHN-*toh*] discount
descuidado, -a [*dehs-kwee*-DAH-*doh, -dah*] careless
descuidar [*dehs-kwee*-DAHR] to neglect
★ **desde** [DEHS-*deh*] since, from
 ¿desde cuándo? [DEHS-*deh* KWAHN-*doh*] since when?
 desde entonces [DEHS-*deh ehn*-TOHN-*thehs*] since then
 ¡desde luego! [DEHS-*deh* LWEH-*goh*] of course!
desdicha [*dehs*-DEE-*chah*] misfortune
desdichado, -a [*dehs-dee*-CHAH-*doh, -dah*] unfortunate
¡dése prisa! [DEH-*seh* PREE-*sah*] hurry up!
deseable [*deh-seh*-AH-*bleh*] desirable
desear [*deh-seh*-AHR] to desire, to wish
 ¿Qué deseaba Ud.? [*keh deh-seh*-AH-*bah oos*-TEHD] What were you wishing? (Equivalent to "May I help you?")
desembarcar [*deh-sehm-bahr*-KAHR] to disembark
desembolso [*deh-sehm*-BOHL-*soh*] expenditure
desempacar [*deh-sehm-pah*-KAHR] to unpack
desempeñar [*deh-sehm-peh-n'*YAHR] to perform, to carry out
desempleo [*deh-sehm*-PLEH-*oh*] unemployment
deseo [*deh*-SEH-*oh*] desire, wish
deseoso, -a [*deh-seh*-OH-*soh, -sah*] desirous, willing
desequilibrado, -a [*deh-seh-kee-lee*-BRAH-*doh, -dah*] unbalanced
desertar [*deh-sehr*-TAHR] to desert, to abandon
desesperación (f) [*deh-sehs-peh-rah-th'*YOHN] despair
desesperado, -a [*deh-sehs-peh*-RAH-*doh, -dah*] desperate
desfavorable [*dehs-fah-voh*-RAH-*bleh*] unfavorable
desfile (m) [*dehs*-FEE-*leh*] parade, review
desgastar(se) [*dehs-gahs*-TAHR*(seh)*] to wear out or away

desgaste (m) [*dehs*-GAHS-*teh*] waste
desgracia [*dehs*-GRAH-*th'yah*] misfortune
¡Qué desgracia! [*keh dehs*-GRAH-*th'yah*] What a shame!
desgraciadamente [*dehs-grah-th'yah-dah*-MEHN-*teh*] unfortunately
desgraciado, -a [*dehs-grah-th'*YAH-*doh, -dah*] unfortunate, unlucky
deshacer [*dehs-ah*-THEHR] to undo, to unwrap
deshecho, -a [*dehs*-EH-*choh, -chah*] undone
deshonra [*dehs*-OHN-*rah*] dishonor, disgrace
desierto [*deh-s'*YEHR-*toh*] desert
designar [*deh-seeg*-NAHR] to designate
desigual [*deh-see*-GWAHL] unequal, not the same
desilusión (f) [*deh-see-loo-s'*YOHN] disillusion
desilusionar [*deh-see-loo-s'yoh*-NAHR] to disillusion
desinfectar [*deh-seen-fehk*-TAHR] to disinfect
desistir [*deh-sees*-TEER] to desist
desleal [*dehs-leh*-AHL] disloyal
desmayar(se) [*dehs-mah*-YAHR-*(seh)*] to faint
desmontar [*dehs-mohn*-TAHR] to dismount, to disassemble
desmoralizar [*dehs-moh-rah-lee*-THAHR] to demoralize
desnudo, -a [*dehs*-NOO-*doh, -dah*] nude, bare
desobedecer [*deh-soh-beh-deh*-THEHR] to disobey
desobediente [*deh-soh-beh-d'*YEHN-*teh*] disobedient
desocupado, -a [*deh-soh-koo*-PAH-*doh, -dah*] unemployed, vacant
desorden (m) [*deh*-SOHR-*dehn*] disorder
desorganizar [*deh-sohr-gah-nee*-THAHR] to disorganize
★ **despacio** [*dehs*-PAH-*th'yoh*] slowly
despachar [*dehs-pah*-CHAHR] to send, to ship
despacho [*dehs*-PAH-*choh*] office, shipment (of goods)
despedir [*dehs-peh*-DEER)] to discharge, to dismiss, to see (someone) off
despensa [*dehs*-PEHN-*sah*] pantry
desperdicio [*dehs-pehr*-DEE-*th'yoh*] waste, garbage
despertador [*dehs-pehr-tah*-DOHR] alarm clock

despertar [*dehs-pehr*-TAHR] to wake up
despertarse [*dehs-pehr*-TAHR-*seh*] to wake up (oneself)
despierto, -a [*dehs-p'*YEHR-*toh, -tah*] awake, clever
despreciable [*dehs-preh-th'*YAH-*bleh*] despicable
desprecio [*dehs*-PREH-*th'yoh*] scorn
después [*dehs*-PWEHS] after, afterward
  después de usted [*dehs*-PWEHS *deh oos*-TEHD] after you
destapar [*dehs-tah*-PAHR] to open (a container)
desteñir(se) [*dehs-teh-n'*YEHR-*(seh)*] to fade
destinar [*dehs-tee*-NAHR] to destine, to designate
destino [*dehs*-TEE-*noh*] destiny, fate, destination
destornillador [*dehs-tohr-nee-l'yah*-DOHR] screw driver
destrozar and **destruir** [*dehs-troh*-THAHR] and [*dehs-troo*-EER] to destroy
desván (m) [*dehs*-VAHN] attic
desventaja [*dehs-vehn*-TAH-*hah*] disadvantage
desvestir(se) [*dehs-vehs*-TEER-*(seh)*] to undress
detalle (m) [*deh*-TAH-*l'yeh*] detail, retail (commercial)
detective [*deh-tehk*-TEE-*veh*] detective
detener [*deh-teh*-NEHR] to arrest, to stop (someone else)
detenerse [*deh-teh*-NEHR-*seh*] to stop (oneself)
determinación (f) [*deh-tehr-mee-nah-th'*YOHN] determination
determinar [*deh-tehr-mee*-NAHR] to determine
detestar [*deh-tehs*-TAHR] to detest
★ **detrás de** [*deh*-TRAHS *deh*] in back of, behind
deuda [DEH-*oo-dah*] debt
devoción (f) [*deh-voh-th'*YOHN] devotion
devolver [*deh-vohl*-VEHR] to return (something), to refund
★ **día** (m) [DEE-*ah*] day
  todo el día [TOH-*doh ehl* DEE-*ah*] all day
  todos los días [TOH-*dohs lohs* DEE-*ahs*] every day
  día de trabajo [DEE-*ah deh trah*-BAH-*hoh*] work day
  día festivo [DEE-*ah fehs*-TEE-*voh*] holiday
diablo [*d'*YAH-*bloh*] devil
dialecto [*d'yah*-LEHK-*toh*] dialect
diálogo [*d'*YAH-*loh-goh*] dialogue
diamante (m) [*d'yah*-MAHN-*teh*] diamond

diámetro [*d'*YAH-*meh-troh*] diameter
diario [*d'*YAH-*r'yoh*] daily newspaper
diario, -ria [*d'*YAH-*r'yoh, -r'yah*] daily, every day
dibujante [*dee-boo-*HAHN-*teh*] draftsman
dibujar [*dee-boo-*HAHR] to draw
dibujo [*dee-*BOO-*hoh*] drawing
diccionario [*deek-th'yoh-*NAH-*r'yoh*] dictionary
diciembre [*dee-th'*YEHM-*breh*] December
dictado [*deek-*TAH-*doh*] dictation
dictar [*deek-*TAHR] to dictate
dicha [DEE-*chah*] happiness
dicho (n) [DEE-*choh*] saying (proverb)
dichoso, -a [*dee-*CHOH-*soh, -sah*] fortunate, happy
★ **diecinueve** [*d'yeh-thee-*NWEH-*veh*] nineteen
★ **dieciocho** [*d'yeh-thee-*OH-*choh*] eighteen
★ **dieciséis** [*d'yeh-thee-*SEH-*ees*] sixteen
★ **diecisiete** [*d'yeh-thee-s'*YEH-*teh*] seventeen
diente (m) [*d'*YEHN-*teh*] tooth
diestro, -a [*d'*YEHS-*troh, -trah*] skillful
dieta [*d'*YEH-*tah*] diet
★ **diez** [*d'yehth*] ten
  son las diez [*sohn lahs d'yehth*] it is ten o'clock
diferencia [*dee-feh-*REHN-*th'yah*] difference
★ **diferente** [*dee-feh-*REHN-*teh*] different
★ **difícil** [*dee-*FEE-*theel*] difficult
dificultad (f) [*dee-fee-kool-*TAHD] difficulty
difunto, -ta [*dee-*FOON-*toh, -tah*] deceased (dead person)
difusión (f) [*dee-foo-s'*YOHN] broadcast, diffusion
dígame [DEE-*gah-meh*] (from *decir*) tell me
dígale [DEE-*gah-leh*] tell him (her)
  ¡no me diga! [*noh meh* DEE-*gah*] you don't say!
(se) dice [*seh* DEE-*theh*] it is said
digerir [*dee-heh-*REER] to digest
digestión (f) [*dee-hehs-t'*YOHN] digestion
dignidad (f) [*deeg-nee-*DAHD] dignity
digno, -a [DEEG-*noh, -nah*] worthy
diligencia [*dee-lee-*HEHN-*th'yah*] diligence
diluir [*dee-loo-*EER] to dilute

dimensión (f) [*dee-mehn-s'*YOHN] dimension
diminutivo [*dee-mee-noo-*TEE-*voh*] diminutive
Dinamarca [*dee-nah-*MAHR-*kah*] Denmark
dinamita [*dee-nah-*MEE-*tah*] dynamite
★ **dinero** [*dee-*NEH-*roh*] money
dinero contante [*dee-*NEH-*roh kohn-*TAHN-*teh*] cash
★ **Dios** [D'YOHS] God
¡Dios mío! [D'YOHS MEE-*oh*] Good Heavens!
NOTE: Frequent references to the Deity are not considered profane in Spanish.
¡Por Dios! [*pohr-*D'YOHS] For heavens sake!
Si Dios quiere [*see* D'YOHS *k'*YEH-*reh*] If God wills
diploma (m) [*dee-*PLOH-*mah*] diploma
diplomático (n and adj) [*dee-ploh-*MAH-*tee-koh*] diplomat, diplomatic
dirección (f) [*dee-rehk-th'*YOHN] direction, address
★ **directo, -a** [*dee-*REHK-*toh, -tah*] direct
director, -a [*dee-rehk-*TOHR, *-ah*] director, directress
director de orquesta [*dee-rehk-*TOHR *deh ohr-*KEHS-*tah*] orchestra conductor
dirigir [*dee-ree-*HEER] to direct, to lead
dirigir la palabra [*dee-ree-*HEER *lah pah-*LAH-*brah*] to make an address, to address
dirigir(se) [*dee-ree-*HEER*(seh)*] to address
disciplina [*dees-thee-*PLEE-*nah*] discipline
discípulo, -a [*dees-*THEE-*poo-loh, -lah*] pupil
disco [DEES-*koh*] disk, phonograph record
discreción (f) [*dees-kreh-th'*YOHN] discretion
discreto, -a [*dees-*KREH-*toh, -tah*] discreet
disculpa [*dees-*KOOL-*pah*] apology
disculpar [*dees-kool-*PAHR] to excuse, to apologize
discúlpeme [*dees-*KOOL-*peh-meh*] excuse me
discurso [*dees-*KOOR-*soh*] speech
discusión (f) [*dees-koo-s'*YOHN] discussion
discutir [*dees-koo-*TEER] to discuss, to argue
diseñar [*dee-seh-n'*YAHR] to sketch, to design
diseño [*dee-*SEH-*n'yoh*] sketch, design
disfraz (m) [*dees-*FRATH] mask, disguise

disfrutar [*dees-froo*-TAHR] to enjoy, to benefit by
disgustar(se) [*dees-goos*-TAHR-*(seh)*] to be offended, d s-pleased
disminuir [*dees-mee-noo*-EER] to decrease, to diminish
disparar [*dees-pah*-RAHR] to shoot
disparate (m) [*dees-pah*-RAH-*teh*] nonsense
disparo [*dees*-PAH-*roh*] shot
★ **¡dispense!** or **¡dispénseme!** [*dees*-PEHN-*seh-meh*] excuse me!
¡Está dispensado! [*ehs*-TAH *dees-pehn*-SAH-*doh*] You are excused!
disponer [*dees-poh*-NEHR] to dispose
Está a su disposición [*ehs*-TAH *ah soo dees-poh-see-th'*YOHN] It is at your service
disponible [*dees-poh*-NEE-*bleh*] available
dispuesto, -a [*dees*-PWEHS-*toh, -tah*] ready
disputar [*dees-poo*-TAHR] to argue
distancia [*dees*-TAHN-*th'yah*] distance
distante [*dees*-TAHN-*teh*] distant
distinción (f) [*dees-teen-th'*YOHN] distinction
distinguido, -a [*dees-teen*-GHEE-*doh, -dah*] distinguish
distinto, -a [*dees*-TEEN-*toh, -tah*] distinct, different
distribuidor [*dees-tree-boo-ee*-DOHR] distributor
distribuir [*dees-tree-boo*-EER] to distribute
diversión (f) [*dee-vehr-s'*YOHN] amusement, diversion
diverso, -a [*dee*-VEHR-*soh, -sah*] different
divertido, -a [*dee-vehr*-TEE-*doh, -dah*] amusing
divertir [*dee-vehr*-TEER] to amuse
divertir(se) [*dee-vehr*-TEER-*(seh)*] to have a good time
¡Diviértase mucho! [*dee-v'*YEHR-*tah-seh* MOO-*choh*] Have a good time!
dividir [*dee-vee*-DEER] to divide
divino, -a [*dee*-VEE-*noh, -nah*] divine
división (f) [*dee-vee-s'*YOHN] division
divorcio [*dee*-VOHR-*th'yoh*] divorce
doblar [*doh*-BLAHR] to double, to fold
★ **doce** [DOH-*theh*] twelve
Son las doce [*sohn lahs* DOH-*theh*] It is twelve o'clock
docena [*doh*-THEH-*nah*] dozen

dócil [DOH-*theel*] docile, gentle
doctor, -a [*dohk*-TOHR, *-rah*] doctor (m and f)
documento [*doh-koo*-MEHN-*toh*] document
doler [*doh*-LEHR] to ache, to hurt
  ¿Dónde le duele? [DOHN-*deh leh* DWEH-*leh*] Where does it hurt you?
dolor (m) [*doh*-LOHR] pain, sorrow
  dolor de cabeza [*doh*-LOHR *deh kah*-BEH-*thah*] headache
  dolor de estómago [*doh*-LOHR *deh ehs*-TOH-*mah-goh*] stomach ache
doméstico, -a [*doh*-MEHS-*tee-koh, -kah*] domestic
domicilio [*doh-mee*-THEE-*l'yoh*] home, residence
dominar [*doh-mee*-NAHR] to dominate, to master
★ **domingo** [*doh*-MEEN-*goh*] Sunday
dominio [*doh*-MEE-*n'yoh*] dominion, control
don (m) **doña** (f) [*dohn*, DOH-*n'yah*]
  NOTE: *Don* and *doña* are titles of respect that are prefaced to first names; e.g., *Doña Clara, Don Roberto.*
★ **donde** (adv) [DOHN-*deh*] where
★ **¿dónde?** [DOHN-*deh*] where?
  ¿dónde está? [DOHN-*deh ehs*-TAH] where is it?
dondequiera [DOHN-*deh*-K'YEH-*rah*] anywhere, wherever
dorado, -a [*doh*-RAH-*doh, -dah*] gilded
★ **dormir** [*dohr*-MEER] to sleep
dormir(se) [*dohr*-MEER*(seh)*] to go to sleep, to fall asleep
dormitorio [*dohr-mee*-TOH-*r'yoh*] bedroom
★ **dos** [*dohs*] two
doscientos, -as [*dohs-th'*YEHN-*tohs, -tahs*] two hundred
dosis [DOH-*sees*] dose
doy [DOH-*ee*] I give (see *dar*)
drama (m) [DRAH-*mah*] drama, play
droga [DROH-*gah*] drug
ducha [DOO-*chah*] shower bath
duda [DOO-*dah*] doubt
dudar [*doo*-DAHR] to doubt
dudoso, -a [*doo*-DOH-*soh, -sah*] doubtful

duelo [DWEH-*loh*] grief, mourning, duel
duende (m) [DWEHN-*deh*] ghost
dueño, -a (m and f) [DWEH-*n'yoh, -n'yah*] owner, proprietor
dulce (n and adj) [DOOL-*theh*] sweet, candy
dulzura [*dool*-THOO-*rah*] sweetness
duplicado, -a [*doo-plee*-KAH-*doh, -dah*] duplicate
duque (m) [DOO-*keh*] duke
duquesa [*doo*-KEH-*sah*] duchess
duración (f) [*doo-rah-th'*YOHN] duration
durante [*doo*-RAHN-*teh*] during
durar [*doo*-RAHR] to last
durazno [*doo*-RAHTH-*noh*] peach
★ **duro, -a** [DOO-*roh, -rah*] hard

E

e [*eh*] and
NOTE: A variant of *y* (and) to be used when the following word begins with *i*.
eclipse (m) [*eh*-KLEEP-*seh*] eclipse
eco [EH-*koh*] echo
económico, -a [*eh-koh*-NOH-*mee-koh, -kah*] economic, low priced
economizar [*eh-koh-noh-mee*-THAHR] to save
echar [*eh*-CHAHR] to throw
echar una carta al correo [*eh*-CHAHR OO-*nah* KAHR-*tah ahl koh*-RREH-*oh*] to mail a letter
echar de menos [*eh*-CHAHR *deh* MEH-*nohs*] to miss (someone or something)
Ecuador [*eh-kwa*-DOHR] Ecuador
ecuatoriano, -a [*eh-kwah-toh*-R'YAH-*noh, -nah*] Ecuadorian
edad (f) [*eh*-DAHD] age
edición (f) [*eh-dee-th'*YOHN] edition
edificar [*eh-dee-fee*-KAHR] to build
edificio [*eh-dee*-FEE-*th'yoh*] building
editar [*eh-dee*-TAHR] to publish

editor [*eh-dee*-TOHR] publisher
editorial [*eh-dee-toh-r'*YAHL] editorial; publishing house
educación (f) [*eh-doo-kah-th'*YOHN] education; good breeding
educar [*eh-doo*-KAHR] to educate, instruct
efectivo, -a [*eh-fehk*-TEE-*voh, -vah*] effective
  en efectivo [*ehn eh-fehk*-TEE-*voh*] in cash
efecto [*eh*-FEHK-*toh*] effect
  efectos personales [*eh*-FEHK-*tohs pehr-soh*-NAH-*lehs*] personal effects
eficaz [*eh-fee*-KATH] effective
eficiente [*eh-fee-th'*YEHN-*teh*] efficient
egipcio, -a [*eh*-HEEP-*th'yoh, -th'yah*] Egyptian
Egipto [*eh*-HEEP-*toh*] Egypt
egoísta (m) [*eh-goh*-EES-*tah*] selfish
ejecución (f) [*eh-heh-koo-th'*YOHN] execution
ejemplar [*eh-hehm*-PLAHR] model; copy
ejemplo [*eh*-HEHM-*ploh*] example
ejercer [*eh-hehr*-THEHR] to practise
ejercicio [*eh-hehr*-THEE-*th'yoh*] exercise
ejército [*eh*-HEHR-*thee-toh*] army
★ **el** [*ehl*] (m, singular) the
★ **él** [*ehl*] he
  a él [*ah ehl*] to him, him
El Salvador [*ehl sahl-vah*-DOHR] El Salvador
elástico, -a [*eh*-LAHS-*tee-koh, -kah*] elastic
elección (f) [*eh-lehk-th'*YOHN] election, choice
electricidad (f) [*eh-lehk-tree-thee*-DAHD] electricity
eléctrico, -a [*eh*-LEHK-*tree-koh, -kah*] electric
elefante [*eh-leh*-FAHN-*teh*] elephant
elegancia [*eh-leh*-GAHN-*th'yah*] elegance
elegante [*eh-leh*-GAHN-*teh*] elegant
elegir [*eh-leh*-HEER] to choose, to elect
elemental [*eh-leh-mehn*-TAHL] elementary
elemento [*eh-leh*-MEHN-*toh*] element
eliminar [*eh-lee-mee*-NAHR] to eliminate
elogio [*eh*-LOH-*h'yoh*] praise

★ **ella** [EH-*l'yah*] she
a ella [*ah* EH-*l'yah*] to her, her (obj)
★ **ellas** [EH-*l'yahs*] they (f, plural)
a ellas [*ah* EH-*l'yahs*] to them, them
ello [EH-*l'yoh*] it (neuter)
★ **ellos** [EH-*l'yohs*] they (m, plural)
a ellos [*ah* EH-*l'yohs*] to them, them
embajada [*ehm-bah-*HAH-*dah*] embassy
embajador, -a [*ehm-bah-hah-*DOHR, -DOH-*rah*] ambassador
embalar [*ehm-bah-*LAHR] to pack
embarcar [*ehm-bahr-*KAHR] to embark
(sin) embargo [*seen ehm-*BAHR-*goh*] however, nevertheless
embarque (m) [*ehm-*BAHR-*keh*] shipment
embestir [*ehm-behs-*TEER] to attack
emborrachar(se) [*ehm-boh-rrah-*CHAHR*(seh)*] to get drunk
embromado [*ehm-broh-*MAH-*doh*] annoyed
embromar [*ehm-broh-*MAHR] to play jokes on, to annoy
embrutecer(se) [*ehm-broo-teh-*THEHR*(seh)*] to become brutalized
embudo [*ehm-*BOO-*doh*] funnel
embustero [*ehm-boos-*TEH-*roh*] liar
emergencia [*eh-mehr-*HEHN-*th'yah*] emergency
emigración (f) [*eh-mee-grah-th'*YOHN] emigration
emisora [*eh-mee-*SOH-*rah*] broadcasting station
emitir [*eh-mee-*TEER] to issue
emoción (f) [*eh-moh-th'*YOHN] emotion
emocionante [*eh-moh-th'yoh-*NAHN-*teh*] touching, exciting
empacar [*ehm-pah-*KAHR] to pack, to bale
empanada [*ehm-pah-*NAH-*dah*] meat pie, croquette
• **empaquetar** [*ehm-pah-keh-*TAHR] to pack
emparedado [*ehm-pah-reh-*DAH-*doh*] sandwich
emparentado, -a [*ehm-pah-rehn-*TAH-*doh, -dah*] related

NOTE: *Relacionado* also means "related" but not by family ties, as does *emparentado*.

empastar [*ehm-pahs*-TAHR] to fill (a tooth)
empeorar [*ehm-peh-oh*-RAHR] to grow worse
emperador (m) [*ehm-peh-rah*-DOHR] emperor
emperatriz (f) [*ehm-peh-rah*-TREETH] empress
empeñar [*ehm-peh-n'*YAHR] to pawn
★ **empezar** [*ehm-peh*-THAHR] to begin
empleado, -a [*ehm-pleh*-AH-*doh, -dah*] employee
emplear [*ehm-pleh*-AHR] to employ
empleo [*ehm*-PLEH-*oh*] employment
empolvar [*ehm-pohl*-VAHR] to powder
emprender [*ehm-prehn*-DEHR] to undertake
empresa [*ehm*-PREH-*sah*] enterprise
empresario [*ehm-preh*-SAH-*r'yoh*] promoter, impresario
empréstito [*ehm*-PREHS-*tee-toh*] loan
empujar [*ehm-poo*-HAHR] to push
¡empuje! [*ehm*-POO-*heh*] Push!
★ **en** [*ehn*] in, into, at, on
enamorado, -a (adj) [*eh-nah-moh*-RAH-*doh, -dah*] in love
encabezamiento [*ehn-kah-beh-thah-m'*YEHN-*toh*] headline (of newspaper), heading (of letter)
encaje [*ehn*-KAH-*heh*] lace
encantado, -a [*ehn-kahn*-TAH-*doh, -dah*] enchanted, charmed
Note: Often used to acknowledge an introduction or acceptance.
encantador, -a [*ehn-kahn-tah*-DOHR, *-ah*] charming
encantar [*ehn-kahn*-TAHR] to charm
Note: Can be used with indirect object to express liking. *Eso me encanta:* "I like that very much."
encanto [*ehn*-KAHN-*toh*] charm
encargado, -a [*ehn-kahr*-GAH-*doh, -dah*] in charge
encargar [*ehn-kahr*-GAHR] to entrust
encargo [*ehn*-KAHR-*goh*] charge, commission
encarnado, -a [*ehn-kahr*-NAH-*doh, -dah*] red
encendedor [*ehn-thehn-deh*-DOHR] cigarette lighter
encender [*ehn-thehn*-DEHR] to light
enchilada [*ehn-chee*-LAH-*dah*] (Mexican dish of stuffed *tortillas*)

enchufe [*ehn*-CHOO-*feh*] plug (electric)
encima [*ehn*-THEE-*mah*] above
★ **encima de** [*ehn*-THEE-*mah deh*] on, over
★ **encontrar** [*ehn-kohn*-TRAHR] to find; to meet
encontrarse [*ehn-kohn*-TRAHR-*seh*] to come upon, to find oneself, to run into someone
¿Cómo se encuentra? [KOH-*moh seh ehn*-KWEHN-*trah*] How do you feel?
encrucijada [*ehn-kroo-thee*-HAH-*dah*] crossroads or cross street
encuentro [*ehn*-KWEHN-*troh*] meeting, encounter
endosar [*ehn-doh*-SAHR] to indorse
enemigo [*eh-neh*-MEE-*goh*] enemy
energía [*eh-nehr*-HEE-*ah*] energy
enero [*eh*-NEH-*roh*] January
enfadarse [*ehn-fah*-DAHR-*seh*] to become angry
enfadado, -da [*ehn-fah*-DAH-*doh, -dah*] angry
énfasis [EHN-*fah-sees*] emphasis
enfermar(se) [*ehn-fehr*-MAHR*(seh)*] to fall ill
enfermedad (f) [*ehn-fehr-meh*-DAHD] illness, sickness
enfermo, -a [*ehn*-FEHR-*moh, -ah*] ill, sick
enfrente [*ehn*-FREHN-*teh*] in front
enfriar [*ehn-free*-AHR] to cool
engañar [*ehn-gah-n'*YAHR] to deceive
engaño [*eh*-GAH-*n'yoh*] deceit
engordar [*ehn-gohr*-DAHR] to get fat
engranaje [*ehn-grah*-NAH-*heh*] gears (of a car)
engrasar [*ehn-grah*-SAHR] to oil, to grease
enhorabuena [*eh-noh-rah*-BWEH-*nah*] congratulations
enloquecer [*ehn-loh-keh*-THEHR] to become insane
enmendar [*ehn-mehn*-DAHR] to amend, to reform
enojado, -a [*eh-noh*-HAH-*doh, -dah*] angry
enojar(se) [*eh-noh*-HAHR-*seh*] to become angry
¡No se enoje! [*noh seh eh*-NOH-*heh*] Don't be angry!
enojo [*eh*-NOH-*hoh*] anger
enorme [*eh*-NOHR-*meh*] enormous
enredar [*ehn-reh*-DAHR] to involve in difficulties, to entangle

enriquecer(se) [*ehn-ree-keh-*THEHR-*seh*] to become rich
ensalada [*ehn-sah-*LAH-*dah*] salad
ensayar [*ehn-sah-*YAHR] to try; to rehearse
ensayo [*ehn-*SAH-*yoh*] essay; trial, rehearsal
enseñanza [*ehn-seh-n'*YAHN-*thah*] teaching
enseñar [*ehn-seh-n'*YAHR] to teach; to show
ensuciar [*ehn-soo-th'*YAHR] to soil, to dirty
★ **entender** [*ehn-tehn-*DEHR] to understand
  ¿entiende Ud.? [*ehn-t'*YEHN-*deh oos-*TEHD] Do you understand?
  está entendido [*ehs-*TAH *ehn-tehn-*DEE-*doh*] it is understood
enteramente [*ehn-téh-rah-*MEHN-*teh*] entirely
enterar(se) de [*ehn-teh-*RAHR-*seh deh*] to find out
entero, -a [*ehn-*TEH-*roh, -rah*] entire
entierro [*ehn-t'*YEHR-*roh*] burial
★ **entonces** (adv) [*ehn-*TOHN-*thehs*] then
  desde entonces [DEHS-*deh ehn-*TOHN-*thehs*] since then
entrada [*ehn-*TRAH-*dah*] entrance, ticket (for show)
  Se prohibe la entrada [*seh proh-*EE-*beh lah ehn-*TRAH-*dah*] No admittance
entrante [*ehn-*TRAHN-*teh*] next (week, month, year, etc.)
★ **entrar** [EHN-*trahr*] to enter
★ **¡entre!** [EHN-*treh*] Come in!
  ¿Se puede entrar? [*seh* PWEH-*deh ehn-*TRAHR] May one come in?
★ **entre** [EHN-*treh*] among, between
entreacto [*ehn-treh-*AHK-*toh*] intermission
entregar [*ehn-treh-*GAHR] to deliver; to yield
entretanto [*ehn-treh-*TAHN-*toh*] meanwhile
entretenido, -a [*ehn-treh-teh-*NEE-*doh, -dah*] entertaining, amusing
entrevista [*ehn-treh-*VEES-*tah*] interview
entusiasmo [*ehn-too-s'*YAHS-*moh*] enthusiasm
★ **enviar** [*ehn-v'*YAHR] to send; to ship
envidia [*ehn-*VEE-*d'yah*] envy
envidioso, -a [*ehn-vee-d'*YOH-*soh, -sah*] envious

envío [*ehn*-VEE-*oh*] shipment
envolver [*ehn-vohl*-VEHR] to wrap
época [EH-*poh-kah*] epoch, period of time
equipaje (m) [*eh-kee*-PAH-*heh*] baggage, luggage
equipo [*eh*-KEE-*poh*] equipment; team
equivalente [*eh-kee-vah*-LEHN-*teh*] equivalent
equivocado, -a [*eh-kee-voh*-KAH-*doh, -dah*] mistaken
equivocar(se) [*eh-kee-voh*-KAHR*(seh)*] to make a mistake, to be wrong
era [EH-*rah*] era, age
error (m) [*eh*-RROHR] error, mistake
★ **es** [*ehs*] (you) are, (he, she, it) is
★ **esa** (f), **esas** (plural) [EH-*sah*, EH-*sahs*] that (adj)
ésa (f), **ésas** (plural) [EH-*sah*, EH-*sahs*] that (one) (demonstrative pron)
escabeche [*ehs-kah*-BEH-*cheh*] pickled fish
escala [*ehs*-KAH-*lah*] ladder; scale
escalera [*ehs-kah*-LEH-*rah*] staircase
escalofrío [*ehs-kah-loh*-FREE-*oh*] shiver
escándalo [*ehs*-KAHN-*dah-loh*] scandal
escapar [*ehs-kah*-PAHR] to escape
escaparate (m) [*ehs-kah-pah*-RAH-*teh*] cabinet, display window
escaso, -a [*ehs*-KAH-*soh, -sah*] scarce
escena [*ehs*-THEH-*nah*] stage; scene
esclavo [*ehs*-KLAH-*voh*] slave
escoba [*ehs*-KOH-*bah*] broom
escoger [*ehs-koh*-HEHR] to choose
esconder [*ehs-kohn*-DEHR] to hide
escopeta [*ehs-koh*-PEH-*tah*] shotgun
★ **escribir** [*ehs-kree*-BEER] to write
  ¡escríbalo! [*ehs*-KREE-*bah-loh*] write it!
  escribir a máquina [*ehs-kree*-BEER *ah* MAH-*kee-nah*] to type
  por escrito [*pohr ehs*-KREE-*toh*] in writing
escritor, -a [*ehs-kree*-TOHR, *-ah*] writer
escritorio [*ehs-kree*-TOH-*r'yoh*] writing desk

★ **escuchar** [*ehs-koo*-CHAHR] to listen to
escudo [*ehs*-KOO-*doh*] shield; coat of arms
★ **escuela** [*ehs*-KWEH-*lah*] school
escultor [*ehs-kool*-TOHR] sculptor
escupir [*ehs-koo*-PEER] to spit
★ **ese** (m), **esos** (plural) [EH-*seh,* EH-*sohs*] that
ése (m), **esos** (plural) [EH-*seh,* EH-*sohs*] that (one) (demonstrative pron)
esencial [*eh-sehn-th'*YAHL] essential
esfuerzo [*ehs*-FWEHR-*thoh*] effort
esmalte [*ehs*-MAHL-*teh*] enamel
esmerado, -a [*ehs-meh*-RAH-*doh, -dah*] careful, painstaking
esmeralda [*ehs-meh*-RAHL-*dah*] emerald
★ **eso** [EH-*soh*] it, that (thing)

NOTE: Used when antecedent has not been specifically identified as masculine or feminine. *¿Qué es eso?* "What is that?"

espacio [*ehs*-PAH-*th'yoh*] space; room, capacity
espada [*ehs*-PAH-*dah*] sword
espalda [*ehs*-PAHL-*dah*] back
espantar [*ehs-pahn*-TAHR] to scare
espantoso, -a [*ehs-pahn*-TOH-*soh, -sah*] frightful
España [*ehs*-PAH-*n'yah*] Spain
español, -a [*ehs-pah-n'*YOHL, *-lah*] (adj) Spanish, (n) Spaniard
esparcir [*ehs-pahr*-THEER] to scatter; to spread
espárrago [*ehs*-PAH-*rrah-goh*] asparagus
especial [*ehs-peh-th'*YAHL] special, particular
especificar [*ehs-peh-thee-fee*-KAHR] to specify
espectáculo [*ehs-pehk*-TAH-*koo-loh*] spectacle, show
espejo [*ehs*-PEH-*hoh*] mirror
esperanza [*ehs-peh*-RAHN-*thah*] hope (also a girl's name)

★ **esperar** [*ehs-peh-*RAHR] to hope; to expect; to wait
¡espére un momento! [*ehs-*PEH-*reh oon moh-*MEHN-*toh*] Wait a moment!
espeso, -a [*ehs-*PEH-*soh, -sah*] thick
espía (m or f) [*ehs-*PEE-*ah*] spy
espina [*ehs-*PEE-*nah*] thorn, fishbone
espíritu (m) [*ehs-*PEE-*ree-too*] spirit
espléndido, -a [*ehs-*PLEHN-*dee-doh, -dah*] splendid
esposo, esposa [*ehs-*POH-*soh, ehs-*POH-*sah*] husband, wife
espuma [*ehs-*POO-*mah*] foam
esqueleto [*ehs-keh-*LEH-*toh*] skeleton
esquina [*ehs-*KEE-*nah*] corner
ésta [EHS-*tah*] this one
está [*ehs-*TAH] (you) are (he, she, it) is
¿Cómo está Ud.? [KOH-*moh ehs-*TAH *oos-*TEHD] How are you?
Está de viaje. [*ehs-*TAH *deh v'*YAH-*heh*] (He) (she) is on a trip.
Está de vuelta. [*ehs-*TAH *deh* VWEHL-*tah*] (He) (she) is back.
Está en la calle. [*ehs-*TAH *ehn lah* KAH-*l'yeh*] (He) (she) is out (literally "in the street")
estación (f) [*ehs-tah-th'*YOHN] station, season
estacionar [*ehs-tah-th'yoh-*NAHR] to park (a car, etc.)
estado [*ehs-*TAH-*doh*] state
estallar [*ehs-tah-l'*YAHR] to explode, to burst
estampilla [*ehs-tahm-*PEE-*l'yah*] stamp
estaño [*ehs-*TAH-*n'yoh*] tin
★ **estar** [*ehs-*TAHR] to be (for location or position)
estatua [*ehs-*TAH-*too-ah*] statue
★ **este** (m) [EHS-*teh*] East
★ **este** (m), **esta** (f) [EHS-*teh,* EHS-*tah*] this (m and f, adj)
éste (m) **ésta** (f) [EHS-*teh,* EHS-*tah*] this, this one; the latter (m and f, pron)
estilo [*ehs-*TEE-*loh*] style
y así por el estilo [*ee ah-*SEE *pohr ehl ehs-*TEE-*loh*] and so on

estimación (f) [*ehs-tee-mah-th'*YOHN] esteem, appraisal
estimar [*ehs-tee-*MAHR] to estimate, to respect
estirar [*ehs-tee-*RAHR] to stretch
★ **esto** [EHS-*toh*] this

NOTE: *Esto* is used when the gender is not specified and in general expressions. Ex.: *¿Qué es esto?*—"What is this?" *Esto me gusta.*—"I like this."

estómago [*ehs-*TOH-*mah-goh*] stomach
estornudar [*ehs-tohr-noo-*DAHR] to sneeze
estos (m, plural), **estas** (f, plural) [EHS-*tohs,* EHS-*tahs*] these (m and f plural adj)
★ **estos** (m, plural), **estas** f, (plural) [EHS-*tohs,* EHS-*tahs*] these, the latter (m and f, plural pron)
estoy [*ehs-*TOH-*ee*] I am (see *estar*)
estrecho, -a [*ehs-*TREH-*choh, -chah*] narrow
estrella [*ehs-*TREH-*l'yah*] star
estrenar [*ehs-treh-*NAHR]
NOTE: No exact equivalent; signifies to use, wear or do something for the first time.
estreno [*ehs-*TREH-*noh*] première (of a show, etc.)
estribo [*ehs-*TREE-*boh*] stirrup
estricto, -a [*ehs-*TREEK-*toh, -tah*] strict
estropear [*ehs-troh-peh-*AHR] to damage; to ruin
estudiante (m and f) [*ehs-too-d'*YAHN-*teh*] student
estudiar [*ehs-too-d'*YAHR] to study
estudio [*ehs-*TOO-*d'yoh*] study
estufa [*ehs-*TOO-*fah*] stove
estupendo, -a [*ehs-too-*PEHN-*doh, -dah*] stupendous
estúpido, -a [*ehs-*TOO-*pee-doh, -dah*] stupid
eterno, -a [*eh-*TEHR-*noh, -nah*] eternal, everlasting
etiqueta [*eh-tee-*KEH-*tah*] etiquette, label
Europa [*eh-oo-*ROH-*pah*] Europe
europeo, -a [*eh-oo-roh-*PEH-*oh, -ah*] European

evaporar(se) [*eh-vah-poh*-RAHR-*(seh)*] to evaporate
evento [*eh*-VEHN-*toh*] event
evidente [*eh-vee*-DEHN-*teh*] evident
evitar [*eh-vee*-TAHR] to avoid
exactamente [*ehg-sahk-tah*-MEHN-*teh*] exactly
exacto, -a [*ehk*-SAHK-*toh, -tah*] exact
exageración (f) [*ehk-sah-heh-rah*-TH'YOHN] exaggeration
examen (m) [*ehk*-SAH-*mehn*] examination
examinar [*ehk-sah-mee*-NAHR] to examine
exceder [*ehks-theh*-DEHR] to exceed, surpass
excelencia [*ehks-theh*-LEHN-*th'yah*] excellence; excellency
excelente [*ehks-theh*-LEHN-*teh*] excellent
excepción (f) [*ehks-thehp*-TH'YOHN] exception
excepcional [*ehks-thehp-th'yoh*-NAHL] exceptional
excepto [*ehks*-THEHP-*toh*] except
excesivo, -a [*ehks-theh*-THEE-*voh, -vah*] excessive
exceso [*ehks*-THEH-*soh*] excess; surplus
exceso de equipaje [*ehks*-THEH-*soh deh eh-kee*-PAH-*heh*] excess baggage
excitar [*ehks-thee*-TAHR] to excite
exclamar [*ehks-sklah*-MAHR] to exclaim
excluir [*ehks-skloo*-EER] to exclude
exclusivamente [*ehks-skloo-see-vah*-MEHN-*teh*] exclusively
exclusivo, -a [*ehks-skloo*-SEE-*voh, -vah*] exclusive
excursión (f) [*ehks-skoor-s'*YOHN] excursion
excusa [*ehks*-KOO-*sah*] excuse
excusado [*ehks-koo*-SAH-*doh*] toilet
excusar [*ehks-koo*-SAHR] to excuse
exento, -a [*ehk*-SEHN-*toh, -tah*] exempt; freed
exhibición (f) [*ehk-see-bee-th'*YOHN] exhibition
exigente [*ehk-see*-HEHN-*teh*] demanding
existencia [*ehk-sees*-TEHN-*th'yah*] existence (comm.: supply, stock)
existir [*ehk-sees*-TEER] to exist
éxito [EHK-*see-toh*] success
expedición (f) [*ehks-peh-dee-th'*YOHN] expedition
expediente (m) [*ehks-peh-d'*YEHN-*teh*] expedient; record

expedir [*ehks-peh-*DEER] to expedite, to issue, to ship
experiencia [*ehks-peh-r'*YEHN-*th'yah*] experience
experimento [*ehks-peh-ree-*MEHN-*toh*] experiment
explicación (f) [*ehks-plee-kah-th'*YOHN] explanation
explicar [*ehks-plee-*KAHR] to explain
explorar [*ehks-ploh-*RAHR] to explore
explotar [*ehks-ploh-*TAHR] to explode, also to exploit
exponer [*ehks-poh-*NEHR] to expose, to show
exportación (f) [*ehks-pohr-tah-th'*YOHN] exportation
exportador [*ehks-pohr-tah-*DOHR] exporter
exportar [*ehks-pohr-*TAHR] to export
exposición [*ehks-poh-see-th'*YOHN] show, exhibition
expresar [*ehks-preh-*SAHR] to express
expresión (f) [*ehks-preh-s'*YOHN] expression
expresivo, -a [*ehks-preh-*SEE-*voh, -ah*] expressive, affectionate
expreso [*ehks-*PREH-*soh*] express
exprimir [*ehks-pree-*MEER] to squeeze
expuesto, -a [*ehks-*PWEHS-*toh, -tah*] on display; exposed
expulsar [*ehks-pool-*SAHR] to expel
exquisito, -a [*ehks-kee-*SEE-*toh, -tah*] exquisite
extender [*ehks-tehn-*DEHR] to extend
extensión (f) [*ehks-tehn-s'*YOHN] extension
extenso, -a [*ehks-*TEHN-*soh, -sah*] extended
exterior [*ehks-teh-r'*YOHR] exterior
extinguir [*ehks-teen-*GHEER] to extinguish
extra [EHKS-*trah*] extra
extranjero, -a [*ehks-trahn-*HEH-*roh, -rah*] foreigner
  al extranjero [*ahl ehks-trahn-*HEH-*roh*] abroad
extrañar [*ehks-trah-n'*YAHR] to wonder at; to miss (to be lonely for)
extraño, -a [*ehks-*TRAH-*n'yoh, -n'yah*] strange
extraordinario, -a [*ehks-trah-ohr-dee-*NAH-*r'yoh, -ah*] extraordinary
extraviar [*ehks-trah-v'*YAHR] to misplace
extremadamente [*ehks-treh-mah-dah-*MEHN-*teh*] extremely
extremo [*ehks-*TREH-*moh*] extreme

F

fábrica [FAH-*bree-kah*] factory
fabricante [*fah-bree*-KAHN-*teh*] manufacturer
fabricar [*fah-bree*-KAHR] to manufacture
fábula [FAH-*boo-lah*] fable, tale
fabuloso, -a [*fah-boo*-LOH-*soh, -sah*] fabulous; marvellous
★ **fácil** [FAH-*seel*] easy
facilmente [*fah-theel*-MEHN-*teh*] easily
factura [*fahk*-TOO-*rah*] invoice, bill
facultad (f) [*fah-kool*-TAHD] faculty
faja [FAH-*hah*] band, girdle
falda [FAHL-*dah*] skirt
falso, -a [FAHL-*soh, -sah*] false
falta [FAHL-*tah*] lack, defect
faltar [*fahl*-TAHR] (to be) lacking
fallar [*fah-l'*YAHR] to fail
fallecer [*fah-l'yeh*-THEHR] to die

NOTE: The past participle of *fallecer, fallecido,* is frequently used in newspapers and announcements of death.

fama [FAH-*mah*] fame
★ **familia** [*fah*-MEE-*l'yah*] family
familiar (m and f) [*fah-mee-l'*YAHR] familiar
famoso, -a [*fah*-MOH-*soh, -sah*] famous
fanático, -a [*fah*-NAH-*tee-koh, -kah*] fanatic (also used for sports and bullfight fan)
fango [FAHN-*goh*] mud
fantasma (m) [*fahn*-TAHS-*mah*] phantom, ghost
NOTE: Although it ends in *a fantasma* is masculine
fantástico, -a [*fahn*-TAHS-*tee-koh, -kah*] fantastic
farmacia [*fahr-mah*-THEE-*ah*] drugstore

farol (m) [*fah*-ROHL] street lamp
farsa [FAHR-*sah*] farce
farsante [*fahr*-SAHN-*teh*] fraud
fascinar [*fahs-see*-NAHR] to fascinate
fastidiar [*fahs-tee-d'*YAHR] to bother, to bore
fastidioso, -a [*fahs-tee-d'*YOH-*soh, -sah*] tedious, tiresome
fatal [*fah*-TAHL] fatal
fatigar [*fah-tee*-GAHR] to tire
favor (m) [*fah*-VOHR] favor
★ **por favor** [*pohr fah*-VOHR] please
favorable (m and f) [*fah-voh*-RAH-*bleh*] favorable
favorito, -a [*fah-voh*-REE-*toh, -tah*] favorite
fe [*feh*] faith
fecha [FEH-*chah*] date
felicidad (f) [*feh-lee-thee*-DAHD] happiness
felicitaciones (f, plural) [*feh-lee-thee-tah-th'*YOH-*nehs*] congratulations
felicitar [*feh-lee-thee*-TAHR] to congratulate
★ **feliz** [*feh*-LEETH] happy
¡Feliz Cumpleaños! [*fee*-LEETH *koom-pleh*-AH-*n'yohs*] Happy Birthday!
¡Felices Pascuas! [*feh*-LEE-*thehs* PAHS-*kwahs*] Merry Christmas! (also) Happy Easter!
femenino, -a [*feh-meh*-NEE-*noh, -nah*] feminine
fenómeno [*feh*-NOH-*meh-noh*] phenomenon
★ **feo, -a** [FEH-*oh, -ah*] ugly
feria [FEH-*r'yah*] market, fair
feroz [*feh*-ROTH] ferocious, fierce
ferretería [*feh-rreh-teh*-REE-*ah*] hardware shop
ferrocarril (m) [*feh-rroh-kah*-RREEL] railroad
festejar [*fehs-teh*-HAHR] to celebrate
(al) fiado [*ahl f'*YAH-*doh*] on credit
fianza [*f'*YAHN-*thah*] guarantee
fiar [*f'yahr*] to trust
fideo [*fee*-DEH-*oh*] noodle
fiebre [F'YEH-*breh*] fever
fiel [*f'yehl*] faithful, loyal
fiera [*f'*YEH-*rah*] wild beast

fiesta [*f'*YEHS-*tah*] party, feast, celebration
figura [*fee*-GOO-*rah*] figure; shape
figurar(se) [*fee-goo*-RAHR-*(seh)*] to imagine
fijar(se) [*fee*-HAHR-*(seh)*] to note, to look at
fijar [f*ee*-HAHR] to fasten
fijo [FEE-*hoh*] fixed
fila [FEE-*lah*] row
filete (m) [*fee*-LEH-*teh*] steak
Filipinas [*fee-lee*-PEE-*nahs*] Philippines
filipino, -a [*fee-lee*-PEE-*noh, -nah*] Filipino
filosofía [*fee-loh-soh*-FEE-*ah*] philosophy
filósofo [*fee*-LOH-*soh-foh*] philosopher
filtro [FEEL-*troh*] filter
★ **fin** (m) [*feen*] end
  a fin de [*ah* FEEN *deh*] in order to
  al fin [*ahl* FEEN] at last
final (m and f) [*fee*-NAHL] final
finalmente [*fee-nahl*-MEHN-*teh*] finally
finca [FEEN-*kah*] farm, estate
fingir [*feehn*-HEER] to pretend
fino, -a [*fee-noh, -nah*] fine

NOTE: Has the sense of "delicate" or "fine" (thin) rather than of "fine" (good).

firma [FEER-*mah*] company, firm, (also) signature
firme (m and f) [FEER-*meh*] firm
flaco, -a [FLAH-*koh, -kah*] thin; lean
flan (m) [*flahn*] custard
flecha [FLEH-*chah*] arrow
flete (m) [FLEH-*teh*] freight
flojo, -a [FLOH-*hoh, -hah*] loose, lax (col. "lazy")
flor (f) [*flohr*] flower
florería [*floh-reh*-REE-*ah*] flower shop
flota [FLOH-*tah*] fleet

flotar [*floh*-TAHR] to float
foca [FOH-*kah*] seal
folleto [*foh-l'*YEH-*toh*] pamphlet, booklet
fonda [FOHN-*dah*] inn
fondo [FOHN-*doh*] bottom, back, fund
fonógrafo [*foh*-NOH-*grah-foh*] phonograph
forma [FOHR-*mah*] form; shape
formal [*fohr*-MAHL] formal
formalidad (f) [*fohr-mah-lee*-DAHD] formality
formar [*fohr*-MAHR] to form
formidable [*fohr-mee*-DAH-*bleh*] formidable
fórmula [FOHR-*moo-lah*] formula
formulario [*fohr-moo*-LAH-*r'yoh*] form for filling out
forro [FOH-*rroh*] lining
fortaleza [*fohr-tah*-LEH-*thah*] fortress
fortuna [*fohr*-TOO-*nah*] fortune
forzosamente [*fohr-thoh-sah*-MEHN-*teh*] necessarily
fósforo [FOHS-*foh-roh*] match, phosphorus
fotografía [*foh-toh-grah*-FEE-*ah*] photograph
fotografiar [*foh-toh-grah-f'*YAHR] to take a photograph of
fotógrafo [*foh*-TOH-*grah-foh*] photographer
fracasar [*frah-kah*-SAHR] to fail
fracaso [*frah*-KAH-*soh*] failure
fracción (f) [*frahk-th'*YOHN] fraction
fractura [*frahk*-TOO-*rah*] break, fracture
frágil [FRAH-*heel*] fragile
frambuesa [*frahm-b'*WEH-*sah*] raspberry
francamente [*frahn-kah*-MEHN-*teh*] frankly
francés, francesa [*frahn*-THEHS, *frahn*-THEH-*sah*] (adj) French; (n) Frenchman, Frenchwoman
Francia [FRAHN-*th'yah*] France
franco, -a [FRAHN-*koh, -kah*] frank, free
franqueo [*frahn*-KEH-*oh*] postage
frasco [FRAHS-*koh*] small bottle
frase (f) [FRAH-*seh*] phrase
frazada [*frah*-THAH-*dah*] blanket
frecuencia [*freh*-KWEHN-*th'yah*] frequency
frecuentemente [*freh-kwehn-teh*-MEHN-*teh*] frequently

fregar [*freh*-GAHR] to scrub; to wash (dishes)
freír [*freh*-EER] to fry
freno [FREH-*noh*] brake (of car), bridle (of horse)
frente (f) [FREHN-*teh*] forehead
fresa [FREH-*sah*] strawberry
fresco, -a [FREHS-*koh, -kah*] fresh; cool
frijol (m) [*free*-HOHL] bean
★ **frío, -a** [FREE-*oh, -ah*] cold
(**hacer**) **frío** [*ah*-THEHR FREE-*oh*] to be cold (weather)
(**tener**) **frío** [*teh*-NEHR FREE-*oh*] to be cold, to feel cold
frito, -a [FREE-*toh, -tah*] fried
frívolo, -a [FREE-*voh-loh, -lah*] frivolous
frontera [*frohn*-TEH-*rah*] frontier, border
frontón (m) [*frohn*-TOHN] Court for playing jai alai, a Basque ball game.
fruta [FROO-*tah*] fruit
frutería [*froo-teh*-REE-*ah*] fruit store
★ **fuego** [*f'*WEH-*goh*] fire
fuente (f) [*f'*WEHN-*teh*] fountain
fuera [*f'*WEH-*rah*] out, outside
fuerte (n or adj) [*f'*WEHR-*teh*] (as adj) strong, (as n) fort (m and f)
fuerza [*f'*WEHR-*thah*] force; strength
fugar(se) [*foo*-GAHR-*seh*] to flee
Fulano [*foo*-LAH-*noh*]
(also) **Fulano de Tal** [*foo*-LAH-*noh deh tahl*]

NOTE: A proper name used to indicate a name not known, like "Mr. So and So."

fumar [*foo*-MAHR] to smoke
función (f) [*foon-th'*YOHN] function, show
funcionar [*foon-th'yoh*-NAHR] to work, to function
fundador [*foon-dah*-DOHR] founder

fundar [*foon*-DAHR] to found
furioso, -a [*foo-r'*YOH-*soh, -sah*] furious
fusil (m) [*foo*-SEEL] rifle, gun
fusilar [*foo-see*-LAHR] to shoot (execute)
fútbol [FOOT-*bohl*] football (refers to soccer, not American football)
futuro, -a [*foo*-TOO-*roh, -rah*] future
  en lo futuro [*ehn loh foo*-TOO-*roh*] in the future

G

gabinete (m) [*gah-bee*-NEH-*teh*] cabinet
gafas (f plural) [GAH-*fahs*] spectacles
galante (adj) [*gah*-LAHN-*teh*] gallant
galería [*gah-leh*-REE-*ah*] gallery
galleta [*gah-l'*YEH-*tah*] cracker
gallina [*gah-l'*YEE-*nah*] hen
gallo [GAH-*l'yoh*] cock, rooster
  pelea de gallos [*peh*-LEH-*ah deh* GAH-*l'yohs*] cock fights
gana [GAH-*nah*] appetite, desire
  tener ganas de [*teh*-NEHR GAH-*nahs deh*] to desire to, to feel like
ganado [*gah*-NAH-*doh*] cattle
ganador, -a [*gah-nah*-DOHR, *-rah*] winner
ganancia [*gah*-NAHN-*th'yah*] profit, gain
ganar [*gah*-NAHR] to win, to gain
gancho [GAHN-*choh*] hook
ganga [GAHN-*gah*] bargain
ganso [GAHN-*soh*] goose
garage [*gah*-RAH-*heh*] garage
garantía [*gah-rahn*-TEE-*ah*] guarantee
garantizar [*gah-rahn-tee*-THAHR] to guarantee
garbanzo [*gahr*-BAHN-*zoh*] chickpea
gardenia [*gahr*-DEH-*n'yah*] gardenia
garganta [*gahr*-GAHN-*tah*] throat
garra [GAH-*rrah*] claw

gas (m) [*gahs*] gas
gasolina [*gah-soh-*LEE*-nah*] gasoline
gastar [*gahs-*TAHR] to spend, to waste
gasto [GAHS*-toh*] expense
gatillo [*gah-*TEE*-l'yoh*] trigger
★ **gato, -a** [GAH*-toh, -tah*] cat
gaucho [GOW*-choh*] cowboy (Argentina and some neighboring countries)
gaveta [*gah-*VEH*-tah*] drawer
gaviota [*gah-v'*YOH*-tah*] seagull
gemelo [*heh-*MEH*-loh*] twin
gemir [*heh-*MEER] to groan
general (n and adj) [*heh-neh-*RAHL] general
  en general [*ehn-heh-neh-*RAHL] in general
  por lo general, generalmente [*pohr loh heh-neh-*RAHL, *heh-neh-rahl-*MEHN*-teh*] generally
género [HEH*-neh-roh*] class, kind
generoso, -a [*heh-neh-*ROH*-soh, -sah*] generous
genio [HEH*-n'yoh*] genius, temper
★ **gente** (f) [HEHN*-teh*] people
  NOTE: Always feminine even if referring to men.
gentil [*hehn-*TEEL] gracious, kind
gentileza [*hehn-tee-*LEH*-thah*] graciousness, politeness
genuino, -a [*heh-noo-*EE*-noh, -nah*] genuine
geografía [*heh-oh-grah-*FEE*-ah*] geography
gerente (m) [*heh-*REHN*-teh*] manager
gigante (m) (n and adj) [*hee-*GAHN*-teh*] giant
gimnasio [*heem-*NAH*-s'yoh*] gymnasium, school
giro [HEE*-roh*] turn, money order
gitano, -a [*hee-*TAH*-noh, -nah*] gipsy
globo [GLOH*-boh*] globe
gloria [GLOH*-r'yah*] glory (Also a girl's name)
gobernador [*goh-behr-nah-*DOHR] governor
gobernar [*goh-behr-*NAHR] to govern, to rule
gobierno [*goh-b'*YEHR*-noh*] government
golfo [GOHL*-foh*] gulf
golondrina [*goh-lohn-*DREE*-nah*] swallow (bird)

golpe (m) [GOHL-*peh*] blow
goma [GOH-*mah*] gum, rubber
★ gordo, -a [GOHR-*doh, -dah*] fat
gorra [GOH-*rrah*] cap
gorrión (m) [*goh-rr'*YOHN] sparrow
gota [GOH-*tah*] drop (liquid)
gozar [*goh*-THAHR] to enjoy
gracia [GRAH-*th'yah*] grace, wit
★ gracias [GRAH-*th'yahs*] thanks
gracioso, -a [*grah-th'*YOH-*soh, -sah*] graceful, witty, funny
grado [GRAH-*doh*] degree
graduar(se) [*grah*-DWAHR-*(seh)*] to graduate
gramática [*grah*-MAH-*tee-kah*] grammar
★ gran or grande [*grahn,* GRAHN-*deh*] great, large, big

NOTE: *Gran* is used in front of the noun while *grande* is used after. *Gran* usually means "great."

granizo [*grah*-NEE-*thoh*] hail
granja [GRAHN-*hah*] farm, barn
grano [GRAH-*noh*] grain
grasa [GRAH-*sah*] grease
gratis [GRAH-*tees*] gratis, free
grato, -a [GRAH-*toh, -tah*] pleasant
grave [GRAH-*veh*] grave, serious
Grecia [GREH-*th'yah*] Greece
griego, -a [*gr'*YEH-*goh, -ah*] Greek
grifo [GREE-*foh*] faucet
★ gris (m and f) [*grees*] gray
grito [GREE-*toh*] cry, scream
grosero, -a [*groh*-SEH-*roh, -rah*] coarse, rough
grueso, -a [GRWEH-*soh, -sah*] thick
grupo [GROO-*poh*] group
gruta [GROO-*tah*] cavern

guante (m) [GWAHN-*teh*] glove
guapo, -a [GWAH-*poh, -pah*] good looking
guardafango [*gwahr-dah*-FAHN-*goh*] mudguard
guardar [*gwahr*-DAHR] to guard, to keep
guardarropa [*gwahr-dah*-RROH-*pah*] closet
Guatemala [*gwah-teh*-MAH-*lah*] Guatemala
guatemalteco, -a [*gwah-teh-mahl*-TEH-*koh, -kah*] Guatemalan
★ **guerra** [GHEH-*rrah*] war
guerra mundial [GHEH-*rrah moon-d'*YAHL] world war
guerrero [*gheh*-RREH-*roh*] warrior
guía [GHEE-*ah*] guide

NOTE: Masculine or feminine depending of the person who is the guide. If a written guide, then feminine.

guía telefónica [GHEE-*ah teh-leh*-FOH-*nee-kah*] telephone book
guiar [*ghee*-AHR] to guide, to lead
guisar [*ghee*-SAHR] to cook
guisante (m) [*ghee*-SAHN-*teh*] pea
guitarra [*ghee*-TAH-*rrah*] guitar
guitarrista (m or f) [*ghee-tah*-RREES-*tah*] guitar player
gusano [*goo*-SAH-*noh*] worm
★ **gustar** [*goos*-TAHR] to taste, to like
NOTE: When meaning "to like" *gustar* is used with indirect object pronouns.
¿Le gusta? [*leh* GOOS-*tah*] Do you like?
¿Le gustaría? [*leh goos-tah*-REE-*ah*] Would you like?
No me gusta . . . [*noh meh* GOOS-*tah*] I don't like . . .
gusto [GOOS-*toh*] taste
mucho gusto [MOO-*choh* GOOS-*toh*] much pleasure (Said on acknowledging introductions)
gustosamente [*goos-toh-sah*-MEHN-*teh*] gladly

H

haba [AH-*bah*] lima bean
★ **haber** [*ah*-BEHR] to have

NOTE: *Haber* is used only as an auxiliary in compound tenses. The regularly used verb for "to have" is *tener*.

habichuela [*ah-bee*-CHWEH-*lah*] string bean
hábil [AH-*beel*] capable, skillful
habitación (f) [*ah-bee-tah-th'*YOHN] room, chamber
habitante [*ah-bee*-TAHN-*teh*] inhabitant
habitar [*ah-bee*-TAHR] to live in
★ **hablar** [*ah*-BLAHR] to speak, to talk
¿Habla usted castellano? [AH-*blah oos*-TEHD *kahs-teh-l'*YAH-*noh*] Do you speak Spanish?
★ **hacer** [*ah*-THEHR] to make, to do
hace buen tiempo [AH-*theh bwehn t'*YEHM-*poh*] it is good weather
hace calor [AH-*theh kah*-LOHR] it is hot
hace frío [AH-*theh* FREE-*oh*] it is cold
hace mal tiempo [AH-*theh mahl t'*YEHM-*poh*] it is bad weather
hace mucho tiempo [AH-*theh* MOO-*choh t'*YEHM-*poh*] a long time ago
hace sol [AH-*theh sohl*] it is sunny
hace viento [AH-*theh v'*YEHN-*toh*] it is windy
hacer mal [*ah*-THEHR *mahl*] to do wrong
hacer(se) [*ah*-THEHR-*(seh)*] to become
★ **hacia** [AH-*th'yah*] toward
hacienda [*ah-th'*YEHN-*dah*] farm, ranch, estate
hacha [AH-*chah*] axe
NOTE: Feminine but uses *el* in the singular.

haga el favor de [AH-*gah ehl fah*-VOHR *deh*] please

NOTE: This expression is followed by the infinitive of the next verb. EX.: *Haga el favor de salir.*—"Do me the favor of leaving."

Haití [*eye*-TEE] Haiti

haitiano, -a [*eye-t'*YAH-*noh, -nah*] Haitian

halar [*ah*-LAHR] to pull, to haul

hallar [*ah-l'*YAHR] to find

hamaca [*ah*-MAH-*kah*] hammock

hambre [AHM-*breh*] hunger

NOTE: Feminine but uses *el* in the singular.

tener hambre [*teh*-NEHR AHM-*breh*] to be hungry

harina [*ah*-REE-*nah*] flour

★ **hasta** [AHS-*tah*] until, up to

hasta ahora [AHS-*tah ah*-OH-*rah*] up to now

hasta la fecha [AHS-*tah lah* FEH-*chah*] up to now

hasta otro día [AHS-*tah* OH-*troh* DEE-*ah*] until another day

hasta pronto [AHS-*tah* PROHN-*toh*] till soon

★ **hay** [*eye*] there is, there are, is there? are there?

NOTE: Does not change for singular or plural. Can be made interrogative voice inflection. *Hay café:* "There is coffee." *¿Hay café?* "Is there any coffee?"

he aquí [*eh ah*-KEE] here is

hecho [EH-*choh*] deed (n), done, made (adj and part)

hecho a mano [EH-*choh ah* MAH-*noh*] hand-made

helado [*eh*-LAH-*doh*] ice cream (n), frozen (adj)

helar [*eh*-LAHR] to freeze

hélice (f) [EH-*lee-theh*] propeller

hembra [EHM-*brah*] female

hemisferio [*eh-mees*-FEH-*r'yoh*] hemisphere

heredar [*eh-reh*-DAHR] to inherit

heredero, -a [*eh-reh*-DEH-*roh, -rah*] heir (heiress)

herida [*eh*-REE-*dah*] wound

heridos, -a [*eh*-REE-*doh, -dah*] wounded
herir [*eh*-REER] to wound, to hurt
★ **hermano (hermana)** [*ehr*-MAH-*noh, -nah*] brother (sister)
★ **hermoso, -a** [*ehr*-MOH-*soh, -sah*] beautiful, handsome
héroe (heroína) [EH-*roh-eh, (eh-roh*-EE-*nah)*] hero (heroine)
herramienta [*eh-rrah-m'*YEHN-*tah*] tool
hervir [*ehr*-VEER] boil
hielo [YEH-*loh*] ice
hierba [YEHR-*bah*] grass
hierbabuena [*yehr-bah*-BWEH-*nah*] mint
hierro [YEH-*rroh*] iron
hígado [EE-*gah-doh*] liver
higo [EE-*goh*] fig
★ **hijo (hija)** [EE-*hoh, -hah*] son (daughter)
hilo [EE-*loh*] thread
hinchado, -a [*een*-CHAH-*doh, -dah*] swollen
hipo [EE-*poh*] hiccup
hipócrita [*ee*-POH-*kree-tah*] hypocrite and hypocritic (always retains *a* as ending)
hipódromo [*ee*-POH-*droh-moh*] hippodrome, racetrade
hispano, -a [*ees*-PAH-*noh, -nah*] (Adjective denoting descent from Spanish culture or civilization.)
hispanoamericano, -a [*ees-pah-noh-ah-meh-ree*-KAH-*noh, -nah*] Spanish-American
historia [*ees*-TOH-*r'yah*] history
hogar [*oh*-GAHR] home, hearth
hoja [OH-*hah*] leaf
¡hola! [OH-*lah*] hello!
Holanda [*oh*-LAHN-*dah*] Holland
holandés, holandesa [*oh-lahn*-DEHS, *oh-lahn*-DEH-*sah*] Dutch
★ **hombre** (m) [OHM-*breh*] man
hombro [OHM-*broh*] shoulder
homenaje (m) [*oh-meh*-NAH-*heh*] homage (party in honor of someone)
hondo, -a [OHN-*doh, -dah*] deep
Honduras [*ohn*-DOO-*rahs*] Honduras
hondureño, -a [*ohn-doo*-REH-*n'yoh, -n'yah*] Honduran
honor [*oh*-NOHR] honor

honorable [*oh-noh-*RAH-*bleh*] honorable
honorarios [*oh-noh-*RAH-*r'yohs*] fee
honradez (f) [*ohn-rrah-*DEHTH] probity, integrity
honrado, -a [*ohn-*RRAH-*doh, -dah*] honest, honorable
★ **hora** [OH-*rah*] hour
Es hora de . . . [*ehs* OH-*rah deh*] It is time to . . .
¿Qué hora es? [*keh* OH-*rah ehs*] What time is it?
horario [*oh-*RAH-*r'yoh*] schedule, time table
horizonte (m) [*oh-ree-*THOHN-*teh*] horizon
hormiga [*ohr-*MEE-*gah*] ant
horno [OHR-*noh*] oven
horrible [*oh-*RREE-*bleh*] horrible
horror (m) [*oh-*RROHR] horror
hospedarse [*ohs-peh-*DAHR-*seh*] to stop at (hotel, etc.)
hospital (m) [*ohs-pee-*TAHL] hospital
hotel [*oh-*TEHL] hotel
★ **hoy** [*oy*] today
de hoy en adelante [*deh oy ehn ah·deh-*LAHN-*teh*] from today on
hoyo [OH-*yoh*] hole
hoz (f) [*oth*] scythe, sickle
hueco, -a [WEH-*koh, -kah*] hollow
huele [WEH-*leh*] it smells (see *oler*)
huelga [WELL-*gah*] strike (of workers)
huelguista (m and f) [*well-*GHEES-*tah*] striker
huella [WEH-*l'yah*] footprint, impression, track, trace
huérfano, -a [WEHR-*fah-noh, -nah*] orphan
huerta or **huerto** [WEHR-*tah*] vegetable garden
hueso [WEH-*soh*] bone
huésped (m and f) [WEHS-*pehd*] guest
★ **huevo** [WEH-*voh*] egg
huevos fritos [WEH-*vohs* FREE-*tohs*] fried eggs
huevos pasados por agua [WEH-*vohs pah-*SAH-*dohs pohr* AH-*gwah*] soft-boiled eggs
huevos revueltos [WEH-*vohs reh-*VWEHL-*tohs*] scrambled eggs
tortilla de huevos [*tohr-*TEE-*l'yah deh* WEH-*vohs*] omelet

huir [*oo*-EER] to flee
humanidad (f) [*oo-mah-nee*-DAHD] humanity
humano, -a [*oo*-MAH-*noh, -nah*] human
  un ser humano [*oon sehr oo*-MAH-*noh*] a human being
humedad (f) [*oo-meh*-DAHD] humidity
húmedo [OO-*meh-doh*] humid, moist, damp
humilde [*oo*-MEEL-*deh*] humble
humo [OO-*moh*] smoke
humor [*oo*-MOHR] humor
hundir(se) [*oohn*-DEER-*(seh)*] to sink
húngaro, -a [OON-*gah-roh, -rah*] Hungarian
Hungría [*oon*-GREE-*ah*] Hungary
huracán (m) [*oo-rah*-KAHN] hurricane

I

ida [EE-*dah*] departure
  ida y vuelta [EE-*dah ee v'*WEHL-*tah*] round trip
idea [*ee*-DEH-*ah*] idea
ideal (n and adj) [*ee-deh*-AHL] ideal
identitad [*ee-dehn-tee*-TAHD] identity
  cédula de identitad [THEH-*doo-lah deh ee-dehn-tee*-TAHD] identification card
identificar [*ee-dehn-tee-fee*-KAHR] to identify
idiota (m and f) [*ee-d'*YOH-*tah*] idiot
★ **iglesia** [*ee*-GLEH-*s'yah*] church
ignorancia [*eeg-noh*-RAHN-*th'yah*] ignorance
ignorante [*eeg-noh*-RAHN-*teh*] ignorant
igual [*ee*-GWAHL] equal
  igualmente [*ee-gwahl*-MEHN-*teh*] equally, as well
ilegal [*ee-leh*-GAHL] illegal
ileso, -a [*ee*-LEH-*soh, -sah*] unharmed
iluminar [*ee-loo-mee*-NAHR] to illuminate, to light
ilusión (f) [*ee-loo-s'*YOHN] illusion
ilustración (f) [*ee-loos-trah-th'*YOHN] illustration
ilustrado, -a [*ee-loos*-TRAH-*doh, -dah*] illustrated

ilustre [*ee-*LOOS*-treh*] illustrious
imaginar(se) [*ee-mah-hee-*NAHR*-seh*] to imagine
imaginario, -a [*ee-mah-hee-*NAH*-r'yoh, -r'yah*] imaginary
imbécil (n, masc and fem, and adj) [*eem-*BEH*-theel*] imbecile
imitación (f) [*ee-mee-tah-th'*YOHN] imitation
imitar [*ee-mee-*TAHR] to imitate
impaciencia [*eem-pah-th'*YEHN*-th'yah*] impatience
impaciente [*eem-pah-th'*YEHN*-teh*] impatient, anxious
impedir [*eem-peh-*DEER] to prevent
imperativo, -a [*eem-peh-rah-*TEE*-voh, -vah*] imperative
imperfecto [*eem-pehr-*FEHK*-toh*] imperfect
imperial [*eem-peh-r'*YAHL] imperial
imperio [*eem-*PEH*-r'yoh*] empire
impermeable (m) [*eem-pehr-meh-*AH*-bleh*] raincoat
impertinente [*eem-pehr-tee-*NEHN*-teh*] impertinent
importante [*eem-pohr-*TAHN*-teh*] important
importar [*eem-pohr-*TAHR] to be important
  no importa [*noh eem-*POHR*-tah*] never mind (or) it doesn't matter
  ¿qué importa? [*keh eem-*POHR*-tah?*] what does it matter?
importe (m) [*eem-*POHR*-teh*] amount; price, cost
imposible [*eem-poh-*SEE*-bleh*] impossible
impresión (f) [*eem-preh-s'*YOHN] impression
impreso, -a [*eem-*PREH*-soh, -sah*] printed matter, publication printed
imprevisto, -a [*eem-preh-*VEES*-toh, -tah*] unforeseen
impuesto [*eem-p'*WEHS*-toh*] tax
impulsivo, -a [*eem-pool-*SEE*-voh, -vah*] impulsive
inaugurar [*ee-now-goo-*RAHR] to inaugurate
incansable [*een-kahn-*SAH*-bleh*] untiring
incapaz [*een-kah-*PATH] incapable, incompetent
incendio [*een-*THEHN*-d'yoh*] fire
incidente (m) [*een-thee-*DEHN*-teh*] incident
incierto, -a [*een-th'*YEHR*-toh, -tah*] uncertain
inclinación (f) [*een-klee-nah-th'*YOHN] inclination
incluir [*een-kloo-*EER] to include
inclusive [*een-kloo-*SEE*-veh*] inclusive

incomodar [*een-koh-moh*-DAHR] to disturb, to trouble
No se incomode [*noh seh een*-KOH-*moh-deh*] Don't trouble yourself
incómodo, -a [*een*-KOH-*moh-doh, -dah*] uncomfortable
incompleto, -a [*een-kohm*-PLEH-*toh, -tah*] incomplete
inconsciente [*een-kohn-th'*YEHN-*teh*] unconscious
inconveniente (m) [*een-kohn-veh*-N'YEHN-*teh*] inconvenient
incorrecto, -a [*een-koh*-RREHK-*toh, -tah*] improper
incredulidad (f) [*een-kreh-doo-lee*-DAHD] incredulity
increíble [*een-kreh*-EE-*bleh*] unbelievable, incredible
indecente [*een-deh*-THEHN-*teh*] indecent
indecisión (f) [*een-deh-thee-s'*YOHN] indecision
indefinido, -a [*een-deh-fee*-NEE-*doh, -dah*] indefinite
independencia [*een-deh-pehn*-DEHN-*th'yah*] independence
independiente [*een-deh-pehn-d'*YEHN-*teh*] independent
India [EEN-*d'yah*] India
indicar [*een-dee*-KAHR] to indicate
indiferente [*een-dee-feh*-REHN-*teh*] indifferent
indigno, -a[*een*-DEEG-*noh, -nah*] unworthy
indio, -a [EEN-*d'yoh, -d'yah*] Indian
indirecta [*een-dee*-REHK-*tah*] hint, allusion
indiscreto, -a [*een-dees*-KREH-*toh, -tah*] indiscreet
indispuesto, -a [*een-dees*-PWEHS-*toh, -tah*] indisposed
individualmente [*een-dee-vee-dwahl*-MEHN-*teh*] individually
individuo [*een-dee*-VEE-*dwoh*] individual
índole (f) [EEN-*doh-leh*] kind, sort
indudablemente [*een-doo-dah-bleh*-MEHN-*teh*] doubtlessly
indulgente [*een-dool*-HEHN-*teh*] indulgent
industria [*een*-DOOS-*tr'yah*] industry
industrial [*een-doos-tr'*YAHL] industrial, industrialist
inesperadamente [*ee-nehs-peh-rah-dah*-MEHN-*teh*] unexpectedly
inevitable [*ee-neh-vee*-TAH-*bleh*] unavoidable
infancia [*een*-FAHN-*th'yah*] childhood
infantería [*een-fahn-teh*-REE-*ah*] infantry
infección (f) [*een-fehk-th'*YOHN] infection

infeliz [*een-feh-*LEETH] unhappy
inferior [*een-feh-r'*YOHR] inferior
inferioridad (f) [*een-feh-r'yoh-ree-*DAHD] inferiority
inferir [*een-feh-*REER] to infer
infierno [*een-f'*YEHR-*noh*] hell
infinitamente [*een-fee-nee-tah-*MEHN-*teh*] infinitely
influencia [*een-floo-*EHN-*th'yah*] influence
influir [*een-floo-*EER] to influence
información (f) [*een-fohr-mah-th'*YOHN] information
informal [*een-fohr-*MAHL] unreliable
NOTE: in spite of its spelling it does *not* mean "informal."
informar [*een-fohr-*MAHR] to inform
ingeniería [*een-heh-n'yeh-*REE-*ah*] engineering
ingeniero [*een-heh-*N'YEH-*roh*] engineer
ingenioso, -a [*een-heh-n'*YOH-*soh, -sah*] clever, ingenious
ingenuo, -a [*een-*HEH-*n'woh, -wah*] naive
Inglaterra [*een-glah-*TEH-*rrah*] England
inglés, inglesa [*een-*GLEHS, *een-*GLEH-*sah*] English (adj) (noun) Englishman, -woman
ingrato, -a [*een-*GRAH-*toh, -tah*] ungrateful
ingresar [*een-greh-*SAHR] to enter (an institution)
ingreso [*een-*GREH-*soh*] entrance; revenue, income
inicial [*ee-nee-th'*YAHL] (noun m) initial, (adj) starting, initial
injuriar [*een-hoo-r'*YAHR] to insult
injusticia [*een-hoos-*TEE-*th'yah*] injustice
injusto, -a [*een-*HOOS-*toh, -tah*] unjust
inmediatamente [*een-meh-d'yah-tah-*MEHN-*teh*] immediately
inmediato, -a [*een-meh-d'*YAH-*toh, -tah*] immediate
inmenso, -a [*een-*MEHN-*soh, -sah*] immense
inmigración (f) [*een-mee-grah-th'*YOHN] immigration
inmigrante [*een-mee-*GRAHN-*teh*] immigrant
inmoral [*een-moh-*RAHL] immoral
inmortal [*een-mohr-*TAHL] immortal
innecesario, -a [*een-neh-theh-*SAH-*r'yoh, -r'yah*] unnecessary

inocencia [*ee-noh-*THEHN-*th'yah*] innocence
inocente [*ee-noh-*THEHN-*teh*] innocent
inofensivo, -a [*ee-noh-fehn-*SEE-*voh, -vah*] inoffensive; harmless
inolvidable [*een-ohl-vee-*DAH-*bleh*] unforgettable
inquietar(se) [*een-k'yeh-*TAHR-*seh*] to worry, to become worried
inquieto [*een-k'*YEH-*toh*] restless
inquilino, -a [*een-kee-*LEE-*noh, -nah*] lodger, tenant
inscribir(se) [*een-skree-*BEER-*seh*] to register
inscripción (f) [*een-skreep-th'*YOHN] inscription
insecto [*een-*SEHK-*toh*] insect
inseguro, -a [*een-seh-*GOO-*roh, -rah*] insecure
insensible [*een-sehn-*SEE-*bleh*] unfeeling
insertar [*een-sehr-*TAHR] to insert
insignia [*een-*SEEG-*n'yah*] insignia
insignificante [*een-see-gnee-fee-*KAHN-*teh*] insignificant
insistir [*een-sees-*TEER] to insist
insolente [*een-soh-*LEHN-*teh*] insolent
insoportable [*een-soh-pohr-*TAH-*bleh*] unbearable
inspección (f) [*een-spehk-th'*YOHN] inspection
inspector (m) [*een-spehk-*TOHR] inspector
inspirar [*een-spee-*RAHR] to inspire
instalar [*een-stah-*LAHR] to install
instante (m) [*een-*STAHN-*teh*] instant
  al instante [*ahl een-*STAHN-*teh*] instantly
instinto [*een-*STEEN-*toh*] instinct
instituto [*een-stee-*TOO-*toh*] institute, school
instrucción (f) [*een-strook-th'*YOHN] instruction
instructor [*een-strook-*TOHR] instructor, teacher
instruir [*eens-troo-*EER] to instruct
instrumento [*eens-troo-*MEHN-*toh*] instrument
insuficiente [*een-soo-fee-th'*YEHN-*teh*] insufficient
insulto [*een-*SOOL-*toh*] insult
intacto, -a [*een-*TAHK-*toh, -tah*] intact
intelectual [*een-teh-lehk-t'*WAHL] intellectual
inteligencia [*een-teh-lee-*HEHN-*th'yah*] intelligence
inteligente [*een-teh-lee-*HEHN-*teh*] intelligent

intención (f) [*een-tehn-th'*YOHN] intention
intentar [*een-tehn-*TAHR] to try
intento [*een-*TEHN-*toh*] intent
intenso, -a [*een-*TEHN-*soh, -sah*] intent
intercambio [*een-tehr-*KAHM-*b'yoh*] interchange
interés (m) [*een-teh-*REHS] interest
interesante [*een-teh-reh-*SAHN-*teh*] interesting
interesar [*een-teh-reh-*SAHR] to interest
interesar(se) en [*een-teh-reh-*SAHR-*seh ehn*] to be interested in
interior (m) [*een-teh-r'*YOHR] interior (n and adj)
intermedio, -a [*een-tehr-*MEH-*d'yoh, -d'yah*] intermediate
internacional [*een-tehr-nah-th'yoh-*NAHL] international
interpretar [*een-tehr-preh-*TAHR] to interpret
intérprete (m or f) [*een-*TEHR-*preh-teh*] interpreter
interrogar [*een-teh-rroh-*GAHR] to question
interrumpir [*een-teh-rroom-*PEER] to interrupt
intestino [*een-tehs-*TEE-*noh*] intestine
íntimo, -a [EEN-*tee-moh, -mah*] intimate
intolerante [*een-toh-leh-*RAHN-*teh*] intolerant
intranquilo, -a [*een-trahn-*KEE-*loh, -lah*] worried, troubled
introducir [*een-troh-doo-*THEER] to introduce into
inundación (f) [*een-noon-dah-th'*YOHN] flood
inútil [*ee-*NOO-*teel*] useless
inutilmente [*ee-noo-teel-*MEHN-*teh*] uselessly
inválido, -a [*een-*VAH-*lee-doh, -dah*] invalid
invariable [*een-vah-r'*YAH-*bleh*] invariable
invención (f) (also) **invento** [*een-vehn-th'*YOHN, *een-*VEHN-*toh*] invention
inventar [*een-vehn-*TAHR] to invent
inverso [*een-*VEHR-*soh*] inverse, inverted
invertir [*een-vehr-*TEER] to invest
investigación [*een-vehs-tee-gah-th'*YOHN] investigation
investigar [*een-vehs-tee-*GAHR] to investigate
★ **invierno** [*een-v'*YEHR-*noh*] winter
invisible [*een-vee-*SEE-*bleh*] invisible
invitación (f) [*een-vee-tah-th'*YOHN] invitation

invitar [*een-vee-*TAHR] to invite
inyección (f) [*een-yehk-th'*YOHN] injection
iodo (yodo) [YOH-*doh*] iodine
★ **ir** [*eer*] to go
irse [EER-*seh*] to go off, to go away
ira [EE-*rah*] anger, rage
Irlanda [*eer-*LAHN-*dah*] Ireland
irlandés, -a [*eer-lahn-*DEHS, *-sah*] Irish
ironía [*ee-roh-*NEE-*ah*] irony
irresponsable [*ee-rrehs-pohn-*SAH-*bleh*] irresponsible
irritar [*ee-rree-*TAHR] to irritate
★ **isla** [EES-*lah*] island
Italia [*ee-*TAH-*l'yah*] Italy
italiano, -a [*ee-tah-l'*YAH-*noh, -nah*] Italian
itinerario [*ee-tee-neh-*RAH-*r'yoh*] itinerary
izquierdista (m and f) [*eeth-k'yehr-*DEES-*tah*] (politics) leftist, radical
★ **izquierdo, -a** [*eeth-k'*YEHR-*doh, -dah*] left

J

jabón (m) [*hah-*BOHN] soap
jalea [*hah-*LEH-*ah*] jelly
★ **jamás** [*hah-*MAHS] never
jamón (m) [*hah-*MOHN] ham
Japón [*hah-*POHN] Japan
japonés, -a [*hah-poh-*NEHS, *-sah*] Japanese
jarabe (m) [*hah-*RAH-*beh*] sirup
jardín (m) [*hahr-*DEEN] flower garden
jardinero, -a [*hahr-dee-*NEH-*roh, -rah*] gardener
jarra [HAH-*rrah*] pitcher
jarro [HAH-*rroh*] jug, jar
jaula [HOW-*lah*] cage
jazmín (m) [*hahth-*MEEN] jasmine
jefe (m) [HEH-*feh*] chief, leader, boss (col)
jerez (m) [*heh-*RETH] sherry

Jesús [*heh*-SOOS] Jesus

NOTE: Often said after a person sneezes or even as a mild exclamation. Also frequently used as a man's name.

jinete (m) [*hee*-NEH-*teh*] horseman
jira [HEE-*rah*] tour
jirafa [*hee*-RAH-*fah*] giraffe
joroba [*hoh*-ROH-*bah*] hump
joven [HOH-*vehn*] (m and f) young
joya [HOH-*yah*] jewel, gem
joyería [*hoh-yeh*-REE-*ah*] jewelry shop, jewelry
júbilo [HOOH-*bee-loh*] glee, joy
★ **juego** [HWEH-*goh*] sport, game, gambling, set (plates, silver, etc.)
★ **jueves** [HWEH-*vehs*] Thursday
juez (m) [*hwehth*] judge
jugador [*hoo-gah*-DOHR] player; gambler
jugar [*hoo*-GAHR] to play; to gamble
jugo [HOO-*goh*] juice
juguete (m) [*hoo*-GHEH-*teh*] toy
juguetería [*hoo-gheh-teh*-REE-*ah*] toyshop
juicio [HWEE-*th'yoh*] judgment, trial (in court)
julio [HOO-*l'yoh*] July (also a man's name corresponding to Julius.)
junio [HOO-*n'yoh*] June
junta [HOON-*tah*] board, council
junta de comercio [HOON-*tah deh koh*-MEHR-*th'yoh*] board of trade
junta de educación (f) [HOON-*tah deh eh-doo-kah-th'*YOHN] board of education
juntar [*hoon*-TAHR] to join
juntar(se) [*hoon*-TAHR-*(seh)*] to get together
junto, -a [HOON-*toh, -tah*] close to, together, joined
jurado [*hoo*-RAH-*doh*] jury

juramento [*hoo-rah-*MEHN*-toh*] oath
jurar [*hoo-*RAHR] to swear
justicia [*hoos-*TEE*-th'yah*] justice
justo, -a [HOOS*-toh, -tah*] just, fair
juventud (f) [*hoo-vehn-*TOOD] youth
juzgado [*hooth-*GAH*-doh*] court (of justice)
juzgar [*hooth-*GAHR] to judge

K

kilo [KEE*-loh*] **kilogramo** [*kee-loh-*GRAH*-moh*] kilogram
(See metric table at back of dictionary.)
kilómetro [*kee-*LOH*-meh-troh*] kilometer
(See metric table at back of dictionary.)
kiosco [*k'*YOHS*-koh*] newsstand

L

★ **la** [*lah*] the (feminine); her, it (as direct object)
labio [LAH*-b'yoh*] lip
laboratorio [*lah-boh-rah-*TOH*-r'yoh*] laboratory
lado [LAH*-doh*] side
ladrar [*lah-*DRAHR] to bark
ladrillo [*lah-*DREE*-l'yoh*] brick
ladrón (ladrona) [*lah-*DROHN, *lah-*DROH*-nah*] thief
lagarto [*lah-*GAHR*-toh*] lizard
lago [LAH*-goh*] lake
lágrima [LAH*-gree-mah*] tear
laguna [*lah-*GOO*-nah*] pond, puddle
lamentar [*lah-mehn-*TAHR] to regret
★ **lámpara** [LAHM*-pah-rah*] lamp
lana [LAH*-nah*] wool
lancha [LAHN*-chah*] launch, boat
langosta [*lahn-*GOHS*-tah*] lobster
lanza [LAHN*-thah*] lance, spear

lanzar [*lahn*-THAHR] to throw; to launch
★ **lápiz** (m) [LAH-*peeth*] pencil
★ **largo, -a** [LAHR-*goh, -gah*] long
★ **las** [*lahs*] (feminine, plural); them, you (as direct object)
lástima [LAHS-*tee-mah*] pity, shame
¡Qué lástima! [*keh* LAHS-*tee-mah*] What a pity!
lastimar [*lahs-tee*-MAHR] to hurt
lata [LAH-*tah*] tin, (col) nuisance
látigo [LAH-*tee-goh*] whip
latín [*lah*-TEEN] Latin (language)
latino, -a [*lah*-TEE-*noh, -nah*] Latin (adj)
latir [*lah*-TEER] to palpitate, to beat
lavabo [*lah*-VAH-*boh*] washbasin, lavatory
lavandera [*lah-vahn*-DEH-*rah*] laundress
lavandería [*lah-vahn-deh*-REE-*ah*] laundry
★ **lavar** [*lah*-VAHR] to wash
lavar(se) [*lah*-VAHR-*seh*] to wash (oneself)
lazo [LAH-*thoh*] bow, tie
★ **le** [*leh*] (as direct object) him; (as indirect object) to him, to her, to it.
leal [*leh*-AHL] loyal
lección (f) [*lehk-th'*YOHN] lesson
lectura [*lehk*-TOO-*rah*] reading
★ **leche** (f) [LEH-*cheh*] milk
lechería [*leh-cheh*-REE-*ah*] dairy
lechero [*leh*-CHEH-*roh*] milkman
lecho [LEH-*choh*] bed, bed of a river
lechón (m) [*leh*-CHOHN] suckling pig (culinary specialty)
lechuga [*leh*-CHOO-*gah*] lettuce
★ **leer** [*leh*-EHR] to read
legal [*leh*-GAHL] legal
legalizar [*leh-gah-lee*-THAHR] to legalize
legumbre (f) [*leh*-GOOM-*breh*] vegetable
lejano, -a [*leh*-HAH-*noh, -nah*] far off
★ **lejos** [LEH-*hohs*] far
está lejos [*ehs*-TAH LEH-*hohs*] it is far off
lengua [LEHN-*gwah*] tongue, language
lentamente [*lehn-tah*-MEHN-*teh*] slowly

lenteja [*lehn*-TEH-*hah*] lentil
★ **lento, -a** [LEHN-*toh, -tah*] slow
leña [LEH-*n'yah*] firewood
león, leona [*leh*-OHN, *leh*-OH-*nah*] lion, lioness
leopardo [*leh-oh*-PAHR-*doh*] leopard
★ **les** [*lehs*] to them (indirect object)
letra [LEH-*trah*] letter
  letra de crédito [LEH-*trah deh* KREH-*dee-toh*] letter of credit
letrero [*leh*-TREH-*roh*] sign, shop sign
levantar [*leh-vahn*-TAHR] to lift
levantar(se) [*leh-vahn*-TAHR-*seh*] to get up
ley (f) [*lay*] law
leyenda [*leh*-YEHN-*dah*] legend
liberación (f) [*lee-beh-rah-th'*YOHN] liberation
liberal [*lee-beh*-RAHL] liberal
libertad (f) [*lee-behr*-TAHD] liberty, freedom
libertador [*lee-behr-tah*-DOHR] liberator
libra [LEE-*brah*] pound

NOTE: Most Spanish-speaking countries usually use kilos for measuring weight. See metric table at back of book.

libre [LEE-*breh*] free
librería [*lee-breh*-REE-*ah*] bookstore
libreta [*lee*-BREH-*tah*] notebook
★ **libro** [LEE-*broh*] book
licencia [*lee*-THEHN-*th'yah*] license
licenciado [*lee-thehn-th'*YAH-*doh*] (title given to lawyers)
licorería [*lee-koh-reh*-REE-*ah*] liquor shop
líder [LEE-*dehr*] leader
liebre (f) [*l'*YEH-*breh*] hare
liga [LEE-*gah*] league (also garter)
ligero, -a [*lee*-HEH-*roh, -rah*] light, fast
lila [LEE-*lah*] lilac

lima [LEE-*mah*] file; lime
limitar [*lee-mee*-TAHR] to limit
límite (m) [LEE-*mee-teh*] limit
limón (m) [*lee*-MOHN] lemon
limonada [*lee-moh*-NAH-*dah*] lemonade
limosna [*lee*-MOHS-*nah*] alms, money given to beggars
limpiabotas [*leem-p'yah*-BOH-*tahs*] shoe shine boy
limpiar [*leem-p'*YAHR] to clean
★ **limpio, -a** [LEEM-*p'yoh, -yah*] clean
★ **lindo, -a** [LEEN-*doh, -dah*] pretty, lovely
 ¡Qué linda! [*keh* LEEN-*dah*] How pretty!
línea [LEE-*neh-ah*] line
lino [LEE-*noh*] linen
linterna [*leen*-TEHR-*nah*] lantern
lío [LEE-*oh*] bundle, (coll) mess, difficulty
liquidación (f) [*lee-kee-dah-th'*YOHN] liquidation; bargain sale
líquido [LEE-*kee-doh*] liquid
lirio [LEE-*r'yoh*] lily
liso, -a [LEE-*soh, -sah*] smooth
lisonjero, -a [*lee-sohn*-HEH-*roh, -rah*] (adj) flattering; (noun) flatterer
lista [LEES-*tah*] list, menu
 lista de correos [LEES-*tah deh koh*-RREH-*ohs*] general delivery
listo, -a [LEES-*toh, -tah*] ready
literario, -a [*lee-teh*-RAH-*r'yoh, -yah*] literary
literatura [*lee-teh-rah*-TOO-*rah*] literature
litro [LEE-*troh*] liter (Approximately 1 quart, see metric measures at end of book.)
liviano, -a [*lee-v'*YAH-*noh, -nah*] light (not heavy)
llama [*l'*YAH-*mah*] llama (Andean animal)
llamada [*l'yah*-MAH-*dah*] call, knock
★ **llamar** [*l'yah*-MAHR] to call, to knock
★ **llamar(se)** [*l'yah*-MAHR-*seh*] to be called, to be named
 ¿Cómo se llama Ud.? [KOH-*moh seh l'*YAH-*mah oos* TEHD] What is your name?
llano, -a [*l'*YAH-*noh, -nah*] smooth, level

llave (f) [*l'*YAH-*veh*] key, switch
llegada [*l'yeh*-GAH-*dah*] arrival
★ **llegar** [*l'yeh*-GAHR] to arrive
llenar [*l'yeh*-NAHR] to fill, to fill out
lleno, -a [*l'*YEH-*noh, -nah*] full
★ **llevar** [*l'yeh*-VAHR] to carry, to take to, to wear
llevar(se) [*l'yeh*-VAHR-*seh*] to take off, to take away
llorar [*l'yoh*-RAHR] to cry
★ **llover** [*l'yoh*-VEHR] to rain
llueve [*l'*WEH-*veh*] it is raining
llovizna [*l'yoh*-VEETH-*nah*] drizzle
lluvia [*l'*YOO-*v'yah*] rain
★ **lo** [*loh*] (as direct object) him, it (as article used abstractly) the: Ex.: *Lo bueno*—"The good," *Lo interesante*—"The interesting (thing)."
lobo [LOH-*boh*] wolf
local (m) [*loh*-KAHL] place, premises
localizar [*loh-kah-lee*-THAHR] to locate
locamente [*loh-kah*-MEHN-*teh*] crazily
loción (f) [*loh-th'*YOHN] lotion
loco, -a [LOH-*koh, -kah*] crazy
locura [*loh*-KOO-*rah*] insanity
locutor [*loh*-KOO-*tohr*] radio announcer or speaker
lodo [LOH-*doh*] mud
lógico, -a [LOH-*hee-koh, -kah*] logical
lograr [*loh*-GRAHR] to achieve, to obtain
loma [LOH-*mah*] hill
lomo [LOH-*moh*] back (of an animal)
loro [LOH-*roh*] parrot
los [*lohs*] the (plural); them (as direct object)
lotería [*loh-teh*-REE-*ah*] lottery
lubricar [*loo-bree*-KAHR] to lubricate
lucir [*loo*-THEER] to shine, to glow
lucha [LOO-*chah*] struggle
luchar [*loo*-CHAHR] to struggle, to wrestle
★ **luego** [*l'*WEH-*goh*] then, later, soon
Desde luego [DEHS-*deh l'*WEH-*goh*] of course

★ **¡Hasta luego!** [AHS-*tah l'*WEH-*goh*] So long!
★ **lugar** [*loo*-GAHR] place
en lugar de [*ehn loo*-GAHR *deh*] in place of
lugarteniente (m) [*loo-gahr-teh-n'*YEHN-*teh*] lieutenant
lujo [LOO-*hoh*] luxury
lujoso, -a [*loo*-HOH-*soh, -sah*] luxurious
lumbre (f) [LOOM-*breh*] fire (in stove, fireplace, etc.)
★ **luna** [LOO-*nah*] moon
luna de miel [LOO-*nah deh m'yehl*] honeymoon
(estar en la) luna [*ehs*-TAHR *ehn la* LOO-*nah*] to be distracted, absent-minded
★ **lunes** (m) [LOO-*nehs*] Monday
luneta [*loo*-NEH-*tah*] (theat) orchestra seat
luto [LOO-*toh*] mourning
★ **luz** (f) [*looth*] light (Also used as girl's name)

M

machacar [*mah-chah*-KAHR] to pound, to crush
machete (m) [*mah*-CHEH-*teh*] long cutting knife
macho [MAH-*choh*] male
★ **madera** [*mah*-DEH-*rah*] wood
madrastra [*mah*-DRAHS-*trah*] stepmother
★ **madre** [MAH-*dreh*] mother
madreselva [*mah-dreh*-SEHL-*vah*] honeysuckle
madrina [*mah*-DREE-*nah*] godmother, patroness
madrugada [*mah-droo*-GAH-*dah*] early morning, time before dawn
maduro, -a [*mah*-DOO-*roh, -rah*] ripe
maestro, -a [*mah*-EHS-*troh, -trah*] teacher
mágico, -a [MAH-*hee-koh, -kah*] magic
magnífico, -a [*mah*-GNEE-*fee-koh, -kah*] magnificent
mago [MAH-*goh*] magician
mahometano, -a [*mah-oh-meh*-TAH-*noh, -nah*] Mohammedan
maíz (m) [*mah*-EETH] corn

majestad (f) [*mah-hehs*-TAHD] majesty
★ **mal** (adv) [*mahl*] badly
mal (n) [*mahl*] evil
mal hecho, -a [*mahl* EH-*choh, -chah*] badly done
malcriado, -a [*mahl-kr'*YAH-*doh, -dah*] ill bred, rude
maldecir [*mahl-deh*-THEER] to curse
maldito, -a [*mahl*-DEE-*toh, -tah*] damned, accursed
malestar [*mah-lehs*-TAHR] uncomfortable feeling, sickness
maleta [*mah*-LEH-*tah*] suitcase
maletero [*mah-leh*-TEH-*roh*] porter (for carrying bags)
malicioso, -a [*mah-lee-th'*YOH-*soh, -sah*] malicious
★ **malo, -a** [MAH-*loh, -lah*] bad

NOTE: When *malo* precedes a noun, it is shortened to *mal. Mala*, however, does not change.

malsano, -a [*mahl*-SAH-*noh, -nah*] unhealthy
maltratar [*mahl-trah*-TAHR] to mistreat
manada [*mah*-NAH-*dah*] flock, herd
manantial (m) [*mah-nahn-t'*YAHL] spring (water)
mancha [MAHN-*chah*] spot, stain
mandar [*mahn*-DAHR] to order, to command
como Ud. mande [KOH-*moh oos*-TEHD MAHN-*deh*] "As you command"
mandar a decir [*mahn*-DAHR *ah deh*-THEER] to send word
mande Ud. [MAHN-*deh oos*-TEHD] "Command me" (Tell me what you wish)
mandarina [*mahn-dah*-REE-*nah*] tangerine
manecilla [*mah-neh*-THEE-*l'yah*] hand of watch or clock
manejar [*mah-neh*-HAHR] to manage, to drive
★ **manera** [*mah*-NEH-*rah*] manner, way
de esta manera [*deh* EHS-*tah mah*-NEH-*rah*] in this way
de cualquier manera [*deh kwahl-k'*YEHR *mah*-NEH-*rah*] anyhow
de todas maneras [*deh* TOH-*dahs mah*-NEH-*rahs*] anyway

manga [MAHN-*gah*] sleeve
mango [MAHN-*goh*] handle, tropical fruit
manifestar [*mah-nee-fehs*-TAHR] to inform, to declare
★ **mano** (f) [MAH-*noh*] hand
NOTE: *Mano* is feminine although it ends in "o."
manso, -a [MAHN-*soh, -sah*] tame, gentle
manta [MAHN-*tah*] blanket, shawl
mantel (m) [*mahn*-TEHL] table cloth
mantener [*mahn-teh*-NEHR] to maintain, to keep up
mantequilla [*mahn-teh*-KEE-*l'yah*] butter
mantilla [*mahn*-TEE-*l'yah*] head shawl, mantilla
manuscrito [*mah-noos*-KREE-*toh*] manuscript
manzana [*mahn*-THAH-*nah*] apple, block (of houses)
★ **mañana** (adv) [*mah-n'*YAH-*nah*] tomorrow
★ **mañana** (noun f) [*mah-n'*YAH-*nah*] morning
mañana por la mañana [*mah-n'*YAH-*nah pohr lah mah-n'*YAH-*nah*] tomorrow morning
por la mañana [*pohr lah mah-n'*YAH-*nah*] in the morning
mapa (m) [MAH-*pah*] map
NOTE: *Mapa* is masculine despite the "a" ending.
maquillaje [*mah-kee-l'*YAH-*heh*] make up, cosmetics
máquina [MAH-*kee-nah*] machine, engine
máquina de coser [MAH-*kee-nah deh koh*-SEHR] sewing machine
máquina de escribir [MAH-*kee-nah deh ehs-kree*-BEER] typewriter
maquinilla de afeitar [*mah-kee*-NEE-*l'yah deh ah-fay*-TAHR] safety razor
★ **mar** [*mahr*] sea
NOTE: May be either masculine or feminine.
maravilla [*mah-rah*-VEE-*l'yah*] marvel, wonder
maravilloso, -a [*mah-rah-vee-l'*YOH-*soh, -sah*] wonderful
¡Qué maravilloso! [*keh-mah-rah-vee-l'*YOH-*soh*] How wonderful!
marca [MAHR-*kah*] mark, brand
marco [MAHR-*koh*] frame
marchar [*mahr*-CHAHR] to march, to function

mareado, -a [*mah-reh-*AH*-doh, -dah*] seasick
marfil [*mahr-*FEEL] ivory
margarita [*mahr-gah-*REE*-tah*] daisy (Also a girl's name)
marido [*mah-*REE*-doh*] husband
marina de guerra [*mah-*REE*-nah deh* GHEH*-rrah*] navy
marina mercante [*mah-*REE*-nah mehr-*KAHN*-teh*] merchant marine
marinero [*mah-ree-*NEH*-roh*] sailor
mariposa [*mah-ree-*POH*-sah*] butterfly
marisco [*mah-*REES*-koh*] shellfish
mármol (m) [MAHR*-mohl*] marble
marqués (marquesa) [*mahr-*KEHS, *mahr-*KEH*-sah*] marquis (marquise)
★ **marrón** [*mah-*RROHN] brown
★ **martes** [MAHR*-tehs*] Tuesday
martillo [*mahr-*TEE*-l'yoh*] hammer
marzo [MAHR*-thoh*] March
mas (conj) [*mahs*] but
★ **más** (adv) [*mahs*] more
más bien [*mahs b'yehn*] rather
más o menos [*mahs oh* MEH*-nohs*] more or less
¿qué más? [*keh mahs*] what else?
más adelante [*mahs ah-deh-*LAHN*-teh*] later on
algo más [AHL*-goh mahs*] something more
masaje (m) [*mah-*SAH*-heh*] massage
máscara [MAHS*-kah-rah*] mask
masculino, -a [*mahs-koo-*LEE*-noh, -nah*] masculine
masticar [*mahs-tee-*KAHR] to chew
mata [MAH*-tah*] shrub, bush
matadero [*mah-tah-*DEH*-roh*] slaughter house
matador [*mah-tah-*DOHR] killer, matador (bullfighter who kills the bull)
matar [*mah-*TAHR] to kill
matemáticas [*mah-teh-*MAH*-tee-kahs*] mathematics
materia [*mah-*TEH*-r'yah*] material, matter
materia prima [*mah-*TEH*-r'yah* PREE*-mah*] raw material
material (m) [*mah-teh-r'*YAHL] material

matricularse [*mah-tree-koo-*LAHR*-seh*] to register, to enroll
matrimonio [*mah-tree-*MOH*-n'yoh*] marriage, married couple
máximo, -a (adj) [MAHK*-see-moh, -mah*] greatest
máximo (n) [MAHK*-see-moh*] maximum
mayo [MAH*-yoh*] May
mayor [*mah-*YOHR] greater, larger, elder

NOTE: Preceded by an article it means "the largest," "the eldest."

(la) mayor parte de [*(lah) mah-*YOHR PAHR*-teh deh*] most of, the majority
mayordomo [*mah-yohr-*DOH*-moh*] butler, manager
mayoría [*mah-yoh-*REE*-ah*] majority
★ **me** [*meh*] to me, me, (as reflexive) myself
mecánico, -a (adj) [*meh-*KAH*-nee-koh, -kah*] mechanical
mecánico (n) [*meh-*KAH*-nee-koh*] mechanic
mecanógrafo, -a [*meh-kah-*NOH*-grah-foh, -fah*] typist
medalla [*meh-*DAH*-l'yah*] medal
media [MEH*-d'yah*] stocking
(a) mediados de . . . [*ah meh-d'*YAH*-dohs deh*] about the middle of . . .
mediano, -a [*meh-d'*YAH*-noh, -nah*] medium, mediocre
medianoche [*meh-d'yah-*NOH*-cheh*] midnight
medicina [*meh-dee-*THEE*-nah*] medicine
médico [MEH*-dee-koh*] doctor, physician
medida [*meh-*DEE*-dah*] measure, size
★ **medio, -a** [MEH*-d'yoh, -d'yah*] half, middle
a medias [*ah-*MEH*-d'yahs*] by halves
medio asado [MEH*-d'yoh ah-*SAH*-doh*] medium (meat)
por medio de [*pohr* MEH*-d'yoh deh*] by means of
mediodía [*meh-d'yoh-*DEE*-ah*] noon
medir [*meh-*DEER] to measure

mejilla [*meh*-HEE-*l'yah*] check
★ **mejor** [*meh*-HOHR] better
NOTE: When preceded by *el* or *la* it means "the best."
a lo mejor [*ah loh meh*-HOHR] probably
mejor dicho [*meh*-HOHR DEE-*choh*] rather
tanto mejor [TAHN-*toh meh*-HOHR] so much the better
mejorar [*meh-hoh*-RAHR] to improve, to get better
melancólico, -a [*meh-lahn*-KOH-*lee-koh, -kah*] sad, melancholy
melocotón (m) [*meh-loh-koh*-TOHN] peach
melodía [*meh-loh*-DEE-*ah*] melody
melón (m) [*meh*-LOHN] melon
melón de agua (m) [*meh*-LOHN *deh* AH-*gwah*] watermelon
mellizo, -a [*meh-l'*YEE-*thoh, -thah*] twin
memoria [*meh*-MOH-*r'yah*] memory
mencionar [*mehn-th'yoh*-NAHR] to mention
mendigo, -a [*mehn*-DEE-*goh, -gah*] beggar
menester (m) [*meh-nehs*-TEHR] need, want

NOTE: *es menester,* followed by the infinitive of a verb, means "it is necessary to ..."

menor [*meh*-NOHR] smaller, younger
NOTE: When preceded by *el* or *la* it means "the smallest," "the youngest."
★ **menos** [MEH-*nohs*] less, fewer
NOTE: When preceded by article it means "the least."
a menos que ... [*ah* MEH-*nohs keh*] unless
al menos [*ahl* MEH-*nohs*] at least
más o menos [*mahs oh* MEH-*nohs*] more or less
por lo menos [*pohr loh* MEH-*nohs*] at least
mensaje (m) [*mehn*-SAH-*heh*] message
mensajero, -a [*mehn-sah*-HEH-*roh, -rah*] messenger

mensual [*mehn*-SWAHL] monthly, by the month
menta [MEHN-*tah*] peppermint
mentar [*mehn*-TAHR] to mention, to name
mentir [*mehn*-TEER] to lie
mentira [*mehn*-TEE-*rah*] lie
menú [*meh*-NOO] menu
menudo, -a [*meh*-NOO-*doh, -dah*] small (as n) change
a menudo [*ah meh*-NOO-*doh*] frequently
mercado [*mehr*-KAH-*doh*] market
mercancía [*mehr-kahn*-THEE-*ah*] merchandise
merecer [*meh-reh*-THEHR] to deserve, to be worthy of
merienda [*meh-r'*YEHN-*dah*] light meal
mérito [MEH-*ree-toh*] merit
mero, -a [MEH-*roh, -rah*] mere, simple
★ **mes** (m) [*mehs*] month
el mes pasado [*ehl mehs pah*-SAH-*doh*] last month
el mes que viene [*ehl mehs keh v'*YEH-*neh*] next month
★ **mesa** [MEH-*sah*] table
la mesa está puesta [*lah*-MEH-*sah-ehs*-TAH-PWEHS-*tah*] the table is set
mestizo, -a [*mehs*-TEE-*thoh, -thah*] half breed
meta [MEH-*tah*] goal, aim
metal (m) [*meh*-TAHL] metal
meter [*meh*-TEHR] to put in, to insert
método [MEH-*toh-doh*] method
metro [MEH-*troh*] meter
NOTE: A little over a yard. See table at end of book. Also, abbreviation for *Metropolitana,* name given to subway in some countries.
mexicano, -a [*meh-hee*-KAH-*noh, -nah*] Mexican
Mexico [MEH-*hee-koh*] Mexico
mezclar [*mehth*-KLAHR] to mingle, to blend
★ **mi** [*mee*] my
mí [*mee*] **a mi** [*ah mee*] me, to me (Used after prepositions *a, de, para, por*)
miedo [*m'*YEH-*doh*] fear
tener miedo de [*teh*-NEHR *m'*YEH-*doh deh*] to be afraid of
miel (f) [*m'yehl*] honey

miembro [*m'*YEHM-*broh*] member
mientras [*m'*YEHN-*trahs*] while
mientras tanto [*m'*YEHN-*trahs* TAHN-*toh*] meanwhile
mientras que [*m'*YEHN-*trahs keh*] while
★ **miércoles** (m) [*m'*YEHR-*koh-lehs*] Wednesday
★ **mil** (m) [*meel*] thousand
milagro [*mee*-LAH-*groh*] miracle
Milagros is used as a girl's name.
militar (adj) [*mee-lee*-TAHR] military
militar (n) [*mee-lee*-TAHR] soldier
milla [MEE-*l'yah*] mile
NOTE: Most Spanish speaking countries use *kilómetros,* approximately five-eights of a mile.
millón [*mee-l'*YOHN] million
millonario, -ria [*mee-l'yoh*-NAH-*r'yoh, -r'yah*] millionaire
mimado, -da [*mee*-MAH-*doh, -dah*] overindulged, spoiled (as a child)
mina [MEE-*nah*] mine
mineral (adj) [*mee-neh*-RAHL] mineral
mineral (n) [*mee-neh*-RAHL] ore
mínimo, -a (adj) [MEE-*nee-moh, -mah*] least
mínimo, -a (n) [MEE-*nee-moh, -mah*] minimum
ministerio [*mee-nees*-TEH-*r'yoh*] ministry
Ministerio de Estado [*mee-nees*-TEH-*r'yoh deh ehs*-TAH-*doh*] State Department
Ministerio de Hacienda [*mee-nees*-TEH-*r'yoh deh ah-th'*YEHN-*dah*] Treasury Department
Ministerio de Sanidad [*mee-nees*-TEH-*r'yoh deh sah-nee*-DAHD] Public Health Department
ministro [*mee*-NEES-*troh*] minister
minoría [*mee-noh*-REE-*ah*] minority
minuto [*mee*-NOO-*toh*] minute
mío (plural **míos**) [*mee-oh*] mine
★ **mirar** [*mee*-RAHR] to look, to look at
mirar(se) [*mee*-RAHR-*(seh)*] to look at oneself
★ **¡mire!** (familiar form: **¡mira!**) [MEE-*reh*] look!
mis [*mees*] my (when object possessed is plural)
misa [MEE-*sah*] mass (religious ceremony)
miserable [*mee-seh*-RAH-*bleh*] miserable

misericordia [*mee-seh-ree-*KOHR*-d'yah*] mercy, pity
misión (f) [*mee-s'*YOHN] mission, errand
☆ **mismo, -a** [MEES*-moh, -mah*] same, similar
  ahora mismo [*ah-*OH*-rah* MEES*-moh*] right now
  eso mismo [EH*-soh* MEES*-moh*] that very thing
  lo mismo [*loh* MEES*-moh*] the same
  lo mismo me da [*loh* MEES*-moh meh dah*] it's the same to me
    NOTE: *Mismo* added to the personal pronouns as in the case of *yo mismo, Ud. mismo,* etc. is translated as "I myself," "you yourself," etc.
misterio [*mees-*TEH*-r'yoh*] mystery
mitad (f) [*mee-*TAHD] half
moda [MOH*-dah*] style, mode
  a la moda [*ah lah* MOH*-dah*] in style
  la última moda [*lah* OOL*-tee-mah* MOH*-dah*] the latest style
  pasado de moda [*pah-*SAH*-doh deh* MOH*-dah*] out of style
modales (m plural) [*moh-*DAH*-lehs*] manners
modelo (m) [*moh-*DEH*-loh*] model
    NOTE: When model is a girl—*la modelo.*
moderno, -a [*moh-*DEHR*-noh, -nah*] modern
modestia [*moh-*DEHS*-t'yah*] modesty
modesto, -ta [*moh-*DEHS*-toh, -tah*] modest
modificar [*moh-dee-fee-*KAHR] modify
modista [*moh-*DEES*-tah*] dressmaker, milliner
★ **modo** [MOH*-doh*] way, manner
  de cualquier modo [*deh kwahl-k'*YEHR MOH*-doh*] anyway
  de modo que [*deh* MOH*-doh keh*] so that
  de ningún modo [*deh neen-*GOON MOH*-doh*] in no way
  de todos modos [*deh* TOH*-dohs* MOH*-dohs*] anyway
mojado, -a [*moh-*HAH*-doh, -dah*] wet
mojar [*moh-*HAHR] to wet, to drench
mojar(se) [*moh-*HAHR*-(seh)*] to get wet
molestar [*moh-lehs-*TAHR] to annoy
  ¡No se moleste! [*noh seh moh-*LEHS*-teh*] Don't bother yourself.
  No molestar. [*noh moh-lehs-*TAHR] Do not disturb.
molestia [*moh-*LEHS*-t'yah*] annoyance

molino [*moh*-LEE-*noh*] mill

★ **momento** [*moh*-MEHN-*toh*] moment

En cualquier momento [*ehn kwahl-k'*YEHR *moh*-MEHN-*toh*] at any moment

¡Espere un momento! [*ehs*-PEH-*reh oon moh*-MEHN-*toh*] Wait a moment!

monarquía [*moh-nahr*-KEE-*ah*] monarchy

moneda [*moh*-NEH-*dah*] currency, coin

monja [MOHN-*hah*] nun

monje (m) [MOHN-*heh*] monk

mono, -a (n) [MOH-*noh, -nah*] monkey

mono, -a (colloquial adj) [MOH-*noh, -nah*] "cute" (colloquial)

monótono, -a [*moh*-NOH-*toh-noh, -nah*] monotonous

monstruo [MOHNS-*troo-oh*] monster

montaña [*mohn*-TAH-*n'yah*] mountain

montar [*mohn*-TAHR] to mount, to ride

montar a caballo [*mohn*-TAHR *ah kah*-BAH-*l'yoh*] to ride horseback

monte (m) [MOHN-*teh*] mountain, woods

montón (m) [*mohn*-TOHN] heap, pile

montura [*mohn*-TOO-*rah*] saddle

monumento [*moh-noo*-MEHN-*toh*] monument

mora [MOH-*rah*] blackberry

morado, -a [*moh*-RAH-*doh, -dah*] purple

moral (f) [*moh*-RAHL] moral, ethics

morder [*mohr*-DEHR] to bite

mordida [*mohr*-DEE-*dah*] bite

mordida (coll) [*mohr*-DEE-*dah*] bribe

moreno, -a [*moh*-REH-*noh, -nah*] brown, dark skinned, brunette

morir [*moh*-REER] to die

moro, -a [MOH-*roh, -rah*] Moorish

mortal [*mohr*-TAHL] mortal

mosca [MOHS-*kah*] fly

mosquito [*mohs*-KEE-*toh*] mosquito

mostaza [*mohs*-TAH-*thah*] mustard

mostrador [*mohs-trah*-DOHR] counter

mostrar [*mohs*-TRAHR] to show
motivo [*moh*-TEE-*voh*] reason, motive
motocicleta [*moh-toh-thee*-KLEH-*tah*] motorcycle
motor (m) [*moh*-TOHR] motor, engine
mover [*moh*-VEHR] to move
movimiento [*moh-vee-m'*YEHN-*toh*] movement
mozo, -a (adj) [MOH-*thoh, -thah*] young
mozo, -a [MOH-*thoh, -thah*] young man, young woman; waiter, waitress
buen mozo, buena moza [*bwehn* MOH-*thoh,* BWEH-*nah* MOH-*thah*] good looking
★ **muchacho, -a** [*moo*-CHAH-*choh, -chah*] boy, girl
muchísimo, -a [*moo*-CHEE-*see-moh, -mah*] (adj) very much (adj plural) very many, (adv) a very great deal
★ **mucho, -a** [MOO-*choh, -chah*] (adj) much, a great deal of, (adv) a great deal
★ **muchos, -as** (adj, plural) [MOO-*chohs, -chahs*] many
★ **con mucho gusto** [*kohn* MOO-*choh* GOOS-*toh*] with much pleasure
mucho más [MOO-*choh mahs*] much more
mucho menos [MOON-*choh* MEH-*nohs*] much less
mucho tiempo [MOO-*choh t'*YEHM-*poh*] a long time
mudar(se) [*moo*-DAHR*(seh)*] to change (clothes), to move
mudo, -a [MOO-*doh, -dah*] dumb, silent
mueble (m) [MWEH-*bleh*] furniture
mueblería [*mweh-bleh*-REE-*ah*] furniture shop
muela [MWEH-*lah*] rear tooth, molar
muelle (m) [MWEH-*l'yeh*] dock, pier
muerte (f) [MWEHR-*teh*] death
muerto, -a [MWEHR-*toh, -tah*] dead
muestra [MWEHS-*trah*] sample
★ **mujer** (f) [*moo*-HEHR] woman, wife
NOTE: As *mujer* means both "woman" and "wife" the exact meaning must come from the context. See *esposa*.
muleta [*moo*-LEH-*tah*] cloth used by bullfighter before kill
mulo, -a [MOO-*loh, -lah*] mule
multa [MOOL-*tah*] fine

multitud (f) [*mool-tee-*TOOD] multitude, crowd
★ **mundo** [MOON-*doh*] world
muñeca [*moon-n'*YEH-*kah*] wrist; doll
muralla [*moo-*RAH-*l'yah*] wall (of a city or castle)
murmullo [*moor-*MOO-*l'yoh*] murmur
músculo [MOOS-*koo-loh*] muscle
museo [*moo-*SEH-*oh*] museum
música [MOO-*see-kah*] music
musical (adj) [*moo-see-*KAHL] musical
músico (n) [MOO-*see-koh*] musician
muslo [MOOS-*loh*] thigh
mutuo, -a [MOO-*twoh, -twah*] mutual
★ **muy** [*mooy*] very, greatly
muy bien [*mooy b'yehn*] very well
muy mal [*mooy mahl*] very badly
NOTE: *Muy señor mio* (or *nuestro*), *Muy señora mía* (or *nuestra*) and *Muy señores nuestros* are the accepted ways of saying "Dear Sir," "Dear Madam," or "Gentlemen," at the beginning of a letter.

N

nacer [*nah-*THEHR] to be born
¿Dónde nació Ud.? [DOHN-*deh nah-th'*YOH *oos-*TEHD] Where were you born?
nacido, -a [*nah-*THEE-*doh, -dah*] born
nación (f) [*nah-th'*YOHN] nation
Naciones Unidas [*nah-*TH'YOH-*nehs oo-*NEE-*dahs*] United Nations
nacional [*nah-th'yoh-*NAHL] national
nacionalidad (f) [*nah-th'yoh-nah-lee-*DAHD] nationality
★ **nada** [NAH-*dah*] nothing
★ **de nada** [*deh* NAH-*dah*] you are welcome
nada de nuevo [NAH-*dah deh n'*WEH-*voh*] nothing new
nada de particular [NAH-*dah deh pahr-tee-koo-*LAHR] nothing in particular
★ **nada más** [NAH-*dah mahs*] nothing more
nadador, -a [*nah-dah-*DOHR, *-rah*] swimmer

nadar [*nah*-DAHR] to swim
★ **nadie** [NAH-*d'yeh*] nobody
naipe (m) [NIGH-*peh*] playing card
naranja [*nah*-RAHN-*hah*] orange
naranjada [*nah-rahn*-HAH-*dah*] orangeade
narcótico, -a [*nahr*-KOH-*tee-koh, -kah*] narcotic (adj and n)
nariz (f) [*nah*-REETH] nose
narrar [*nah*-RRAHR] to tell, to relate
nativo, -a [*nah*-TEE-*voh, -vah*] native
natural [*nah-too*-RAHL] natural
  natural de [*nah-too*-RAHL *deh*] native of
naturaleza [*nah-too-rah*-LEH-*thah*] nature
naturalizado, -a [*nah-too-rah-lee*-THAH-*doh, -dah*] naturalized
naufragio [*now*-FRAH-*h'yoh*] shipwreck
navaja [*nah*-VAH-*hah*] razor, knife
navegación [*nah-veh-gah-th'*YOHN] navigation
navegar [*nah-veh*-GAHR] to sail, to navigate
Navidad [*nah-vee*-DAHD] Christmas
  Feliz Navidad [*feh*-LEETH *nah-vee*-DAHD] Merry Christmas
neblina [*neh*-BLEE-*nah*] mist, fog
necesario, -a [*neh-theh*-SAH-*r'yoh, -yah*] necessary
necesidad (f) [*neh-theh-see*-DAHD] need, necessity
necesitar [*neh-theh-see*-TAHR] to need, to be in want of
necio, -a [NEH-*th'yoh, -th'yah*] foolish, stupid
negar [*neh*-GAHR] to deny
negativa [*neh-gah*-TEE-*vah*] negative, refusal
negligencia [*neh-glee*-HEHN-*th'yah*] negligence
negocio [*neh*-GOH-*th'yoh*] business
  de negocios [*deh neh*-GOH-*th'yohs*] on business
★ **negro, -a** [NEH-*groh, -grah*] black, Negro
nene, nena [NEH-*neh*, NEH-*nah*] (col) infant, child
nervio [NEHR-*v'yoh*] nerve
nervioso, -a [*nehr-v'*YOH-*soh, -sah*] nervous
neumático (n) [*neh-oo*-MAH-*tee-koh*] tire
neutral [*neh-oo*-TRAHL] neutral
nevada [*neh*-VAH-*dah*] snowfall

nevar [*neh*-VAHR] to snow
nevera [*neh*-VEH-*rah*] ice box
★ **ni** [*nee*] nor
ni . . . ni [*nee . . . nee . . .*] neither . . . nor
ni uno ni otro [*nee* OO-*noh nee* OH-*troh*] neither the one nor the other
ni siquiera [*nee see-k'*YEH-*rah*] not even
Nicaragua [*nee-kah*-RAH-*gwah*] Nicaragua
nicaragüense (m and f) [*nee-kah-rah*-GWEHN-*seh*] Nicaraguan
nido [NEE-*doh*] nest
niebla [*n'*YEH-*blah*] fog, haze
nieto, -a [*n'*YEH-*toh, -tah*] grandson (granddaughter)
nieve (f) [*n'*YEH-*veh*] snow
ningún [*neen*-GOON] not one, no
NOTE: Used *before* a masculine noun.
de ningún modo [*deh neen*-GOON MOH-*doh*] in no way
ninguno, -a [*neen*-GOO-*noh, -nah*] no, not any, not one
★ **niña** [NEE-*n'yah*] young girl, little girl
niñera [*nee-n'*YEH-*rah*] nurse for children
niñez (f) [*nee-n'*YEHTH] childhood
★ **niño** [NEE-*n'yoh*] child, little boy
nivel (m) [*nee*-VEHL] level
nivel del mar [*nee*-VEHL *dehl mahr*] sea level
★ **no** [*noh*] no, not
★ **no hay** [*noh eye*] there isn't, there aren't (any)
no hay de que [*noh eye deh keh*] you are welcome
no hay nada [*noh eye* NAH-*dah*] there isn't anything
no hay nadie [*noh eye* NAH-*d'yeh*] there isn't anyone
no importa [*noh eem*-POHR-*tah*] it doesn't matter
¡No me diga! [*noh meh* DEE-*gah*] You don't say!
¡no obstante! [*noh ohbs*-TAHN-*teh*] nevertheless

NOTE: "Does not" and "do not" when used as negations are expressed simply by *no*. "He does not speak"—*No habla.*

no todavía [*noh toh-dah-*VEE-*ah*] not yet
ya no [*yah noh*] no longer
noble [NOH-*bleh*] noble
nocivo, -a [*noh-*THEE-*voh, -vah*] harmful
★ **noche** (f) [NOH-*cheh*] night
★ **Buenas noches** [*b'*WEH-*nahs* NOH-*chehs*] Good evening, good night
de noche [*deh* NOH-*cheh*] at night
Nochebuena [NOH-*cheh-b'*WEH-*nah*] Christmas Eve
por la noche [*pohr lah* NOH-*cheh*] at night
nombramiento [*nohm-brah-m'*YEHN-*toh*] nomination, appointment
★ **nombre** (m) [NOHM-*breh*] name, noun
nombre de pila [NOHM-*breh deh* PEE-*lah*] given name
nombre y apellido [NOHM-*breh ee ah-peh-l'*YEE-*doh*] first and last name
normal [*nohr-*MAHL] normal
★ **norte** (m) [NOHR-*teh*] north
norteamericano, -a [*nohr-teh-ah-meh-ree-*KAH-*noh, -nah*] North American
NOTE: Usually applied only to citizens of the U.S.A.
Noruega [*noh-*RWEH-*gah*] Norway
noruego, -a [*noh-*RWEH-*goh, -gah*] Norwegian
nos [*nohs*] us, to us; (ref) ourselves
nosotros, -as [*nohs-*OH-*trohs, -trahs*] we
a nosotros [*ah-noh-*SOH-*trohs*] to us, us
nostalgia [*nohs-*TAHL-*h'yah*] homesickness, nostalgia
nota [NOH-*tah*] note
notar [*noh-*TAHR] to note, to observe
notario [*noh-*TAH-*r'yoh*] notary public
noticia [*noh-*TEE-*th'yah*] news, news item
¿Qué noticias hay? [*keh noh-*TEE-*th'yahs eye*] What is the news?
notificar [*noh-tee-fee-*KAHR] to notify
novecientos, -as [*noh-veh-th'*YEHN-*tohs, -tahs*] nine hundred
novedad [*noh-veh-*DAHD] novelty, news, change
sin novedad [*seen noh-veh-*DAHD] nothing new

novela [*noh*-VEH-*lah*] novel
noveno, -a [*noh*-VEH-*noh, -nah*] ninth
novia [NOH-*v'yah*] bride, fiancée
noviazgo [*noh-v'*YAHTH-*goh*] engagement
noviembre [*noh-v'*YEHM-*breh*] November
novio [NOH-*v'yoh*] bridegroom, fiancé
nube [(f) [NOO-*beh*] cloud
nublado, -a [*noo*-BLAH-*doh, -dah*] cloudy
nudo [NOO-*doh*] bow, knot
nuera [*n'*WEH-*rah*] daughter-in-law
★ **nuestro, -a** [*n'*WEHS-*troh, -trah*] our (when article possessed is singular)
nuestros, -as [*n'*WEHS-*trohs, -trahs*] our (when article possessed is plural)
★ **nueve** [*n'*WEH-*veh*] nine
★ **nuevo, -a** [*n'*WEH-*voh, -vah*] new
nuez (f) [*nwehth*] nut
★ **número** [NOO-*meh-roh*] number
numeroso, -a [*noo-meh*-ROH-*soh, -sah*] numerous
ñame (m) [*n'*YAH-*meh*] yam

O

★ **o** [*oh*] or, either
obedecer [*oh-beh-deh*-THEHR] to obey
obediente [*oh-beh-d'*YEHN-*teh*] obedient
obispo [*oh*-BEES-*poh*] bishop
objeto [*ohb*-HEH-*toh*] object
obligación (f) [*oh-blee-gah-th'*YOHN] obligation
obligado, -a [*oh-blee*-GAH-*doh, -dah*] obliged

NOTE: Use *estar* when combined with "to be." "I am obliged to go"—*Estoy obligado a ir.*

obligar [*oh-blee-*GAHR] to oblige
obra [OH-*brah*] work, labor
obra maestra [OH-*brah mah-*EHS-*trah*] masterpiece
obras públicas [OH-*brahs* POO-*blee-kahs*] public works
obrero [*oh-*BREH-*roh*] worker
obscurecer [*ohbs-koo-reh-*THEHR] to darken, to dim
obscuro, -a [*ohbs-*KOO-*roh, -rah*] obscure, dark
NOTE: The *b* can be dropped: *oscuro.*
observación (f) [*ohb-sehr-vah-*TH'YOHN] observation
observador, -a [*ohb-sehr-vah-*DOHR, *-rah*] observer
observar [*ohb-sehr-*VAHR] to observe
observatorio [*ohb-sehr-vah-*TOH-*r'yoh*] observatory
obstáculo [*ohb-*STAH-*koo-loh*] obstacle
obstinado, -a [*ohb-stee-*NAH-*doh, -dah*] obstinate
obstrucción (f) [*ohb-strook-th'*YOHN] obstruction
obtener [*ohb-teh-*NEHR] to obtain
obvio, -a [OHB-*v'yoh, -yah*] obvious
ocasión (f) [*oh-kah-s'*YOHN] opportunity, occasion
occidental [*ohk-thee-dehn-*TAHL] western, occidental
océano [*oh-*THEH-*ah-noh*] ocean
ocio [OH-*th'yoh*] leisure
octavo, -a [*ohk-*TAH-*voh, -vah*] eighth
octubre [*ohk-*TOO-*breh*] October
oculista (m) [*oh-koo-*LEES-*tah*] oculist
ocultar [*oh-kool-*TAHR] to hide
ocupación (f) [*oh-koo-pah-th'*YOHN] occupation
ocupado, -a [*oh-koo-*PAH-*doh, -dah*] occupied, busy
ocupar [*oh-koo-*PAHR] to occupy
ocurrente [*oh-koo-*RREHN-*teh*] humorous, witty
ocurrir [*oh-koo-*RREER] to occur
¿Qué ocurre? [*keh oh-*KOO-*rreh*] What is going on?
★ **ochenta** [*oh-*CHEHN-*tah*] eighty
★ **ocho** [OH-*choh*] eight
odiar [*oh-d'*YAHR] to hate
odio [OH-*d'yoh*] hatred
odioso, -a [*oh-d'*YOH-*soh, -sah*] hateful
★ **oeste** [*oh-*EHS-*teh*] West
ofender [*oh-fehn-*DEHR] to offend

ofensivo, -a [*oh-fehn*-SEE-*voh, -vah*] offensive
oferta [*oh*-FEHR-*tah*] offer
¿Qué se le ofrece? [*keh seh leh oh*-FREH-*theh*] What can one offer you?
oído [*oh*-EE-*doh*] hearing, ear

NOTE: There are two words for "ear": *oído* for the inner ear and *oreja* for the visible part.

★ **¡oiga!** [OY-*gah*] listen!
★ **oir** [*oh*-EER] to hear, to listen
★ **¡ojalá!** [*oh-hah*-LAH] I hope so! Would that!
ojalá que no [*oh-hah*-LAH *keh noh*] I hope not
★ **ojo** [OH-*hoh*] eye
¡ojo! [OH-*hoh*] Look out! Be careful!
ola [OH-*lah*] wave
oler [*oh*-LEHR] to smell
olfato [*ohl*-FAH-*toh*] sense of smell
oliva [*oh*-LEE-*vah*] olive, olive tree
olor [*oh*-LOHR] smell, fragrance
★ **olvidar** (or) **olvidar(se)** [*ohl-vee*-DAHR-*(seh)*] to forget
olvido [*ohl*-VEE-*doh*] forgetfulness
olla [OH-*l'yah*] pot
omisión (f) [*oh-mee-s'*YOHN] omission
omitir [*oh-mee*-TEER] to omit
ómnibus (m) [OHM-*nee-boos*] bus
★ **once** [OHN-*theh*] eleven
onda [OHN-*dah*] wave
onda corta [OHN-*dah* KOHR-*tah*] short wave
onza [OHN-*thah*] ounce
NOTE: Nearest equivalent weight is 28 *graines*. See table at rear of book.
ópera [OH-*peh-rah*] opera
operación (f) [*oh-peh-rah-th'*YOHN] operation
opinar [*oh-pee*-NAHR] to judge, to have an opinion

opinión [*oh-pee-n'*YOHN] opinion
oponer [*oh-poh-*NEHR] oppose
oportunidad [*oh-pohr-too-nee-*DAHD] opportunity
oposición [*oh-poh-see-th'*YOHN] opposition
oprimir [*oh-pree-*MEER] to oppress
optimista (m) [*ohp-tee-*MEES-*tah*] optimist
óptimo [OHP-*tee-moh*] the best, very good
opuesto, -a [*oh-p'*WEHS-*toh, -tah*] opposite, contrary
oración (f) [*oh-rah-th'*YOHN] (gram) sentence, prayer
orden (m) [OHR-*dehn*] order (arrangement)
orden (f) [OHR-*dehn*] order (command)
  a sus órdenes [*ah soos* OHR-*deh-nehs*] at your orders
ordenar [*ohr-deh-*NAHR] to arrange
ordinario, -a [*ohr-dee-*NAH-*r'yoh, -r'yah*] ordinary
★ **oreja** [*oh-*REH-*hah*] ear (visible part), see *oído.*
organización (f) [*ohr-gah-nee-thah-th'*YOHN] organization
organizado, -a [*ohr-gah-nee-*THAH-*doh, -dah*] organized
organizar [*ohr-gah-nee-*THAHR] to organize
órgano [OHR-*gah-noh*] organ
orgulloso, -a [*ohr-goo-l'*YOH-*soh, -sah*] proud
oriental [*oh-r'yehn-*TAHL] eastern, oriental
Oriente (m) [*oh-r'*YEHN-*teh*] East, Orient
origen (m) [*oh-*REE-*hehn*] origin
original [*oh-ree-hee-*NAHL] original
orilla [*oh-*REE-*yah*] edge, bank, shore
★ **oro** [OH-*roh*] gold
  (de) oro [*deh* OH-*roh*] of gold, golden
orquesta [*ohr-*KESS-*tah*] orchestra
orquídea [*ohr-*KEE-*deh-ah*] orchid
ortografía [*ohr-toh-grah-*FEE-*ah*] spelling
os [*ohs*] you (as direct object), to you (familiar and also rhetorical style)
osado, -a [*oh-*SAH-*doh, -dah*] daring, bold
oso [OH-*soh*] bear
ostión (and) **ostra** [*ohs-*T'YOHN, OHS-*trah*] oyster
★ **otoño** [*oh-*TOH-*n'yoh*] fall, autumn
otorgar [*oh-tohr-*GAHR] to grant, to agree to
★ **otro, -a** [OH-*troh, -trah*] other, another

el otro día [*ehl* OH-*troh* DEE-*ah*] the other day
otro día [OH-*troh* DEE-*ah*] another day
otra vez [OH-*trah vehth*] again, another time
por otra parte [*pohr* OH-*trah* PAHR-*teh*] on the other hand
otra cosa [OH-*trah* KOH-*sah*] something else
otros, -as [OH-*trohs, -trahs*] other, different (in plural)
oveja [*oh*-VEH-*hah*] sheep
oxidar(se) [*oh-ksee*-DAHR-*(seh)*] to become rusty
oxígeno [*oh*-KSEE-*heh-noh*] oxygen
★ **¡oye!** [OH-*yeh*] listen! (familiar form)

P

paciencia [*pah-th'*YEHN-*th'yah*] patience
paciente (m and f) [*pah-th'*YEHN-*teh*] patient (adj and n)
pacífico, -a [*pah*-THEE-*fee-koh, -kah*] pacific, tranquil
padecer [*pah-deh*-THEHR] to suffer
padrastro [*pah*-DRAHS-*troh*] stepfather
★ **padre** (m) [PAH-*dreh*] father
padrino [*pah*-DREE-*noh*] godfather
paella [*pah*-EH-*l'yah*] a famous rice, chicken and shellfish dish of Valencia
pagadero, -a [*pah-gah*-DEH-*roh, -rah*] payable to, payable
pagado, -a [*pah*-GAH-*doh, -dah*] paid
pagador [*pah-gah*-DOHR] paymaster, teller
★ **pagar** [*pah*-GAHR] to pay
página [PAH-*hee-nah*] page
pago [PAH-*goh*] payment
país [*pah*-EES] nation, country
paisaje [*pie*-SAH-*heh*] landscape
paisano, -a [*pie*-SAH-*noh, -nah*] from the same country, fellow citizen
paja [PAH-*hah*] straw
pájaro [PAH-*hah-roh*] bird
pala [PAH-*lah*] shovel
★ **palabra** [*pah*-LAH-*brah*] word

palabra de honor [*pah*-LAH-*brah deh oh*-NOHR] word of honor
palacio [*pah*-LAH-*th'yoh*] palace
palanca [*pah*-LAHN-*kah*] bar, crow bar
palco [PAHL-*koh*] box (theatre)
pálido, -a [PAH-*lee-doh, -dah*] pale
palma [PAHL-*mah*] palm tree, palm (of hand)
palo [PAH-*loh*] stick, pole, log
paloma [*pah*-LOH-*mah*] dove
palpitar [*pahl-pee*-TAHR] to beat, to palpitate
paludismo [*pah-loo*-DEES-*moh*] malaria
pampa [PAHM-*pah*] plain (especially in Argentina)
★ **pan** (n) [*pahn*] bread
pan con mantequilla [*pahn kohn mahn-teh*-KEE-*l'yah*] bread and butter
pan tostado [*pahn tohs*-TAH-*doh*] toast
panadería [*pah-nah-deh*-REE-*ah*] bakery
Panamá [*pah-nah*-MAH] Panama
panameño, -a [*pah-nah*-MEH-*n'yoh, -n'yah*] Panamanian
pandereta [*pahn-deh*-REH-*tah*] tamborine
pandilla [*pahn*-DEE-*l'yah*] gang
panecillo [*pah-neh*-THEE-*l'yoh*] roll (bread)
pánico [PAH-*nee-koh*] panic
pantalón (m) [*pahn-tah*-LOHN] pants
pantalla [*pahn*-TAH-*l'yah*] screen, lampshade
pañal [*pah-n'*YAHL] diaper (for baby)
paño [PAH-*n'yoh*] cloth, wool material
pañuelo [*pah-n'yoo*-EH-*loh*] handkerchief
Papa [PAH-*pah*] Pope
papa [PAH-*pah*] potato
NOTE: In Spain, *patata* is the word used.
papá (m) [*pah*-PAH] (coll) father
★ **papel** (m) [*pah*-PEHL] paper, rôle (theatre)
papel de escribir [*pah*-PEHL *deh ehs-kree*-BEER] writing paper
papel de seda [*pah*-PEHL *deh* SEH-*dah*] tissue paper
papelería (f) [*pah-peh-leh*-REE-*ah*] stationery store
paquete (m) [*pah*-KEH-*teh*] package

par (adj) [*pahr*] even, equal, (n) pair

★ **para** [PAH-*rah*] for, to, in order to

¿para cuándo? [PAH-*rah* KWAHN-*doh?*] when? (in the future)

★ **¿para qué?** [PAH-*rah keh*] what for?

¿para quién? [PAH-*rah k'*YEHN] for whom?

para siempre [PAH-*rah s'*YEHM-*preh*] forever

parabrisa (m) [*pah-rah* BREE-*sah*] windshield

paracaídas (m) [*pah-rah-kah*-EE-*dahs*] parachute

NOTE: *Paracaídas* and *paraguas* are masculine singular and plural even though they appear to be plural only.

parada [*pah*-RAH-*dah*] stop, stay

parado, -a [*pah*-RAH-*doh, -dah*] stopped

paraguas (m) [*pah*-RAH-*gwahs*] umbrella

paraíso [*pah-rah*-EE-*soh*] heaven, paradise

paralelo, -a [*pah-rah*-LEH-*loh, -lah*] parallel

paralizado, -a [*pah-rah-lee*-THAH-*doh, -dah*] paralysed

Paraguay [*pah-rah-g'*WHY] Paraguay

paraguayo, -a [*pah-rah*-GWAH-*yoh, -yah*] Paraguayan

★ **parar** [*pah*-RAHR] to stop

parar(se) [*pah*-RAHR-*(seh)*] to stop, to stand up

parcialmente [*pahr-th'yahl*-MEN-*teh*] partially

★ **pardo, -a** [PAHR-*doh, -dah*] brown, grey

★ **parecer** [*pah-reh*-THEHR] to appear, to seem

Me parece que . . . [*meh pah*-REH-*theh keh*] It seems to me that . . .

¿Qué le parece? [*keh leh pah*-REH-*theh*] What do you think? How does it seem to you?

parecer(se) [*pah-reh*-THEHR-*(seh)*] to look alike, to resemble

Se parece a su madre. [*seh pah*-REH-*theh ah soo* MAH-*dreh*] He looks like his mother. (She looks like her mother.)

parecido, -a [*pah-reh*-THEE-*doh, -dah*] like, similar to

pared (f) [*pah*-REHD] wall
pareja [*pah*-REH-*hah*] pair, couple
parentesco [*pah-rehn*-TEHS-*koh*] family relationship
pariente [*pah-r'*YEHN-*teh*] family relation

NOTE: Does not designate "parent" in sense of "mother" and "father." "Parents" is translated by *padres*.

parir [*pah*-REER] to give birth to
parque (m) [PAHR-*keh*] park
parrilla [*pah*-RREE-*l'yah*] broiler, grate
★ **parte** (f) [PAHR-*teh*] part, share
  dar parte a [*dahr* PAHR-*teh ah*] to notify
  de parte de [*deh* PAHR-*teh deh*] on the part of, from
  en alguna parte [*ehn ahl*-GOO-*nah* PAHR-*teh*] somewhere
  en todas partes [*ehn* TOH-*dahs* PAHR-*tehs*] everywhere
★ **la mayor parte** [*lah mah*-YOHR PAHR-*teh*] the majority
  por otra parte [*pohr* OH-*trah* PAHR-*teh*] on the other hand
participar [*pahr-tee-thee*-PAHR] to participate
particular (adj) [*pahr-tee-koo*-LAHR] particular; (n) person
partida [*pahr*-TEE-*dah*] departure
partido [*pahr*-TEE-*doh*] game, party
partido, -a [*pahr*-TEE-*doh, -dah*] divided, broken
partir [*pahr*-TEER] to divide, to split, to depart
  a partir de [*ah pahr*-TEER *deh*] starting from
pasa [PAH-*sah*] raisin
pasado, -a [*pah*-SAH-*doh, -dah*] past
  pasado mañana [*pah*-SAH-*doh mah-n'*YAH-*nah*] the day after tomorrow
  pasado de moda [*pah*-SAH-*doh deh* MOH-*dah*] out of style
pasaje (m) [*pah*-SAH-*heh*] passage, fare
pasajero, -a [*pah-sah*-HEH-*roh, -rah*] passenger
pasaporte (m) [*pah-sah*-POHR-*teh*] passport

★ **pasar** [*pah*-SAHR] to pass, to go across, to happen
Pase por aquí. [PAH-*seh pohr ah*-KEE] Come along here.
Que lo pase bien. [*keh loh* PAH-*seh b'yehn*] Have a good time.
★ **¿Qué pasa?** [*keh* PAH-*sah?*] What is going on?
Que pase buenas noches. [*keh* PAH-*seh* BWEH-*nahs* NOH-*chehs*] Have a good night.
¿Qué pasó? [*keh pah*-SOH?] What happened?
pasatiempo [*pah-sah-t'*YEHM-*poh*] hobby, pastime
Pascuas [PAHS-*kwahs*] Christmas *and* Easter
Felices Pascuas [*feh*-LEE-*thehs* PAHS-*kwahs*] Merry Christmas or Happy Easter
pase (m) [PAH-*seh*] permit; pass (in bullfight)
pasear [*pah-seh*-AHR] to take a walk or side
paseo [*pah*-SEH-*oh*] stroll, walk
pasillo [*pah*-SEE-*l'yoh*] passage, corridor
pasión (f) [*pah-s'*YOHN] passion, emotion
paso [PAH-*soh*] step, pass
a cada paso [*ah* KAH-*dah* PAH-*soh*] at each step
a pocos pasos [*ah* POH-*kohs* PAH-*sohs*] at a short distance
de paso [*deh* PAH-*soh*] by the way, passing through
prohibido el paso [*proh-ee*-BEE-*doh ehl* PAH-*soh*] keep out
pasta [PAHS-*tah*] paste
pasta de dientes [PAHS-*tah deh d'*YEHN-*tehs*] toothpaste
pastelería [*pahs-teh-leh*-REE-*ah*] pastry shop, pastry
pastilla [*pahs*-TEE-*l'yah*] tablet, drop
pata [PAH-*tah*] foot (of animal), leg (of table, etc.)
meter la pata [*meh*-TEHR *lah* PAH-*tah*] to put one's foot in it
patata [*pah*-TAH-*tah*] (Spain) potato (see *papa*)
patín (m) [*pah*-TEEN] skate
patines de hielo [*pah*-TEE-*nehs deh* YEH-*loh*] ice skates
patinar [*pah-tee*-NAHR] to skate, to skid
pato [PAH-*toh*] duck
patria [PAH-*tr'yah*] fatherland, native country
patriótico, -a [*pah-tree*-OH-*tee-koh, -kah*] patriotic
patrocinar [*pah-troh-thee*-NAHR] to sponsor

patrón (patrona) (f) [*pah*-TROHN, *pah*-TROH-*nah*] pattern, boss, landlord (-lady)
pausa [POW-*sah*] pause
pavo [PAH-*voh*] turkey
payaso [*pah*-YAH-*soh*] clown
★ **paz** (f) [*pahth*] peace
pecado [*peh*-KAH-*doh*] sin
peculiar [*peh-koo-l'*YAHR] peculiar
pecho [PEH-*choh*] chest, breast
pechuga [*peh*-CHOO-*gah*] breast (of fowl)
pedazo [*peh*-DAH-*thoh*] piece, morsel
pedido [*peh*-DEE-*doh*] demand; (com) order, request
★ **pedir** [*peh*-DEER] to ask for, request, order
pedir prestado [*peh*-DEER *prehs*-TAH-*doh*] to borrow
pegar [*peh*-GAHR] to glue, stick, attach, hit
pegar fuego a [*peh*-GAHR FWEH-*goh ah*] to set fire to
peinado [*pay*-NAH-*doh*] hair dressing, hair style
peinar [*pay*-NAHR] to comb
peine (m) [PAY-*neh*] comb
pelar [*peh*-LAHR] to skin, to pluck, to peal
pelea [*peh*-LEH-*ah*] fight, quarrel
pelea de gallos [*peh*-LEH-*ah deh* GAH-*l'yohs*] cock fight
peletería [*peh-leh-teh*-REE-*ah*] fur shop, leather goods shop
película [*peh*-LEE-*koo-lah*] film
peligro [*peh*-LEE-*groh*] danger
★ **peligroso, -a** [*peh-lee*-GROH-*soh, -sah*] dangerous
★ **pelo** [PEH-*loh*] hair
tomar el pelo [*toh*-MAHR *ehl* PEH-*loh*] to "pull one's leg"
pelota [*peh*-LOH-*tah*] ball
peludo, -a [*peh*-LOO-*doh, -dah*] shaggy, hairy
peluquería [*peh-loo-keh*-REE-*ah*] barber shop, beauty shop
pellizcar [*peh-l'yeeth*-KAHR] to pinch
pena [PEH-*nah*] pain, punishment, grief
Me da mucha pena. [*meh dah* MOO-*chah* PEH-*nah*] I am very sorry.
No vale la pena. [*noh* VAH-*leh lah* PEH-*nah*] It isn't worth while.
pendiente (adj) [*pehn-d'*YEHN-*teh*] pending (n. m)

penetrar [*peh-neh*-TRAHR] to penetrate
península [*peh*-NEEN-*soo-lah*] peninsula
penoso, -a [*peh*-NOH-*soh, -sah*] painful, distressing
pensamiento [*pehn-sah-m'*YEHN-*toh*] thought, mind, pansy
★ **pensar** [*pehn*-SAHR] to think
¿En qué piensa? [*ehn keh p'*YEHN-*sah*] What are you thinking about?
¿Qué piensa de esto? [*keh p'*YEHN-*sah deh* EHS-*toh?*] What do you think about this?
pensión (f) [*pehn-s'*YOHN] pension, boarding house
peña [PEH-*n'yah*] rock
★ **peor** [*peh*-OHR] worse
NOTE: When preceded by *el la* or *lo* means "the worst."
tanto peor [TAHN-*toh peh*-OHR] so much the worse
pepino [*peh*-PEE-*noh*] cucumber
★**pequeño, -a** [*peh*-KEH-*n'yoh, -n'yah*] (adj) small, (n) child
pera [PEH-*rah*] pear
percibir [*pehr-thee*-BEER] to perceive, collect
percha [PEHR-*chah*] perch, clothes rack
★ **perder** [*pehr*-DEHR] to lose
perder de vista [*pehr*-DEHR *deh* VEES-*tah*] to lose sight of
perder el juicio [*pehr*-DEHR *ehl* HWEE-*th'yoh*] to lose one's mind
perder la vista [*pehr*-DEHR *lah* VEES-*tah*] to lose one's sight
¡pierda Ud. cuidado! [*p'*YEHR-*dah oos*-TEHD *kwee*-DAH-*doh*] don't worry!
perder(se) [*pehr*-DEHR-*(seh)*] to get lost
pérdida [PEHR-*dee-dah*] loss
★ **perdido, -a** [*pehr*-DEE-*doh, -dah*] lost
perdón [*pehr*-DOHN] pardon
perdonar [*pehr-doh*-NAHR] to pardon
perejil [*peh-reh*-HEEL] parsley
perezoso, -a [*peh-reh*-THOH-*soh, -sah*] lazy
perfeccionar [*pehr-fehk-th'yoh*-NAHR] to improve, to make perfect

perfecto, -a [*pehr*-FEHK-*toh, -tah*] perfect
perfume (m) [*pehr*-FOO-*meh*] perfume
perfumería [*pehr-foo-meh*-REE-*ah*] perfume shop
periódico, -a [*peh-ree*-OH-*dee-koh, -kah*] (adj) periodic; (n, m) newspaper
periodista (m or f) [*peh-r'yoh*-DEES-*tah*] journalist
período [*peh*-REE-*oh-doh*] period (But not period at end of sentence, which is *punto*)
perjuicio [*pehr*-HWEE-*th'yoh*] hurt, damage
perla [PEHR-*lah*] pearl
permanacer [*pehr-mah-nah*-THEHR] to stay, to remain
permanente [*pehr-mah*-NEHN-*teh*] permanent
permiso [*pehr*-MEE-*soh*] permission, leave
¡con permiso! [*kohn pehr*-MEE-*soh*] Excuse me!
★ **permitir** [*pehr-mee*-TEER] to permit
¿Se permite fumar? [*seh pehr*-MEE-*teh foo*-MAHR?] Is smoking allowed?
★ **pero** [PEH-*roh*] but (see *sino*)
No hay pero que valga [*noh eye* PEH-*roh keh* VAHL-*gah*] There are no buts about it.
perpetuo, -a [*pehr*-PEH-*too-oh, -ah*] perpetual
★ **perro, perra** [PEH-*rroh, -rrah*] dog
perseguir [*pehr-seh*-GHEER] to persue, to persecute
persistente [*pehr-sees*-TEHN-*teh*] persistent
persona [*pehr*-SOH-*nah*] person
personal [*pehr-soh*-NAHL] (adj) personal, (n) personnel
personalidad [*pehr-soh-nah-lee*-DAHD] personality
persuadir [*pehr-swah*-DEER] to persuade
persuadir(se) [*pehr-swah*-DEER-*(seh)*] to be persuaded
★ **pertenecer** [*pehr-teh-neh*-THEHR] to belong to
¿A quién pertenece esto? [*ah k'yehn pehr-teh*-NEH-*theh* EHS-*toh?*] To whom does this belong?
pertinente [*pehr-tee*-NEHN-*teh*] pertinent
(el) **Perú** [*peh*-ROO] Peru
peruano, -a [*peh*-RWAH-*noh, -nah*] Peruvian
perverso, -a [*pehr*-VEHR-*soh, -sah*] perverse, wicked
pesadilla [*peh-sah*-DEE-*l'yah*] nightmare

pesado, -a [*peh*-SAH-*doh, -dah*] heavy, tedious
  ¡no sea pesado! [*noh* SEH-*ah peh*-SAH-*doh, -dah*] Don't be tiresome!
pésame [PEH-*sah-meh*] condolence
pesar [*peh*-SAHR] to weigh
  a pesar de [*ah-peh*-SAHR-*deh*] in spite of
pesca [PEHS-*kah*] fishing
★ **pescado** [*pehs*-KAH-*doh*] fish
  NOTE: Refers to fish *after* it is out of water. See *pez.*
pescuezo [*pehs*-KWEH-*thoh*] neck
peseta [*peh*-SEH-*tah*] Spanish money (See table at end of book.)
pesimista [*peh-see*-MEES-*tah*] (n and adj) pessimist, pessimistic
peso [PEH-*soh*] weight, unit of currency
  peso neto [PEH-*soh* NEH-*toh*] net weight
  peso bruto [PEH-*soh* BROO-*toh*] gross weight
pestaña [*pehs*-TAH-*n'yah*] eyelash
petición (f) [*peh-tee-th'*YOHN] petition, request
petróleo [*peh*-TROH-*leh-oh*] oil, petroleum
petrolero [*peh-troh*-LEH-*roh*] (adj) oil, (n) person in oil industry
★ **pez** (m) [*pehth*] fish (when alive in water)
pianista (m and f) [*p'yah*-NEES-*tah*] pianist
piano (m) [*p'*YAH-*noh*] piano
picado, -a [*pee*-KAH-*doh, -dah*] hurt, stung, pricked
picador (m) [*pee-kah*-DOHR] (in bullfight) horseman with spear
picante [*pee*-KAHN-*teh*] stinging, highly seasoned
picar [*pee*-KAHR] to prick, to sting, to itch
pícaro, -a [PEE-*kah-roh, -rah*] mischievous, sly
picazón (m) [*pee-kah*-THOHN] itching
pico [PEE-*koh*] point, pickaxe, beak (of bird)
  y pico [*ee* PEE-*koh*] and still a little bit
pichón (m) [*pee*-CHOHN] pigeon
★ **pie** (m) [*p'yeh*] foot
  a los pies de Ud. [*ah lohs p'yehs deh oos*-TEHD] at your feet

NOTE: A very polite formula on being introduced to ladies.

andar a pie [*ahn*-DAHR *ah p'yeh*] to walk
de pie [*deh p'yeh*] standing
★ **piedad** [*p'yeh*-DAHD] piety (Also a girl's name).
★ **piedra** [*p'*YEH-*drah*] stone
piel (f) [*p'yehl*] fur, skin, leather
★ **pierna** [*p'*YEHR-*nah*] leg
pieza [*p'*YEH-*thah*] piece, room, part (of machine)
pijama (m) [*pee*-HAH-*mah*] pajamas
pilar (m) [*pee*-LAHR] pillar (Also used as girl's name.)
píldora [PEEL-*doh-rah*] pill
piloto [*pee*-LOH-*toh*] pilot, ship's mate
pimienta [*pee-m'*YEHN-*tah*] pepper (black)
pimiento [*pee-m'*YEHN-*toh*] pepper (red or green)
piña [PEE-*n'yah*] pineapple
pincel (m) [*peen*-THEHL] artist's paint brush
pinchar [*peen*-CHAHR] to pinch, to puncture
pinchazo [*peen*-CHAH-*thoh*] (colloquial) flat tire
pino [PEE-*noh*] pine
pintado, -a [*peen*-TAH-*doh, -dah*] painted
pintar [*peen*-TAHR] to paint
pintor, -a [*peen*-TOHR, *-rah*] painter
pintura [*peen*-TOO-*rah*] painting
pinzas [PEEHN-*thahs*] tweezers, pincers
pipa [PEE-*pah*] pipe (for smoking)
pirámide (f) [*pee*-RAH-*mee-deh*] pyramid
piropo [*pee*-ROH-*poh*] compliment
pisar [*pee*-SAHR] to step on
piscina [*pees*-THEE-*nah*] swimming pool
piso [PEE-*soh*] floor, story, apartment
pista [PEES-*tah*] trail, track
pistola [*pees*-TOH-*lah*] pistol

pito [PEE-*toh*] whistle
pizarra [*pee*-THAH-*rrah*] blackboard
placa [PLAH-*kah*] license plate, plaque
placer (m) [*plah*-THEHR] pleasure
plan (m) [*plahn*] plan, design
plancha [PLAHN-*chah*] iron (for ironing clothes)
planchar [*plahn*-CHAHR] to iron (clothes)
planeta (m) [*plah*-NEH-*tah*] planet
NOTE: Masculine in spite of *a* ending.
planilla [*plah*-NEE-*l'yah*] application blank, list
plano, -a [PLAH-*noh, -nah*] smooth, plain
planta [PLAHN-*tah*] sole of foot, plant
plástico [PLAHS-*tee-koh*] plastic (adj)
plata [PLAH-*tah*] silver, money
plátano [PLAH-*tah-noh*] banana
plato [PLAH-*toh*] plate, dish
plato del día [PLAH-*toh dehl* DEE-*ah*] special dish of the day
playa [PLAH-*yah*] beach
plaza [PLAH-*thah*] plaza, town square
plaza de toros [PLAH-*thah deh* TOH-*rohs*] bull ring
plazo [PLAH-*thoh*] term of payment, credit, length of time
a plazos [*ah* PLAH-*thohs*] on credit
plegar [*pleh*-GAHR] to fold
pleito [PLAY-*toh*] law suit
pleno, -a [PLEH-*noh, -nah*] full
plomo [PLOH-*moh*] lead
pluma [PLOO-*mah*] pen, feather
pluma fuente [PLOO-*mah* FWEHN-*teh*] fountain pen
población (f) [*poh-blah-th'*YOHN] town, population
pobre [POH-*breh*] poor
pobreza [*poh*-BREH-*thah*] poverty
★ **poco, -a** [POH-*koh, -kah*] a little
poco a poco [POH-*koh ah* POH-*koh*] little by little
poco más o menos [POH-*koh mahs oh* MEH-*nohs*] more or less
★ **pocos, -as** [POH-*kohs, -ahs*] few, some
pocas veces [POH-*kahs* VEH-*thehs*] a few times

poder [*poh*-DEHR] to be able, can, may

NOTE: When followed by another verb, the second verb must be in the infinitive. *¿Puedo entrar?*– "May I come in?"

poesía [*poh-eh*-SEE-*ah*] poetry
polaco, -a [*poh*-LAH-*koh, -kah*] Polish
policía (f) [*poh-lee*-THEE-*ah*] police force
policía (m) [*poh-lee*-THEE-*ah*] policeman
política [*poh*-LEE-*tee-kah*] politics, policy
póliza (de seguros) [POH-*lee-thah (deh seh*-GOO-*rohs)*] (insurance) policy
Polonia [*poh*-LOH-*n'yah*] Poland
polvo [POHL-*voh*] powder, dust
pollo [POH-*l'yoh*] chicken
★ **poner** [*poh*-NEHR] to put, to place
poner al corriente [*poh*-NEHR *ahl koh*-RR'YEHN-*teh*] to inform
poner un telegrama [*poh*-NEHR *oon teh-leh*-GRAH-*mah*] to send a telegram
¡póngalo aquí! [POHN-*gah-loh ah*-KEE] put it here!
poner(se) [*poh*-NEHR-*(seh)*] to become, to set (the sun), to put on
popular [*poh-poo*-LAHR] popular
poquito, -a [*poh*-KEE-*toh, -tah*] very little, a bit
★ **por** [*pohr*] by, through, for, over, in
por aquí [*pohr ah*-KEE] over here
por dentro [*pohr* DEHN-*troh*] on the inside
¡por Dios! [*pohr d'*YOHS] For heaven's sake!
por escrito [*pohr ehs*-KREE-*toh*] in writing
por esto [*pohr* EHS-*toh*] for this reason
por fuera [*pohr* FWEH-*rah*] on the outside
por la mañana [*pohr lah mah-n'*YAH-*nah*] in the morning
★ **¿por qué?** [*pohr* KEH?] why?
por si acaso [*pohr see ah*-KAH-*soh*] in case
por supuesto [*pohr soo*-PWEHS-*toh*] of course

★ **porque** [POHR-*keh*] because
porquería [*pohr-keh*-REE-*ah*] worthless thing, dirty act
portamonedas (m) [*pohr-tah-moh*-NEH-*dahs*] purse, pocketbook
portar(se) [*pohr*-THAR-*(seh)*] to behave
portero [*pohr*-TEH-*roh*] janitor
Portugal [*pohr-too*-GAHL] Portugal
portugués, -a [*pohr-too*-GHEHS, *-sah*] Portuguese
poseer [*poh-seh*-EHR] to possess
★ **posible** [*poh*-SEE-*bleh*] possible
positivo, -a [*poh-see*-TEE-*voh, -vah*] positive
postizo, -a [*pohs*-TEE-*thoh, -thah*] artificial
postre (m) [POHS-*treh*] desert
potente [*poh*-TEHN-*teh*] potent, powerful
pozo [POH-*thoh*] well (for water)
práctico, -a [PRAHK-*tee-koh, -kah*] practical
prado [PRAH-*doh*] lawn, field
precedente [*preh-theh*-DEHN-*teh*] preceding
★ **precio** [PREH-*th'yoh*] price
  precio de venta [PREH-*th'yoh deh* VEHN-*tah*] sales price
precioso, -a [*preh-th'*YOH-*soh, -sah*] precious, beautiful
preciso, -a [*preh*-THEE-*soh, -sah*] precise, necessary
prefacio [*preh*-FAH-*th'yoh*] preface
preferible [*preh-feh*-REE-*bleh*] preferable
preferir [*preh-feh*-REER] to prefer
pregunta [*preh*-GOON-*tah*] question
★ **preguntar** [*preh-goon*-TAHR] to ask, to question
preguntar(se) [*preh-goon*-TAHR-*(seh)*] to wonder
premio [PREH-*m'yoh*] prize, reward
prenda [PREHN-*dah*] pledge, garment, piece of jewellery
prender [*prehn*-DEHR] to seize
  prender fuego [*prehn*-DEHR FWEH-*goh*] to catch on fire
prendido [*prehn*-DEE-*doh*] ladies' attire
prensa [PREHN-*sah*] press, printing press
preocupado, -a [*preh-oh-koo*-PAH-*doh, -dah*] preoccupied, worried

preocupar(se) [*preh-oh-koo-*PAHR*-(seh)*] to be worried
  ¡No se preocupe! [*noh seh preh-oh-*KOO*-peh*] Don't worry!
preparado, -a [*preh-pah-*RAH*-doh, -dah*] prepared
preparar [*preh-pah-*RAHR] to prepare, to get ready
preposición [*preh-poh-see-th'*YOHN] preposition
presenciar [*preh-sehn-th'*YAHR] to attend, to witness
presentar [*preh-sehn-*TAHR] to present, to display
presente (adj and n, m) [*preh-*SEHN*-teh*] present, current
  al presente [*ahl preh-*SEHN*-teh*] at the present
  tener presente [*teh-*NEHR *preh-*SEHN*-teh*] to bear in mind
presidente, -a [*preh-see-*DEHN*-teh*] president
preso, -a [PREH*-soh, -sah*] convict, prisoner
prestado, -a [*prehs-*TAH*-doh, -dah*] loaned
prestar [*prehs-*TAHR] to lend
prestigio [*prehs-*TEE*-h'yoh*] prestige
presupuesto [*preh-soo-*PWEHS*-toh*] budget
pretendiente [*preh-tehn-d'*YEHN*-teh*] pretender, suitor
prevenir [*preh-veh-*NEER] to prevent, to prepare, to warn
★ **primavera** [*pree-mah-*VEH*-rah*] spring
★ **primero, -a** [*pree-*MEH*-roh, -rah*] first, former
  de primera [*deh pree-*MEH*-rah*] of the best
  el primero del mes [*ehl pree-*MEH*-roh dehl mehs*] the first of the month
  primeros auxilios [*pree-*MEH*-rohs ow-*KSEE*-l'yohs*] first aid

NOTE: All days of the month except the first are expressed by the number only: "May 1st": *El primero de Mayo.* "May 2nd": *El dos de Mayo.*

primo, -a [PREE*-moh, -mah*] cousin
princesa [*preen-*THEH*-sah*] princess
principal (m) [*preen-thee-*PAHL] principal (n and adj)
príncipe (m) [PREEN*-thee-peh*] prince
principio [*preen-*THEE*-p'yoh*] beginning, principle

prisa [PREE-*sah*] hurry, haste
¡dése prisa! [DEH-*seh* PREE-*sah*] hurry up!
tener prisa [*teh*-NEHR PREE-*sah*] to be in a hurry
prisionero, -a [*pree-s'yoh*-NEH-*roh, -rah*] prisoner
privado, -a [*pree*-VAH-*doh, -dah*] private
privilegio [*pree-vee*-LEH-*h'yoh*] privilege
probable [*proh*-BAH-*bleh*] probable, likely
probablemente [*proh-bah-bleh*-MEHN-*teh*] probably
probar [*proh*-BAHR] to try, to taste
proceder [*proh-theh*-DEHR] to proceed
proceso [*proh*-THEH-*soh*] law suit, trial
proclamar [*proh-klah*-MAHR] to proclaim
producción [*proh-dook-th'*YOHN] production
producir [*proh-doo*-THEER] to produce
producto [*proh*-DOOK-*toh*] product
profesión (f) [*proh-feh-s'*YOHN] profession
profesor, -a [*proh-feh*-SOHR, *-rah*] professor
profundo, -a [*proh*-FOON-*doh, -dah*] deep, profound
progreso [*proh*-GREH-*soh*] progress
prohibir [*proh-ee*-BEER] to prohibit, to forbid
se prohibe fumar [*seh proh*-EE-*beh foo*-MAHR] no smoking
se prohibe la entrada [*seh proh*-EE-*beh lah ehn*-TRAH-*dah*] no admittance
★ **prohibido, -a** [*proh-ee*-BEE-*doh, -dah*] forbidden
prohibido pasar [*proh-ee*-BEE-*doh pah*-SAHR] no thoroughfare
prolongar [*proh-lohn*-GAHR] to prolong, to extend
promedio [*proh*-MEH-*d'yoh*] average
prometer [*proh-meh*-TEHR] to promise
prometido, -a [*proh-meh*-TEE-*doh, -dah*] promised, betrothed
pronombre [*proh*-NOHM-*breh*] pronoun
★ **pronto, -a** [PROHN-*toh, -tah*] ready, fast, quick
tan pronto como [*tahn* PROHN-*toh* KOH-*moh*] as soon as
pronunciación (f) [*proh-noon-th'yah-th'*YOHN] pronunciation

propiedad (f) [*proh-p'yeh*-DAHD] property
propietario, -a [*proh-p'yeh*-TAH-*r'yoh, -r'yah*] proprietor
propio, -a [PROH-*p'yoh, -p'yah*] own
  en sus propias manos [*ehn soos* PROH-*p'yahs* MAH-*nohs*] right into his hands
  mi propia casa [*mee* PROH-*p'yah* KAH-*sah*] my own house
proporcionar [*proh-pohr-th'yoh*-NAHR] to supply, to procure
propósito [*proh*-POH-*see-toh*] intention, aim
  (a) propósito [*ah proh*-POH-*see-toh*] by the way, on purpose
próspero, -a [PROHS-*peh-roh, -rah*] prosperous
proteger [*proh-teh*-HEHR] to protect
protestante [*proh-tehs*-TAHN-*teh*] Protestant
protestar [*proh-tehs*-TAHR] to protest
provecho [*proh*-VEH-*choh*] advantage, profit
  ¡Buen provecho! [*b'wehn proh*-VEH-*choh*] Have a good meal!
proverbio [*proh*-VEHR-*b'yoh*] proverb
provincia [*proh*-VEEN-*th'yah*] province
próximo, -a [PROH-*xee-moh, -mah*] next, close, near
proyecto (m) [*proh*-YEHK-*toh*] plan, project
prudente [*proo*-DEHN-*teh*] prudent
prueba [PRWEH-*bah*] proof, test
publicar [*poo-blee*-KAHR] to publish
público, -a [POO-*blee-koh, -kah*] public
puchero [*poo*-CHEH-*roh*] pot, stew
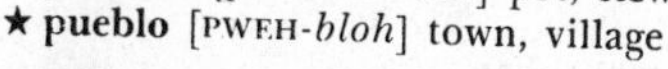
★ **pueblo** [PWEH-*bloh*] town, village

NOTE: Also means "people" when referring to a nation as a whole. *El pueblo español.*—"The Spanish people."

puente (m or f) [PWEHN-*teh*] bridge
★ **puerta** [PWEHR-*tah*] door
puerto [PWEHR-*toh*] port

★ **pues** [*pwehs*] for, because, inasmuch as, then

pues vamos [*pwehs* VAH-*mohs*] Then let's go

NOTE: *Pues* is also used as a "hesitation" word, to bridge over a gap and in this sense approximates "well...."

¿pues qué? [*pwehs keh*] What of it?

pues sí [*pwehs see*] Yes, indeed

puesto [PWEHS-*toh*] (as n) stand, booth, (as adj) placed, put

puesto que [PWEHS-*toh keh*] inasmuch as

pulga [POOL-*gah*] flea

pulmón (m) [*pool*-MOHN] lung

pulmonía [*pool-moh*-NEE-*ah*] pneumonia

pulsera [*pool*-SEH-*rah*] bracelet

puño [POO-*n'yoh*] fist, handful, cuff

punta [POON-*tah*] point (sharp end)

punto [POON-*toh*] point, period

puro, -a [POO-*roh, -rah*] pure, (as n, m) cigar

Q

★ **que** [*keh*] that, which, who, whom, than

el que [*ehl keh*] he who, the one that

la que [*lah keh*] she who, the one that

lo que [*loh keh*] that which

los que, las que [*lohs keh, lahs keh*] they who, the ones that

★ **más que** [*mahs keh*] more than

★ **menos que** [MEH-*nohs keh*] less than

★ **¿qué?** [*keh*] what? how?

¡Qué barbaridad! [*keh bahr-bah-ree*-DAHD] How terrible!

¿Qué hay? [*keh eye*] What is there?

¿Qué hora es? [*keh* OH-*rah ehs*] What time is it?

¿Qué pasa? [*keh* PAH-*sah*] What is going on?

¿Qué sé yo? [*keh seh yoh*] How do I know?

¿Qué tal? [*keh tahl*] How goes it?

¡Qué va! [*keh vah*] Nonsense!

quebrar [*keh*-BRAHR] to break, to crush

★ **quedar** [*keh*-DAHR] to stay, to stop, to be

NOTE: *quedar* is sometimes used for "to be" as a substitute for *estar*. "Where is the station?"—*¿Dónde queda la estación?*

quedar(se) [*keh*-DAHR-*(seh)*] to remain

quedar en [*keh*-DAHR *ehn*] to agree

quedar(se) con [*keh*-DAHR-*(seh) kohn*] to keep

queja [KEH-*hah*] complaint

quejar(se) [*keh*-HAHR-*(seh)*] to complain

quemar [*keh*-MAHR] to burn

★ **querer** [*keh*-REHR] to want, to wish, to love

NOTE: The only way to tell whether *querer* means "to want" or "to love" is according to how it is used. *Quiero un vaso de agua.*—"I want a glass of water." *Te quiero.*—"I love you."

querer decir [*keh*-REHR *deh*-THEER] to mean

querido, -a [*keh*-REE-*doh, -dah*] dear, darling

queso [KEH-*soh*] cheese

★ **quien** (singular), **quienes** (plural) [*k'yehn, k'*YEH-*nehs*] who

a quien [*ah k'yehn*] whom

de quien [*deh k'yehn*] of whom

★ **¿quién?** (singular), **¿quiénes?** (plural) [*k'yehn, k'*YEH-*nehs*] who?

¿a quién? [*ah k'yehn*] whom?

¿de quién? [*deh k'yehn*] whose?

¿quién sabe? [*k'yehn* SAH-*beh*] who knows?

quiero [*k'*YEH-*roh*] I want, I love

quieto, -a [*k'*YEH-*toh, -tah*] quiet

química [KEE-*mee-kah*] chemistry

químico, -a [KEE-*mee-koh, -kah*] (adj) chemical, (n) chemist

★ **quince** [KEEN-*theh*] fifteen

quinientos, -as [*kee-n'*YEHN-*tohs, -tahs*] five hundred

quinina [*kee*-NEE-*nah*] quinine

quinto, -a [KEEN-*toh, -tah*] fifth

NOTE: *Quinta* as noun means "country house."

quiosco [*k'*YOHS-*koh*] newsstand

quitar [*kee*-TAHR] to take away

quitar(se) [*kee*-TAHR-*(seh)*] to take off, to get rid of

★ **quizá, quizás** [*kee*-THAH, *kee*-THAHS] perhaps

R

rábano [RAH-*bah-noh*] radish
rabia [RAH-*b'yah*] rage, anger
rabo [RAH-*boh*] tail
radiador [*rah-d'yah*-DOHR] radiator
radio [RAH-*d'yoh*] radius, radium, radio
radiodifusión (f) [*rah-d'yoh-dee-foos-s'*YOHN] broadcast
raíz (f) [*rah*-EETH] root
rajar [*rah*-HAHR] to split, to crack
rama (also **ramo**) [RAH-*mah*, RAH-*moh*] branch
rana [RAH-*nah*] frog
ranchero [*rahn*-CHEH-*roh*] farmer, rancher
rancho [RAHN-*choh*] hut, ranch
rápidamente [*rah-pee-dah*-MEHN-*teh*] rapidly
rápido, -a [RAH-*pee-doh, -dah*] rapid, fast
raramente [*rah-rah*-MEHN-*teh*] rarely
raro, -a [RAH-*roh, -rah*] scarce, rare, queer
  ¡Qué raro! [*keh* RAH-*roh*] How queer!
  rara vez [RAH-*rah vehth*] seldom
rascacielos [*rahs-kah-th'*YEH-*lohs*] skyscraper
rascar [*rahs*-KAHR] to scratch
rasgo [RAHS-*goh*] feature, characteristic
rasguño [*rahs*-GOO-*n'yoh*] scratch
rastro [RAHS-*troh*] track, trail, sake
rata [RAH-*tah*] rat
rato [RAH-*toh*] moment, short while
  al poco rato [*ahl* POH-*koh* RAH-*toh*] in a short while
  pasar el rato [*pah*-SAHR *ehl* RAH-*toh*] to pass time
ratón (m) [*rah*-TOHN] mouse
raya [RAH-*yah*] stroke, dash, line, stripe
rayo [RAH-*yoh*] ray, beam
raza [RAH-*thah*] race, lineage
razón (f) [*rah*-THOHN] reason
  dar la razón a [*dahr lah rah*-THOHN *ah*] to agree with
  tener razón [*teh*-NEHR *rah*-THOHN] to be right

real (adj) [*reh*-AHL] royal, real
realidad (f) [*reh-ah-lee*-DAHD] reality
realizar [*reh-ah-lee*-THAHR] to fulfill, to carry out
NOTE: "To realize" or "become conscious of" is expressed by *darse cuenta de.*
rebaja [*reh*-BAH-*hah*] reduction
rebaño [*reh*-BAH-*n'yoh*] flock, herd
rebelde [*reh*-BEHL-*deh*] rebellious
recado [*reh*-KAH-*doh*] message
recámara [*reh*-KAH-*mah-rah*] dressing room
recargo [*reh*-KAHR-*goh*] overload
receptor [*reh-thehp*-TOHR] receiver
receta [*reh*-THEH-*tah*] prescription, recipe
★ **recibir** [*reh-thee*-BEER] to receive
recibo [*reh*-THEE-*boh*] receipt
acusar recibo [*ah-koo*-SAHR *reh*-THEE-*boh*] to acknowledge receipt
recién [*reh-th'*YEHN] recently
recién casado, -a [*reh-th'*YEHN *kah*-SAH-*doh, -dah*] newly wed
recién nacido, -a [*reh-th'*YEHN *nah*-THEE-*doh, -dah*] newly born
reclamar [*reh-klah*-MAHR] to claim, to demand
recobrar [*reh-koh*-BRAHR] to recover, to regain
recoger [*reh-koh*-HEHR] to gather
recomendación [*reh-koh-mehn-dah-th'*YOHN] recommendation
recomendar [*reh-koh-mehn*-DAHR] to recommend
recompensa [*reh-kohm*-PEHN-*sah*] compensation, reward
reconocer [*reh-koh-noh*-THEHR] to recognize
★ **recordar** [*reh-kohr*-DAHR] to remember
recorrido [*reh-koh*-RREE-*doh*] course, route
recorte [*reh*-KOHR-*teh*] clipping, outline
recreo [*reh*-KREH-*oh*] recreation
recto, -a [REHK-*toh, -tah*] straight, just
recuerdo [*reh*-KWEHR-*doh*] memory, keepsake, souvenir
recuperar [*reh-koo-peh*-RAHR] to recuperate
recurso [*reh*-KOOR-*soh*] resource, recourse

red (f) [*rehd*] net, network
★ **redondo, -a** [*reh-*DOHN-*doh, -dah*] round
reducir [*reh-doo-*THEER] to reduce
reembolso [*reh-ehm-*BOHL-*soh*] refund
referir [*reh-feh-*REER] to refer
refinado, -a [*reh-fee-*NAH-*doh, -dah*] refined
refinería [*reh-fee-neh-*REE-*ah*] refinery
refresco [*reh-*FREHS-*koh*] refreshment
refugio [*reh-*FOO-*h'yoh*] refuge, shelter
regalar a [*reh-gah-*LAHR *ah*] to make a present to
regalo [*reh-*GAH-*loh*] present, gift
regañar [*reh-gah-n'*YAHR] to scold
regimiento [*reh-hee-m'*YEHN-*toh*] regiment
regio, -a [REH-*h'yoh, -h'yah*] royal, magnificent
región [*reh-h'*YOHN] region
registrar [*reh-hees-*TRAHR] to examine, to inspect
regla [REH-*glah*] rule, regulation
  por regla general [*pohr* REH-*glah heh-neh-*RAHL] as a general rule
★ **regresar** [*reh-greh-*SAHR] to return
regreso [*reh-*GREH-*soh*] return
regular [*reh-goo-*LAHR] regular, common
reina [REY-*nah*] queen
reino [REY-*noh*] kingdom
★ **reír** [*reh-*EER] to laugh
reja [REH-*hah*] railing, window bars
relación [*reh-lah-th'*YOHN] relation, connection (*not* relative)
religión (f) [*reh-lee-h'*YOHN] religion
religioso, -a [*reh-lee-*H'YOH-*soh, -sah*] religious
★ **reloj** (m) [*reh-*LOHKH] clock, watch
  reloj pulsera [*reh-*LOHKH *pool-*SEH-*rah*] wrist watch
relleno [*reh-l'*YEH-*noh*] stuffing
remar [*reh-*MAHR] to row
remate (m) [*reh-*MAH-*teh*] end, finish, auction
remedio [*reh-*MEH-*d'yoh*] remedy, medicine
  No hay remedio [*noh eye reh-*MEH-*d'yoh*] There is no help for it

remitir [*reh-mee-*TEER] to remit, to forward
remolacha [*reh-moh-*LAH-*chah*] beet
remordimiento [*reh-mohr-dee-m'*YEHN-*toh*] remorse
rendido, -a [*rehn-*DEE-*doh, -dah*] devoted, worn out
rendir [*rehn-*DEER] to give up, to render
renovar [*reh-noh-*VAHR] to renew, to renovate
renta [REHN-*tah*] income, profit
renuncia [*reh-*NOON-*th'yah*] resignation
reñir [*reh-n'*YEER] to quarrel, to scold
reparar [*reh-pah-*RAHR] to repare, to stop at
repartir [*reh-pahr-*TEER] to divide, to distribute
reparto [*reh-*PAHR-*toh*] cast (theatre)
repaso [*reh-*PAH-*soh*] review, inspection
(de) repente [*deh reh-*PEHN-*teh*] suddenly
repetir [*reh-peh-*TEER] to repeat, to rehearse
repollo [*reh-*POH-*l'yoh*] cabbage
reponer [*reh-poh-*NEHR] to replace
reponer(se) [*reh-poh-*NEHR-*(seh)*] to recover
reporte [*reh-*POHR-*teh*] report, news
reposo [*reh-*POH-*soh*] repose
representación (f) [*reh-preh-sehn-tah-s'*YOHN] representation; performance (theatre)
representante (m) [*reh-preh-sehn-*TAHN-*teh*] representative, agent
representar [*reh-preh-sehn-*TAHR] to represent
reproducción (f) [*reh-proh-dook-th'*YOHN] reproduction
república [*reh-*POO-*blee-kah*] republic
República Dominicana [*reh-*POO-*blee-kah doh-mee-nee-*KAH-*nah*] Dominican Republic
republicano, -a [*reh-poo-blee-*KAH-*noh, -nah*] republican
repuesto [*reh-*PWEHS-*toh*] stock, supply, cupboard
  de repuesto [*deh reh-*PWEHS-*toh*] spare, extra
repugnante [*reh-poog-*NAHN-*teh*] disgusting, repugnant
reputación (f) [*reh-poo-tah-th'*YOHN] reputation
requerir [*reh-keh-*REER] to require
res (f) [*rehs*] head of cattle, beef
resbalar [*rehs-bah-*LAHR] to slip
reservar [*reh-sehr-*VAHR] to reserve

reservación (f) [*reh-sehr-vah-th'*YOHN] reservation
resfriado [*rehs-free-*AH-*doh*] cold (sickness)
residente (adj) [*reh-see-*DEHN-*teh*] residing (n), resident
residir [*reh-see-*DEER] to reside
resistente [*reh-sees-*TEHN-*teh*] resistant, strong
resistir [*reh-sees-*TEER] to resist
resolver [*reh-sohl-*VEHR] to solve
respectivo, -a [*rehs-pehk-*TEE-*voh, -vah*] respective
respecto [*rehs-*PEHK-*toh*] relation
respeto [*rehs-*PEH-*toh*] respect, regard
respirar [*rehs-pee-*RAHR] to breathe
responder [*rehs-pohn-*DEHR] to reply, to answer
responsabilidad (f) [*rehs-pohn-sah-bee-lee-*DAHD] responsibility
respuesta [*rehs-*PWEHS-*tah*] reply, answer
★ **restaurante** (m) [*rehs-tow-*RAHN-*teh*] restaurant
resuelto, -a [*reh-*SWEHL-*toh, -tah*] resolved
resultado [*reh-sool-*TAH-*doh*] result
resultar [*reh-sool-*TAHR] to result, to turn out
retardo [*reh-*TAHR-*doh*] delay
retener [*reh-teh-*NEHR] to retain, to keep back
retirado, -a [*reh-tee-*RAH-*doh, -dah*] retired, remote
retrasado, -a [*reh-trah-*SAH-*doh, -dah*] late, tardy
retrato [*reh-*TRAH-*toh*] picture
reunión (f) [*reh-oo-n'*YOHN] meeting
reunir [*reh-oo-*NEER] to unite
reunir(se) [*reh-oo-*NEER-*(seh)*] to meet, to get together
reventar [*reh-vehn-*TAHR] to burst
revés (m) [*reh-*VEHS] reverse, back
revisar [*reh-vee-*SAHR] to revise, to inspect
revista [*reh-*VEES-*tah*] review, magazine
revolución (f) [*reh-voh-loo-th'*YOHN] revolution
revolver [*reh-vohl-*VEHR] to mix
revólver (m) [*reh-*VOHL-*vehr*] revolver
revuelta [*reh-*VWEHL-*tah*] revolt
rey (m) [*ray*] king
rezar [*reh-*THAHR] to pray
rico, -a [REE-*koh, -kah*] rich; (col) delicious

ridículo, -a [*ree*-DEE-*koo-loh, -lah*] ridiculous
rienda [*r'*YEHN-*dah*] rein
riesgo [*r'*YEHS-*goh*] risk
rifle [REE-*fleh*] rifle
rincón (m) [*reen*-KOHN] corner (of a room, etc.)
riña [REE-*n'yah*] quarrel
riñón (m) [*ree-n'*YOHN] kidney
★ **río** [REE-*oh*] river
riqueza [*ree*-KEH-*thah*] wealth
risa [REE-*sah*] laughter
ritmo [REET-*moh*] rhythm
rival (m) [*ree*-VAHL] rival
rizo [REE-*thoh*] curl
robar [*roh*-BAHR] to rob
robo [ROH-*boh*] robbery, theft
roca [ROH-*kah*] rock
rodar [*roh*-DAHR] to roll, to revolve
rodear [*roh-deh*-AHR] to surround, to round up
rodilla [*roh*-DEE-*l'yah*] knee
rogar [*roh*-GAHR] to request, to beg
★ **rojo, -a** [ROH-*hoh, -hah*] red
romántico ,-a [*roh*-MAHN-*tee-koh, -kah*] romantic
romper [*rohm*-PEHR] to break
ron (m) [*rohn*] rum
roncar [*rohn*-KAHR] to snore
★ **ropa** [ROH-*pah*] clothes, clothing
  ropa hecha [ROH-*pah* EH-*chah*] ready made clothes
  ropa interior [ROH-*pah een-teh-r'*YOHR] underwear
  ropa vieja [ROH-*pah v'*YEH-*hah*] old clothes *or* minced meat
ropero [*roh*-PEH-*roh*] closet
rosa [ROH-*sah*] rose
rosario [*roh*-SAH-*r'yoh*] rosary (also a girl's name)
rostro [ROHS-*troh*] face
★ **roto, a** [ROH-*toh, -tah*] broken, torn
rótulo [ROH-*too-loh*] label, poster
rubí (m) [*roo*-BEE] ruby
rubio, -a [ROO-*b'yoh, -b'yah*] blond

rúbrica [ROO-*bree-kah*] caption

NOTE: Also a flourish added to one's signature and a legal part of it.

rueda [RWEH-*dah*] wheel
ruido [RWEE-*doh*] noise
ruina [RWEE-*nah*] ruin
Rumanía [*roo-mah*-NEE-*ah*] Roumania
rumano, -a [*roo*-MAH-*noh, -nah*] Roumanian
rumba [ROOM-*bah*] (dance from Cuba)
rumbo [ROOM-*boh*] course, route
con rumbo a [*kohn* ROOM-*boh ah*] in the direction of
rumor (m) [*roo*-MOHR] rumor, murmur
Rusia [ROO-*s'yah*] Russia
ruso, -a [ROO-*soh, -sah*] Russian
ruta [ROO-*tah*] route, way
rutina [*roo*-TEE-*nah*] routine

S

★ **sábado** [SAH-*bah-doh*] Saturday
sábana [SAH-*bah-nah*] sheet
★ **saber** [*sah*-BEHR] to know
¿quién sabe? [*k'yehn* SAH-*beh*] who knows?
sabe Dios [SAH-*beh* D'YOHS] God knows
¿sabe Ud. nadar? [SAH-*beh oos*-TEHD *nah*-DAHR] Do you know how to swim?

NOTE: *Saber* means "to know" in the sense of knowing how to do something or to know a fact. To indicate that you are acquainted with someone, use *conocer*.

sabio, -a [SAH-*b'yoh, -b'yah*] wise, learned
sabor [*sah*-BOHR] flavor
sabroso, -a [*sah*-BROH-*soh, -sah*] delicious
sacar [*sah*-KAHR] to pull out, to take out
sacar una fotografía [*sah*-KAHR OO-*nah foh-toh-grah*-FEE-*ah*] to take a picture

sacerdote (m) [*sah-thehr-*DOH-*teh*] priest
saco [SAH-*koh*] sack, bag, suit coat
sacrificar [*sah-kree-fee-*KAHR] to sacrifice
sacudir [*sah-koo-*DEER] to shake
sagrado, -a [*sah-*GRAH-*doh, -dah*] sacred
sal (f) [*sahl*] salt, wit
sala [SAH-*lah*] living room
salario [*sah-*LAH-*r'yoh*] salary
salchicha [*sahl-*CHEE-*chah*] sausage (small)
salchichón (m) [*sahl-chee-*CHOHN] sausage (large)
saldo [SAHL-*doh*] balance (com)
★ **salida** [*sah-*LEE-*dah*] exit, departure
★ **salir** [*sah-*LEER] to leave, to go out, to rise (sun)
¿Cuándo sale? [KWAHN-*doh* SAH-*leh*] When are you (he, she) leaving? When does it leave?
salmón (m) [*sahl-*MOHN] salmon
salón (m) [*sah-*LOHN] living room
salsa [SAHL-*sah*] sauce, gravy
saltar [*sahl-*TAHR] to jump
¡Salta a la vista! [SAHL-*tah ah lah* VEES-*tah*] It's very obvious!
salto [SAHL-*toh*] jump, leap
salud (f) [*sah-*LOOD] health
estar bien de salud [*ehs-*TAHR *b'yehn deh sah-*LOOD] to be in good health

NOTE: *¡Salud!* or *¡a su salud!* is frequently used as a toast. Another variant is *¡Salud y pesetas!* ("Health and money!")

saludar [*sah-loo-*DAHR] to greet, to salute
saludo [*sah-*LOO-*doh*] greeting
déle mis saludos [DEH-*leh mees sah-*LOO-*dohs*] give him (her) my greetings
salvaje [*sahl-*VAH-*heh*] savage
salvar [*sahl-*VAHR] to save, to rescue

salvar(se) [*sahl*-VAHR-*(seh)*] to be saved
salvavidas (m) [*sahl-vah*-VEE-*dahs*] life preserver
salvo [SAHL-*voh*] except
salvo, -a [SAHL-*voh, -vah*] saved, safe
sandalia [*sahn*-DAH-*l'yah*] sandal
sandía [*sahn*-DEE-*ah*] watermelon
sangre (f) [SAHN-*greh*] blood
  sangre fría [SAHN-*greh* FREE-*ah*] calmness
sanidad (f) [*sah-nee*-DAHD] sanitation
sano, -a [SAH-*noh, -nah*] sound, healthy
santo, -a [SAHN-*toh, -tah*] saint
sapo [SAH-*poh*] toad
sarampión (m) [*sah-rahm-p'*YOHN] measles
sardina [*sahr*-DEE-*nah*] sardine
sargento [*sahr*-HEHN-*toh*] sergeant
sartén (m) [*sahr*-TEHN] frying pan
sastre (m) [SAHS-*treh*] tailor
sastrería [*sahs-treh*-REE-*ah*] tailor shop
satisfacción (f) [*sah-tees-fahk-th'*YOHN] satisfaction
satisfacer [*sah-tees-fah*-THEHR] to satisfy
satisfecho, -a [*sah-tees*-FEH-*choh, -chah*] satisfied
saya [SAH-*yah*] skirt
★ **se** [*seh*]

NOTE: *Se* has several distinct uses.

1. As reflexive pronoun used before verb, meaning himself, herself, itself or themselves. Ex.:
   Se lavó—"He washed himself."
2. As an indirect object pronoun used to replace *le* and avoid excessive use of the letter *l*. Ex.:
   El se lo dió—"He gave it to her."
3. As an impersonal pronoun, used in expressions like "they say," "it is said," etc.
   Aquí se habla español—"Spanish is spoken here."
   Se prohibe estacionar—"Parking is forbidden."

★ **sé** [*seh*] I know (see *saber*)
  No sé [*noh seh*] I don't know
secar [*seh*-KAHR] to dry
sección (f) [*sehk-th'*YOHN] section

seco, -a [SEH-*koh, -kah*] dry
secretario, -a [*seh-kreh*-TAH-*r'yoh, -r'yah*] secretary
secreto [*seh*-KREH-*toh*] secret
secuestro [*seh*-KWEHS-*troh*] kidnapping
sed (f) [*sehd*] thirst
  tener sed [*teh*-NEHR *sehd*] to be thirsty
seda [SEH-*dah*] silk
★ **(en) seguida** [*ehn seh*-GHEE-*dah*] right away
seguido, -a [*seh*-GHEE-*doh, -dah*] straight, successive
★ **seguir** [*seh*-GHEER] to follow
★ **según** [*seh*-GOON] according to
segundo, -a [*seh*-GOON-*doh, -dah*] second
seguramente [*seh-goo-rah*-MEHN-*teh*] surely
seguridad (f) [*seh-goo-ree*-DAHD] security, safety
  caja de seguridad [KAH-*hah deh seh-goo-ree*-DAHD] safe, safety deposit box
seguro, -a [*seh*-GOO-*roh, -rah*] safe, sure
  seguro de vida [*seh*-GOO-*roh deh* VEE-*dah*] life insurance
★ **seis** [SEH-*ees*] six
  son las seis [*sohn lahs* SEH-*ees*] it is six o'clock
seiscientos, -as [*say-th'*YEHN-*tohs, -tahs*] six hundred
selección (f) [*seh-lehk-th'*YOHN] choice
selva [SEHL-*vah*] forest, woods
sellar [*seh-l'*YAHR] to seal
sello [SEH-*l'yoh*] stamp
★ **semana** [*seh*-MAH-*nah*] week
  A la semana [*ah lah seh*-MAH-*nah*] for the week
  la semana que viene [*lah seh*-MAH-*nah keh v'*YEH-*neh*] next week
  Semana Santa [*seh*-MAH-*nah* SAHN-*tah*] Holy week
sembrar [*sehm*-BRAHR] to sow
semejante [*seh-meh*-HAHN-*teh*] similar
semilla [*seh*-MEE-*l'yah*] seed
senador (m) [*seh-nah*-DOHR] senator
sencillo, -a [*sehn*-THEE-*l'yoh, -l'yah*] simple
seno [SEH-*noh*] bosom, (also) cavity
sensato, -a [*sehn*-SAH-*toh, -tah*] sensible
sensible [*sehn*-SEE-*bleh*] sensitive

sentado, -a [*sehn*-TAH-*doh, -dah*] seated
★ **sentar** [*sehn*-TAHR] to fit, to seat
sentar(se) [*sehn*-TAHR-*(seh)*] to sit down
sentido [*sehn*-TEE-*doh*] sense, feeling, meaning
sentimiento [*sehn-tee-m'*YEHN-*toh*] sentiment, feeling
sentir [*sehn*-TEER] to feel; to regret
Lo siento mucho [*loh s'*YEHN-*toh* MOO-*choh*] I am very sorry
seña [SEH-*n'yah*] sign, trace
NOTE: In plural *señas* can mean "address."
señalar [*seh-n'yah*-LAHR] to point out, to mark
★ **señor (Sr.)** [*seh-n'*YOHR] gentleman, Mr., Sir
★ **señora (Sra.)** [*seh-n'*YOH-*rah*] lady, Mrs., Madam
★ **señorita (Srta.)** [*seh-n'yoh*-REE-*tah*] young lady, Miss
separado, -a [*seh-pah*-RAH-*doh, -dah*] separated
por separado [*pohr seh-pah*-RAH-*doh*] separately
separar [*seh-pah*-RAHR] to separate, to divide
septiembre [*sehp-t'*YEHM-*breh*] September
séptimo, -a [SEHP-*tee-moh, -mah*] seventh
★ **ser** [*sehr*] to be

NOTE: *Ser* and *estar* both mean "to be." *Ser* is generally used for description while *estar* is used for location, condition and position.

ser humano [*sehr oo*-MAH-*noh*] human being
será [*seh*-RAH] will be
NOTE: This form can be used for "you," "he," "she" and "it." For other forms see verb table at back of book.
serenata [*seh-reh*-NAH-*tah*] serenade
sereno, -a [*seh*-REH-*noh, -nah*] serene; (as n, m) watchman
serie (f) [SEH-*r'yeh*] series
serio, -a [SEH-*r'yoh, -r'yah*] serious
serpiente [*sehr-p'*YEHN-*teh*] snake
servicio [*sehr*-VEE-*th'yoh*] service

servidor, -a [*sehr-vee-*DOHR, *-rah*]
NOTE: Although *servidor* means servant it is used only in acknowledging introductions, *servidor de Ud.* or at the end of letters: *Atento y seguro servidor.*

servilleta [*sehr-vee-l'*YEH-*tah*] napkin

★ **servir** [*sehr-*VEER] to serve, to wait on, to be good for
No sirve para nada [*noh* SEER-*veh* PAH-*rah* NAH-*dah*] It isn't good for anything
¿para qué sirve esto? [PAH-*rah keh* SEER-*veh* EHS-*toh*] What is this good for?

★ **sesenta** [*seh-*SEHN-*tah*] sixty

sesión (f) [*seh-s'*YOHN] session

seso [SEH-*soh*] brain

seta [SEH-*tah*] mushroom

severo, -a [*seh-*VEH-*roh, -rah*] severe

sexo [SEHK-*soh*] sex

sexto, -a [SEHKS-*toh, -tah*] sixth

★ **sí** [*see*] yes

NOTE: *Sí* as a reflexive pronoun used after a preposition means "himself," "herself," "oneself" or "itself." *Para sí*—"For himself," etc.

★ **si** [*see*] if, whether

★ **siempre** [*s'*YEHM-*preh*] always
siempre que [*s'*YEHM-*preh keh*] whenever, provided

sierra [*s'*YEH-*rrah*] saw, mountain range

siesta [*s'*YEHS-*tah*] nap

★ **siete** [*s'*YEH-*teh*] seven
son las siete [*sohn lahs s'*YEH-*teh*] it is seven o'clock
a las siete [*ah lahs s'*YEH-*teh*] at seven o'clock

★ **¡siga!** [SEE-*gah*] go on! go ahead! (see *seguir*)

siglo [SEE-*gloh*] century

significado [*seek-nee-fee-*KAH-*doh*] meaning

significar [*seek-nee-fee-*KAHR] to mean

signo [SEEK-*noh*] sign, signal

siguiente [*see-gh'*YEHN-*teh*] following
sílaba [SEE-*lah-bah*] syllable
silbido [*seel-*BEE-*doh*] whistle
silencio [*see-*LEHN-*th'yoh*] silence
silla [SEE-*l'yah*] chair, saddle
simpatía [*seem-pah-*TEE-*ah*] liking
simpático, -a [*seem-*PAH-*tee-koh, -kah*] pleasant, (col) nice
simple [SEEM-*pleh*] simple, silly
simplemente [*seem-pleh-*MEHN-*teh*] simply
★ **sin** [*seen*] without
sin duda [*seen* DOO-*dah*] doubtlessly
sin embargo [*seen ehm-*BAHR-*goh*] nevertheless
sin falta [*seen* FAHL-*tah*] without fail
sinceridad (f) [*seen-theh-ree-*DAHD] sincerity
sincero, -a [*seen-*THEH-*roh, -rah*] sincere
singular [*seen-goo-*LAHR] singular, unusual
★ **sino** [*see-*NOH] but

NOTE: *Sino* is used after a negative. *No soy español sino cubano.* "I am not Spanish but Cuban" (otherwise "but" is translated by *pero*).

sinvergüenza [*seen-vehr-*GWEHN-*thah*] scoundrel, shameless person
siquiera [*see-k'*YEH-*rah*] at least, although, even
sirena [*see-*REH-*nah*] siren, foghorn
★ **sírvase** [SEER-*vah-seh*] please
NOTE: *Sírvase* comes from *servir* and must be followed by an infinitive. *¡Sírvase entrar!*—"Please come in!"
sirviente, -a [*seer-v'*YEHN-*teh, -tah*] servant
sistema (m) [*sees-*TEH-*mah*] system
sitio [SEE-*t'yoh*] place, spot, room
situación (f) [*see-twah-th'*YOHN] situation
soberbio, -a [*soh-*BEHR-*b'yoh, -b'yah*] proud, grand, magnificent

(de) sobra [*(deh)*-SOH-*brah*] in excess, superfluous
★ **sobre** [SOH-*breh*] over, on, upon
sobrecama [*soh-breh*-KAH-*mah*] bedspread
sobrecargar [*soh-breh-kahr*-GAHR] to overload
sobremanera [*soh-breh-mah*-NEH-*rah*] exceedingly
sobrepasar [*soh-breh-pah*-SAHR] to exceed
sobresaliente [*soh-breh-sah-l'*YEHN-*teh*] outstanding
sobretodo [*soh-breh*-TOH-*doh*] overcoat
sobrino, -a [*soh*-BREE-*noh, -nah*] nephew (niece)
socialista (m and f) [*soh-th'yah*-LEES-*tah*] socialist
sociedad (f) [*soh-th'yeh*-DAHD] society, company
sociedad anónima (S.A.) [*soh-th'yeh*-DAHD *ah*-NOH-*nee-mah*] corporation
socio, -a [SOH-*th'yoh, -ah*] partner, member
socorro [*soh*-KOH-*rroh*] help, aid
NOTE: Also used as a girl's name.
sofá (m) [*soh*-FAH] sofa
soga [SOH-*gah*] rope
★ **sol** (m) [*sohl*] sun, sunlight
al sol [*ahl*-SOHL] under the sun
NOTE: *Sol* is also the Peruvian unit of currency.
solamente [*soh-lah*-MEHN-*teh*] only
solapa [*soh*-LAH-*pah*] lapel
soldado [*sohl*-DAH-*doh*] soldier
soledad (f) [*soh-leh*-DAHD] solitude (also a girl's name)
solicitar [*soh-lee-thee*-TAHR] to apply for
solicitud (f) [*soh-lee-thee*-TOOD] application, request
sólido, -a [SOH-*lee-doh, -dah*] solid
solitario, -a [*soh-lee*-TAH-*r'yoh, -r'yah*] solitary
★ **solo, -a** [SOH-*loh, -lah*] alone
a solas [*ah* SOH-*lahs*] alone
sentir(se) solo [*sehn*-TEER-*(seh)* SOH-*loh*] to feel lonely
★ **sólo** [SOH-*loh*] only
soltar [*sohl*-TAHR] to untie, to turn loose
soltero, -a [*sohl*-TEH-*roh, -rah*] unmarried (m and f)
solterón, -a [*sohl-teh*-ROHN, -OH-*nah*] old bachelor, old maid
solución (f) [*soh-loo-th'*YOHN] solution

sombra [SOHM-*brah*] shade, shadow
★ sombrero [*sohm*-BREH-*roh*] hat
someter [*soh-meh*-TEHR] to subject, to submit
★ somos [SOH-*mohs*] (we) are
son (m) [*sohn*] sound
★ son [*sohn*] (you, they) are
sonar [*soh*-NAHR] to sound, to strike
sonrisa [*sohn*-REE-*sah*] smile
soñar [*soh-n'*YAHR] to dream
sopa [SOH-*pah*] soup
soplar [*soh*-PLAHR] to blow
soportar [*soh-pohr*-TAHR] to support, to bear
sordo, -a [SOHR-*doh, -dah*] deaf
sorprendido, -a [*sohr-prehn*-DEE-*doh, -dah*] surprised
sorpresa [*sohr*-PREH-*sah*] surprise
sorteo [*sohr*-TEH-*oh*] drawing, raffle
sortija [*sohr*-TEE-*hah*] ring
soso, -a [SOH-*soh, -sah*] insipid
sospechar [*sohs-peh*-CHAHR] to suspect
sospechoso, -a [*sohs-peh*-CHOH-*soh, -sah*] suspicious
sostener [*sohs-teh*-NEHR] to sustain, to hold up
sótano [SOH-*tah-noh*] cellar, basement
★ soy [*soy*] I am (see *ser*)
★ su, sus [*soo, soos*] his, her, your, its, their

NOTE: When the thing possessed is singular, use *su*. When the thing possessed is plural use *sus*. "His book"—*Su libro*. "His books"—*Sus libros*.

suave [SWAH-*veh*] smooth, soft, gentle
subasta [*soo*-BAHS-*tah*] auction
★ subir [*soo*-BEER] to rise, to climb, to go up
súbitamente [*soo-bee-tah*-MEHN-*teh*] suddenly
súbito [soo-*bee-toh*] sudden
submarino [*soob-mah*-REE-*noh*] submarine
subrayar [*soob-rah*-YAHR] to underline

substancia [*soobs*-TAHN-*th'yah*] substance
substituir [*soobs-tee-too*-EER] to substitute
subteniente [*soob-teh-n'*YEHN-*teh*] (second) lieutenant
subterráneo, -a [*soob-teh*-RRAH-*neh-oh, -neh-ah*] underground
NOTE: Often used to indicate subway.
suburbio [*soo*-BOOR-*b'yoh*] suburb
★ **suceder** [*soo-theh*-DEHR] to follow, to happen
¿Qué sucedió? [*keh soo-theh-d'*YOH] What happened?
suceso [*soo*-THEH-*soh*] happening, event
sucesores (sucs.) [*soo-theh*-SOH-*rehs*] (com) successors to a firm
sucio, -a [SOO-*th'yoh, -th'yah*] dirty
sucre [SOO-*kreh*] currency unit of Ecuador
sucursal (f) [*soo-koor*-SAHL] branch (of business)
sudar [*soo*-DAHR] to sweat, to perspire
Suecia [SWEH-*th'yah*] Sweden
sueco [SWEH-*koh*] Swedish
suegro, -a [SWEH-*groh, -grah*] father-in-law, mother-in-law
sueldo [SWEHL-*doh*] salary
suelo [SWEH-*loh*] soil, ground
suelto, -a [SWEHL-*toh, -tah*] loose, free
suelto [SWEHL-*toh*] small change (money)
sueño [SWEH-*n'yoh*] dream, sleep
suerte (f) [SWEHR-*teh*] luck, chance
suficiente [*soo-fee-th'*YEHN-*teh*] sufficient
sufrir [*soo*-FREER] to suffer
sugerencia [*soo-heh*-REHN-*th'yah*] suggestion
sugerir [*soo-heh*-REER] to suggest
suicidio [*soo-ee*-THEE-*d'yoh*] suicide
Suiza [SWEE-*thah*] Switzerland
suizo, -a [SWEE-*thoh, -thah*] Swiss
sujeto, -a [*soo*-HEH-*toh, -tah*] subject (to), liable
suma [SOO-*mah*] sum
sumar [*soo*-MAHR] to add
suministrar [*soo-mee-nees*-TRAHR] to supply, to provide
superar [*soo-peh*-RAHR] to exceed, to surpass

superficial [*soo-pehr-fee-th'*YAHL] superficial
superficie (f) [*soo-pehr-*FEE-*th'yeh*] area
superintendente (m) [*soo-pehr-een-tehn-*DEHN-*teh*] superintendent
superior [*soo-peh-r'*YOHR] superior, upper
suplicar [*soo-plee-*KAHR] to entreat, to request
suponer [*soo-poh-*NEHR] to suppose
supremo, -a [*soo-*PREH-*moh, -mah*] supreme
suprimir [*soo-pree-*MEER] to suppress
supuesto, -a [*soo-*PWEHS-*toh, -tah*] supposed
★ **sur** (m) [*soor*] south
surtido [*soor-*TEE-*doh*] stock, assortment
suspender [*soos-pehn-*DEHR] to suspend
suspiro [*soos-*PEE-*roh*] sigh
susto [SOOS-*toh*] fright, shock
sutil [*soo-*TEEL] subtle
suyo, -a (singular) [SOO-*yoh, -yah*] his, hers, its, yours, theirs
suyos, -as (plural) [SOO-*yohs, -yahs*] his, hers, its, yours, theirs

NOTE: *Suyo* is used after the noun. *Esta casa es suya* —"This house is yours." *Suyo* is frequently used with the definite article *el, la, los, las.* "Which is yours?"—*¿Cuál es el suyo?*

T

taladro [*tah-*LAH-*droh*] bore, bit, drill
talentoso, -a [*tah-lehn-*TOH-*soh, -sah*] talented
talla [TAH-*l'yah*] carving, height size (in clothes)
taller (m) [*tah-l'*YEHR] workshop, factory
tamaño [*tah-*MAH-*n'yoh*] size
también [*tahm-b'*YEHN] also, too
tambor (m) [*tahm-*BOHR] drum

tampoco [*tahm*-POH-*koh*] neither, not either

NOTE: Generally used with another negative. *Ni yo tampoco*—"Nor I" (either).

★ **tan** [*tahn*] as, so, so much
NOTE: Used idiomatically to intensify an adjective: *¡Qué niña tan guapa!*—"What a pretty girl."
tanque [*tahn-keh*] tank, reservoir
tanto, -a [TAHN-*toh, -tah*] so much, as much
por lo tanto [*pohr loh* TAHN-*toh*] therefore
tanto gusto [TAHN-*toh* GOOS-*toh*] (on being introduced)—So much pleasure
tanto mejor [TAHN-*toh meh*-HOHR] so much the better
tantos, -as [TAHN-*tohs, -tahs*] so many, as many
tapa [TAH-*pah*] lid, cover
tapar [*tah*-PAHR] to cover, to hide
tapón (m) [*tah*-POHN] cork, stopper
taquígrafa [*tah*-KEE-*grah-fah*] stenographer
taquilla [*tah*-KEE-*l'yah*] ticket office
tardar [*tahr*-DAHR] to delay
a más tardar [*ah mahs tahr*-DAHR] at the very latest
★ **tarde** (f) [TAHR-*deh*] afternoon
por la tarde [*pohr lah* TAHR-*deh*] in the afternoon
tarde [TAHR-*deh*] late
se hace tarde [*seh* AH-*seh* TAHR-*deh*] it is growing late
tarifa (f) [*tah*-REE-*fah*] fare
tarjeta [*tahr*-HEH-*tah*] card
tarjeta postal [*tahr*-HEH-*tah pohs*-TAHL] post card
taxi (m) [TAHK-*see*] taxi
taza [TAH-*thah*] cup
té (m) [*teh*] tea
te [*teh*] you, to you, yourself
NOTE: This is the familiar form of "you." See *usted*

teatro [*teh*-AH-*troh*] theatre
técnico, -a [TEHK-*nee-koh, -kah*] technical
techo [TEH-*choh*] roof, ceiling
teja [TEH-*hah*] tile
tejido [*teh*-HEE-*doh*] fabric, weaving
tela [TEH-*lah*] cloth, material
telefonear [*teh-leh-foh-neh*-AHR] to telephone
telefonista [*teh-leh-foh*-NEES-*tah*] telephone operator
teléfono [*teh*-LEH-*foh-noh*] telephone
telegrama (m) [*teh-leh*-GRAH-*mah*] telegram
televisión (f) [*teh-leh-vee-s'*YOHN] television
telón [*teh*-LOHN] curtain (theatre)
tema (m) [TEH-*mah*] theme, subject
temblor (m) [*tehm*-BLOHR] tremor
  temblor de tierra [*tehm*-BLOHR *deh t'*YEH-*rrah*] earthquake
temer [*teh*-MEHR] to fear
temor (m) [*teh*-MOHR] fear
temperatura [*tehm-peh-rah*-TOO-*rah*] temperature
tempestad [*tehm-pehs*-TAHD] tempest, storm
temporada [*tehm-poh*-RAH-*dah*] season
temprano, -a [*tehm*-PRAH-*noh, -nah*] early
tendencia [*tehn*-DEHN-*th'yah*] tendency
tenedor [*teh-neh*-DOHR] fork
  tenedor de libros [*teh-neh*-DOHR *deh* LEE-*brohs*] bookkeeper
tener [*teh*-NEHR] to have, to hold

NOTE: Many uses of *tener* correspond to the use of "to be" in English.

  tener calor [*teh*-NEHR *kah*-LOHR] to be hot
  tener éxito [*teh*-NEHR EHK-*see-toh*] to be successful
  tener frío [*teh*-NEHR FREE-*oh*] to be cold
  tener ganas de [*teh*-NEHR GAH-*nahs deh*] to want to

tener hambre [*teh*-NEHR HAHM-*breh*] to be hungry
tener lugar [*teh*-NEHR *loo*-GAHR] (to) take place
tener miedo [*teh*-NEHR *m'*YEH-*doh*] to be afraid
tener prisa [*teh*-NEHR PREE-*sah*] to be in a hurry
tener que [*teh*-NEHR *keh*] to have to (followed by infinitive)
tener razón [*teh*-NEHR *rah*-THOHN] to be right
tener sed [*teh*-NEHR *sehd*] to be thirsty
tener sueño [*teh*-NEHR SWEH-*n'yoh*] to be sleepy
¡tenga! [TEHN-*gah*] Here you are!
tengo [TEHN-*goh*] I have
teniente (m) [*teh-n'*YEHN-*teh*] lieutenant
teñir [*teh-n'*YEER] to tint, to dye
tercero, -a [*tehr*-THEH-*roh, -rah*] third
terciopelo [*tehr-th'yoh*-PEH-*loh*] velvet
terminado, -a [*tehr-mee*-NAH-*doh, -dah*] finished
terminar [*tehr-mee*-NAHR] to finish
término [TEHR-*mee-noh*] end, term
término medio [TEHR-*mee-noh* MEH-*d'yoh*] average
termómetro [*tehr*-MOH-*meh-troh*] thermometer
ternera [*tehr*-NEH-*rah*] veal
ternura [*tehr*-NOO-*rah*] tenderness
terraza [*teh*-RRAH-*thah*] terrace
terremoto [*teh-rreh*-MOH-*toh*] earthquake
terreno [*teh*-RREH-*noh*] land, ground
terrible [*teh*-RREE-*bleh*] terrible
territorio [*teh-rree*-TOH-*r'yoh*] territory
terror (m) [*teh*-RROHR] terror
tertulia [*tehr*-TOO-*l'yah*] party, entertainment
tesoro [*teh*-SOH-*roh*] treasure
testamento [*tehs-tah*-MEHN-*toh*] testament, will
testarudo, -a [*tehs-tah*-ROO-*doh, -dah*] stubborn
testigo [*tehs*-TEE-*goh*] witness
texto [TEX-*toh*] text, textbook
ti [*tee*] to you, you (familiar form)
a ti [*ah tee*] to you
tía [TEE-*ah*] aunt
tibio, -a [TEE-*b'yoh, -b'yah*] warm

tiburón (m) [*tee-boo*-ROHN] shark
★ **tiempo** [*t'*YEHM-*poh*] time, weather

NOTE: Not to be used for asking the time. "What time is it?"—*¿Qué hora es?*

a tiempo [*ah t'*YEHM-*poh*] on time
hace algún tiempo [AH-*theh ahl*-GOON *t'*YEHM-*poh*] a short time ago
hace buen tiempo [AH-*theh bwehn t'*YEHM-*poh*] the weather is good
★ **tienda** [*t'*YEHN-*dah*] shop
tierno, -a [*t'*YEHR-*noh, -nah*] tender
★ **tierra** [*t'*YEH-*rrah*] earth, land
por tierra [*pohr t'*YEH-*rrah*] by land
tigre (m) [TEE-*greh*] tiger
tijeras [*tee*-HEH-*rahs*] scissors
timbre (m) [TEEM-*breh*] stamp, bell
tímido, -a [TEE-*mee-doh, -dah*] timid
tinta [TEEN-*tah*] ink
tinto, -a [TEEN-*toh, -tah*] red (wine), dark (coffee)
tío [TEE-*oh*] uncle, (coll) fellow
tipo [TEE-*poh*] type, (coll) fellow
buen tipo [*bwehn* TEE-*poh*] good looking
tiranía [*tee-rah*-NEE-*ah*] tyranny
tirar [*tee*-RAHR] to throw, to shoot
tiro [TEE-*roh*] shot, throw
título [TEE-*too-loh*] title
tiza [TEE-*thah*] chalk
toalla [*toh*-AH-*l'yah*] towel
tocador (n) [*toh-kah*-DOHR] dressing room
tocante a [*toh*-KAHN-*teh ah*] referring to
★ **tocar** [*toh*-KAHR] to touch, to play (an instrument)
tocar a la puerta [*toh*-KAHR *ah lah* PWEHR-*tah*] to knock at the door
tocino [*to*-THEE-*noh*] bacon

★ **todavía** [*toh-dah-*VEE-*ah*] still, yet
★ **todavía no** [*toh-dah-*VEE-*ah noh*] not yet
★ **todo, -a** [TOH-*doh, -dah*] every, each, all
con todo [*kohn* TOH-*doh*] nevertheless
después de todo [*dehs-*PWEHS *deh* TOH-*doh*] after all
sobre todo [SOH-*breh* TOH-*doh*] especially
todo el mundo [TOH-*doh ehl* MOON-*doh*] everyone
todos, -as [TOH-*dohs, -dahs*] all
tolerante [*toh-leh-*RAHN-*teh*] tolerant
tolerar [*toh-leh-*RAHR] to tolerate
★ **tomar** [*toh-*MAHR] to take
¡Tome asiento! [TOH-*meh ah-s'*YEHN-*toh*] Have a seat!

NOTE: Also means "to drink" or "to eat" in the sense of taking food or drink.

¿Qué quiere tomar? [*keh k'*YEH-*reh toh-*MAHR] What will you have?
tomate (m) [*toh-*MAH-*teh*] tomato
tonelada [*toh-neh-*LAH-*dah*] ton
tono [TOH-*noh*] tone
tonto, -a [TOHN-*toh, -tah*] silly, foolish
torcer [*tohr-*THEHR] to twist
torear [*toh-reh-*AHR] to fight bulls
torero [*toh-*REH-*roh*] bullfighter
tormenta [*tohr-*MEHN-*tah*] storm
tornillo [*tohr-*NEE-*l'yoh*] screw
toro [TOH-*roh*] bull
toronja [*toh-*ROHN-*hah*] grapefruit
torpe [TOHR-*peh*] dull, stupid
torre (f) [TOH-*rreh*] tower
torta, tortita [TOHR-*tah, tohr-*TEE-*tah*] cake, small cake
tortilla [*tohr-*TEE-*l'yah*] omelet, pancake
tortuga [*tohr-*TOO-*gah*] turtle
torturar [*tohr-too-*RAHR] to torture

tos (f) [*tohs*] cough
tostada [*tohs*-TAH-*dah*] toast
tostado, -a [*tohs*-TAH-*doh, -dah*] toasted, sunburned
total (m) [*toh*-TAHL] total
★ **trabajar** [*trah-bah*-HAHR] to work
trabajo [*trah*-BAH-*hoh*] work
tradicional [*trah-dee-th'yoh*-NAHL] traditional
traducción (f) [*trah-dook-th'*YOHN] translation
traducir [*trah-doo*-THEER] to translate
traer [*trah*-EHR] to bring, to wear, to carry
tráfico [TRAH-*fee-koh*] traffic (exchange, see *tránsito*)
tragar [*trah*-GAHR] to swallow
tragedia [*trah*-HEH-*d'yah*] tragedy
★ **traje** [TRAH-*heh*] suit, dress
traje de baño [TRAH-*heh deh* BAH-*n'yoh*] bathing suit
traje de etiqueta [TRAH-*heh deh eh-tee*-KEH-*tah*] evening dress
trámite [TRAH-*mee-teh*] transaction, proceedings
trampa [TRAHM-*pah*] trap, snare
tranquilo, -a [*trahn*-KEE-*loh, -lah*] quiet
tranquilizar(se) [*trahn-kee-lee*-THAHR-*seh*] to calm down
transeúnte [*trahn-seh*-OON-*teh*] passer-by, transient
transferir [*trahns-feh*-REER] to transfer
transformar [*trahns-fohr*-MAHR] to transform
tránsito [TRAHN-*see-toh*] transit, traffic
se prohibe el tránsito [*seh proh*-EE-*beh ehl* TRAHN-*see-toh*] no thoroughfare
transporte (m) [*trahns*-POHR-*teh*] transportation, transport
tranvía (m) [*trahn*-VEE-*ah*] streetcar
trapo [TRAH-*poh*] rag
tras [*trahs*] after, behind
trasero, -a [*trah*-SEH-*roh, -rah*] rear
trasladar [*trahs-lah*-DAHR] to move, to postpone
trastorno [*trahs*-TOHR-*noh*] upheaval, disturbance
tratado [*trah*-TAH-*doh*] treaty
tratamiento [*trah-tah-m'*YEHN-*toh*] treatment
tratar [*trah*-TAHR] to treat
tratar de [*trah*-TAHR *deh*] to try, to treat of, to deal with

trato [TRAH-*toh*] treatment, agreement
(a) **través de** [*ah trah*-VEHS *deh*] across
travesía [*trah-veh*-SEE-*ah*] crossing, passage
travieso, -a [*trah-v'*YEH-*soh, -sah*] mischievous
★ **trece** [TREH-*theh*] thirteen
trecientos, -as [*treh-th'*YEHN-*tohs, -tahs*] three hundred
trecho [TREH-*choh*] distance, lapse
★ **treinta** [TRAYN-*tah*] thirty
tremendo, -a [*treh*-MEHN-*doh, -dah*] tremendous
tren (m) [*trehn*] train
  tren expreso [*trehn ehks*-PREH-*so*] express train
  tren ómnibus [*trehn* OHM-*nee-boos*] local train
trenza [TREHN-*thah*] brand
★ **tres** [*trehs*] three
triángulo [*tree*-AHN-*goo-loh*] triangle
tribu [TREE-*boo*] tribe
tribunal [*tree-boo*-NAHL] court (of law)
trigo [TREE-*goh*] wheat
trigueño, -a [*tree*-GWEH-*n'yoh, -yah*] brunette, dark
trinidad [*tree-nee*-DAHD] trinity (Also a girl's name)
tripa [TREE-*pah*] tripe
tripulación (f) [*tree-poo-lah-th'*YOHN] crew
★ **triste** [TREES-*teh*] sad
triunfar [*tree-oon*-FAHR] to triumph, to succeed
triunfo [*tree*-OON-*foh*] triumph
tronco [TROHN-*koh*] trunk (of tree)
trono [TROH-*noh*] throne
tropa [TROH-*pah*] troop
tropezar [*troh-peh*-THAHR] to stumble
tropical [*troh-pee*-KAHL] tropical
trópico [TROH-*pee-koh*] the Tropics
trozo [TROH-*thoh*] piece, bit
trucha [TROO-*chah*] trout
trueno [*troo*-EH-*noh*] thunder
★ **tú** [*too*] you
  NOTE: This form of "you" is for members of the family, close friends and children. When in doubt use *usted.*

★ **tu** [*too*] your (when object possessed is singular)
tubo [TOO-*boh*] tube, pipe
tuerto, -a [TWEHR-*toh, -tah*] one-eyed
tulipán (m) [*too-lee*-PAHN] tulip
tumba [TOOM-*bah*] tomb
tumbar [*toom*-BAHR] to knock down
túnel (m) [TOO-*nehl*] tunnel
tupido, -a [*too*-PEE-*doh, -dah*] thick, dense
turco, -a [TOOR-*koh, -kah*] Turkish
turista [*too*-REES-*tah*] tourist

NOTE: Use appropriate article for masculine or feminine.

turno [TOOR-*noh*] turn
Turquía [*toor*-KEE-*ah*] Turkey
turrón (m) [*too*-RROHN] almond paste
tus [*toos*] your (when object possessed is plural)
tuyo, -a [TOO-*yoh, -yah*] yours (familiar form)
plural **tuyos, -as** [TOO-*yohs, -yahs*]

NOTE: Is also used with the definite article: *Este es el mío no el tuyo*—This is mine, not yours.

U

ubicado, -a [*oo-bee*-KAH-*doh, -dah*] located
Ud. [*oos*-TEHD] you (abbreviation of *usted*).
Uds. [*oos*-TEH-*dehs*] you (abbreviation of *ustedes*).
ultimamente [*ool-tee-mah*-MEHN-*teh*] lately
último, -a [OOL-*tee-moh, -mah*] last
última moda [OOL-*tee-mah* MOH-*dah*] latest style
★ **un** [*oon*] one, a

NOTE: *Un,* the abbreviated form of *uno* is always used before a masculine noun. *un señor:* "a man."

un poco [*oon* POH-*koh*] a little, a little bit
único, -a [OO-*nee-koh, -kah*] only, sole
unidad (f) [*oo-nee*-DAHD] unity, unit
unido, -a [*oo*-NEE-*doh, -dah*] united
uniforme (m) [*oo-nee*-FOHR-*meh*] uniform
unión (f) [*oo-n'*YOHN] union
unir [*oo*-NEER] to unite
universal [*oo-nee-vehr*-SAHL] universal
universidad (f) [*oo-nee-vehr-see*-DAHD] university
★ **uno, -a** [OO-*noh, -nah*] one, a
la una [*lah* OO-*nah*] one o'clock
uña [OO-*n'yah*] finger nail, claw
urbanización [*oor-bah-nee-zah-th'*YOHN] civic development
Uruguay [*oo-roog*-WHY] Uruguay
uruguayo, -a [*oo-roo*-GWAH-*yoh, -yah*] Uruguayan
usado, -da [*oo*-SAH-*doh, -dah*] used, worn out
★ **usar** [*oo*-SAHR] to use
uso [OO-*soh*] use
★ **usted** (singular) [*oos*-TEHD] you
★ **ustedes** (plural) [*oos*-TEH-*dehs*] you

NOTE: *Usted* is the polite form for "you" and is abbreviated variously as *Ud., Vd., V.* in the singular and *Uds., Vds.* or *UU.* in the plural.

útil [OO-*teel*] useful
uva [OO-*vah*] grape

V

★ **va** [*vah*] (he, she, it) goes, (you) go
★ **vaca** [VAH-*kah*] cow
vacío, -a [*vah*-THEE-*oh, -ah*] vacant, empty
vacuna [*vah*-KOO-*nah*] vaccination

vago, -a [VAH-*goh, -gah*] vague, (colloquial) lazy, (as n, m) a tramp
vagón (m) [*vah*-GOHN] car (railroad)
vajilla [*vah*-HEE-*l'yah*] table set
vale (m) [VAH-*leh*] I.O.U., voucher
★ **valer** [*vah*-LEHR] to be worth
¿Cuánto vale? [KWAHN-*toh* VAH-*leh?*] How much is it?
más vale [*mahs* VAH-*leh*] it is better
vale la pena [VAH-*leh lah* PEH-*nah*] it is worth the trouble
¡Válgame Dios! [VAHL-*gah-meh d'yohs*] Good Heavens!
válido, -a [VAH-*lee-doh, -dah*] valid
valiente [*vah-l'*YEHN-*teh*] brave, courageous
valor (m) [*vah*-LOHR] value
válvula [VAHL-*voo-lah*] valve
valle (m) [VAH-*l'yeh*] valley
★ **vamos** [VAH-*mohs*] we go
NOTE: Also used as exclamation indicating "Go on!", "Come on!", "Well!" etc.
★ **van** [*vahn*] they go, you go (plural)
vanidoso, -a [*vah-nee*-DOH-*soh, -sah*] vain
(en) vano [*ehn* VAH-*noh*] in vain
vapor (m) [*vah*-POHR] steam, ship
vaquero [*vah*-KEH-*roh*] cowboy
vara [VAH-*rah*] staff, rod (unit of measure: 2.8 ft.)
variar [*vah-r'*YAHR] to vary, to change
variedad (f) [*vah-r'yeh*-DAHD] variety
varilla [*vah*-REE-*l'yah*] rod, bar
varios, -as [VAH-*r'yohs, -r'yahs*] several
varón (m) [*vah*-ROHN] male
vasco, -a [VAHS-*koh, -kah*] Basque
vaso [VAH-*soh*] glass (for drinking)
vaya [VAH-*yah*] well! indeed!
¡váyase! [VAH-*yah-seh*] go away (formal)
vecindad (f) [*veh-theen*-DAHD] neighborhood
vecino, -a [*veh*-THEE-*noh, -nah*] neighbor, neighboring
vegetal (m) [*veh-heh*-TAHL] vegetable

★ **veinte** [VAYN-*teh*] twenty

NOTE: Numbers like twenty-one, twenty-two etc. can be written either as *veintiuno, veintidos,* etc. or in separated fashion such as *veinte y uno, veinte y dos,* etc.

vejez (f) [*veh*-HEHTH] old age
vela [VEH-*lah*] sail, vigil, candle
velocidad (f) [*veh-loh-thee*-DAHD] speed
  límite de velocidad [LEE-*mee-teh deh- veh-loh-thee*-DAHD] speed limit
vena [VEH-*nah*] vein
vencedor, -a [*vehn-theh*-DOHR, *-ah*] winner
vencer [*vehn*-THEHR] to win, conquer
vencido, -a [*vehn*-THEE-*doh, -dah*] beaten, payable (com)
vendaje (m) [*vehn*-DAH-*heh*] bandage
vendedor, -a [*vehn-deh*-DOHR *-ah*] salesman; saleswoman
★ **vender** [*vehn*-DEHR] to sell
  vender al contado [*vehn*-DEHR *ahl kohn*-TAH-*doh*] to sell for cash
  vender al por mayor [*vehn*-DEHR *ahl pohr mah*-YOHR] to sell wholesale
  vender al por menor [*vehn*-DEHR *ahl pohr meh*-NOHR] to sell retail
veneno [*veh*-NEH-*noh*] poison
venenoso, -a [*veh-neh*-NOH-*soh, -sah*] poisonous
venezolano, -a [*veh-neh-thoh*-LAH-*noh, -nah*] Venezuelan
Venezuela [*veh-neh*-THWEH-*lah*] Venezuela
★ **¡venga!** [VEHN-*gah*] come!
venganza [*vehn*-GAHN-*thah*] vengeance
★ **venir** [*veh*-NEER] to come
  ¿cuándo vendrá? [KWAHN-*doh vehn*-DRAH] When will you (he, she) come?
  la semana que viene [*lah seh*-MAH-*nah keh v'*YEH-*neh*] next week
venta [VEHN-*tah*] sale

★ **ventana** [*vehn*-TAH-*nah*] window
ventanilla [*vehn-tah*-NEE-*l'yah*] (ticket) window
ventilador (m) [*ven-tee-lah*-DOHR] fan, ventilator
ventura [*vehn*-TOO-*rah*] luck, happiness
★ **ver** [*vehr*] to see, look at
  ¡a ver! [*ah vehr*] let's see
  ¡vamos a ver! [VAH-*mohs ah vehr*] let's see
★ **ver(se)** [VEHR-*seh*] to see each other, to appear
★ **verano** [*veh*-RAH-*noh*] summer
¿(de) veras? [*deh* VEH-*rahs*] really?
verbo [VEHR-*boh*] verb
★ **verdad** (f) [*vehr*-DAHD] truth

NOTE: *Verdad* is one of the words most frequently heard in conversation. As a question it means "isn't it so?" or "really?" and is often used in the form *¿no es verdad?*

verdaderamente [*ver-dah-deh-rah*-MEHN-*teh*] truly, really
★ **verde** [VEHR-*deh*] green
verdura [*vehr*-DOO-*rah*] vegetables, greens
vereda [*veh*-REH-*dah*] path
vergüenza [*vehr*-GWEHN-*thah*] shame
  tener vergüenza [*teh*-NEHR *vehr*-GWEHN-*thah*] to be ashamed
  ¡Qué vergüenza! [*keh vehr*-GWEHN-*thah*] What a disgrace!
verificar [*veh-ree-fee*-KAHR] to check, confirm
verso [VEHR-*soh*] verse
verter [*vehr*-TEHR] to pour
vertical [*vehr-tee*-KAHL] vertical
vértigo [VEHR-*tee-goh*] dizziness
vestido [*vehs*-TEE-*doh*] dress, suit
vestir [*vehs*-TEER] to dress
vestir(se) [*vehs*-TEER-*(seh)*] to get dressed
¡vete! [VEH-*teh*] go away! (familiar form)
★ **vez** [*vehth*] time, occasion

dos veces [*dohs* VEH-*thehs*] twice
muchas veces [MOO-*chahs* VEH-*thehs*] often
alguna vez [*ahl*-GOO-*nah vehth*] ever (used in questions)
a veces [*ah* VEH-*thehs*] sometimes
de vez en cuando [*deh vehth ehn* KWAHN-*doh*] sometimes
otra vez [OH-*trah vehth*] again
tal vez [*tahl vehth*] perhaps
vía [VEE-*ah*] track, way
vía aérea [VEE-*ah-ah*-EH-*reh-ah*] by air
★ **viajar** [*v'yah*-HAHR] to travel
viaje (m) [*v'*YAH-*heh*] voyage, trip
¡buen viaje! [*bwehn v'*YAH-*heh*] (Have a) good trip!
viajero, -a [*v'yah*-HEH-*roh, -rah*] traveler
vicio [VEE-*th'yoh*] vice
víctima [VEEK-*tee-mah*] victim
NOTE: Always feminine, even if the victim is male.
victoria [*veek*-TOH-*r'yah*] victory
vicuña [*vee*-KOO-*n'yah*] Andean animal used for wool.
vidriera [*vee-dr'*YEH-*rah*] show case, window
★ **viejo, -a** [*v'*YEH-*hoh, -hah*] old
viento [*v'*YEHN-*toh*] wind
★ **viernes** (m) [*v'*YEHR-*nehs*] Friday
viga [VEE-*gah*] beam, girder
vigilar [*vee-hee*-LAHR] to watch over
vigoroso, -a [*vee-goh*-ROH-*soh, -sah*] vigorous
villa [VEE-*l'yah*] small town; country house
vinagre (m) [*vee*-NAH-*greh*] vinegar
viña [VEE-*n'yah*] vineyard
vino [VEE-*noh*] wine
violento, -a [*v'yoh*-LEHN-*toh, -tah*] violent
violín (m) [*v'yoh*-LEEN] violin
virar [*vee*-RAHR] to turn
virgen (f) [VEER-*hehn*] virgin
virtud (f) [*veer*-TOOD] virtue (*Virtudes* is a girl's name also)
visa [VEE-*sah*] visa
visión (f) [*vee-s'*YOHN] vision
visita [*vee*-SEE-*tah*] visit

vista [VEES-*tah*] sight, view
  a la vista [*ah lah* VEES-*tah*] in sight
★ **hasta la vista** [AHS-*tah lah* VEES-*tah*] goodby
visto, -a [VEES-*toh, -tah*] seen, clear, obvious
  por lo visto [*pohr loh* VEES-*toh*] apparently, judging from the facts
  visto bueno [VEES-*toh*-BWEH-*noh*] approved
viuda [*v'*YOO-*dah*] widow
viudo [*v'*YOO-*doh*] widower
★ **¡viva!** [VEE-*vah*] Long live! Hurray!
víveres (m, plural) [VEE-*veh-rehs*] foodstuffs, provisions
★ **vivir** [*vee*-VEER] to live
vivo, -a [VEE-*voh, -vah*] alive, lively
volar [*voh*-LAHR] to fly
volcán (m) [*vohl*-KAHN] volcano
volcar [*vohl*-KAHR] to overturn
volumen (m) [*voh*-LOO-*mehn*] volume (size)
voluntad (m) [*voh-loon*-TAHD] desire, will
  de buena voluntad [*deh* BWEH-*nah voh-loon*-TAHD] willingly
★ **volver** [*vohl*-VEHR] to return, to turn
  volver en sí [*vohl*-VEHR *ehn see*] to regain consciousness
  volver(se) [*vohl*-VEHR-*(seh)*] to turn, to become
  volver(se) loco, -a [*vohl*-VEHR-*(seh)* LOH-*koh, -kah*] to become crazy
vosotros, -as [*voh*-SOH-*trohs, -trahs*] you

NOTE: *Vosotros* is the plural of the familiar form of "you"—*tú*. It is frequently employed in speeches, public addresses and writing.

votar [*voh*-TAHR] to vote
voto [VOH-*toh*] vote
★ **voy** [VOH-*ee*] I go, I am going (see *ir*)
★ **voz** (f) [*vohth*] voice (plural *voces*)
vuelo [VWEH-*loh*] flight

★ **vuelta** [VWEHL-*tah*] turn, return
a la vuelta [*ah lah* VWEHL-*tah*] on returning; round the corner
dar una vuelta [*dahr* OO-*nah* VWEHL-*tah*] to take a stroll
dar vueltas [*dahr* VWEHL-*tahs*] to turn round, to hang around
estar de vuelta [*ehs*-TAHR *deh* VWEHL-*tah*] to be back
vuelto [VWEHL-*toh*] change (money)
vuelve [VWEHL-*veh*] he, (she) returns
vuestro, -a [VWEHS-*troh, -trah*] your (plural of familiar form. See *vosotros.*)
vulgar [*vool*-GAHR] vulgar, ordinary

Y

★ **y** [*ee*] and
★ **ya** [*yah*] already, now, finally, once
Ya es tarde. [*yah ehs* TAHR-*deh*] It's already late.
ya no [*yah noh*] no longer
Ya voy. [*yah* VOH-*ee*] I'm coming.

NOTE: *Ya* is also used as an expletive to add force to other words.

¡Ya está! [*yah ehs*-TAH] There, it's done!
¡ya lo creo! [*yah loh* KREH-*oh*] of course!
yarda [YAHR-*dah*] yard
NOTE: *Metro* is the Spanish measure nearest to yard. See metric table at rear of book.
yegua [YEH-*gwah*] mare
yerno [YEHR-*noh*] son-in-law
yeso [YEH-*soh*] plaster
★ **yo** [*yoh*] I
yo mismo [*yoh* MEES-*moh*] I myself

Z

zafiro [*zah*-FEE-*roh*] sapphire
zafra [ZAH-*frah*] sugar harvest
zaguán (m) [*thah*-GWAHN] foyer
zanahoria [*thah-nah*-OH-*r'yah*] carrot
zanja [THAN-*hah*] ditch, drain
zapatería [*thah-pah-teh*-REE-*ah*] shoe shop
zapatero [*thah-pah*-TEH-*roh*] shoe maker
zapatilla [*thah-pah*-TEE-*l'yah*] slipper
zapato [*thah*-PAH-*toh*] shoe
zarpar [*thahr*-PAHR] to sail (departure)
zarzuela [*thahr*-THWEH-*lah*] a Spanish type of musical comedy
zona [THOH-*nah*] zone
(jardín) zoológico [*thoh-oh*-LOH-*hee-koh*] zoo
zorro [THOH-*rroh*] fox
zurcir [*thoor*-THEER] to mend
zutano [*thoo*-TAH-*noh*] So and So (col)

A FEW WORDS ON VERBS

The Spanish verb changes its ending according to its subject, that is, the "person" used with it. Here is the present tense of the verb *hablar,* "(to) speak":

yo hablo, I speak
tú hablas, you speak (familiar)
Ud. (el, ella) habla, you speak he, she speaks

nosotros hablamos, we speak
vosotros habláis, you speak
Uds. (ellos, ellas) hablan, you, they (m and f) speak

Notice that there is no word for "it" as "it" is always masculine or feminine and therefore translated by the third person singular, without the pronoun. Moreover as the progressive tense is not used so frequently as in English, *hablo* means either "I speak" or "I am speaking." Of all the various forms of "you," *Ud.* and its plural *Uds.* are the most important as its use by the speaker implies a certain respect.

Out of eighteen Spanish tenses, some of which are very rarely used, we have selected the eight most frequently employed and therefore the most important for everyday conversation. Here is an example of each with the equivalent English meaning.

Infinitive: *hablar,* "(to) speak"
Present indicative: *yo hablo,* "I speak *or* I am speaking"
Past: *yo hablé,* "I spoke"
Perfect: *yo he hablado,* "I have spoken"
Future: *yo hablaré,* "I shall speak"
Imperfect: *yo hablaba,* "I was speaking *or* I used to speak"
Past perfect: *yo había hablado,* "I had spoken"
Present conditional: *yo hablaría,* "I would speak"
Present subjunctive: *(que) yo hable,* "(that) I speak"

The Subjunctive, although practically nonexistent in English, has been included because of its importance in Spanish. It is principally used after impersonal expressions introduced by *que* (that) such as *para que* (so that), (it is necessary that) etc., as well as expressions of emotion such as "I am happy (or sad) that..." etc. It can also be used to give commands.

Whenever you look up a verb in this dictionary you find it in the infinitive. (For example: *hablar,* "to speak"; *vender,* "to sell"; *vivir,* "to live.") All Spanish verbs are divided into three groups, for purposes of furnishing a conjugation pattern. In other words, learn the group pattern and you will know how to conjugate any verb. The first group includes all verbs with infinitives ending in *-ar,* the second group those ending in *-er* and the third group those ending in *-ir.*

On the following pages you will see at a glance the pattern into which these groups fall as well as the special behavior of the "auxiliary" *haber* and the two verbs meaning "to be," *ser* and *estar. Haber* is used to form the perfect and the past perfect as well as other tenses not shown here.

Irregular verbs

Aside from the three verb groups there also exist the inevitable "irregular verbs." They are called irregular because they vary in some form or other from the established three-group pattern. Some change their endings in a different way while others modify their roots or otherwise change their spelling. You will find the important form of the principal irregular verbs following this discussion.

Reflexive verbs

These verbs can be recognized by the *-se* ending attached to their infinitive, which precedes them in the dictionary (*lavarse, vestirse,* etc.). This simply means that every pronoun preceding the verb must be followed by an additional reflexive pronoun placed between it and the verb. Observe how this works with *lavarse:*

yo me lavo, I wash myself
tú te lavas, you wash yourself (familiar)
Ud. (él, ella) se lava, you wash yourself; (he, she) washes (himself, herself)

nosotros nos lavamos, we wash ourselves
vosotros os laváis, you wash yourselves (fam. pl.)
Uds. (ellos, ellas) se lavan, you (they) wash themselves

The imperative mood

The most important imperative is that for *Ud.* which is the same as the third person present subjunctive. The imperative for *tú* is generally the same as the second person present indicative form, *without* the *s.*

The present participle

The present participle of all verbs ends in *-ando* or *-iendo,* for example: *acabando* (finishing), *lloviendo* (raining), *recibiendo* (receiving).

The present participle can be used to form verbal phrases. Thus: "While finishing *or* by finishing": *acabando;* "While receiving *or* in receiving": *recibiendo.*

Moreover, the present participle can be used, together with the verb *estar* (to be), to form the progressive mood of all verbs, and, in this, follows the familiar English pattern, except that its use is not so general. Examples:

"I am writing," *(yo) estoy escribiendo*
"I was writing," *(yo) estaba escribiendo*

REMEMBER: Verbs are the heart of any language. Master *them* and the rest is easy.

REGULAR VERBS

		1ST GROUP Hablar, "(to) speak"	2ND GROUP Comer, "(to) eat"	3RD GROUP Vivir, "(to) live"
INDICATIVE				
Present	yo	hablo	como	vivo
	tú	hablas	comes	vives
	usted, él, ella	habla	come	vive
	nosotros	hablamos	comemos	vivimos
	vosotros	habláis	coméis	vivís
	ustedes, ellos, ellas	hablan	comen	viven
Past	yo	hablé	comí	viví
	tú	hablaste	comiste	viviste
	Ud., él, ella	habló	comió	vivió
	nosotros	hablamos	comimos	vivimos
	vosotros	hablasteis	comisteis	vivisteis
	Uds., ellos, ellas	hablaron	comieron	vivieron
Perfect (*Present of "haber" plus past participle*)				
	yo	he hablado	he comido	he vivido
Future	yo	hablaré	comeré	viviré
	tú	hablarás	comerás	vivirás
	Ud., él, ella	hablará	comerá	vivirá
	nosotros	hablaremos	comeremos	viviremos
	vosotros	hablaréis	comeréis	viviréis
	Uds., ellos, ellas	hablarán	comerán	vivirán
Imperfect	yo	hablaba	comía	vivía
	tú	hablabas	comías	vivías
	Ud., él, ella	hablaba	comía	vivía
	nosotros	hablábamos	comíamos	vivíamos
	vosotros	hablabais	comíais	vivíais
	Uds., ellos, ellas	hablaban	comían	vivían
Pluperfect (*Imperfect of "haber" plus past participle*)				
	yo	había hablado	había comido	había vivido

		1ST GROUP Hablar, "(to) speak"	2ND GROUP Comer, "(to) eat"	3RD GROUP Vivir, "(to) live"
CONDITIONAL				
Present	yo	hablaría	comería	viviría
	tú	hablarías	comerías	vivirías
	Ud., él, ella	hablaría	comería	viviría
	nosotros	hablaríamos	comeríamos	viviríamos
	vosotros	hablaríais	comeríais	viviríais
	Uds., ellas, ellas	hablarían	comerían	vivirían
SUBJUNCTIVE				
Present	yo	hable	coma	viva
	tú	hables	comas	vivas
	Ud., él, ella	hable	coma	viva
	nosotros	hablemos	comamos	vivamos
	vosotros	habléis	comáis	viváis
	Uds., ellos, ellas	hablen	coman	vivan

AUXILIARY VERB AND TWO FORMS OF "TO BE"

		Haber, "(to) have" (auxiliary)	Estar, "(to) be" (location)	Ser, "(to) be" (description)
INDICATIVE				
Present	yo	he	estoy	soy
	tú	has	estás	eres
	usted, él, ella	ha	está	es
	nosotros	hemos	estamos	somos
	vosotros	habéis	estáis	sois
	ustedes, ellos, ellas	han	están	son
Past	yo	hube	estuve	fuí
	tú	hubiste	estuviste	fuiste
	Ud., él, ella	hubo	estuvo	fué
	nosotros	hubimos	estuvimos	fuimos
	vosotros	hubisteis	estuvisteis	fuisteis
	Uds., ellos, ellas	hubieron	estuvieron	fueron
Perfect	yo	he habido	he estado	he sido
Future	yo	habré	estaré	seré
	tú	habrás	estarás	serás
	Ud., él, ella	habrá	estará	será
	nosotros	habremos	estaremos	seremos
	vosotros	habréis	estaréis	seréis
	Uds., ellos, ellas	habrán	estarán	serán
Imperfect	yo	había	estaba	era
	tú	habías	estabas	eras
	Ud., él, ella	había	estaba	era
	nosotros	habíamos	estábamos	éramos
	vosotros	habíais	estabais	erais
	Uds., ellos, ellas	habían	estaban	eran
Pluperfect	yo	había habido	había estado	había sido

		Haber, "(to) have" (auxiliary)	Estar, "(to) be" (location)	Ser, "(to) be" (description)
CONDITIONAL				
Present	yo	habría	estaría	sería
	tú	habrías	estarías	serías
	Ud., él, ella	habría	estaría	sería
	nosotros	habríamos	estaríamos	seríamos
	vosotros	habríais	estaríais	seríais
	Uds., ellos, ellas	habrían	estarían	serían
SUBJUNCTIVE				
Present	yo	haya	esté	sea
	tú	hayas	estés	seas
	Ud., él, ella	haya	esté	sea
	nosotros	hayamos	estemos	seamos
	vosotros	hayáis	estéis	seáis
	Uds., ellos, ellas	hayan	estén	sean

IRREGULAR

PRESENT INDICATIVE		IMPERFECT*	FUTURE*
Abrazar—(to) embrace (*past participle:* abrazado) *same as:* **Adelgazar, Alcanzar, Cazar, Cruzar,** etc.			
abrazo	abrazamos	abrazaba	abrazaré
abrazas	abrazáis		
abraza	abrazan		
Andar—(to) walk			
ando	andamos	andaba	andaré
andas	andáis		
anda	andan		
Caer—(to) fall (*past participle:* caído)			
caigo	caemos	caía	caeré
caes	caéis		
cae	caen		
Coger—(to) seize (*past participle:* cogido) *same as:* **Acoger, Escoger, Encoger, Proteger,** etc.			
cojo	cogemos	cogía	cogeré
coges	cogéis		
coge	cogen		
Conocer—(to) know (*past participle:* conocido) *same as:* **Agradecer, Complacer, Crecer, Nacer,** etc.			
conozco	conocemos	conocía	conoceré
conoces	conocéis		
conoce	conocen		
Construir—(to) construct (*past participle:* construído) *same as:* **Concluir, Contribuir, Huir, Sustituir,** etc.			
construyo	construímos	construía	construiré
construyes	construís		
construye	construyen		
Contar—(to) count (*past participle:* contado) *same as:* **Acordar, Acostar(se), Costar, Probar, Sonar,** etc.			
cuento	contamos	contaba	contaré
cuentas	contáis		
cuenta	cuentan		

VERBS

PAST		PRESENT SUBJUNCTIVE	
abracé	abrazamos	abrace	abracemos
abrazaste	abrazasteis	abraces	abracéis
abrazó	abrazaron	abrace	abracen
anduve	anduvimos	ande	andemos
anduviste	anduvisteis	andes	andéis
anduvo	anduvieron	ande	anden
caí	caímos	caiga	caigamos
caíste	caisteis	caigas	caigáis
cayó	cayeron	caiga	caigan
cogí	cogimos	coja	cojamos
cogiste	cogisteis	cojas	cojáis
cogió	cogieron	coja	cojan
conocí	conocimos	conozca	conozcamos
conociste	conocistéis	conozcas	conozcáis
conoció	conocieron	conozca	conozcan
construí	construímos	construya	construyamos
construiste	construísteis	construyas	construyáis
construyó	construyeron	construya	construyan
conté	contamos	cuente	contemos
contaste	contasteis	cuentes	contéis
contó	contaron	cuente	cuenten

* *The forms of this tense are regularly formed as shown on pages 326-7.*

PRESENT INDICATIVE		IMPERFECT*	FUTURE*

Corregir—(to) correct (*past participle:* corregido) *same as:* **Elegir, Eregir, Regir**

corrijo	corregimos	corregía	corregiré
corriges	corregís		
corrige	corrigen		

Creer—(to) believe (*past participle:* creído) *same as:* **Leer**

creo	creemos	creía	creeré
crees	creéis		
cree	creen		

Dar—(to) give (*past participle:* dado)

doy	damos	daba	daré
das	dais		
da	dan		

Decir—(to) say (*past participle:* dicho)

digo	decimos	decía	diré
dices	decís		
dice	dicen		

Dormir—(to) sleep (*past participle:* dormido) *same as:* **Morir**

duermo	dorminos	dormía	dormiré
duermes	dormís		
duerme	duermen		

Ejercer—(to) practice or (to) perform (*past participle:* ejercido) *same as:* **Convencer, Mecer, Vencer**

ejerzo	ejercemos	ejercía	ejerceré
ejerces	ejercéis		
ejerce	ejercen		

Empezar—(to) begin (*past participle:* empezado) *same as:* **Comenzar, Tropezar,** etc.

empiezo	empezamos	empezaba	empezaré
empiezas	empezáis		
empieza	empiezan		

PAST		PRESENT SUBJUNCTIVE	
corregí	corregimos	corrija	corrijamos
corregiste	corregisteis	corrijas	corrijáis
corrigió	corrigieron	corrija	corrijan
creí	creímos	crea	creamos
creíste	creísteis	creas	creáis
creyó	creyeron	crea	crean
dí	dimos	dé	demos
diste	disteis	des	deis
dió	dieron	dé	den
dije	dijimos	diga	digamos
dijiste	dijisteis	digas	digáis
dijo	dijeron	diga	digan
dormí	dormimos	duerma	durmamos
dormiste	dormisteis	duermas	durmáis
durmió	durmieron	duerma	duerman
ejercí	ejercimos	ejerza	ejerzamos
ejerciste	ejercisteis	ejerzas	ejerzáis
ejerció	ejercieron	ejerza	ejerzan
empecé	empezamos	empiece	empecemos
empezaste	empezasteis	empieces	empecéis
empezó	empezaron	empiece	empiecen

* *The forms of this tense are regularly formed as shown on pages 326-7.*

PRESENT INDICATIVE		IMPERFECT *	FUTURE *
Hacer—(to) do, (to) make (*past participle:* hecho)			
hago	hacemos	hacía	haré
haces	hacéis		
haco	hacen		
Ir—(to) go (*past participle:* ido)			
voy	vamos	iba	iré
vas	vais		
va	van		
Llover—(to) rain (only 3rd pers. sing.) (*past participle:* llovido)			
llueve		llovía	lloverá
Oler—(to) smell (*past participle:* olido)			
huelo	olamos	olía	oleré
hueles	oléis		
huele	huelen		
Pagar—(to) pay (*past participle:* pagado) *same as:* **Tragar, Apagar, Llegar, Castigar, Obligar,** etc.			
pago	pagamos	pagaba	pagaré
pagas	pagáis		
paga	pagan		
Pedir—(to) ask for (*past participle:* pedido) *same as:* **Despedir, Competir, Servir, Teñir,** etc.			
pido	pedimos	pedía	pediré
pides	pedís		
pide	piden		
Pensar—(to) think (*past participle:* pensado) *same as:* **Acertar, Alentar, Apretar, Sentar(se),** etc.			
pienso	pensamos	pensaba	pensaré
piensas	pensáis		
piensa	piensan		
Poder—(to) be able (*past participle:* podido)			
puedo	podemos	podía	podré
puedes	podéis		
puede	pueden		

PAST		PRESENT SUBJUNCTIVE	
hice	hicimos	haga	hagamos
hiciste	hicisteis	hagas	hagáis
hizo	hicieron	haga	hagan
fuí	fuímos	vaya	vayamos
fuiste	fuisteis	vayas	vayáis
fué	fueron	vaya	vayan
llovió		llueva	
olí	olimos	huela	olamos
oliste	olisteis	huelas	oláis
olió	olieron	huela	huelan
pague	pagamos	pague	paguemos
pagaste	pagasteis	pagues	paguéis
pagó	pagaron	pague	paguen
pedí	pedimos	pida	pidamos
pediste	pedisteis	pidas	pidáis
pidió	pidieron	pida	pidan
pensé	pensamos	piense	pensemos
pensaste	pensasteis	pienses	penséis
pensó	pensaron	piense	piensen
pude	pudimos	pueda	podamos
pudiste	pudisteis	puedas	podáis
pudo	pudieron	pueda	puedan

* *The forms of this tense are regularly formed as shown on pages 326-7.*

PRESENT INDICATIVE		IMPERFECT*	FUTURE*
Poner—(to) put (*past participle:* puesto)			
pongo	ponemos	ponía	pondré
pones	ponéis		
pone	ponen		
Producir—(to) produce (*past participle:* producido) *same as:* **Conducir, Introducir, Reproducir, Traducir,** etc.			
produzco	producimos	producía	produciré
produces	producís		
produce	producen		
Querer—(to) want (*past participle:* querido)			
quiero	queremos	quería	querré
quieres	queréis		
quiere	quieren		
Reir—(to) laugh (*past participle:* reído) *same as:* **Sonreír, Freir,** etc.			
río	reímos	reía	reirá
ríes	reís		
ríe	ríen		
Saber—(to) know (*past participle:* sabido)			
sé	sabemos	sabía	sabré
sabes	sabéis		
sabe	saben		
Sacar—(to) take out (*past participle:* sacado) *same as:* **Aplicar, Buscar, Explicar, Secar,** etc.			
saco	sacamos	sacaba	sacaré
sacas	sacáis		
saca	sacan		
Salir—(to) leave (*past participle:* salido)			
salgo	salimos	salía	saldré
sales	salís		
sale	salen		

PAST		PRESENT SUBJUNCTIVE	
puse	pusimos	ponga	pongamos
pusiste	pusisteis	pongas	pongáis
puso	pusieron	ponga	pongan
produje	produjimos	produzca	produzcamos
produjiste	produjisteis	produzcas	produzcáis
produjo	produjeron	produzca	produzcan
quise	quisimos	quiera	queramos
quisiste	quisisteis	quieras	queráis
quiso	quisieron	quiera	quieran
reí	reímos	ría	ríamos
reíste	reísteis	rías	ríais
rió	rieron	ría	rían
supe	supimos	sepa	sepamos
supiste	supisteis	sepas	sepáis
supo	supieron	sepa	sepan
saqué	sacamos	saque	saquemos
sacaste	sacasteis	saques	saquéis
sacó	sacaron	saque	saquen
salí	salimos	salga	salgamos
saliste	salisteis	salgas	salgáis
salió	salieron	salga	salgan

* *The forms of this tense are regularly formed as shown on pages 326-7.*

PRESENT INDICATIVE		**IMPERFECT***	**FUTURE***
Seguir—(to) follow (*past participle:* seguido) *same as:* **Conseguir, Proseguir, Perseguir,** etc.			
sigo	seguimos	seguía	seguiré
sigues	seguís		
sigue	siguen		
Sentir—(to) feel (*past participle:* sentido) *same as:* **Advertir, Herir, Preferir, Referir,** etc.			
siento	sentimos	sentía	sentiré
sientes	sentís		
siente	sienten		
Tener—(to) have (*past participle:* tenido) *same as:* **Contener, Detener,** etc.			
tengo	tenemos	tenía	tendré
tienes	tenéis		
tiene	tienen		
Traer—(to) bring (*past participle:* traído)			
traigo	traemos	traía	traeré
traes	traéis		
trae	traen		
Venir—(to) come (*past participle:* venido)			
vengo	venimos	venía	vendré
vienes	venís		
viene	vienen		
Ver—(to) see (*past participle:* visto) *same as:* **Convenir, Intervenir, Prevenir,** etc.			
veo	vemos	veía	veré
ves	veis		
ve	ven		
Volver—(to) return (*past participle:* vuelto) *same as:* **Revolver, Resolver,** etc.			
vuelvo	volvemos	volvía	volveré
vuelves	volvéis		
vuelve	vuelven		

PAST		PRESENT SUBJUNCTIVE	
seguí	seguimos	siga	sigamos
seguiste	seguís	sigas	sigáis
siguió	siguen	siga	sigan
sentí	sentimos	sienta	sintamos
sentiste	sentisteis	sientas	sintáis
sintió	sintieron	sienta	sientan
tuve	tuvimos	tenga	tengamos
tuviste	tuvisteis	tengas	tengáis
tuve	tuvieron	tenga	tengan
traje	trajimos	traiga	traigamos
trajiste	trajisteis	traigas	traigáis
trajo	trajeron	traiga	traigan
vine	vinimos	venga	vengamos
viniste	vinisteis	vengas	vengáis
vino	vinieron	venga	vengan
vi	vimos	vea	veamos
viste	visteis	veas	veáis
vió	vieron	vean	vean
volví	volvimos	vuelva	volvamos
volviste	volvisteis	vuelvas	volváis
volvió	volvieron	vuelva	vuelvan

* *The forms of this tense are regularly formed as shown on pages 326-7.*

METRIC MEASURES

In Spanish countries everything is measured according to the metric system whether the subject under consideration is the size of a shirt or the distance between towns.

But before you complain about Spanish-speaking people perversely measuring and weighing everything in an unnatural way—as the metric system may seem to you—you must realize that is we, not they, who are clinging to an outmoded system.

Which is easier: to count 12 inches to a foot, 3 feet to a yard, 5,280 feet to a mile, or to measure 100 centimeters to a meter and 1000 meters to a kilometer? The Spanish way, *¿no es verdad?* In any case, the following table will help you accustom yourself to the Spanish (also international) way of measuring.

1 centimeter	.39 inches
1 meter	39.37 inches
1 kilometer	.62 miles
1 kilogram	1.05 quarts (liquid)
1 inch	2.54 centimeters
1 foot	.304 meter
1 yard	.91 meter
1 mile	1.61 kilometers
1 pound	.46 kilogram
1 quart	.95 liter (liquid)